D0939021

FOUNDATIONS
OF
AMERICAN
FOREIGN
POLICY

Other Books by the Author

Empire on the Pacific: A Study in American Continental Expansion (1955, 1983).
The New Isolationism: A Study in Politics and Foreign Policy Since 1950 (1956).
Cold War Diplomacy: American Foreign Policy, 1945–1975 (1962, 1977).
A History of the United States, 2 vols. (1970). With Gilbert C. Fite and Philip L. White.
A History of the American People (1970, 1975). With Gilbert C. Fite and Philip L. White.
Recent United States History (1972). With Gilbert C. Fite.
The Age of Global Power: The United States Since 1939 (1979). American Republic Series.
America as a World Power: A Realist Appraisal from Wilson to Reagan (1984).

Books Edited

The Enduring Lincoln (1959).
Politics and the Crisis of 1860 (1961).
An Uncertain Tradition: American Secretaries of State in the Twentieth Century (1961).
The Cold War: A Conflict of Ideology and Power (1963, 1976).
Ideas and Diplomacy: Readings in the Intellectual Tradition of American Foreign Policy (1964).
Manifest Destiny (1968).
Nationalism and Communism in Asia: The American Response (1977).
Freedom in America: A 200-Year Perspective (1977).
American Diplomatic History to 1900 (1978). Goldentree Bibliographies in American History.
Traditions and Values: American Diplomacy, 1790–1865 (1985).
Traditions and Values: American Diplomacy, 1865–1945 (1985).
National Security: Its Theory and Practice in the United States, 1945–1960 (1985).

FOUNDATIONS OF AMERICAN FOREIGN POLICY

A Realist Appraisal from Franklin to McKinley

Essays by
Norman A. Graebner

SR *Scholarly Resources Inc.*
Wilmington, Delaware

© 1985 by Norman A. Graebner
All rights reserved
First published 1985
Printed and bound in the United States of America

Scholarly Resources Inc.
104 Greenhill Avenue
Wilmington, Delaware 19805

Library of Congress Cataloging-in-Publication Data

Graebner, Norman A.
  Foundations of American foreign policy.

  Includes bibliographies and index.
  1. United States—Foreign relations—Addresses,
essays, lectures.   I. Title.
E183.7.G723   1985   327.73   85-14394
ISBN 0-8420-2244-9
ISBN 0-8420-2245-7 (pbk.)

Contents

Foreword

NORMAN A. GRAEBNER was born in Kingman, Kansas, on October 19, 1915 but lived eight of his early years in Coffeyville before his family moved to Milwaukee, Wisconsin, in January 1926. There, upon graduation from Washington High School, he pursued his post-high school education at Milwaukee State Teachers College (now the University of Wisconsin-Milwaukee), from which he graduated in 1939. His studies continued at the University of Oklahoma where he received his master's degree in 1940. After teaching for two years, one in a small Oklahoma high school and the other at Oklahoma College for Women, he entered the U.S. Army. His active service included fourteen months as a lieutenant in the Pacific Theater, initially in the Philippines and then in Japan for the first ten months of the occupation. In Yokohama he established Japan's first school for American soldiers, and for that accomplishment General Robert Eichelberger, Eighth Army Commander, awarded him a special citation. Returning home in the summer of 1946, he taught another year at Oklahoma College for Women.

Entering the University of Chicago in 1947, he studied primarily under the direction of a trio of American historians—Avery Craven, Thomas Hutchinson, and Walter Johnson—and received his Ph.D. in 1949. Having focused on American history, he was exposed only later to the developing theories of Chicago's noted political scientist, Hans J. Morgenthau. Meanwhile, in 1948, he had undertaken his teaching duties at Iowa State College, Ames, where he spent the next eight years, broken only by one year at Stanford University. In 1956 he moved to the University of Illinois as professor of history; there he remained for eleven years, serving that department as chairman in 1961–63. In 1967 the University of Virginia invited him to accept a chair as Edward R. Stettinius, Jr., Professor of Modern American History, and in 1982 he became the Randolph P. Compton Professor of

History and Public Affairs at the University of Virginia where he presently teaches.

Throughout his career Professor Graebner has devoted consuming energy to his teaching. Encouraged by the responsiveness of students at Iowa State, he developed special lecturing skills at the outset. At the University of Illinois, as his reputation spread across the campus, his classes grew to such size that both his survey course in American history and his upper division and graduate courses in diplomatic history were moved in order to accommodate the demand for enrollment. Teaching assistants assigned to his classes still remember vividly the dynamism that flowed from the lectern and the incredible response from the undergraduates. Invariably the last lecture of the semester brought forth a standing ovation from the class. Fifteen years after he left the University of Illinois, Jim Vermette, a former student and now president of that university's Alumni Association, introduced an appeal to the alumni with these words:

> Did you know Norman Graebner?
>
> Lean, dark, and dynamic. His eyes fixed your attention and his fast-moving words fastened your mind to his thoughts. His subjects were American history and international diplomacy, his real love was teaching, and how I and other students appreciated him! He made us see the forces that shaped this country and how it relates to the world in a way that I had never realized.

While he was at Illinois, one of the greatest compliments to Professor Graebner's pedagogic and speaking abilities came from the Speech Department where graduate students were encouraged to attend his diplomacy courses in order to study his lecturing style. As a teacher, his reputation preceded him to the University of Virginia where his classes were large from the beginning.

Further testimony to Norman Graebner's teaching skills rests on the fact that he has received distinguished teaching awards wherever he has been, including the first Outstanding Teacher Award given at the University of Illinois, the Z Society and IMP Society awards, and the Alumni Association Distinguished Professor Award at Virginia. Not only has he been a distinguished lecturer to undergraduate students but also his seminars have been model laboratories for the training of more than thirty graduate students he has guided to receiving their Ph.D. degrees at Illinois and Virginia. Together with his wife Laura, a historian in her own right, Professor Graebner has been both friend and mentor to these men and women who recently established the Norman and Laura Graebner Distinguished Service Award through the Society for Historians of American Foreign Relations. This award will be given for the first time after Professor Graebner's retirement from teaching in 1986.

Norman Graebner has reached one of the widest audiences of any American historian of modern times. He has lectured at some two hundred colleges and universities in the United States, Western Europe, and the Far East. In thirty-nine years of college teaching his under-graduate enrollments have reached approximately 30,000, as his classes in all but seminars have exceeded 250 students since the early 1950s and often have reached 500. His perspectives have gained an even wider audience through his writings on politics and diplomatic history. Since 1951 he has published eight books, twelve edited volumes, and over one hundred articles, essays, and booklets. In 1958–59 and again in 1966, his University of Illinois course in U.S. diplomatic history was broadcast from the classroom to an estimated regular listening audience of 75,000. From 1958 to 1960 he had a weekly radio program over WBBM, Chicago, entitled "Background of the News."

If Professor Graebner's prowess as a teacher recommended him to an expansive lectureship around the world, his many writings on the history of American foreign relations established his reputation as a scholar. Possessing ideas and the ability to communicate them, he has received many special invitations to visit other institutions. He was the Commonwealth Fund Lecturer, University College, London, in 1958; he delivered the Walter Linwood Fleming Lectures at Louisiana State University in 1962; he was a Fulbright Lecturer at the University of Queensland, Brisbane, Australia, in 1963; and served again as a Fulbright Lecturer at the University of Sydney in the summer of 1983. He was the Distinguished Visiting Professor of History, Pennsylvania State University, 1975–76, where he directed that university's award-winning bicentennial program, "Freedom: Then, Now, and Tomor-row." He also was selected for the prestigious Harold Vyvyan Harmsworth Professorship of American History at Oxford University, 1978–79. Most recently he was the Pettyjohn Distinguished Lecturer at Washington State University in 1980 and Visiting Professor of History at the U.S. Military Academy, West Point, in 1981–82, for the purpose of directing the special year-long symposium on "The Theory and Practice of National Security, 1945–1960." For this he received the Outstanding Civilian Service Medal from West Point after his return to Virginia. In 1985 he was the Thomas Jefferson Visiting Scholar at Downing College, Cambridge.

Among the numerous expressions of esteem that have come to Norman Graebner are several that reflect his stature in the academic community. In 1972 he was elected as one of the earliest presidents of the Society for Historians of American Foreign Relations. Also he was awarded the Litt.D. degree by Albright College in 1976 and the Doctor of Humane Letters degree by the University of Pittsburgh and Valparaiso University in 1981. That spring the University of Virginia chapter of Phi Beta Kappa made him an honorary member of that fraternity. During the 1981–82 academic year he served as a Phi Beta Kappa Visiting Scholar, traveling to nine colleges and universities. In 1983 he was elected to membership in the highly respected Massachusetts Historical Society and also has long been a member of the Society of American Historians. Professor Graebner has been very active in professional affairs. He has appeared on more than two dozen sessions of the annual meetings of major historical societies and has sat on a number of permanent and ad hoc committees of these societies. He has served as chairman of the Program and Nominating committees as well as a member of the Executive Board of the Organization of American Historians. For a period of six years each, he represented the Organization of American Historians on the Joint Committee on Historians and Archivists and the American Historical Association on the National Archives Advisory Council. He was also a member of the Advisory Committee for American Studies Abroad for almost a decade.

Perhaps more than any other historian in the United States Professor Graebner has expostulated a realist evaluation of American diplomatic history. Having studied political rather than diplomatic history as a graduate student, he entered the study of international affairs largely through the writings of Hans Morgenthau, Walter Lippmann, and George F. Kennan. To further the efforts of these men to analyze the external expertise of the United States in terms of the historical principles of international politics, Graebner extended his intellectual foundations to include the works of such writers on the European state system as Callières, Fénelon, Bolingbroke, Vattel, Metternich, and Clausewitz, as well as this nation's Founding Fathers who sought to embody the best European thought on international affairs in the early foreign policies of the United States.

Through all the years in which he developed his perspective on effective foreign policy, although he has refined and honed his original conceptual framework, Norman Graebner has been consistent in his insistence that a successful foreign policy rests on balancing ends and means, on preserving a clear understanding of the difference between defensible national interests and national ideals, and on the capacity of leaders to perceive the differences between broadly defined personal ambitions for the nation and precisely defined national needs. He also has lived by the rule that effective assessment of the foreign policy process requires evaluation of a broad range of causes for national behavior which transcend the mere accumulation of empirical data, believed by some to make decision making predictable. Behavioralism, at least in its extreme form, he has argued, assigns far too much rationality to the human species. In the introduction to his text, *Ideas and Diplomacy* (Oxford, 1964), Professor Graebner summed up his advice to both practitioners and students of foreign policy:

> National greatness is determined as much by wisdom as by power. . . . To employ its power wisely a nation must learn from experience. And that experience, if it is to be helpful (for precise situations seldom recur), must lie in the general concepts of diplomacy, power, national interest, and world society which determined the actual decisions and against which their results must then be measured.

It is within this framework that the material in the subsequent pages should be read and absorbed.

Edward M. Bennett
Richard Dean Burns

Introduction

BENJAMIN FRANKLIN observed in his journal of the peace negotiations with Britain in 1782: "Great affairs sometimes take their rise from small circumstances." His neighbor, Madame Brillon, vacationing in Nice, had met members of the English gentry, including Lord Cholmondeley who promised, on his return to England, to visit Franklin, which he did on March 22. "He told me," Franklin recorded, that "he knew Lord Shelburne had a great regard for me, that he was sure his lordship would be pleased to hear from me, and that if I would write a line he should have a pleasure in carrying it."[1] Franklin then penned a note to express the hope that he and the new prime minister might arrange a peace to bring the long Revolutionary War to an end. In April, Shelburne dispatched Richard Oswald, a Scottish merchant, to open conversations in Paris. The United States had reached the point of national independence not only because of its successful exertion of force against Great Britain, but also, more fundamentally, because its leaders understood and respected the European state system and had managed, through ability and good fortune, to turn that system to their advantage.

Victory over Britain required far more military power than the colonies possessed. For that reason the movement for independence was never separable from the international environment in which it occurred. The Declaration of Independence was not a symbolic effort of the United States to escape the demands and vicissitudes of European politics but rather the necessary prelude to the alliance with France. It was the affirmation of a widespread conviction that the interests of the English settlers in the New World required a deeper

[1] "Journal of the Negotiation for Peace with Great Britain," in Albert Henry Smyth, ed., *The Writings of Benjamin Franklin*, 10 vols. (New York, 1905–1907), 8:459–60; Franklin to Lord Shelburne, March 22, 1782, ibid., pp. 460–61.

involvement in the affairs of Europe than membership in the British Empire permitted. Even in the eighteenth century the appreciation of geographic isolation and its advantages were lesser determinants of American behavior than the quest for commercial empire and the direct, purposeful reliance on Europe's power structure. Whatever differences from the European standard actually existed in early American diplomatic practice resulted less from conceptual uniqueness than from the greater freedom of action permitted by the absence of contiguous nations that possessed the power to challenge the American people at every turn.

For America's Founding Fathers the European state system was never a mystery, nor were the brilliant seventeenth- and eighteenth-century writings that described the system and defined the rules that governed it. The Treaty of Westphalia (1648), with its recognition of the sovereignty of nations and the optimum conditions for their security and survival, had perfected the European system. That treaty redistributed western Europe among its several rulers, with the intention that the new status quo would be permanent. The Westphalian system underwrote Europe's emerging stability by imposing order and continuity on the disparate, sovereign elements that comprised its complex political structure. Assuming the inevitability of war, the system emphasized the ending of conflicts under conditions best suited to limit change and reimpose the necessary forms of order. What preserved Europe's remarkable post-Westphalian stability, despite the continuing wars, was the concept of equilibrium or balance. The system sought to check the universal selfishness of men and nations with counterchecks composed of opposing combinations of power. Thus Friedrich von Gentz, the noted Prussian diplomat, defined the balance of power as "that constitution which exists among neighbouring states more or less connected with each other, by virtue of which none of them can violate the independence or the essential rights of another without effective resistance from some quarter and consequent danger to itself."[2] The balance of power as a conscious effort to check the ambitions of any individual state began in the coalition against King Philip II of Spain in the late sixteenth century. The Peace of Westphalia, in terminating Hapsburg pretensions to universal monarchy, recognized the balance of power as an essential institution in European society.[3]

Fundamentally, the objective in maintaining an equilibrium among the powers was the preservation of Europe's international community.

---

[2]Friedrich von Gentz quoted in Moorhead Wright, ed., *Theory and Practice of the Balance of Power* (London, 1975), p. 94.

[3]Hedley Bull, *The Anarchical Society: A Study of Order in World Politics* (London, 1977), p. 32.

The balancing system assumed that each major power formed an essential element within the system. The second objective, then, followed logically from the first: to assure the survival of such individual states by preventing the ascendancy of one over the others with the power to encroach on their sovereignty and ultimately to destroy them. On the day that one country became strong enough to challenge all others combined, the system would cease to exist. Writers on the balance of power assumed that one or more ambitious countries always would seek to enhance, if not to maximize, their power. Therefore, every member state, in its own interest and in the interest of the equilibrium, carried the obligation to prevent any one country from becoming too powerful. Fénelon, in his essays on the balance of power (1720), summarized the demands which the European system placed on its members: "Christendom . . . makes a sort of general republic which has its interests, its dangers, and its policy. All the members of this great body owe to one another for the common good, and to themselves for their particular security, that they oppose the progress of any one member, which may destroy the balance, and tend to the inevitable ruin of the other members."[4] To fulfill their obligations to defend the established distribution of power and territory, nations maintained standing armies and endless diplomatic negotiations requiring permanent legations in the important capitals. Cardinal Richelieu devised this scheme in the seventeenth century to protect France's superiority over its Hapsburg rivals in Spain and Austria.[5] That small states on occasion ceased to exist demonstrated both the subordinate role of independence to the general equilibrium and the predominant role of the great powers as the custodians of international society.[6]

European statesmen recognized movement in history as reflected in the rise and decline of national power and ambition. The constant change in the relationship of nations to the balance of power demanded the vigilance necessary to detect the predominant tendencies within international society and to judge their consequences in terms of the general good. Emmerich de Vattel, the influential author of *The Law of Nations* (1758) and the chief authority of American leaders, argued that the effort to curtail the internal development of any nation would

---

[4] Fénelon, "Two Essays on the Balance of Europe," in Wright, *Theory and Practice of the Balance of Power*, p. 41.

[5] The classic account of seventeenth-century diplomatic method is Monsieur de Callières, *On the Manner of Negotiating with Princes*, trans. A. F. Whyte (Notre Dame, IN, 1963).

[6] Carl von Clausewitz noted that Poland had been a bone of contention among the European powers; the powers divided it to prevent it from becoming a province of Russia. See Clausewitz in Wright, *Theory and Practice of the Balance of Power*, p. 107.

be futile and unjust. It was preferable, he wrote, to overcome discrepancies in power and to counterbalance the growing weight and ambitions of states by forming alliances. The incessant changes in the power and purposes of nations placed a premium on diplomatic flexibility. As the Abbé de Pradt suggested, in any threat to Europe's equilibrium it was imperative that "enemies come together for common defense, and allies momentarily separate for the same reason." There was no room in a balanced system for partiality. Maintaining the equilibrium was more important than peace, pledges, treaties, and friendships. In practice, nations generally supported the causes of others with less energy than they supported their own. Even with such limitations the balancing system sustained Europe's international order. To prevent the unnecessary enlargement of war and the excessive uses of power, writers on the balance encouraged neutrality; the more widespread the neutrality, the more confined the war and the less its impact on international stability. Neutrality would not necessarily please the warring parties. To avoid unwanted involvement in war, a country required sufficient power to make its neutrality effective.

After Westphalia five closely related and generally equal nations—Great Britain, France, Russia, Prussia, and Austria—dominated the European state system. Europe contained a number of secondary and lesser nations, including Turkey, which often played definable roles in the European equilibrium, but the Big Five managed the system and determined its fundamental policies. What contributed to the success of this balancing system was Europe's common culture and the concept of a common destiny, which gave the nations a certain unity of outlook despite their continuing differences. G. F. Von Martens, in his *Summary of the Law of Nations* (1795), stressed this essential unity when he wrote that

> the resemblance in manners and religion, the intercourse of commerce, the frequency of traders of all sorts, and the ties of blood between sovereigns, have so multiplied the relations between each particular state and the rest, that one may consider Europe (particularly the Christian states of it) as a society of nations and states, each of which has its laws, its customs, and its maxims, but which it cannot put in execution without observing a great deal of delicacy towards the rest of society.

Europe, furthermore, was tied together by common experience and common institutions. All member states within the system shared similar diplomatic and economic practices, similar military organizations, and a group consciousness that gave all a mutual interest in the perpetuation of the balance of power structure itself. European civilization was unique, and its perpetuation was the goal of wise statesmanship.

Europe's cosmopolitanism reinforced the equilibrium by encouraging moderation in war. It was an eighteenth-century maxim that victors never crush an aggressor nation in the interest of stern justice but rather perpetuate that country's capacity to play its traditional role in the general balance. "You must take care," argued Fénelon, "that the engagements you lay yourself under, do not reduce your enemy too low, and prove too beneficial to your ally; which may lay you under a necessity either to suffer what may be ruinous to you, or to violate your engagements."[7] Montesquieu once asserted that the "law of nations is naturally founded on this principle, that different nations ought in time of peace to do one another all the good they can and in time of war as little injury as possible, without prejudicing their real interest." In practice, governments limited violence in war by demanding sacrifices from opponents small enough to provoke only limited responses. The smaller the political objective in war, the less would be the resistance and the needed exertion of force to gain it. Thus the political objective, the original motive for war, determined the nature of the resulting conflict and the levels of power that the contestants would unleash. Pursuing limited goals the aggressor might readily give up the effort rather than escalate the costs beyond the value of the objective. To contain the scope of war, nations sought to avoid international animosities that might turn the slightest quarrel into an explosion disproportionate in magnitude to the issues at stake.[8] It was not strange that nations generally sustained their contacts with their enemies even in time of war, the more easily to retrieve a mistaken policy. The essential purpose of the balance of power was to confine national ambition by encouraging moderation. Within the limits imposed by existing moral and political restraints, each nation was free to pursue its own interests as it chose to define them.[9]

II

Before the Treaty of Westphalia two rival dynasties, the French Bourbon and the Austrian Hapsburg, dominated European politics. The region of controversy had been central and southern Europe, but Westphalia established France's dominance on the Continent. Great Britain's subsequent triumphs over the Dutch gave it command of the seas and the power to confront French ambitions in western Europe and in

[7]Fénelon quoted in ibid., p. 42.

[8]On this theme see Carl von Clausewitz, *On War*, ed. and trans. Michael Howard and Peter Paret (Princeton, NJ, 1976), pp. 75–76, 87–88.

[9]For superb studies on the European state system see Edward V. Gulick, *Europe's Classical Balance of Power* (Ithaca, NY, 1955); and Alfred Vagts, "The Balance of Power: Growth of an Idea," *World Politics* 1 (October 1948): 82–101.

the Atlantic. Long before the end of the seventeenth century the burgeoning rivalry between Britain and France replaced France's older competition with the Hapsburgs as the central feature of European politics. If British leaders recognized the importance of the European balance of power, they could not agree on the need of an active British policy to maintain it. Some argued that Britain's insular position offered that country sufficient security, whatever the lack of equilibrium on the Continent.[10] In time France's Continental ambitions denied Britain the luxury of isolation from European politics.

The Anglo-French struggle for leadership in world affairs actually began in North America where the British and French colonies coexisted in a vast wilderness. Following La Salle's overland journey in 1682, the French built a series of posts that followed the arc of their claims through the Great Lakes country and down the Mississippi River to the Gulf of Mexico. Already the contest for the Great Lakes fur trade focused on western New York where the powerful Iroquois, dominating the other tribes, penetrated the lake country and diverted much of the lucrative fur trade from Montreal and Paris to Albany and London. Facing an unwanted conflict in the American wilderness, Britain and France signed the Treaty of Whitehall in November 1686. This agreement pledged the two nations to live in "peace, union, concord, and good correspondence" in the New World. Should any rupture occur in Europe between them, they agreed additionally that "true and firm peace and neutrality shall continue in America . . . as if no rupture had occurred in Europe."[11] The treaty had little effect simply because the stakes of empire in America were much too high. The War of the Spanish Succession (1701–1713) was preeminently a war to reestablish Europe's equilibrium by preventing a union between France and Spain. Despite its importance, the British victory would not resolve the contest in America for control of the back country.

During Britain's continuing wars with France, the seaboard colonies from Massachusetts to Virginia recognized the French challenge to their interests in the region of the Ohio and the Great Lakes. English colonies claimed the great inland empire, and they regarded the French as intruders. Many anticipated the time when Britain alone would control the vast wealth of North America. To avoid further conflict over the fur trade, Britain and France agreed not to molest the Indians residing within the dominions of the other, but after the War of the Spanish Succession, the two powers penetrated the Indian buffer zone with additional forts in preparation for an eventual showdown. The

    [10]On the theme of Britain's insular position see Felix Gilbert, *To the Farewell Address: Ideas of Early American Foreign Policy* (Princeton, NJ, 1961), pp. 19–43.
    [11]Max Savelle, *The Origins of American Diplomacy: The International History of Anglo-america, 1492–1763* (New York, 1967), pp. 182–83.

French added Fort Niagara in 1720, and New York, on its own initiative, countered with the erection of Fort Oswego on Lake Ontario.
The Indian barrier itself now became the area of friction and strife,
with the bitter skirmishes along the frontier creating a violent reaction
in New England, New York, and Virginia. For colonial leaders determined to secure their borders and control the fur trade, it seemed
essential that the English colonies break the French hold on the St.
Lawrence and the Great Lakes trading routes.[12] Thus the struggle for
the wilderness was primarily an issue between the English and the
French residing in the New World. Not until its final stages did this
contest become part of the worldwide imperial competition between
the two great European rivals.

French officials, conscious of the colonial threat to their empire,
prepared for the inescapable British-American assault on their New
World possessions. American traders established a post on the Great
Miami River which the French destroyed in 1751. Then in 1754 the
French erected Fort Duquesne at the forks of the Ohio to strengthen
their claims to the Ohio watershed. Virginia accepted the challenge by
dispatching George Washington and a small military force to argue the
French into withdrawal; instead, the French drove Washington and
his men from the region. This threat to the British position in America
was too patent to be ignored by the London government which sent
General Edward Braddock with an army to drive the French from the
Ohio Valley. The dismal failure of his campaign did not end the struggle; French ambition simply exceeded what the British would tolerate.
For American imperialists only British power could now resolve the
contest for the North American continent. To their immense satisfaction
London fully committed itself to the struggle for the American wilderness with the outbreak of Europe's Seven Years' War in 1756.

During the subsequent years of fighting in America, which culminated in the British capture of Louisbourg in 1758 and the fall of
Quebec in 1759, colonial spokesmen argued the American case for the
total removal of the French from North America. In 1757 John Mitchell,
a British botanist and cartographer who had spent many years in
Virginia, declared that France had no rights on the North American
continent. At stake in the war, wrote Mitchell, was control of the entire
Continent with all its wealth and commerce. If Britain failed to eliminate the French from its New World domain, it would eventually lose
it all. Franklin attacked the popular notion that Britain should retain
Guadeloupe rather than Canada lest the American people, no longer

---

[12]For a brief but excellent account of American efforts to squeeze the French out
of North America see Richard W. Van Alstyne, *Empire and Independence: The International
History of the American Revolution* (New York, 1965), pp. 2–11.

fearful of French encroachment, become dangerous to Britain itself. Only by acquiring Canada, he warned, would the British avoid future wars in defense of their New World empire.[13] In December 1762, Lord Shelburne proclaimed his conviction in Parliament that Britain had fought the war for the security of its American colonies; that purpose required the exclusion of France from North America. What gave Britain its leverage in the peace negotiations to deprive France of its North American empire was the successes not only of its armies in the New World but also those of its European ally, Frederick the Great of Prussia, which compelled France to waste its energies in a futile war on the Continent.

American imperialists had their way. The Peace of Paris (1763) transferred Canada and all French territory east of the Mississippi River, with the exception of New Orleans and the fishing islands of St. Pierre and Miquelon south of Newfoundland, to Great Britain. This treaty marked the ultimate triumph of the first American venture into international affairs. With good reason the war years from 1754 to 1760 provoked an unprecedented burst of goodwill and patriotism toward the British Empire. Franklin expressed the feeling well when he wrote to an English friend in 1760:

> No one can more sincerely rejoice than I do, on the reduction of Canada; and this not merely as I am a colonist, but as I am a Briton. I have long been of [the] opinion, that the foundations of the future grandeur and stability of the British empire lie in America; and though, like other foundations, they are low and little seen, they are nevertheless, broad and strong enough to support the greatest political structure human wisdom ever erected. . . . All the country from the St. Lawrence to the Mississippi will in another century be filled with British people. Britain itself will become vastly more populous, by the immense increase of its commerce; the Atlantic sea will be covered with your trading ships; and your naval power, then continually increasing, will extend your influence round the whole globe, and awe the world![14]

III

Americans emerged from the French and Indian War generally content with their position in the British Empire. They shared Franklin's deep satisfaction with British policy that had freed the frontiers from French encroachments. The Navigation Acts, which confined colonial trade to

[13]"The Interest of Great Britain Considered With Regard to Her Colonies," Smyth, *Writings of Benjamin Franklin*, 4:40–81.

[14]Franklin to Lord Kames, January 3, 1760, in Leonard W. Labaree, ed., *The Papers of Benjamin Franklin* (New Haven, 1966), 9:6–7.

the ports and ships of the empire, were not onerous; those that might have been troublesome the British tended to neglect. During the Seven Years' War colonial merchants profited handsomely from both their trade with the enemy and their expanded smuggling operations. In 1760 the London government ordered the colonial governors to tighten up the customs service, but without success. Americans had become adept at subverting any imperial regulations that the British sought to enforce, employing techniques of obstruction and delay to defend their commercial interests. Assured access to both British markets and defense, Americans agreed that the advantages of membership in the British Empire far outweighed the liabilities. Unfortunately, the long war against France had overextended Britain's financial needs and the burdens of empire. The British national debt had doubled during the war; the carrying charge alone absorbed more than half the annual budget. The London government, moreover, assumed the responsibility for keeping an army in America to enforce the Proclamation Line of 1763 along the ridge of the Appalachians which was designed to guarantee the Indians the possession of their lands on the frontier. To relieve British taxpayers and control American commerce, the George Grenville ministry secured passage of the Sugar Act in 1764.[15]

Suddenly cords of empire that appeared indestructible began to unravel. Parliament's new regulatory and taxing policies, backed by more effective methods of enforcement, came with such speed and force that they rendered the older colonial strategies almost totally obsolete. Whether the new program was fair was scarcely the issue. For a people accustomed to the benefits of empire with little obligation, any controls or taxes would have set dangerous precedents. When London again discovered that its controls were no match for the new refined techniques of smuggling in America, it turned to the Stamp Act, an internal tax on newspapers, legal documents, and other items. This time the reaction went beyond boycotts and the refusal to cooperate. Soon argument drifted into physical violence, reducing the act to a nullity. Convinced that the strategic advantage had passed to America, British leaders advised an end to all parliamentary impositions, and in 1766 Parliament repealed the Stamp Act. One year later the Townshend Acts—a body of external taxes—faced the customary resistance. Before the end of the decade Parliament had lifted most regulations, permitting the profitable empire trade to resume much of its traditional pattern.[16]

---

[15]For the postwar problems confronting Britain see Van Alstyne, *Empire and Independence*, pp. 24–25.

[16]In the colonial resistance to all British efforts at taxing and regulation, the Americans revealed little feeling of gratitude toward Britain for having driven the French from North America. See ibid., pp. 21, 25–26.

Why Parliament could no longer resolve its quarrel with the colonies was already obvious. At issue in London's postwar commercial and taxing policies were infringements not only on American interests but also on American authority. Sir Francis Bernard, the Massachusetts governor, detected the nature of the confrontation when he wrote to Lord Barrington, the secretary at war, on November 23, 1765:

> All the political evils in America arise from the want of ascertaining the relation between Great Britain and the American colonies. . . . In Britain the American governments are considered as corporations empowered to make bye-laws, existing only during the pleasure of Parliament. . . . In America they claim . . . to be perfect states, not otherwise dependent upon Great Britain than by having the same King; which having compleat legislatures within themselves, are no ways subject to that of Great Britain. In a difference so very wide who shall determine?

Parliament, in its Declaratory Act of 1766, asserted that it had the full power to bind the colonies in all cases. Such claims to sovereignty provided the colonies with no legal defense against unjust legislation and thus rendered parliamentary authority a potential danger to liberty itself. For colonial spokesmen the challenge was clear: How could they limit Parliament's legal jurisdiction in colonial matters without denying its historic supremacy in the British constitutional system? To divide authority left unresolved the question of sovereignty. Governor Thomas Hutchinson of Massachusetts carried the debate to its logical conclusion in 1773 when he declared that there was "no line that can be drawn between the supreme authority of Parliament and the total independence of the colonies: it is impossible there should be two independent legislatures in one and the same state for . . . two legislative bodies will make two governments as distinct as the kingdomes of England and Scotland before the Union."[17]

This confrontation over constitutional principles might have drifted on indefinitely had not a handful of Boston citizens in December 1773 chosen to defy Parliament's remaining tax on tea by dumping 342 chests of East India Company tea into the harbor. In England Parliament viewed the Boston Tea Party for what it was—a direct assault on its authority. Lord North informed Parliament that the question was no longer one of legislation or taxation but "whether or not we have any authority there; that it is very clear we have none, if we suffer the

---

[17]Thomas Hutchinson quoted in Bernard Bailyn, *The Ideological Origins of the American Revolution* (Cambridge, MA, 1967), p. 220.

property of our subjects to be destroyed." The ministry's opposition suggested that Parliament show its goodwill be repealing the tax on tea. "If you give up this tax," Solicitor General Alexander Wedderburn stormed back, "you will be required to give up much more, nay, to give up all." Parliament buried the tea tax repeal by a vote of 182 to 49.[18] For Britain the choices that the Americans offered were narrowing. Parliament would now exert its will or yield a portion of the empire. In March 1774 it voted overwhelmingly to punish Boston and then imposed the Quebec Act, which placed the lands to the west of Pennsylvania under the control of the Catholic province of Quebec.

To answer the British challenge colonial leaders assembled the First Continental Congress in Philadelphia on September 5, 1774. Joseph Galloway, leader of the Conservatives, argued that the colonies could not expect to enjoy the privileges of membership in the British Empire without showing some allegiance to it. In the crisis some colonists advocated royal authority in imperial affairs, assuming that the king would be more restrained and accommodating than Parliament. This was scarcely an alternative, as Parliament would not compromise its long-established authority, nor would the king request it. For Americans, as for the British, the choices were narrow: they would accept parliamentary authority or prepare for war. As King George III wrote to Lord North on September 11, 1774, "The dye is now cast, the colonies must either submit or triumph." Lord Mansfield, Britain's chief justice, agreed that there could be no division of authority in the empire. "We are reduced," he declared, "to the alternative of adopting coercive measures, or of forever relinquishing our claim of sovereignty or dominion over the colonies. . . . [Either] the supremacy of the British legislature must be complete, entire, and unconditional or on the other hand, the colonies must be free and independent."[19] Parliament made its final decision in February 1775 when it adopted Lord North's resolution upholding parliamentary authority.

In Philadelphia the Second Continental Congress adopted the war that began at Lexington and Concord in April 1775. In rejecting Lord North's final resolution of February 20, the Congress reminded the British ministry that it could not accept parliamentary supremacy merely on the assurance that Parliament had no intention of misusing

---

[18]Lord North quoted in Van Alstyne, *Empire and Independence*, p. 36. In the debates on the repeal of the tea tax, Edmund Burke declared that "they tell you that your dignity is tied to it. . . .This dignity is a terrible encumbrance to you for it has of late been ever at war with your interest, your equity and every idea of your policy." Quoted in Barbara W. Tuchman, *The March of Folly: From Troy to Vietnam* (New York, 1984), p. 200.

[19]Lord Mansfield quoted in Van Alstyne, *Empire and Independence*, p. 60.

its power.[20] In response the king accused the colonists of planning a general revolt, leaving London no choice but "to put a speedy end to these disorders by the most decisive exertions." What sustained British as well as American leaders in the crisis, and ruled out any last-minute compromises, was the conviction that war assured the final triumph of their purposes. Many of Britain's political and military leaders assumed that Great Britain would win quickly and easily. In time, declared one member of Parliament, Americans loyal to the king would join the British army, Americanize the war, and permit the British soldiers to return home. Americans were equally conscious of the role of force in international affairs; for years, however, they had insisted that British power rested on the wealth and people of America. To young Alexander Hamilton, writing in February 1775, it seemed strange that Britain would risk war to uphold Parliament's claims. "The consequences to Great Britain," he predicted, "would be too destructive to permit her to proceed to extremities, unless she has lost all just sense of her own interest."[21] The American mood of rebelliousness after 1775 simply reflected such convictions of power and importance. "I do verily believe," wrote Richard Henry Lee of Virginia in April 1776, that "N. America will give law to that proud imperious Island."[22]

What quickly turned American leaders toward a quest for independence was their need for an alliance with France. They understood that Europe's endless search for equilibrium dictated the need for some new coalition to offset the power and prestige of Great Britain. On May 2, 1776, David Hartley advised the House of Commons that "it is next to infatuation and madness, for one moment to suppose that we can have an American without a French and Spanish war."[23] His predictions were not wrong. The Comte de Vergennes, after 1774 the able French minister, was determined to employ all means at hand to

[20]In this resolution Lord North proposed that, if any colony agreed to make a grant for the common defense, Parliament would not assess any other tax for that purpose on the colony. For Americans the resolution changed the form of the tax without lightening the burden. In the Virginia Resolutions on Lord North's Conciliatory Proposal of June 10, 1775, Thomas Jefferson explained why Virginia rejected the resolution: "*Because* to render perpetual our exemption from an unjust taxation, we must saddle ourselves with a perpetual tax adequate to the expectations and subject to the disposal of Parliament alone." For the Virginia resolutions see Julian P. Boyd, ed., *The Papers of Thomas Jefferson* (Princeton, NJ, 1950), 1:171.

[21]"The Farmer Refuted," February 23, 1775, in Harold C. Syrett and Jacob E. Cooke, eds., *The Papers of Alexander Hamilton*, 26 vols. (New York, 1961–1979), 1:160.

[22]Lee to Landon Carter, April 1, 1776, in James Curtis Ballagh, ed., *The Letters of Richard Henry Lee* (New York, 1911), 1:173. The British were equally confident that they could resolve the American problem with force.

[23]Hartley quoted in Van Alstyne, *Empire and Independence*, p. 65. Hamilton also predicted French and Spanish involvement in his "The Farmer Refuted," in Syrett and Cooke, *Papers of Hamilton*, 1:159.

retrieve the fallen glory of the French monarchy. "The deplorable peace of 1763," he reminded the king, "the partition of Poland, and in fact, other causes equally disastrous, have struck the greatest blows to the respect for your crown." The restoration of French prestige required the humiliation of England.[24]

Not all Americans anticipated with elation the internationalization of the war. Loyalists argued that America should not entrust its future to the European balance of power but rather to British protection. Others saw immediately that without France's help the Americans would never win the victories necessary to establish their rights within the British Empire. John Adams readily acknowledged the French interest in the American cause and recorded his arguments in favor of a mission to France: "Interest could not lie. . . . The Interest of France was so obvious, and her motives so cogent, that nothing but a judicial infatuation of her councils could restrain her from embracing US."[25] But Adams feared that the lack of coercive power in the colonies would render France the dominant partner in any alliance. For that reason he argued against a political or military connection with France, preferring only a commercial arrangement. At the same time, Lee advocated a more venturesome approach to Europe. France, he knew, would not break its formal peace with England merely to assure Americans a more favorable status in the British Empire; therefore, the colonies could obtain the needed help from France only by fighting for their independence. On June 2, 1776, he reminded his fellow Virginian, Landon Carter, that only "by a timely alliance with proper and willing powers in Europe" would colonial leaders "secure America from the despotic aims of the British Court. . . . But no State in Europe will either Treat or Trade with us so long as we consider ourselves Subjects of G.B. . . . *It is not choice then but necessity that calls for Independence, as the only means by which foreign Alliance can be obtained.*"[26] On July 2 the Congress declared the United States an independent nation.

IV

Even as American leaders adopted Thomas Jefferson's Declaration of Independence, they were aware of their reliance on France and the need for involving that country in American affairs. Robert Morris

[24]For the French interest in America see Robert Rhodes Crout, "In Search of a 'Just and Lasting Peace': The Treaty of 1783, Louis XVI, Vergennes, and the Regeneration of the Realm," *International History Review* 5 (August 1983): 372–75.

[25]Lyman H. Butterfield, ed., *Diary and Autobiography of John Adams*, 4 vols. (Cambridge, MA, 1961–1966), 3:328–39.

[26]Lee to Landon Carter, June 2, 1776, in Ballagh, *Letters of Richard Henry Lee*, 1:198 (emphasis added).

reminded John Jay of this on September 23, 1776: "It appears clear to me that we may very soon involve all Europe in a War by managing properly the apparent forwardness of the Court of France; it's a horrid consideration that our own Safety should call on us to involve other nations in the Calamities of War. Can this be morally right or have Morality and Policy nothing to do with each other? Perhaps it may not be good Policy to investigate the Question at this time." Members of Congress anticipated a vigorous European response to the threatened breakup of the British Empire. Elbridge Gerry wrote in November that "it is acknowledged on all hands that now is the Time for France and Spain to destroy the Balance of power which has been heretofore said to be preserved in Europe, but considered as preponderating against them."[27] Samuel Adams added in a letter of February 1777 that "the war between Britain and the United States of America will affect the Balance of Power in Europe. Will not the different Powers take different sides to adjust the Balance to their different Interests?" Writing again in April, Adams said: "When it suits the Interest of foreign Powers they will aid us substantially."[28] From the moment of its inception the United States entered the world of diplomacy and power as an active and willful participant.

Franklin landed in France on December 4, 1776 to negotiate an alliance with Vergennes. Behind Franklin's success lay the American promise of full military exertion until the conclusion of the war, the decisive American victory at Saratoga in October 1777, and the growing French interest in severing Britain from its power base in the New World. Already French involvement in American affairs had become so extensive that France either had to turn back ignominiously or fully commit itself to the American cause, even at the risk of war. French and American officials in Paris signed treaties of commerce and alliance on February 6, 1778. The alliance bound the two countries to behave as good and faithful allies, with Article II designed to maintain effectually "the liberty, Sovereignty, and independence absolute and unlimited of the said United States, as well as in Matters of Government as of commerce." The two allies agreed to conclude neither a truce nor peace with Great Britain without the consent of the other; they agreed, in addition, not to lay down their arms until Britain recognized the independence of the United States. In March, Britain and France broke

---

[27]Gerry quoted in James H. Hutson, *John Adams and the Diplomacy of the American Revolution* (Lexington, KY, 1980), p. 9.

[28]Samuel Adams to Samuel Cooper, February 4, 1777, in Harry A. Cushing, ed., *Writings of Samuel Adams*, 4 vols. (New York, 1904–1908), 3:354.

diplomatic relations, and within days both countries were at war.

John Adams quickly deserted his earlier doubts and accepted the alliance with France as a promising response to the challenges of 1778, convinced that the French interest in American independence was sufficient to render France a trustworthy ally. France, having given up all pretension to territory in North America, was not likely to harbor jealousy or animosity toward the new American Republic; thus, Adams foresaw no future American wars except with Britain and its allies. "The United States," he concluded, "will be for ages the natural bulwark of France against the hostile designs of England against her, and France is the natural defense of the United States against the rapacious spirit of Great Britain against them. France is a nation so vastly eminent . . . that united in close alliance with our States, and enjoying the benefit of our trade, there is not the smallest reason to doubt but both will be a sufficient curb upon the naval power of Great Britain."[29] As the new American commissioner, Adams wrote from Paris in August 1778 that "the longer I live in Europe, and the more I consider our Affairs, the more important our Alliance to France appears to me. It is a rock upon which we may safely build."[30]

Still Adams recognized Britain's importance to the European equilibrium. A Dutch merchant in Paris informed him that "they in Holland had regarded England as the Bulwark of the Protestant Religion and the most important Weight in the Ballance of Power in Europe against France." Adams answered that he had been educated from his cradle in the same opinion.[31] He knew that Britain would emerge from the war as an essential element in the European balance and reminded James Warren that "the Annihilation of a Nation never takes place. It depends wholly on herself to determine whether she shall sink down into the Rank of the middling powers of Europe or whether she shall maintain the second place in the Scale."[32]

European diplomacy assumed that interests alone determined the objectives and guided the behavior of nations. Mutual interests, not affection, underwrote the Franco-American alliance. Washington gave this central principle of international politics classic form when he

[29]John Adams to Samuel Adams, July 28, 1778, in Francis Wharton, ed., *The Revolutionary Diplomatic Correspondence of the United States*, 6 vols. (Washington, 1889), 2:668.

[30]Adams to James Warren, August 4, 1778, in *Warren-Adams Letters: Being Chiefly a Correspondence Among John Adams, Samuel Adams, and James Warren* (Boston: Massachusetts Historical Society, 1925), 2:40.

[31]Butterfield, *Diary and Autobiography of John Adams*, 4:38–39.

[32]Adams to Warren, August 4, 1778, in *Warren-Adams Letters*, 2:40.

observed in November 1778: "Hatred of England may carry some to excess of Confidence in France; especially when motives of gratitude are thrown into the scale. . . . I am heartily disposed to entertain the most favourable sentiments of our new ally and to cherish them in others to a reasonable degree; but it is a maxim founded on the universal experience of mankind, that no nation is to be trusted farther than it is bound by its interest; and no prudent statesman or politician will venture to depart from it."[33] When a British general argued before the House of Commons in May 1780 that distance, tradition, language, and religion rendered the Franco-American alliance unnatural, Adams retorted: "I know of no better rule than this,—when two nations have the same interests in general, they are natural allies; when they have opposite interests, they are natural enemies. . . . [But] the habits of affection or enmity between nations are easily changed as circumstances vary, and as essential interests alter."[34] Like all alliances, that with France could be temporary. While earlier France had posed a danger to the English colonies in America, in 1780 common interests rendered it a natural friend.

No less than Adams and Washington, members of Congress welcomed the French alliance because they assumed the existence of strong mutual interests in the struggle against Britain. "We must expect all nations will be influenced by their own interest," wrote William Whipple of New Hampshire in July 1779, "and so far we may expect the Friendship of any power that inclines to form an alliance with us, but if we expect more, we shall certainly be disapppointed."[35] France's decision to entrust its peace efforts to Russia and Prussia as mediating powers in 1781 troubled those who had no confidence in the two continental courts. However, Maryland's Daniel of St. Thomas Jenifer noted in June 1781 that France "must procure us tolerable terms, or She cannot expect to keep us long in her interest, therefore I trust more to her policy than her Justice."[36] Unlike Jenifer, Delaware's Thomas Rodney opposed the instructions of June 1781 which required the American commissioners in Europe to govern themselves ultimately according to the advice of the French court. For him the new orders were dangerous and humiliating. Still he agreed that the mediating powers would readily consent to American independence because "it

[33]Washington to Henry Laurens, November 14, 1778, in John C. Fitzpatrick, ed., *The Writings of George Washington*, 37 vols. (Washington, 1931–1940), 13:256.

[34]Adams to Edmond Charles Genêt, May 17, 1780, in *The Works of John Adams* (Boston, 1853), 7:172–75.

[35]Whipple to Josiah Bartless, July 27, 1779, in Edmund C. Burnett, ed., *Letters of Members of the Continental Congress* (Washington, 1928), 4:346.

[36]Jenifer to George Weedon, June 5, 1781, ibid., 6:112.

will be ever the Interest of France that they should do this lest we should at a future day form an Alliance with great Britain."[37]

V

Historians often have viewed the diplomacy of the American Revolution with cynicism largely because it revealed the intense rivalry of the European powers and their repeated efforts to deny the new American Republic everything that it wanted. That diplomacy demonstrated that even allies can have legitimate interests so much in conflict that no possible settlement can distribute the gains or losses in any equitable fashion. So diverse were the interests of the nations fighting England, so limited their military exertions, that no one could predict the design of the final treaties that would reestablish the peace. At the end Britain faced the United States, France, Spain, and Holland in something approaching a world war. Spain and the United States were allied with France but not with each other; the Dutch were allied to no one. Whatever the differing purposes for which these nations fought, the search for a settlement conformed to traditional principles. For the American commissioners in Europe—Franklin, Adams, and Jay, dispatched to Spain in late 1779—the wartime diplomacy demonstrated in classic fashion not only the close relationship between military and diplomatic success but also the manner in which each nation placed its interests in hierarchical order, readily giving up secondary objectives to assure the achievement of those that mattered. Every country emerged from the war with a respectable settlement. This was the real measure of the competence, moderation, and goodwill that characterized the negotiations. There were no reparations, no special punishments, no lingering desires for revenge; this was peacemaking at its best.

Throughout the wartime negotiations France, the dominant member of the coalition fighting Britain, remained faithful to its commitment to American independence. Vergennes reminded the French minister in America in October 1778 that France would never accept a peace proposal that did not grant absolute independence to the United States. On that point, he wrote, "his majesty could not weaken."[38] That commitment rendered France's needed alliance with Spain elusive. Spain's major interest as a declining power—one far outweighing all others—was the perpetuation of its New World empire. For that reason it had no interest in American independence, surmising accurately that an

---

[37]Rodney to Caesar Rodney, June 15, 1781, ibid., 121–22.

[38]Vergennes to Gérard de Rayneval, October 26, 1778, in John J. Meng, ed., *Dispatches and Instructions of Conrad Alexander Gerard, 1778–1780* (Baltimore, 1939), p. 356.

independent republic in America would soon endanger the Spanish hold on Louisiana. In the Convention of Aranjuez of April 1779, which brought Spain into the war, the French agreed to support the Spanish claims to Gibraltar, Minorca, Mobile, Pensacola, Honduras, and Campeche. France added the transfer of Florida to Spain, but avoided the question of Spanish control of the Mississippi. The French court was not committed to any specific boundaries for the United States; it was concerned only that its ally, Spain, eventually gain a settlement that protected its interests in America. What distracted Vergennes after the convention was the sudden realization that Spain and the United States were in direct conflict over the future of the American West. Congress, in framing its war aims during the spring and autumn of 1779, insisted not only on the Mississippi River as the western boundary of the United States but also on the free navigation of that river between the Florida border and the Gulf of Mexico.[39] It was not strange that Jay, conveying Congress's demands to the Spanish court, could never gain formal recognition or reach an agreement. The Mississippi, declared the Spanish minister, the Count of Floridablanca, "was an object that the king had so much on his heart that he would never relinquish it."[40]

As late as 1782 the London government, with good reason, resisted the granting of independence to the United States. In the American quest for nationhood, the British faced a totally unprecedented challenge to the integrity of their empire. No British official could know where a successful revolution in America might lead. As a minimum, King George predicted in 1779, Britain would lose much of the West Indies as well as Ireland. Still for British leaders time ran out, and in November 1781 London learned not only of the French-American triumph at Yorktown but also of the French victories throughout the West Indies and Minorca. Such British disasters toppled the North government in March 1782. The new government under Lords Rockingham and Shelburne, convinced at last that Britain could no longer withhold the recognition of American independence, opened negotiations in April by sending Oswald to Paris. Vergennes agreed that the Americans should confer directly with the British under their own instructions, provided that the French negotiations proceed at the same pace and that the United States and France sign treaties at the same time.

---

[39]Proceedings of Congress, March–September 1779, in Wharton, *Revolutionary Diplomatic Correspondence*, 3:95–96, 294, 301, 311, 324–26.

[40]The Spanish capture of Mobile in the spring of 1780 caused the Madrid government to become even more demanding. See Henry P. Johnston, ed., *Correspondence and Public Papers of John Jay*, 4 vols. (New York, 1890–1893), 1:386.

Franklin summoned Jay to Paris on April 22. In carrying the burden of American diplomacy because of Franklin's subsequent illness, Jay faced the problem of securing from the British the immediate recognition of American independence, the fisheries along the Newfoundland coast, and the desired boundaries along the Great Lakes, the Mississippi, and the northern border of Florida. At the same time, Jay sought an agreement with the Spanish minister in Paris, the Count d'Aranda, on the question of the Mississippi River boundary and free navigation of that river to the Gulf of Mexico. Aranda, to protect Spanish interests in the West, turned to the French court for support. Versailles still hoped to satisfy the Spanish government. During the summer of 1782, Vergennes's English-speaking undersecretary, Gérard de Rayneval, joined Aranda in proposing a series of compromise boundaries between the Alleghenies and the Mississippi, all of which were designed to keep the United States away from Louisiana.[41] Aranda's line, Jay complained, "would leave near as much country between it and the Mississippi as there is between it and the Atlantic Ocean."[42] France's obvious sympathy for the Spanish position prompted him to ignore Congress's instructions and to seek a solution with Britain without reference to the French court. "We can depend upon the French," he explained, "only to see that we are separated from England, but it is not in their interest that we should become a great and formidable people, and therefore they will not help us to become so."[43]

Jay understood correctly that Great Britain, once committed to American independence, had no desire to keep the United States away from the Mississippi. During the concluding negotiations with Britain, Adams, who arrived in Paris from Holland on October 26, 1782, observed that the American commissioners would obtain the Mississippi River boundary only because they had negotiated independently of France.[44] The final treaty with Britain, signed in Paris on November 30, conveyed to the United States both independence and boundaries bordered by the Great Lakes, the Mississippi, and Florida. Vergennes, reading the text, was astounded. For two years he had assumed that American terms, totally unacceptable to Spain, would in some measure be unacceptable to Britain as well. "You will notice," he informed Gérard de Rayneval, that the "English buy the peace more than they make it.

---

[41]Jay to Robert R. Livingston (secretary of foreign affairs), November 17, 1782, in Wharton, *Revolutionary Diplomatic Correspondence*, 6:22–23.

[42]Jay quoted in Richard B. Morris, *The Peacemakers: The Great Powers and American Independence* (Boston,1983), p. 306.

[43]Jay quoted in ibid., p. 310.

[44]Adams to Livingston, October 31, 1782, in Wharton, *Revolutionary Diplomatic Correspondence*, 5:839.

Their concessions, in fact, exceed all that I should have thought possible."[45] With American independence France also achieved its central
objective in the war, but beyond that it gained little. Shortly after the
Anglo-French negotiations got under way the news of Admiral de
Grasse's stunning defeat in the West Indies reached Europe. From then
on the British made it clear that they expected the American settlement
to follow the Peace of Paris of 1763. France received complete control
of Saint Pierre and Miquelon, some gains in India and Africa, as well
as the promise of a new commercial treaty with Britain.

Given the conflicting purposes of Spain and the United States in
the Mississippi Valley, French diplomacy could not have been more
honest and consistent than it was.[46] With the Spanish failure at Gibraltar in late 1782, France had no choice but to abandon its promise of
Gibraltar to Spain, made in the Convention of Aranjuez. Spain received
other compensations, including Minorca and Florida, but it could not
prevent the extension of the United States to the Mississippi simply
because Britain, in control of that decision, was willing to accept that
boundary. With control of both banks of the Mississippi below 31°,
Spain could compel the United States to negotiate further if it would
acquire free navigation and a commercial depot south of that parallel.
So complete was the American success in reaching the Mississippi that
it left Spain, a cobelligerent, completely distraught. For Spain the defeat
of Britain turned out to be scarcely a victory at all; it sealed the fate
of Spanish Louisiana, Texas, and the far Southwest. At the end Aranda
could observe, with understandable regret, that "this federal republic
is born a pigmy. A day will come when it will be a giant, even a
colossus, formidable in these countries. Liberty of conscience, the facil-
ity for establishing a new population on immense lands, as well as the
advantages of the new government, will draw thither farmers and arti-
sans from all nations. In a few years we shall watch with grief the
tyrannical existence of this same colossus."

Despite their elation the three American commissioners could not
be sure that their accomplishment would stand. The treaty required
the approval of the British government as well as the Continental
Congress at home. In London the arrangement was decidedly unpopular, producing Shelburne's downfall in February 1783. Yet, in the
absence of any clear alternative, Parliament accepted the treaty anyway. The commissioners in Paris were troubled by the possibility that
Congress might reject their work, but the recently arrived Henry Laurens was scarcely worried. "I cannot think our country," he wrote,

[45]Vergennes to Rayneval, December 4, 1782, ibid., 6:107.
[46]See Crout, "In Search of a 'Just and Lasting Peace,' " pp. 396–98.

"will hang their ministers merely for their simplicity in being cheated into independence, the fisheries, and half the Great Lakes." Congress did rebuke the commissioners for departing from their instructions but ultimately, on April 15, 1783, approved the preliminary treaty. Hartley, a friend of both Franklin and America, arrived in Paris to negotiate a definitive treaty with the commissioners; the Americans, however, refused to make any further concessions. On September 3 the British and American negotiators signed the preliminary articles at Hartley's lodgings in the Hôtel de York, and later that day at Versailles the British signed definitive treaties with France and Spain.

VI

With the assurance of independence after November 1782, the United States faced the task of defining its proper relationship to a Europe at peace. How could the new nation best defend its independence, as well as its other interests, against the still great powers of Europe? As late as August 1782, Adams revealed a pervading fear of the British. "They hate us, universally, from the throne to the footstool and would annihilate us, if in their power," he wrote to Jay.[47] But by November Adams had changed his mind, saying that the United States could entrust its future to a policy of neutrality toward Europe's competing factions. The balance of power that had secured American independence would now, by keeping Britain and France at opposite poles, guarantee the status quo in the New World. America, he recalled, "had been a Football between contending Nations from the Beginning, and it was easy to foresee that France and England would endeavor to involve Us in their future Wars. I thought [it] our Interest and Duty to avoid [these] as much as possible and to be compleatly independent and have nothing to do but in Commerce with either of them."[48] One week later he confided to his diary his conviction that the United States should assert its freedom of action in its future relations with Europe:

> You are afraid says Mr. Oswald to day of being made the Tools of the Powers of Europe,—Indeed I am says I.—What Powers says he.—All of them says I. It is obvious that all the Powers of Europe will be continually maneuvering with Us, to work us into their real or imaginary Ballances of Power. They will all wish to make of Us a Make Weight Candle, when they are weighing out their Pounds. Indeed it is not surprising for we shall very often if

[47]Adams to Jay, August 13, 1782, in *Works of John Adams*, 7:610.
[48]Diary of John Adams, November 11, 1782, in Butterfield, *Diary and Autobiography of John Adams*, 3:52.

not always be able to turn the Scale. But I think it ought to be our Rule not to meddle, and that of all the Powers of Europe not to desire Us, or perhaps even to permit Us to interfere, if they can help it.[49]

Adams concluded that Europe's equilibrium placed a premium on American neutrality, that strong ties with some European states would generate animosities in others. "There is a Ballance of Power in Europe," he reminded Warren in March 1783. "Nature has formed it. Practice and Habit have confirmed it, and it must forever exist. It may be disturbed for a time, by the accidental Removal of a Weight from one Scale to the other; but there will be a continual Effort to restore the Equilibrium. The Powers of Europe now think Great Britain too powerful. They will see her Power diminished with pleasure. But they cannot see Us throw ourselves headlong into the Scale of Bourbon without Jealousy and Terror."[50] For Adams it was essential that the United States grant no exclusive arrangements or form perpetual alliances with the powers in one scale. To do so would inevitably make enemies of those in the other. "Congress," he stressed, "adopted these Principles and this System in its purity, and by their Wisdom have succeeded most perfectly in preventing every Power in the World from taking Part against them."

Unlike Adams, Franklin distrusted Britain too deeply to entrust America's future peace and security to a policy of neutrality toward Europe. "It is our firm connection with France," he wrote in late December 1782, that "gives us weight with England, and respect throughout Europe. If we were to break faith with this nation, *on whatever pretence*, England would again trample on us, and every other nation despise us."[51] In November 1783, Franklin reported that the good disposition of France toward the United States would continue into the new era of peace, but he sustained his strong distrust of Britain. "Tho' it has made peace with us," he admonished Thomas Mifflin, "it is not in truth reconcil'd either to us, or to its loss of us, but still flatters itself with Hopes, that some Change in the Affairs of Europe, or some Disunion among ourselves, may afford them an Opportunity of Recovering their Dominion, punishing those who have most offended, and securing our future Dependence."[52] Still Franklin understood that it was the rivalry between Britain and France that had permitted the United States to achieve independence; in some measure, therefore, its

---

[49]Diary, November 18, 1782, ibid., p. 61.

[50]Adams to Warren, March 20, 1783, in *Warren-Adams Letters*, 2:192.

[51]Franklin to Samuel Cooper, December 26, 1782, in Smyth, *Writings of Franklin*, 8:649.

[52]Franklin to Mifflin, December 25, 1783, ibid., 9:131.

continued independence rested on the rivalries and power that had dictated the terms of the recent peace. What disturbed Franklin and others who distrusted Britain was the possibility that France, totally involved on the European continent in some future war, would leave Britain free to deal with the United States alone.

Adams rejected such fears. Nothing disturbed his faith in a policy of neutrality toward the two leading powers of Europe. For him commercial impartiality between them not only would maximize profits but also would reinforce America's political neutrality. He argued in March 1783 that the United States, as an independent country, should extend no trading privileges to either Britain or France. "We are," he wrote, "under no Ties of Honor, Conscience or good Faith, nor of Policy, Gratitude or Politeness, to sacrifice any profits which We can obtain in Trade with Great Britain, merely to promote the Trade of France." It was better, he believed, for the United States to seek the best bargains; the price and quality of goods should be its criterion. "Let the Rivalry of our Trade be free and unrestrained," he concluded. "Let Nations contend which shall furnish Us the best Goods at the cheapest Rate."[53] Adams continued to regard the European equilibrium sufficient to protect American security against the possibility of a major European assault. In his profound disagreement with Franklin, he argued that France had served its own interests admirably in supporting the American cause. Franklin complained that Adams expressed such views openly, sometimes in the presence of English diplomats, and insisted that he could prove French animosity toward the United States with "hundreds of Instances." Franklin feared that Adams's open hostility toward France created the impression in Paris that anti-French views were sufficiently widespread in the United States to endanger the ongoing Franco-American alliance.[54]

Adams cared nothing for France's friendship as he continued to advocate a policy of neutrality. From The Hague in February 1784 he wrote: "May the world continue at peace! But if it should not, I hope we shall have wisdom enough to keep ourselves out of any broil. As I am quite in sentiment with the Baron de Nolken, the Swedish ambassador at St. James's, who did me the honor to visit me, although I had not visited him. 'Sir,' said he, 'I take it for granted, that you will have sense enough to see us in Europe cut each other's throats with a philosophical tranquillity.' "[55] With Europe at peace, nothing in the immediate future, it seemed, would compel the United States to decide whether its interests demanded neutrality or a reaffirmation of the

[53]Adams to Warren, March 20, 1783, in *Warren-Adams Letters*, 2:191–92.
[54]Franklin to Livingston, July 22, 1783, in Smyth, *Writings of Franklin*, 9:61–62.
[55]Adams to the president of Congress, February 10, 1784, in *Works of John Adams*, 8:178.

French alliance, the only real choices before it. Whatever course the nation might choose, its leaders, through a remarkably instructive decade of war and diplomacy, had recognized all the elements of power politics that would determine the success or failure of its future ventures abroad.

CHAPTER ONE

The Trials of Independence*

WITH THEIR INDEPENDENCE IN 1783 the American people accepted the advantages of a separate national existence as well as the inescapable risks. No longer members of the British Empire, they could look to London for neither the sources of power nor the experience in world affairs which, through earlier decades, had guaranteed them not only a high measure of security but also an enriching domestic and foreign trade. Convinced at the end that British commercial restrictions had dimmed their economic future, they anticipated independence as the necessary prelude to the creation of an expanding commercial empire. Thomas Paine had argued in *Common Sense* that the American people, much as they had prospered under British rule, would have flourished even more had they been free of European authority. "The commerce by which [America] hath enriched herself," he wrote, "are the necessaries of life, and will always have a market while eating is the custom of Europe."[1] Supported by the appeal of American products, American merchants would regain their British markets even as they penetrated those of the whole European continent. One Massachusetts newspaper predicted that American commerce, freed of its former shackles, would now "extend to every part of the globe, without passing through the medium of England, that rotten island, absorbed in debt, and crumbling fast to annihilation." Alexander Hamilton predicted confidently in March 1783 that "the acknowledgement of our independence by

---

*Published as "The Trials of Independence," in *Adams and Jefferson in Europe, 1783–1789* (Mary Baldwin College, Staunton, Virginia, 1984). Reprinted by permission.

[1]*Common Sense* (1776), in Moncure Daniel Conway, ed., *The Writings of Thomas Paine* (New York, 1894), 1:86.

Great Britain will facilitate connections and intercourse between these states and the powers of Europe in general."[2] In Paris the recent diplomatic triumphs, which assured America's independence, merely enhanced the mood of confidence. If the nation was small in population, it was large in territory.

America's relations with Europe appeared promising enough, and its three experienced diplomats in Paris—Benjamin Franklin, John Adams, and John Jay—were prepared to extend their earlier successes in negotiating with leading European powers into a new era of peace. As no war was in the offing, the commissioners were free to concentrate their efforts, not on questions of equilibrium and alliances but on the expansion of American commerce with Europe. Trade with France rested on the wartime Treaty of Amity and Commerce, presumably designed to promote commerce between the two countries, but during the war that commerce failed to develop. When peace removed all external restraints, American merchants complained that their efforts in France suffered from numerous internal duties and monopolies embodied in French commercial and financial practice. Franklin hoped that France would remove such impediments quickly so that Franco-American commerce would reach the grandeur promised by the destruction of the British monopoly. Elsewhere the immediate prospects seemed bright. As early as April 1783, Franklin negotiated a commercial treaty with Sweden, one based on existing treaties with France and Holland. "The Treaty with Sweden is made," Adams reported to James Warren on April 12, and "Denmark has ordered our Flag to be respected like that of Republicks of the first order. Portugal has done the same. The Emperor has an Inclination to treat with Us but The House of Austria never makes the first Advances." The Swedish king ratified the new treaty in May; Congress did so in July.[3]

In Paris, Danish, Portuguese, Prussian, Austrian, and other European officials assured Franklin that their rulers desired treaties of friendship and commerce with the United States; even English merchants were eager to resume their commerce with the former colonies.

---

[2]Hamilton to William Floyd and George Clinton, March 17, 1783, in Harold C. Syrett, ed., *The Papers of Alexander Hamilton*, 26 vols. (New York, 1962), 3:290; Massachusetts newspaper quoted in Merrill Jensen, *The New Nation: A History of the United States During the Confederation, 1781–1789* (New York, 1950), p. 154.

[3]Franklin to the Comte de Vergennes, March 16, 1783, in Albert Henry Smyth, ed., *The Writings of Benjamin Franklin*, 10 vols. (New York, 1907), 9:19–20; Franklin to Livingston, April 15, 1783, ibid., p. 30; Adams to Warren, April 12, 1783, in *Warren-Adams Letters: Being Chiefly a Correspondence Among John Adams, Samuel Adams, and James Warren* (Boston: Massachusetts Historical Society, 1925), 2:208; Report on the Treaty With Sweden, July 24, 1783, in William T. Hutchinson and William M. E. Rachal, eds., *The Papers of James Madison* (Chicago, 1971), 7:243–45.

From almost all the ports of Europe, Franklin received applications from persons who desired appointments as American consuls, and, in a letter to Robert R. Livingston, secretary of foreign affairs, he rejoiced over this burgeoning interest in the nation's trade: "Since our trade is laid open, and no longer a Monopoly to England, all Europe seems desirous of sharing in it."[4]

During the final peace negotiations, Congress hoped to add Britain to the short list of countries with which it had achieved bilateral commercial arrangements. Lord Shelburne, who headed the British ministry which recognized American independence, favored a total rapprochement with the United States, including the restitution of all commercial benefits that Americans had enjoyed in the empire. He was even prepared to grant American goods and ships free access to British West Indian and Caribbean ports. Despite his open acceptance of the principle of commercial reciprocity, Shelburne eliminated a commercial arrangement from the preliminary treaty. His negotiators argued, wrote Franklin, that "some statutes were in the way, which must be repealed before a treaty of that kind could be well formed, and that this was a matter to be considered in Parliament."[5] Shelburne introduced a measure to admit American goods and bottoms at least temporarily into British and West Indian ports on the same terms as British goods and ships. With Parliament's approval he hoped to negotiate a full commercial treaty with the United States, but unfortunately the American diplomats, after signing the preliminary peace treaty in November 1782, retained no specific powers to negotiate such a treaty. Adams therefore urged Congress to accredit a minister and instruct him "to enter into a temporary convention for regulating the present trade for a limited number of months or years, or until the treaty of commerce shall be completed."[6] Meanwhile, David Hartley, whose sympathies for the United States matched Shelburne's, remained in Paris to negotiate a commercial treaty with the Americans as soon as they received the necessary commission and instructions.

Parliament was debating the issue of trade with America when the Shelburne ministry fell in February 1783, largely because of its generous behavior toward the United States. Conscious of the rising tide of mercantilism in Great Britain, Adams complained to Warren

---

[4]Franklin to Livingston, April 15, 1783, in Smyth, *Writings of Franklin*, 9:31, 33; Franklin to Livingston, June 12, 1783, ibid., p. 49; Franklin to Livingston, July 22, 1783, ibid., pp. 62, 70.

[5]Franklin to Livingston, December 5, 1782, ibid. (New York, 1907), 8:633.

[6]Adams to the president of Congress, November 9, 1783, in *Works of John Adams* (Boston, 1853), 8:157; Adams to Livingston, February 5, 1783, in Francis Wharton, ed., *The Revolutionary Diplomatic Correspondence of the United States*, 6 vols. (Washington, 1889), 6:242–47.

that Shelburne's refusal to embody a commercial arrangement in the provisional treaty had permitted the critical moment for negotiating a treaty of commerce to pass, apparently forever.[7] Britain's shipping interests now controlled British policy, supported by Lord Sheffield's new pamphlet, *Observations on the Commerce of the American States with Europe and the West Indies* (1783), in which he argued that the Americans, as foreigners, should be excluded from their former colonial trade and that British shipping could gain at American expense and compensate Britain for its financial losses in the war. Sheffield assumed a renewal of the former imperial trade on British terms. As he observed, "At least four-fifths of the importations from Europe into the American States are at all times made upon credit; and undoubtedly the States are in greater want of credit at this time than at former periods. It can be had only in Great Britain." With equal assurance he predicted that Congress was too impotent to retaliate: "It will not be an easy matter to bring the American states to act as a nation. They are not to be feared as such by us. . . . We might as well dread the effects of combinations among the German as among the American states."[8] Parliamentary majorities seemed to agree as they entrusted commercial arrangements to the king in council.

In early May Congress was urged to issue a special commission to Franklin, Adams, and Jay to negotiate a commercial treaty with Britain.[9] It no longer mattered; there would be no commercial arrangement in the final treaty. Free to act, British leadership responded to Parliament's mercantilist preferences by embodying a more and more restrictive policy in a series of orders in council. Following colonial practice, these restrictions permitted American raw materials and foodstuffs, but not manufactured goods, to enter the British home islands in American vessels. Finally, on July 2, 1783, an order in council closed the British West Indies to American ships and goods except for an enumerated list that did not include the country's dominant exports. In Paris the American commissioners responded to the British decrees by advising Congress that they would drop all commercial articles from a definitive treaty with Britain and "leave everything of that kind to a future special treaty, to be made either in America or in Europe, as Congress shall think fit to order." Hartley, unmindful of London's

---

[7]Adams to Warren, March 21, 1783, in *Warren–Adams Letters*, 2:194.

[8]Sheffield quoted in Samuel Flagg Bemis, "John Jay," Bemis, ed., *The American Secretaries of State and Their Diplomacy* (New York, 1928), 1:223–24. See also Richard B. Morris, ed., *John Jay: The Winning of the Peace* (New York, 1980), 2:536–37.

[9]Report on a Treaty of Commerce, May 1, 1783, in Syrett, *Papers of Hamilton*, 3:344–45.

commitment to a mercantilist policy, continued to reassure the American diplomats and to quarrel with his superiors in favor of reciprocity.[10]

Sheffield's predictions soon proved to be disturbingly accurate. In June 1783, Henry Laurens had reported from London that the British government, in rejecting commercial reciprocity with the United States, intended to have the American trade without paying any price for it, especially that of granting American shippers the coveted West Indian carrying trade. As early as May, U.S. ports had been open to British ships; the first imports were enough to reawaken among Americans the general ardor for English products so recently denied them by war and proscription. What drew American trade to British ports, other than habit, was the superior ability of the British manufacturers, which resulted in better goods at lower prices, as well as Britain's greater capital resources and credit facilities. Independence in no way curtailed America's capacity to produce a wide variety of marketable foods and raw materials—fish, tobacco, rice, lumber, furs, and whale oil. To generate prosperity and reasonable profits and to protect its shipping interests, the country required access to foreign markets under conditions that assured fair prices and suitable exchange. London's power to dictate the terms of Anglo-American commercial relations from the outset endangered both the Republic's economic welfare and its standing among the nations of Europe. Americans understood that the negotiation of reciprocal commercial arrangements would comprise, in large measure, Europe's final recognition of the United States as an equal among nations. They discovered not only a contemptuous government in London but also commercial barriers and burdensome trade practices in the Continental states of Europe. Having entered the commercial world of the Atlantic in 1783 as a debtor nation with a colonial economy, the United States faced the insuperable challenge of establishing favorable trade relations in a mercantilist world, without the power to counter the hostile measures of the European governments with mercantile policies of its own.[11]

Especially humiliating for the United States was its troubles with the Barbary pirates. Using them not as independent entrepreneurs but as agents of their governments, the rulers of the North African states—

[10]Franklin, Jay, and Henry Laurens to Livingston, July 27, 1783, in Wharton, *Revolutionary Diplomatic Correspondence*, 6:600; Morris, *John Jay*, 2:537–38; Jay to William Bingham, July 29, 1783, ibid., pp. 571–72; Edward Bancroft to Jay, August 1783, ibid., pp. 575–76; Adams to the president of Congress, November 13, 1783, in *Works of John Adams*, 8:158–59.

[11]Edmund Randolph to James Madison, May 24, 1783, in Hutchinson and Rachal, *Papers of Madison*, 7:73; Virginia Delegates to Benjamin Harrison, August 14, 1783, ibid., p. 275; Madison to Randolph, August 18, 30, 1783, ibid., pp. 281, 295–96; Madison to Thomas Jefferson, September 20, 1783, ibid., p. 353.

Algiers, Tunis, Tripoli, and Morocco—had transformed piracy into a national industry. By capturing merchant vessels, holding sailors and cargoes for ransom, and extorting protection money from nations willing to pay, these petty sultans discouraged European and American sea captains from entering the Mediterranean. Rather than go to war, Europe's maritime powers preferred negotiated arrangements providing for gifts and tribute. As members of the British Empire, colonial merchants sailed the Mediterranean under the protection of British treaties. They had established a lucrative trade with North Africa, averaging generally eighty to one hundred voyages per year. With the war of independence, American sea captains lost their access to admiralty passes; now they faced the pirates, without benefit of treaties or adequate naval protection.

What puzzled Franklin and other American observers was Europe's refusal to combine and destroy the nests and free the Mediterranean of the pirates. Such indulgence gave the United States no apparent choice but to join the other powers in negotiating the necessary tribute to protect its ships. "I think it not improbable," wrote Franklin, "that those Rovers may be privately encouraged by the English to fall upon us, to prevent our Interference in the Carrying Trade; for I have in London heard it as a Maxim among the Merchants, that, *if there were no Algiers, it would be worth England's while to build one.*"[12] Adams was convinced that the Mediterranean trade was worth more than the expense of the tribute required to secure treaties with the pirates; by roaming the seas the corsairs raised the insurance rates on all commerce to a level far beyond the cost of presents. As he wrote to Jay,

> As long as France, England, Holland, the Emperor, etc., will submit to be tributary to these robbers, and even encourage them, to what purpose should we make war upon them? The resolution might be heroic, but would not be wise. The contest would be unequal. They can injure us very sensibly, but we cannot hurt them in the smallest degree. We have, or shall have, a rich trade at sea exposed to their depredations; they have none at all upon which we can made reprisals. . . . Unless it were possible, then, to persuade the great maritime powers of Europe to unite in the suppression of these piracies, it would be very imprudent for us to entertain any thoughts of contending with them, and will only lay a foundation, by irritating their passions, and increasing their insolence and their demands, for long and severe repentance. I hope, therefore, we shall think of nothing but treating with them.[13]

---

[12]Franklin to Livingston, July 25, 1783, in Smyth, *Writings of Franklin*, 9:71–72; Franklin to Thomas Mifflin, December 25, 1783, ibid., p. 133.
[13]Adams to Jay, December 15, 1784, in *Works of John Adams*, 8:218–19.

In September 1783, Franklin, Adams, and Jay met British negotiators in Paris to sign the definitive peace treaty. The experience of
previous months predicted a rough passage from the full establishment
of independence to acceptance as a nation among nations. Only with
difficulty, Adams warned, would the United States maintain the respect
which the exploits of war had excited in Europe. "In the Calm of
peace," he wrote, "little will be said about us in Europe unless we
prepare for it, but by those who have designs upon us. . . . It will become
us, therefore, to do every thing in our power to make reasonable and
just impressions upon the public opinion in Europe." Adams's distrust
of Britain was profound; France, he feared, would join Britain "in all
artifices and endeavors to keep down our reputation at home and
abroad, to mortify our self-conceit, and to lessen us in the opinion of
the world."[14] Russia and Austria, as mediating powers, had officiated
at the signing of the treaty among Britain, France, and Spain at Versailles. Their signatures on the American treaty, Adams believed, would
have made a deep impression in favor of the United States throughout
Europe, but the two imperial courts had refused, thereby leaving the
other Continental governments in a state of doubt concerning their
proper behavior toward the new Republic.

II

The structural defects of the government under the Articles of Confederation diminished the immediate prospect of establishing an American commercial empire based on reciprocity. The articles granted
Congress the power to enter into treaties of commerce but no authority
to control the commercial policies of the states or to threaten other
nations with retaliation. Additionally, Congress received no taxing
power; thus, it had no means to create an army or navy, or even to
reduce its extensive foreign indebtedness. For countless citizens the
nation's decentralized political structure served a variety of speculative,
political, and individual interests and conformed to their notion of an
ideal republic. Those who favored the state sovereignty embodied in
the Articles of Confederation distrusted political power; they denied
that the conduct of foreign affairs required centralized authority capable of mobilizing the nation's power in behalf of common purposes.
Relying on independence and geographical isolation to defend the country's needs abroad, they resisted any move to change the form of the
U.S. government. Conservatives who advocated greater centralization
argued that the constraints on Congress would never enable the United

[14]Adams to the president of Congress, September 5, 1783, ibid., p. 145.

States to defend adequately its external interests. "Every day," Hamilton had observed bitterly in July 1783, "proves the inefficacy of the present confederation, yet the common danger being removed, we are receding instead of advancing in a disposition to amend its defects. The road to popularity in each state is to inspire jealousies of the power of Congress, though nothing can be more apparent than that they have no power."[15]

Older, well-established attachments to Britain and France merely aggravated the new nation's divisions and animosities; Congress, equally divided, possessed no power to counter the jealousy and perversity or to effect a determined course of action. Back in February Thomas Jefferson had complained to Edmund Randolph:

> I find . . . the pride of independence taking deep and dangerous hold on the hearts of the individual states. I know of no danger so dreadful and so probable as that of internal contests. . . . The states will go to war with each other in defiance of Congress; one will call in France to her assistance; another Gr. Britain, and so we shall have all the wars of Europe brought to our own doors. Can any man be so puffed up with his little portion of sovereignty as to prefer this calamitous accompaniment to the parting with a little of his sovereign right and placing it in a council from all the states?[16]

One month later Hamilton reported the same weakening divisions amidst the American people: "We have I fear (among) us and men in trust who have a hankering afte[r] British connection. We have others whose confidence in France savours of credulity. The intrigues of the former and the incautiousness of the latter may be both, though in different degrees, injurious to the American interests; and make it difficult for prudent men to steer a proper course."[17]

During the first months of independence that proper course seemed to demand essentially the congressional control of commerce. Accepting the mercantilist principles of the day, Hamilton had argued in April 1782 that commerce could not flourish without the aid and protection of government, pointing out that Britain's imperial trade had achieved its predominance under government care. Only by regulating the movement of goods could the United States preserve a favorable balance of trade, which for Hamilton was the essential aim of national policy. In

[15]Hamilton to Jay, July 25, 1783, in Syrett, *Papers of Hamilton*, 3:416–17.
[16]Jefferson to Randolph, February 15, 1783, in Julian P. Boyd et al., eds., *The Papers of Thomas Jefferson* (Princeton, 1952), 6:248.
[17]Hamilton to Floyd and Clinton, March 17, 1783, in Syrett, *Papers of Hamilton*, 3:291.

the absence of any central authority to regulate commerce, no state dared to impose duties of its own because other states, by not doing so, would gain too many price advantages.[18]

Conservatives generally accepted the need of a mercantilist policy for a mercantilist world. In a letter of September 1783, James Madison argued for retaliatory power: "The Conduct of G.B. in the negociation with America has shown great unsteadiness if not insidiousness on the subject of commerce: and the . . . proclamation of the 2d. of July is a proof that some experiment is intended on the wisdom, firmness & union of the States, before they will enter into a Treaty in derogation of her Navigation Act." In October, Governor Benjamin Harrison reminded the Virginia delegation in Congress that only an American mercantilist policy, adequately designed and enforced, would compel Britain to alter its trade policies toward the Republic. The British understood the value of American trade; if the United States, he wrote, prohibited "their manufactures or west india commodities except when brought by our own vessels or by those of other nations and thereby oblige them to make their purchases in cash they will very soon come to a compromise."[19] With the achievement of independence, Hamilton argued that Congress should have adjourned and informed the nation forthrightly "of the imperfections of the present system and of the impossibility of conducting the public affairs with honor to themselves and advantage to the community with powers so disproportionate to their responsibility."[20]

By the summer of 1783 the move to strengthen the Articles of Confederation was already a year old. In July 1782 the New York legislature had passed a resolution which declared that the continuance of the constituted government of the United States carried dangers for the safety and independence of the states because it exposed the common interests of the American people to the mercy of events over which they had no control. It seemed essential that the nation "unite in some System more effectual, for producing Energy, Harmony and Consistency of Measures, than that which now exists, and more capable of putting the Common Cause out of Reach of Contingencies." The resolution urged each state to adopt a measure designed to assemble a convention of all the states for the purpose of amending the Articles of Confederation. George Washington shared the concerns of Hamilton and his New York associates. In March 1783 he wrote to Hamilton,

---

[18]*The Continentalist*, no. 4, April 13, 1782, in ibid., pp. 76–77.

[19]Madison to Randolph, September 13, 1783, in Hutchinson and Rachal, *Papers of Madison*, 7:315; Harrison to Virginia Delegates, October 3, 1783, ibid., p. 366.

[20]Hamilton to George Washington, September 30, 1783, in Syrett, *Papers of Hamilton*, 3:462.

saying that "no man in the United States is, or can be more deeply impressed with the necessity of a reform in our present Confederation than myself. No man perhaps has felt the bad effect of it more sensibly; for to the defects thereof, & want of Powers in Congress may justly be ascribed the prolongation of the War, & consequently the Expences occasioned by it."[21] During July 1783, Hamilton prepared his own congressional resolution, which called for a convention to amend the articles, but he withdrew it when he received little support.[22] Finally, in August, Governor George Clinton forwarded the New York resolution to the Continental Congress.

Congress preferred to focus more narrowly on the exclusion of American merchants and shippers from the valuable markets of the West Indies. It postponed action on New York's motion until the states could respond to Madison's resolution of April 18, 1783, which was designed to break the British monopoly in the carrying trade. Under this resolution Congress would possess, for fifteen years, the authority to prohibit the importation and exportation of goods in vessels belonging to the subjects of any country with which the United States had no commercial treaty. Also during this time Congress could forbid the subjects of another nation, unless authorized by treaty, from importing into the United States goods not produced in the country of which they were subjects.[23] The Virginia legislature adopted the resolution in May 1784, and that month Jefferson, as a member of Congress, suggested to Madison that Congress suspend its efforts to obtain treaties of commerce until it wielded sufficient authority to convince Europeans that the United States was capable of protecting its commercial interests.[24] Congress never received the assent of the nine states required to establish its control over the nation's commerce, nor did it act on the resolution which granted it limited power to regulate foreign trade. In November, John F. Mercer expressed the universal anxieties of Conservatives over the determination of the states to cling to their sovereignty. "In my judgement," he confided to Madison, "there never was a crisis, threatening an event more unfavorable to the happiness of the United States, than the present. Those repellent qualities the seeds of which are abundantly sown in the discordant manners & sentiments

---

[21]Resolution of the New York Legislature Calling for a Convention of the States to Revise and Amend the Articles of Confederation, July 20, 1782, ibid., pp. 110–13; Washington to Hamilton, March 31, 1783, ibid., p. 310.

[22]Unsubmitted Resolution Calling for a Convention to Amend the Articles of Confederation, July 1783, ibid., p. 420.

[23]Report on the Public Credit, March 6, 1783, in Hutchinson and Rachal, *Papers of Madison* (Chicago, 1969), 6:313–14.

[24]Jefferson to Madison, May 8, 1784, in Robert A. Rutland and William M. E. Rachal, eds., *The Papers of James Madison* (Chicago, 1973), 8:29.

of the different States, have produc'd great heats & animosities in Congress now no longer under the restraint impos'd by the war—insomuch that I almost despair of seeing that body unite in those decisive, & energetic measures, requisite for the public safety & prosperity."[25]

Livingston resigned as secretary for the Department of Foreign Affairs in May 1783. From the beginning Congress had restricted his activities, even in matters of administration; it assumed both the initiative and the power of decision in all external matters. At times it ignored the secretary and conducted its own direct correspondence with American and foreign diplomats. Livingston, with little power to shape foreign policy, threatened to resign in 1782. Madison introduced a resolution in November, adopted by Congress, which gave the secretary greater freedom in his correspondence and the selection of information which Congress could demand from him. Still Livingston remained severely hampered in the formulation and conduct of policy. Not even in his limited role did he, an admirable administrator, please all members of Congress. One complained that the secretary was often secretive when others had a right to information and open when he should have maintained secrecy. Upon his resignation, Congress thanked Livingston for his services and assured him that it entertained "a high sense of the ability zeal & fidelity with which he had discharged the important trust reposed in him." Congress now sought to strengthen the office. It placed the secretary at the head of the diplomatic corps and declared it "to be his duty from time to time to lay before Congress such plans for conducting the political and commercial intercourse of the United States with foreign nations, as may appear to be conducive to the interests of the said states."[26]

III

Britain exposed American military and diplomatic impotence directly when it refused to fulfill the terms of the peace treaty. Before independence the British had maintained a string of forts from Lake Champlain along the St. Lawrence River and the southern shores of Lake Ontario and Lake Erie to the head of Lake Huron, with the major posts in this

[25]Resolutions to Strengthen Powers of Congress, May 19, 1784, ibid., pp. 38–39; Bill Granting Congress Limited Power to Regulate Commerce, June 5, 1784, ibid., p. 57; Mercer to Madison, November 12, 1784, ibid., pp. 134–35; James Monroe to Madison, December 18, 1784, ibid., 189–90.

[26]Motion Respecting the Secretary of Foreign Affairs, June 4, 1783, in Syrett, *Papers of Hamilton*, 3:374; Report on Peace Arrangements for the Department of Foreign Affairs, May 8, 1783, ibid., p. 351.

chain located at Oswegatchie, Oswego, Niagara, Presque Isle, San-
dusky, Detroit, and Michilimackinac. Article VII of the preliminary
treaty stipulated that the British king would "with all convenient
speed . . . withdraw all his armies, garrisons, and fleets from the said
United States, and from every port, place, and harbour within the
same." Congress prepared to assume command of these frontier posts
as early as May 1783 by providing garrisons consisting of Continental
troops that had enlisted for three years. However, when Baron von
Steuben, the American Revolutionary hero, traveled to Canada to
arrange the transfer of the posts, Governor Sir Frederick Haldimand
in Quebec insisted that he had received no orders except to cease
hostilities. Without specific instructions, he informed Steuben, he would
permit no Americans even to visit the posts.[27] The frontier establishments occupied only small patches of wilderness, but they permitted
the British to control thousands of square miles with their well-traveled
interior routes. Much of the Great Lakes fur trade, valued at £200,000
annually, was a monopoly of the British Northwest Company, with
perhaps two-thirds of the fur coming from the American side of the
boundary. But the British capital invested in the Western country was
not large, nor would the loss of the fur trade to American trappers
necessarily diminish British profits. Whether the pelts reached European markets through Montreal or New York, they would bring the
major rewards to London's fur merchants.

Of greater concern to the British government than the eventual
transfer of its fur trade was its responsibility for the welfare of its Indian
wards. Britain had secured the needed cooperation of the Indians on
the American frontier by promising them protection from encroaching
pioneers. Unfortunately, the British had neglected those Indians south
of the Great Lakes in the peace negotiations; any British move to
relinquish the posts would deliver, of necessity, these faithful allies into
the hands of their dreaded enemies. When Governor Haldimand received
a copy of the preliminary peace terms, he voiced his concern at the
idea of abandoning the posts. "My own anxiety . . . " he reported in
May, "arises from an apprehension of the effects which the prelimi-
naries will have upon the minds of our Indian allies, who will consider
themselves abandoned to the resentment of an ungenerous and implac-
able enemy."[28] Not without reason some British officials feared that

[27]Hamilton to Clinton, October 3, 1783, ibid., p. 465; Virginia Delegates to Harrison, September 8, 1783, in Hutchinson and Rachal, *Papers of Madison*, 7:300–01.
[28]Quoted in A. L. Burt, *The United States, Great Britain and British North America
from the Revolution to the Establishment of Peace After the War of 1812* (New Haven, CT, 1940),
p. 87.

the Indians, if they discovered the treaty terms, would vent their rage on the British garrisons.

For Haldimand the immediate challenge lay in convincing the Indians that Britain would not forsake them. The governor hoped to sustain their confidence, at least momentarily, by plying them with food and munitions. At the same time, he prepared to ease the transfer of the posts—an eventual necessity—by encouraging the Indians to come to terms with the victors in the recent war. Neither policy promised any easy successes. Too much reassurance would encourage the Indians to attack American settlements and possibly involve the British in an unwanted war; too much Indian-American reconciliation would terminate Britain's hold on its allies and endanger the fur trade. Sir John Johnson, the British agent for Indian affairs, assured the Six Nations of the Iroquois at Niagara in late July 1783 that, as they entered a new era of peace, they could continue to rely on the king's protection. He cautioned them, however, to avoid trouble with American settlers by concentrating their villages and avoiding acts of hostility.[29] The Indians suspected that London had betrayed them. Unrestricted military support against the American enemy might have erased their doubts, but such aid no Canadian official could offer.

Trapped between its loyalty to the Indians and its obligations to the United States under Article VII, the British ministry hesitated to act. Finally, in April 1784, London's Colonial Office responded to Canadian remonstrances by ordering the governor of Canada to hold the posts until he received further instructions. This prompted Madison to speculate on British motivation:

> Some suppose it is meant to enforce a fulfillment of the treaty of peace on our part. . . . Others that it is a salve for the wound given the Savages who are made to believe that the posts will not be given up till good terms shall be granted them by Congress. Others that it is the effect merely of omission in the B[ritish] Government to send orders. Others that it is meant to fix the fur trade in the B[ritish] channel and it is even said that the Governor of Canada has a personal interest in securing a monopoly of at least the Crop of this season.[30]

For many Americans, British retention of the posts and reported intrigue with the Indians simply measured the depth of British hostility toward the United States.

---

[29]Johnson's speech quoted in ibid., pp. 88–91.

[30]Madison to Jefferson, October 11, 1784, in Boyd, *Papers of Jefferson* (Princeton, 1953), 7:440; Mercer to Madison, November 12, 1784, in Rutland and Rachal, *Papers of Madison*, 8:134.

British occupation of U.S. territory embraced far more than the frontier posts. In New York, Sir Guy Carleton, the British commander in chief, continued to control an area far more extensive than Governor Clinton believed necessary to protect the security of British troops and stores. By mid-July 1783, Carleton had returned portions of Staten Island and Long Island to their owners, but Clinton still complained that the British held too much territory and, in defiance of the preliminary treaty, had not returned the public records in their possession. American observers noted additionally that British conduct regarding the Negroes under their control departed from the treaty provisions; the treaty had declared specifically that British commanders were to evacuate their troops without carrying away slaves or other property belonging to inhabitants of the thirteen states. Still it was obvious that many Negroes were escaping from their owners through New York's waterfront just as they had earlier through other British-occupied ports. During the late summer Carleton received orders for the immediate evacuation of the city; thereafter, the British withdrawal proceeded rapidly despite the large numbers of Tories who chose to accompany the departing troops.[31]

London officials soon discovered that the United States had neither the power nor the will to force British compliance with the treaty provisions. Still the British government, to avoid an ultimate military confrontation, required a rationale for its decisions that would place responsibility on the new nation. The peace treaty specified that British and American creditors should meet no lawful impediment to the recovery of their debts. During the war various states, mostly in the South, had confiscated debts owed to British creditors; with the peace these states failed to provide payment of these obligations. Congress had no authority to coerce the states, nor could it adequately defend Loyalists from the continuing persecutions, confiscations, and assaults of anti-British extremists. Although the initial British decision to hold the frontier posts rested on imperial considerations, London quickly made the resolution of the debt issue a prerequisite for evacuation. Recognizing the full significance of British complaints against the states, a committee of Congress in May 1783 recommended that the state legislatures execute the treaty provisions for the recovery of debts and the protection of Loyalists.[32]

[31]Joseph Jones to Madison, May 25, 1783, ibid., 7:77; Livingston to Madison, July 19, 1783, ibid., pp. 235–37; Madison to James Madison, Sr., August 30, 1783, ibid., p. 294; Virginia Delegates to Harrison, September 8, 1783, ibid., p. 301. For a record of Carleton's actions in New York see Hugh Hastings and J. A. Holden, eds., *The Public Papers of George Clinton* (Albany, NY, 1904), 8:184–86, 203–04, 207–16.
[32]Report on Measures to be Taken for Carrying Into Effect the Provisional Peace Treaty, May 30, 1783, in Syrett, *Papers of Hamilton*, 3:366.

Hamilton pursued the issue, and in June he reminded Governor Clinton of the widespread and intemperate violations of the peace treaty in New York. For such breaches, wrote Hamilton, the state's government could not escape responsibility. Those whose rights were violated cared little that the government claimed good intentions and then denied that it possessed the power, and thus the responsibility, to restrain its subjects. The United States had limited choices; it had secured a favorable treaty, but it could not coerce Britain to fulfill its provisions. "Great Britain without recommencing hostilities," Hamilton noted, "may evade parts of the treaty. She may keep possession of the frontier posts, she may obstruct the free enjoyment of the fisheries, she may be indisposed to such extensive concessions in matters of commerce as it is our interest to aim at; in all this she would find no opposition from any foreign power; and we are not in a condition to oblige her to any thing." The United States could anticipate no aid from France in another war against England. For British concessions on the posts and the fisheries, the United States could offer the single equivalent of restoring property and avoiding further injury to those protected by the treaty. With their frontier posts in British hands, the people of New York had good reason to furnish Britain no pretext for delaying—or refusing—to execute the treaty.[33]

Hamilton also was troubled by the adverse effect that American failure to control its citizens would have on European opinion. "Will foreign nations," he asked, "be willing to undertake any thing with us or for us, when they find that the nature of our government will allow no dependence to be placed upon our engagements?" In September, Jay wrote from Paris that the reports of American violations in U.S. newspapers were harming the country. "Violences and associations against the Tories," he informed Hamilton, "pay an ill compliment to Government and impeach our good Faith in the opinions of some, and our magnanimity in the opinion of many." In his first "Phocion" letter of January 1784, Hamilton publicly condemned the legislature and citizens of New York for undermining the country's reputation by their refusal to restore confiscated Loyalist property. No treaty, he declared, could bind one side without binding the other. If Britain avoided further compliance with the treaty because of a breach on the part of the American people, Hamilton warned, the nation would sacrifice its interests as well as its character to "the little vindictive selfish mean passions of a few."[34] As late as November 1784, James Monroe reported that Canadian officials defended the British refusal to evacuate the posts

[33]Hamilton to Clinton, June 1, 1783, ibid., p. 370.

[34]Ibid., p. 371; Jay to Hamilton, September 28, 1783, ibid., p. 459; A Letter from Phocion to the Considerate Citizens of New York, January 1–27, 1784, ibid., p. 492.

by citing violations of the treaty, especially in New York and Virginia.[35] Clearly Congress would never settle its outstanding issues with Britain until it could control all internal behavior that affected the country's external relations.

IV

Without instructions to occupy them in Paris, Adams and Jay traveled to England—"unordered and uninvited," as Jefferson put it. Jay went to settle some personal affairs and to relax at Bath; Adams went to see the country. After several weeks, Adams moved to The Hague where, in February 1784, he negotiated a large loan to enable Congress to meet its obligations. The interest rates that the Dutch bankers imposed troubled him. "The credit of the United States must be very low indeed, in this Republic," he wrote to his Dutch agents, "if we must agree to terms so exorbitant as those in the plan you have enclosed to me." Franklin agreed, reminding Adams that "*the foundation of credit abroad must be laid at home*. When the States have not faith enough in a congress of their own choosing to trust with money for the payment of their common debt, how can they expect that the congress should meet with credit, when it wants to borrow more money for their use from strangers?"[36]

Delegates from the necessary nine states did not appear at Annapolis until January 1784 to vote on a unanimous ratification of the Definitive Treaty with Britain. Only six weeks remained to meet the deadline for the exchange of treaties in Paris. Not until the end of March, technically too late, did a copy of the ratified treaty reach Paris, at which time the British minister waived the point. On May 12, Franklin and Jay for the United States and Hartley for Great Britain exchanged ratifications. Even these final ceremonies in Paris could not prompt the British government to send a minister to the United States; should London so decide, quipped one British official, it would require not one but thirteen. Following the exchange Hartley remained in the French capital to negotiate a commercial treaty. Upon hearing of the ceremonies, Adams advised Congress from The Hague that it should

---

[35]Monroe to Jefferson, November 1, 1784, in Boyd, *Papers of Jefferson*, 7:461; Monroe to Madison, November 15, 1784, in Rutland and Rachal, *Papers of Madison*, 8:141.

[36]Franklin to Elias Boudinot, November 1, 1783, in Smyth, *Writings of Franklin*, 9:110–11; Adams to Franklin, December 5, 1783, in *Works of John Adams*, 8:164–65; Adams to Messrs. Willink and others, February 5, 1784, ibid., p. 176; Franklin to Adams, February 5, 1784, ibid., p. 177; Lyman H. Butterfield et al., eds., *Diary and Autobiography of John Adams* (New York, 1964), 3:148–49; Jefferson to Madison, February 20, 1784, in Boyd, *Papers of Jefferson*, 6:546.

address letters to all the sovereigns of Europe, informing them that the United States was a totally independent nation. It was essential, he believed, that the governments of Europe treat all U.S. ambassadors and other public officials as citizens of a sovereign nation in accordance with their status.[37]

Congress agreed in April to seek treaties of amity and commerce with the European countries without waiting for their governments to send ministers. Only special commercial treaties would open new channels of trade, and the accumulating commercial interests of the United States would tolerate no further delay. Early in May Congress adopted a plan for negotiating the desired treaties with the European states as well as with the Barbary powers. At the same time, it pondered the choice between appointing diplomats to particular courts or naming them to a single commission to negotiate jointly with the European countries. Ultimately, Congress made the latter choice and appointed Franklin, Adams, and Jefferson, who was then a member of Congress, to a joint commission to open negotiations with the powers of Europe through their legations in Paris. Jay had asked for his recall and Congress agreed to his return, much to the regret of Franklin and Adams.[38] As Franklin awaited Jay's departure, he complained to Laurens that "I shall be left alone, and with Mr. A[dams], and I can have no favourable opinion of what may be the Offspring of a Coalition between my ignorance and his Positiveness."[39] Jay left Paris on May 16 and sailed from Dover on June 1. Even before he reached American shores, Congress appointed him its new secretary of foreign affairs. "Wisdom and Virtue have tryumphed, for once," Adams observed. "And I hope and believe, he will give an entire new Cast, to the Complexion of our foreign Affairs."[40]

Jefferson received his appointment as commissioner on May 7. Madison rejoiced at the news and promised to keep his fellow Virginian informed of those developments in America that merited his attention. The appointment pleased Adams as well; he wrote to Warren: "He is an old friend, with whom I have had occasion to labor at many a knotty Problem, and in whose Abilities and Steadiness I always found great

[37]Adams to the president of Congress, June 22, 1784, in *Works of John Adams*, 8:204–05.

[38]Monroe to Harrison, February 14, 1784, in Boyd, *Papers of Jefferson*, 6:539; Virginia Delegates to Harrison, May 13, 1784, ibid., 7:248–49.

[39]Franklin to Laurens, April 29, 1784, in Smyth, *Writings of Franklin*, 9:198.

[40]Adams to Warren, June 30, 1784, in *Warren-Adams Letters*, 2:240; Franklin to Adams, July 4, 1784, in *Works of John Adams*, 8:206–07; Franklin to Mifflin, June 16, 1784, in Smyth, *Writings of Franklin*, 9:226; American Commissioners to Jay, March 18, 1785, in Boyd, *Papers of Jefferson* (Princeton, 1953), 8:36.

Cause to confide."[41] In June, Jefferson traveled to Boston, intending to accompany Abigail Adams to Paris, but he found that she already had arranged passage to London and was leaving the following day. He then sailed from Boston on July 5, also bound for London; the trip was fast, lasting nineteen days. At Portsmouth he transferred to another vessel which took him to Le Havre. After a brief stop at Rouen, Jefferson reached Paris on August 6, establishing his residence at the Hôtel d'Orléans adjoining the Palais Royal on the Rue de Richelieu. His reception was cordial; his reputation for enlightenment and integrity, his interest in the arts and sciences, had preceded him. For Jefferson the timing of his arrival was superb. Paris was alive with new construction—streets, boulevards, bridges, churches, public buildings, and elegant private town houses. It was the private residences that he visited, filling his notebook with sketches, diagrams, floor plans, and additional observations which he would use later in designing houses and other buildings in Virginia. Jefferson's favorite, the new Hôtel de Salm located almost directly across the Seine from the Louvre, influenced the design of his own still unfinished Monticello. "While I was in Paris," he wrote to Madame de Tessé, "I was violently smitten with the Hotel de Salm, and used to go to the Tuileries almost daily to look at it." After several weeks in the city, Jefferson moved to the Hôtel de Langeac adjoining the Grille de Chaillot on the Rue de Berri.[42]

After a favorable Atlantic crossing, Abigail Adams reached London on July 20, 1784. When Adams at The Hague learned of her arrival, he set off to meet his wife and daughter and on August 7 was reunited with them after a separation of over four years.[43] The next day the family departed for Paris and there took lodgings near Jefferson's Hôtel d'Orléans. To escape the city the Adamses moved to the Hôtel de Rouhault in Auteuil, a village four miles west of Paris near the Bois de Boulogne, a location that delighted Mrs. Adams, who wrote of her life in France:

> We have a Beautiful wood, cut into walks, within a few rods of our dwelling, which upon this Day, resounds with Musick and Dancing, jollity and Mirth of every kind. In this Wood Booths are erected, where cake, fruit, and wine are sold. . . . I believe this Nation is the only one in the world who could make Pleasure the Business of Life, and yet retain such a relish for it, as never to

[41]Madison to Jefferson, May 15, 1784, in Rutland and Rachal, *Papers of Madison*, 8:35; Adams to Warren, August 27, 1784, quoted in Boyd, *Papers of Jefferson*, 7:382n.
[42]Jefferson to Adams, June 19, 1784, in ibid., 7:309; Jefferson to Adams, July 24, 1784, ibid., p. 382; Jefferson to Monroe, November 11, 1784, ibid., p. 508.
[43]Diaries of John and Abigail Adams in Butterfield, *Diary and Autobiography of John Adams*, 3:166–67, 170–71.

complain of its being tasteless or insipid; the Parisians seem to have exhausted Nature, and Art in this Science; and to be *triste* is a complaint of a most serious Nature.[44]

The three commissioners held their first meeting at Passy near Auteuil, where Franklin maintained his residence at the spacious Hôtel de Valentinois overlooking the Seine. In deference to his gout, they continued to meet at Passy, although Adams had long resented Franklin and his devotion to everything French, including the French court. Jefferson, more tolerant of his fellowmen, associated freely with both but still preferred the company of John and Abigail Adams, whose domestic life conformed far more to his than did that of the less conventional Franklin. The Adams and the Jefferson families were often guests at the home of Thomas Barclay, the American consul general in Paris.[45]

The commission and its instructions reached Paris in July. In preparing the instructions, Jefferson, as a member of Congress, stipulated, in answer to its European critics who insisted that it had no treaty-making power, that foreign nations must treat the United States as one country. These instructions authorized commercial treaties with sixteen European as well as the four Barbary powers. It was an ambitious undertaking in an effort to convert all Europe to the commercial principles of the American Revolution. "You will see," Franklin wrote to Adams, "that a good deal of business is cut out for us—treaties to be made with . . . twenty powers in two years,—so that we are not likely to eat the bread of idleness."[46] The commercial treaties, in principle, would establish the right of each party to carry its own produce, manufactures, and merchandise in its own ships to the ports of the other and then take on the goods of the other, paying duties established by the axiom of the most favored nation. With countries holding territorial possessions in America, the treaties would admit a direct and similar trade, or at least a direct trade between the United States and certain free ports in those possessions.[47]

Following their first meeting at Passy late in August, the commissioners informed Hartley that they were empowered to negotiate

[44]Abigail Adams to Mercy Warren, September 5, 1784, in *Warren-Adams Letters*, 2:243.

[45]See Dumas Malone, *Jefferson and the Rights of Man* (Boston, 1951), pp. 6–7.

[46]Franklin to Comte De Mercy Argenteau, July 30, 1784, in Smyth, *Writings of Franklin*, 9:248–49; Franklin to Adams, August 6, 1784, ibid., p. 250; Commission for Negotiating Treaties of Amity and Commerce, May 12, 1784, in Boyd, *Papers of Jefferson*, 7:262–63. For Jefferson's treaty plans see ibid., pp. 463ff.

[47]Instructions to the Commissioners for Negotiating Treaties of Amity and Commerce, May 7, 1784, ibid., p. 267.

treaties of amity and commerce. At the same time, they told the Danish minister of their powers and requested him to notify his court. For Franklin reconciliation with Britain was the first order of business, and he warned Hartley that "restraints on the freedom of Commerce and intercourse between us can afford no advantage equal to the Mischief they will do by keeping up ill humour, and promoting a total alienation." Hartley, still optimistic, responded that the British court was ready "to receive proposals from the United States for the forming of such regulations as might tend to the mutual and reciprocal advantage of both countries." Because Hartley, now recalled to London, had no power to treat, the commissioners turned to the Duke of Dorset, the British minister in Paris, who advised them that his government was prepared to discuss all the controversies arising from the unfulfilled clauses of the peace treaty. Still Jefferson anticipated no British concessions. "The infatuation of that nation," he confided to Monroe, "seems really preternatural. If anything will open their eyes it will be an application to the avarice of the merchants who are the very people who have opposed the treaty first mediated. . . . Deaf to every principle of common sense, insensible to the feelings of man, they firmly believe they shall be permitted by us to keep all the carrying trade and that we shall attempt no act of retaliation because they are pleased to think it our interest not to do so." On November 24, Dorset informed the commissioners that the British ministry preferred that the United States send an authorized representative to London to negotiate with British officials there. Franklin assured him that the American commissioners would travel to London, but the British government, he complained in January 1785, appointed no one to negotiate.[48]

Dorset offered the commissioners no encouragement when he inquired by letter whether they had received their powers from Congress or from the states. This distinction was critical because the first assumption, if true, suggested that any state could render an agreement ineffectual. By January the commissioners understood what difficulties they faced. "We do not find it easy to make commercial arrangements in Europe," Jefferson wrote; "there is a want of confidence in us." In February he told Monroe: "Our business goes on very slowly. No

[48]Franklin to Adams, July 4, 1784, in *Works of John Adams*, 8:207; Franklin to Hartley, September 6, 1783, in Smyth, *Writings of Franklin*, 9:88; Franklin to Mifflin, June 16, 1784, ibid., pp. 225–26; Hartley to Jay, March 2, 1784, in Morris, *John Jay*, 2:700–01; John B. Church to Hamilton, September 25, 1784, in Syrett, *Papers of Hamilton*, 3:579; aide-mémoire from Hartley, September 16, 1784, in Boyd, *Papers of Jefferson*, 7:422; American commissioners to Dorset, October 28, 1784, ibid., pp. 456, 457–58; American commissioners to the president of Congress, November 11, 1784, ibid., pp. 493–95; Jefferson to Monroe, November 11, 1784, ibid., p. 509; Dorset to the American commissioners, November 24, 1784, ibid., p. 547; Jefferson to Monroe, December 10, 1784, ibid., p. 563; Franklin to Hartley, January 3, 1785, in Smyth, *Writings of Franklin*, 9:284–85.

answers from Spain or Britain. The backwardness of the latter is not new. . . . We have hitherto waited for favorable circumstances to press matters with France. We are now about to do it tho I cannot say the prospect is good."[49] By 1785 much of the earlier desire of the European monarchs to negotiate treaties with the United States had abated. This resulted, Franklin believed, from "the Paines Britain takes to represent us everywhere as distracted with Divisions, discontented with our Governments, the People unwilling to pay taxes, the Congress unable to collect them, and many desiring the Restoration of the old Government, etc. The English Papers are full of this Stuff, and their Ministers get it copied into the foreign Papers." As late as March 18, Jefferson reported that the commissioners still had not heard from London: "Nothing will bring [the British] to reason but physical obstruction, applied to their bodily senses. We must show that we are capable of foregoing commerce with them, before they will be capable of consenting to an equal commerce."[50]

Adams shared Jefferson's conviction that the commissioners in Paris would not accomplish much. "You will negotiate for reciprocities in commerce to very little purpose," he instructed Jay in April, "while the British ministers and merchants are certain that they shall enjoy all the profits of our commerce under their own partial regulations." Adams looked back on his months in Paris as mostly unpleasurable: "Our negotiations in this place have not answered the ends proposed by congress and expected by the people of America, nor is there now scarcely a possibility that they should. . . . But I presume congress will not think it expedient to renew the commissions, or attempt any longer to carry on negotiations with the rest of the world in this place." For Adams the only remaining possibility of coming to terms with Britain and placing American-British relations on a certain footing lay in the appointment of a minister to London. "Whoever goes," he admonished Jay, "will neither find it a lucrative nor a pleasant employment, nor will he be envied by me. . . . But the measure of sending a minister to England appears to me the corner stone of the true American system of politics in Europe; and if it is not done, we shall have cause to repent it for a long time, when it will be too late." One week later he repeated this advice but warned again that anyone sent to London "will probably find himself in a thicket of briars from which he will hardly get free."[51]

[49]Jefferson to Nathanael Greene, January 12, 1785, in Paul Leicester Ford, ed., *The Writings of Thomas Jefferson* (New York, 1894), 4:25; Jefferson to Monroe, February 1785, ibid., pp. 30–31.
[50]Franklin to Jay, February 8, 1785, in Smyth, *Writings of Franklin*, 9:287–88; Jefferson to Madison, March 18, 1785, in Boyd, *Papers of Jefferson*, 8:39–40.
[51]Adams to Jay, April 13, 14, 24, 1785, in *Works of John Adams*, 8:234–37.

These reports of failure in Paris troubled Congress; the British and Spanish courts, it was clear, had no desire to treat with American diplomats.[52] In December, Monroe informed Jefferson that Congress contemplated the appointment of a minister to London as well as a replacement for Franklin, who for one year had asked to be recalled from Paris. "If I am kept here another winter, and as much weakened by it as by the last," he complained as early as May 1784, "I may as well resolve to spend the remainder of my days here; for I shall be hardly able to bear the fatigues of the voyage in returning."[53] Finally, on February 24, 1785, Congress appointed Adams to London and named William Stephens Smith as the secretary of legation. On March 7 Congress granted leave to Franklin; three days later it named Jefferson unanimously as the new minister to Versailles. For Adams and Jefferson the commissions to negotiate commercial treaties remained in force, with the two ministers sharing the task, signing treaties in London or Paris, or separately when they could not meet. Specifically, Congress instructed them to negotiate the best treaties possible with the sixteen European states as well as the four Barbary powers, securing those commercial advantages which the American people were entitled to expect. In a separate action Congress empowered the commissioners to apply whatever money borrowed in Europe, and belonging to the United States, they deemed necessary to negotiate treaties with the Barbary states but not to exceed $80,000. "If we can avoid this humiliating tribute," Adams observed, "I should wish it with all my heart, but am afraid we must sooner or later submit to it."[54]

During June and July, Franklin prepared for his long, difficult voyage back to America; the French king himself furnished the litter that would carry Franklin to the coast. Jefferson cautioned Monroe not to permit his return to pass special notice, explaining later that summer the significance of Franklin's welcome in Philadelphia: "The reception of the Doctor is an object of very general attention, and will

---

[52]Franklin to Jay, February 8, 1785, in Smyth, *Writings of Franklin*, 9:287; Adams to Jay, March 9, 1785, in *Works of John Adams*, 8:228–29. For this reason Adams advocated the appointment of an American minister to London. See Adams to Jay, April 24, 1785, ibid., pp. 236–37.

[53]Monroe to Jefferson, December 14, 1784, in Stanislaus Murray Hamilton, ed., *The Writings of James Monroe* (New York, 1969), 1:54–55; Franklin to Charles Thomson, May 13, 1784, in Smyth, *Writings of Franklin*, 9:213; Franklin to Mr. and Mrs. Jay, May 13, 1784, ibid., p. 214; Franklin to William Franklin, August 16, 1784, ibid., p. 253.

[54]Monroe to Madison, March 6, 1785, in Hamilton, *Writings of Monroe*, 1:64; Monroe to Jefferson, April 12, 1785, ibid., pp. 68–69; Elbridge Gerry to Jefferson, February 25, 1785, in Boyd, *Papers of Jefferson*, 7:652; Jay to the American commissioners, March [11], 1785, ibid., 8:19; Jay to Jefferson, March 15, 1785, ibid., p. 33; Adams to M. Dumas, May 11, 1785, in *Works of John Adams*, 8:247; Adams to Jay, March 9, 1785, ibid., p. 227.

weigh in Europe as an evidence of the satisfaction or dissatisfaction of America with their revolution." Shortly before leaving Paris in July, Franklin had signed a treaty of amity and commerce with Prussia. Jefferson added his signature several days later and forwarded the treaty to London for Adams to sign. William Short, Jefferson's trusted secretary, then carried it to The Hague, where on September 10 Baron Thulemeier signed it for Prussia.[55] That treaty measured the one tangible success of the diplomatic effort in Paris.

[55]Jefferson to Monroe, August 28, 1785, in Ford, *Writings of Jefferson*, 4:87; Franklin to Benjamin Vaughn, July 24, 1785, in Smyth, *Writings of Franklin*, 9:365–66; Franklin to Jay, September 19, 1785, ibid., p. 463.

CHAPTER
TWO

Adams in London*

JOHN ADAMS learned of his appointment as the first U.S. minister to London at the end of April 1785. He was pleased to have the honor of representing the young American Republic at the English court but not necessarily to trade a residence in Paris for one in London. "I exchange a quiet, cheerful mind," he wrote, "for an anxious one, and a life of ease for a scene of perplexity, confusion, and fatigue." Adams scarcely knew what to expect of his new assignment to a court so rich and powerful as that of the recent enemy, and he confessed to Mercy Warren his doubts regarding his own suitability for the office:

> The time is at length come in which the United States of America are to have a Minister at the Court of Great Britain, a time foretold by the Prophets and Seers, and Dreamers of Dreams, but never until very lately stedfastly believed by any to be so near at hand. It is much to be wished that they could have had one . . . more Respectable in many Points than the Person on whom the lot has fallen. It is Fortune and Figure, Birth and Grace, Titles and Ribbons, that make Impressions on Courtiers and succeed with the fair, as they say. This is true in a Sense. But how do they succeed? Why, to be earnestly courted to every Ball, every Entertainment, every Horse Race and Gaming Table, and perhaps to receive certain other Favours which shall be nameless, but all this at the Expense of incessant Fatigue and Chagrin, to the consumption of all his Time and an Inattention to Business and neglect of all his Duties. This is a success of which our Country has no occasion and for which her humble Minister has no Ambition.

*Carroll Lecture, Mary Baldwin College, October 12, 1982. Published as "Adams in London," in *Adams and Jefferson in Europe, 1783–1789* (Mary Baldwin College, Staunton, Virginia, 1984). Reprinted by permission.

What Adams feared in London was the "Groups upon Groups of Tories and Refugees in that Country in the Variety of their Shapes and shades of their Colours, the Numbers of Emissaries from other parts of Europe, the Concourse of unexceptionable Americans, the impassioned English, Scotch and Irish, all watching [my] Motions and most of them wishing and contriving [my] Fall." He added that "whatever lustre in the Eyes of some People there may be in the Feather of being the first Minister to England, you, Madam, will easily see that [my] Situation is more to be dreaded and pitied than envied."[1]

Before he departed for London, Adams confronted the Duke of Dorset, the British minister in Paris, with the accumulating problems raised by the unfulfilled provisions of the peace treaty, especially Britain's possession of the posts along the Great Lakes, the unpaid American debts to British subjects, and the Negroes whom Sir Guy Carleton had carried away from New York at the end of the war. Dorset scarcely commented.[2] Upon receiving good wishes on his new assignment from the Comte de Vergennes at Versailles, Adams noted graciously that it was a form of degradation to go to any European court after being accredited to the king of France. Vergennes retorted that it was "a great Thing to be the first Ambassador from your Country to the Country you sprung from." Before the Adamses departed for London, Thomas Jefferson hosted a dinner for them, attended by such notables as the Marquis de Lafayette and Captain John Paul Jones.[3]

Adams, his wife, and daughter left Auteuil on May 20 and traveled by carriage to Calais. Six days later they arrived in London and took rooms at the Bath Hotel in Piccadilly. That night Adams announced his presence to Lord Carmarthen, the British foreign minister. After house hunting for several days, Mrs. Adams decided on one in the northeast corner of Grosvenor Square.[4] Abigail Adams reported to Jefferson that the contrast between the calm of Auteuil and the bustle of London "almost turned my Brain for the first two or three Days." Recalling Paris, she added: "I think I have somewhere met with the observation that nobody ever leaves Paris but with a degree of tristeness." Still London pleased her: "The figure which this city makes in respect to Equipages is vastly superiour to Paris, and gives one the Idea of superiour wealth and grandeur. I have seen few carriages in

---

[1]Adams to M. Dumas, May 11, 1785, in *The Works of John Adams* (Boston, 1853), 8:247; Adams to Mercy Warren, May 6, 1785, in *Warren-Adams Letters: Being Chiefly a Correspondence Among John Adams, Samuel Adams, and James Warren* (Boston: Massachusetts Historical Society, 1925), 2:255–56.
[2]Adams to John Jay, May 13, 1785, in *Works of John Adams*, 8:248–49.
[3]Lyman H. Butterfield et al., eds., *Diary and Autobiography of John Adams* (New York, 1964), 3:176.
[4]Ibid., pp. 180–81.

Paris and no horses superiour to what are used here for Hackneys." Adams soon missed the walks and pure air at Auteuil. "The Smoke and Damp of this city," he complained to Jefferson, "is ominous to me. London boasts of its Trottoir, but there is a space between it and the Houses through which all the Air from Kitchens, Cellars, Stables and Servants Appartements ascends into the Street and pours directly on the Passanger on Foot. Such Whiffs and puffs assault you every few Steps as are enough to breed the Plague if they do not Suffocate you on the Spot."[5]

On May 27, Adams submitted his credentials to Lord Carmarthen. That day the Dutch minister, after reviewing Adams's early experiences in London, assured him that he had had precisely the same official reception accorded to all other ministries. Adams's high reputation as a diplomatist had preceded him, and during his first week in London he received visits from all the ministers and secretaries of the foreign embassies as well as from some English leaders. Although generally pleased with her husband's reception, Mrs. Adams informed Jefferson that their presence in London did not meet universal approval; she included an item from the *Public Advertiser*:

> An Ambassador from America! Good heavens what a sound! The Gazette surely never announced any thing so extraordinary before, nor once on a day so little expected. This will be such a phenomenon in the Corps Diplomatique that tis hard to say which can excite indignation most, the insolence of those who appoint the Character, or the meanness of those who receive it. Such a thing could never have happened in any former Administration, not even that of Lord North.[6]

Carmarthen informed Adams that on June 1 he would meet King George III. That day the British minister accompanied Adams to the palace where he would present his letter of credence. Members of the diplomatic corps had advised Adams to make a brief speech at court, as complimentary as possible. While waiting for Carmarthen to usher him in to see the king, Adams noted that he was the focus of the eyes of all the ministers, lords, and bishops who crowded the room, but the

---

[5]Abigail Adams to Jefferson, June 6, 1785, in Julian P. Boyd et al., eds., *The Papers of Thomas Jefferson* (Princeton, 1953), 8:178–79; Adams to Jefferson, June 7, 1785, ibid., p. 183.

[6]Adams to Jefferson, May 27, 1785, in *Works of John Adams*, 8:252; Adams to Jay, May 30, 1785, ibid., p. 253; *Public Advertiser* quoted in Abigail Adams to Jefferson, June 6, 1785, in Boyd, *Papers of Jefferson*, 8:179–80.

Swedish and Dutch ministers quickly relieved him of his embarrassment until Carmarthen returned to take him to the royal chamber.[7]
The door was shut, leaving Adams alone with the king and the secretary
of state. Adams made the three reverences established at the courts of
northern Europe: one at the door, one halfway, and one before his
majesty; he then addressed the throne:

> Sir,—The United States of America have appointed me their min-
> ister plenipotentiary to your Majesty, and have directed me to
> deliver to your Majesty this letter which contains the evidence of
> it. It is in obedience to their express commands, that I have the
> honor to assure your Majesty of their unanimous disposition and
> desire to cultivate the most friendly and liberal intercourse between
> your Majesty's subjects and their citizens, and of their best wishes
> for your Majesty's health and happiness, and for that of your royal
> family. The appointment of a minister from the United States to
> your Majesty's Court will form an epoch in the history of England
> and of America. I think myself more fortunate than all my fellow-
> citizens, in having the distinguished honor to be the first to stand
> in your Majesty's royal presence in a diplomatic character; and I
> shall esteem myself the happiest of men, if I can be instrumental
> in recommending my country more and more to your Majesty's
> royal benevolence, and of restoring an entire esteem, confidence,
> and affection, or, in better words, the old good nature and the old
> good humor between people, who, though separated by an ocean,
> and under different governments, have the same language, a sim-
> ilar religion, and kindred blood.[8]

King George listened to every word with dignity and apparent
emotion and then answered the minister with a tremor:

> The circumstances of this audience are so extraordinary, the lan-
> guage you have now held is so extremely proper, and the feelings
> you have discovered so justly adapted to the occasion that I must
> say that I not only receive with pleasure the assurance of the
> friendly dispositions of the United States, but that I am very glad
> the choice has fallen upon you to be their minister. . . . I will be
> very frank with you. I was the last to consent to the separation;
> but the separation having been made, and having become inevi-
> table, I have always said, as I say now, that I would be the first
> to meet the friendship of the United States as an independent
> power. The moment I see such sentiments and language as yours

---

[7]Adams to Franklin and Jefferson, May 29, 1785, ibid., pp. 170–71; Adams to
Jay, June 1, 2, 1785, in *Works of John Adams*, 8:254–56.
[8]Address to the king, June 1, 1785, in ibid., pp. 256–57.

prevail, . . . that moment I shall say, let the circumstances of language, religion, and blood have their natural and full effect.

After this formal exchange of greetings, the king asked Adams if he had last come from France. To an affirmative answer his majesty laughingly said that "there is an opinion among some people that you are not the most attached of all your countrymen to the manners of France." Adams was surprised, not by the accuracy of the statement but by the indiscretion. "That opinion, sir, is not mistaken," he replied, "I must avow to your Majesty, I have no attachment but to my own country." The king retorted that "an honest man will never have any other" and thereupon dismissed Adams. Accompanied by the master of ceremonies, Adams returned to his carriage; his cordial reception at court, he hoped, would silence some English critics.[9]

On June 9, Adams returned to court to meet Queen Charlotte. The audiences, Adams wrote John Jay on the following day, revealed only the intention of the royal family to treat the United States like other foreign powers, but no one should infer from this that the British would relax their commercial policy. "We are sure of one thing," Adams continued, "that a navigation act is in our power, as well as in theirs, and that ours will be more hurtful to them than theirs to us."[10]

After the initial outburst of wonderment that the court had received Adams with a show of civility, the London press viewed the Adamses with growing approval. In late June the *Daily Universal Register* observed that "Mrs. and Miss Adams, wife and daughter to the Ambassador from the American States, are as accomplished women as any in England." The special qualities of Americans who resided in England, declared that journal, suggested that they were people of "fertile invention, exclusive genius, and strong judgment. Mr. Adams, their Ambassador, has been successful in every negotiation he has undertaken; the loan he obtained in Holland astonished the most refined politicians and subtle financiers in Europe."[11]

II

Adams opened his search for accommodation with Britain on June 17. Carmarthen assured him that the British cabinet desired cordial relations with the United States. Adams then listed the unresolved issues that troubled U.S.-British relations: the posts and territories within the

[9]Adams to Jay, June 2, 1785, ibid., pp. 257–58.
[10]Adams to Jay, June 10, 1785, ibid., pp. 265–66.
[11]*Daily Universal Register*, June 21, 22, 1785.

United States still held by British garrisons, the exportation of Negroes and other property in defiance of the seventh article of the treaty of peace, the restrictions on American trade, the seemingly unreasonable British demands for the payment of debts contracted before the war, the British captures on the high seas after the time specified by the treaty, and the liquidation of the charges of prisoners of war. Adams admitted that the negotiation of a commercial treaty would be difficult and time-consuming; the other issues, all flowing from the peace treaty, appeared easier. British concerns over the unpaid debts seemed reasonable to Adams, but the British, by restricting commerce and depriving America of the profits of the fur trade, had made it impossible for such goods to reach England in payment of the debts. The trade had returned to its old patterns, much to the disadvantage of American merchants; relying on British credit, they were going increasingly into debt. "His Lordship heard me very attentively," Adams recorded.[12] Still Carmarthen, predicting that patience would adjust all issues, reminded Adams that there would be many rubs along the way and instructed him to make his inquiries, concerning infringements on the treaty provisions, in writing.

Early in July 1785, Jefferson and Benjamin Franklin sent Adams the draft of a commercial treaty, based generally on the one proposed to Denmark, for him to present to the London government. Adams delivered the treaty draft to Carmarthen late in July,[13] but weeks passed without a response. Adams then wrote in late August that he did not expect an answer from the British government before spring "unless intelligence should arrive of all the States adopting the navigation act, or authorizing congress to do it." On August 24, he had a long conference with William Pitt, the prime minister, who acknowledged that Carmarthen had forwarded the papers which he had written. What had held up the evacuation of the posts, Pitt informed Adams, was the interference of the states in preventing the payment of the debts. He further noted that several states "had interfered, against the treaty, and by acts of their legislatures, had interposed impediments to the recovery of debts."

Adams replied that on the critical issue of payment of interest accrued during the war, American courts had declared that the Revolution, as a social upheaval, had broken all previous contracts and engagements; hence American debtors were not responsible for the interest on their debts during the period of conflict. He insisted that

---

[12]Adams to Jay, June 17, 1785, in *Works of John Adams*, 8:268–72.

[13]Franklin and Jefferson to Adams, July 8, 1785, in Boyd, *Papers of Jefferson*, 8:273; Adams to Carmarthen, July 29, 1785, in *Works of John Adams*, 8:288; Adams to Jay, July 29, 1785, ibid., pp. 288–89.

the difficulty in paying the debts arose from the British restrictions on American trade and argued that the United States had the same right as Britain to control its commerce to its own advantage; to this Pitt agreed. Clearly the issue was not one of rights but one of policy. Adams had little confidence in Pitt, the ministry, or the British public; they all seemed ignorant of the issues in British-American diplomacy. "There is," he wrote, "a prohibition of the truth, arising from popular anger. Printers will print nothing which is true, without pay, because it displeases their readers; while their gazettes are open to lies, because they are eagerly read, and make the paper sell." British factions seemed to be united only on a punitive policy toward America. For Adams the king alone possessed the resolution and energy to carry out a positive course of action, but the factional rivalry isolated him from political reality. Those who surrounded him told him only what he wished to hear.[14]

Adams explained repeatedly that he dominated all conversations with the British because they refused to talk, fearful that they might commit themselves to a position not approved by the cabinet. After weeks of official British silence, he complained to Jay in mid-October 1785: "I can obtain no answer from the ministry to any one demand, proposal, or inquiry." Several days later, in conversation with Carmarthen, he lamented the decline of confidence between the two countries since the peace. "I paused here," wrote Adams, "in hopes his Lordship would have made some reflection, or dropped some hint, from whence I could have drawn some conclusion, excited some hope, or started some fresh topic; but not a word escaped him." Unable to agree on any new course of action, the British, he concluded, "have agreed together to observe a total silence with me until they shall come to a resolution." Again in October Adams reported to Jefferson that "we hold Conferences upon Conferences, but the Ministers either have no Plan or they button it up, closer than their Waistcoats."[15]

Inordinate American addiction to British goods and credit troubled Adams; it undermined his efforts to negotiate a commercial treaty in London. Britain, he admitted regretfully, controlled American commerce: "The superior abilities of the British manufacturers, and the greater capitals of their merchants, have enabled them to give our traders better bargains and longer credit than any others in Europe; . . .

[14]Adams to Jay, August 25, 1785, ibid., pp. 303–05; Adams to Jay, November 4,1785, ibid., p. 337; Adams to Jay, December 3, 1785, ibid., pp. 350–51.
[15]Adams to Jay, August 25, 1785, ibid., p. 309; Adams to Jay, October 15, 1785, ibid., p. 321; Adams to Jay, October 21, 1785, ibid., pp. 326, 331; Adams to Jefferson, October 24, 1785, in Lester J. Cappon, ed., in *The Adams-Jefferson Letters* (Chapel Hill, NC, 1959), 1:86.

Britain has monopolized our trade beyond credibility."[16] So pervading was American partiality for English goods that British merchants could simply assume their continued dominance of the foreign trade of the United States. "The ardor of our citizens in transferring almost the whole commerce of the country here, and voluntarily reviving that monopoly which they had long complained of as a grievance, in a few of the first months of the peace," Adams complained to Jay, "imprudently demonstrated to all the world an immoderate preference of British commerce." Adams wondered whether the British ministry understood that its behavior toward the United States might eventually strengthen America's relations with France and the other powers of Europe. "If we once see a necessity of giving preferences in trade," he observed, "great things may be done."[17]

British merchants and officials reminded Adams that the United States could not exist without British commerce and thus never would unite on any measures of retaliation or any plan to establish its own mercantilist policy. Adams recognized the depth of British conviction and observed bitterly that "if an angel from heaven should declare to this nation that our states will unite, retaliate, prohibit, or trade with France, they would not believe it." He warned that threats of American retaliation would remain ineffective, as long as the British regarded such retaliation as unlikely, and "you will negotiate for reciprocities in commerce to very little purpose, while the British ministers and merchants are certain that they shall enjoy all the profits of our commerce under their own partial regulations."[18]

For Adams the American people still possessed the absolute power to break the British monopoly over them simply by denying themselves the luxuries supplied by British trade and manufactures. To Jay he resignedly wrote:

> But the character of our people must be taken into consideration. They are as aquatic as the tortoises and sea-fowl, and the love of commerce, with its conveniences and pleasures, is a habit in them as unalterable as their natures. It is in vain, then, to amuse ourselves with the thought of annihilating commerce, unless as philosophical speculations. . . . Upon this principle we shall find that we must have connections with Europe, Asia, and Africa; and,

[16]Adams to Jay, May 5, 1785, in *Works of John Adams*, 8:240–41; Adams to Jay, August 6, 1785, ibid., pp. 289–90; Adams to Jefferson, October 3, 1785, in Boyd, *Papers of Jefferson*, 8:577.

[17]Adams to Jay, October 17, 1785, in *Works of John Adams*, 8:323; Adams to Jay, October 21, 1785, ibid., p. 327.

[18]Adams to Jay, May 5, 1785, ibid., p. 241.

therefore, the sooner we form those connections into a judicious system, the better it will be for us and our children.

Adams preferred the disruption of trade to its continuance under Britain's humiliating impositions. "If every ship we have were burnt, and the keel of another never to be laid," he predicted, "we might still be the happiest people upon earth, and, in fifty years, the most powerful."[19] If Americans would not defy British commercial policy by exercising the right not to buy, Adams would counter the foreign impositions with various forms of commercial retaliation. "It is a diplomatic axiom," he reminded Jay, "that he always negotiates ill who is not in a condition to make himself feared." So strong was the mercantile spirit in Britain, he observed in July 1785, that until the states united on a single commercial policy British officials would never take the threat of American prohibitions seriously. "I really believe, it must come to that," he continued. "I have no hopes of a treaty before next spring, nor then, without the most unanimous concurrence of all our States in vigorous measures, which shall put out of all doubt their power and their will to retaliate." Adams hoped that Americans would discard their aversion to monopolies and exclusions and adopt the more selfish principles of the European nations, particularly of France and England.[20] Several weeks later he wrote to Jefferson that "we must not, my Friend, be the bubbles of our own liberal sentiments. If we cannot obtain reciprocal liberalty we must adopt reciprocal prohibitions, exclusions, monopolies, and imposts." Adams argued that nothing less than the monopolization of American commercial policy through navigation acts would protect American rights in English ports. He recommended that members of Congress and the state legislatures study the British acts of navigation and judge the extent to which similar acts would promote the interests of the American people in their commerce with Great Britain.[21] "You may depend upon it," Adams wrote to Jay in October; "the commerce of America will have no relief at present, nor, in my opinion, ever, until the United States shall have generally passed navigation acts." He asked Jay to consider whether the states should give Congress unlimited authority to control the external commerce of all the states for a number of years. If Congress and the states refused to impose

[19]Adams to Jay, December 6, 1785, ibid., p. 357.
[20]Adams to Jay, May 5, 1785, ibid., p. 242; Adams to Jay, July 19, 1785, ibid., p. 283; Adams to Jay, August 8, 1785, ibid., p. 297; Adams to Jay, August 30, 1785, ibid., p. 313.
[21]Adams to Jefferson, August 7, 1785, in Boyd, *Papers of Jefferson*, 8:354–55; Adams to Jefferson, September 4, 1785, ibid., p. 477; Adams to Jefferson, October 3, 1785, ibid., p. 577.

restrictions on British commerce, Adams concluded, there would be no purpose in stationing a minister in London.[22]

III

Adams and Jefferson found the task of freeing American commerce from the curse of the Barbary pirates more and more demanding. What added to their sense of outrage, as well as impotence, was the capture of three American ships. During the previous winter Morocco took the American brig *Betsy*. The Moroccan emperor held the ship and cargo, but he treated the crew with civility, reclothed them, and delivered them to the Spanish minister who sent them to Cadiz. At the same time, the emperor announced that his country would seize no more American vessels until the United States had an opportunity to negotiate a treaty with Morocco.[23] In their instructions from Congress, Adams and Jefferson were to express American satisfaction over the emperor's willingness to enter into a treaty, while Congress authorized the commissioners to appoint an agent to conduct the actual negotiations in their behalf. Because the French court had promised cooperation in the negotiations, Jay suggested that the commissioners seek the advice and assistance of Vergennes, the French foreign minister. On March 20, before he departed for London, Adams consulted the Frenchman, who encouraged the Americans to work through the French consuls but volunteered no information concerning the presents which the king gave to the Barbary rulers. He advised Adams not to invite the emperor of Morocco to send a minister to Paris but rather to dispatch an American negotiator to Morocco.[24]

Shortly after the Moroccan episode Algeria captured two American brigs, the *Maria* and the *Dauphin*, held the crewmen captive, and demanded a heavy ransom for their release. In August 1785 the American captain, Richard O'Brien, informed Jefferson in Paris of the suffering which the Americans had experienced in Algeria and asked him to negotiate for their release. At the news of the captures Jefferson wrote that his mind was "absolutely suspended between indignation

---

[22]Adams to Jay, June 26, 1785, in *Works of John Adams*, 8:273; Adams to Jay, July 19, 1785, ibid., pp. 282–83; Adams to Jay, October 21, 1785, ibid., p. 332.

[23]Jefferson to Madison, September 1, 1785, in Robert A. Rutland and William M. E. Rachal, eds., *The Papers of James Madison* (Chicago, 1973), 8:361.

[24]Jay to the American commissioners, March [11], 1785, in Boyd, *Papers of Jefferson*, 8:19–21; Adams to Franklin and Jefferson, March 20, 1785, ibid., pp. 46–47.

and impotence."[25] The Spanish negotiations with Algeria had disintegrated because the Spanish government refused to pay the required $1 million, in addition to presents; peace with that country would be expensive. "The immense sum said to have been proposed on the part of Spain to Algeria," Jefferson concluded, "leaves us little hope of satisfying their avarice." It would be wiser policy, he had written to James Monroe, to open the Mediterranean with force. "We ought to begin a naval power, if we mean to carry on our own commerce. Can we begin it on a more honorable occasion, or with a weaker foe? I am of opinion Paul Jones with half a dozen frigates would totally destroy their commerce . . . by constant cruising and cutting them to pieces."[26]

Throughout the late summer of 1785, Adams and Jefferson awaited the arrival of Charles Lamb of Connecticut, formerly engaged in the Barbary trade and now appointed by Congress to conduct the negotiations with the North African rulers. To prepare for the forthcoming negotiations, Jefferson, in August, sent Adams the draft of a treaty for the Barbary states for his approval.[27] When Lamb failed to arrive, the two American ministers decided to dispatch Thomas Barclay, a man of proven capabilities, to negotiate a treaty with Morocco. Early in September Jefferson prepared a letter to the emperor, as well as a set of instructions for Barclay, and submitted both to Adams for correction. Barclay's best argument for moderate terms, Adams believed, was the fact that the United States had no ships in the Mediterranean and would have none there until it signed treaties with the Barbary states. The North African corsairs, therefore, could capture U.S. vessels only in the Atlantic where they would be exposed to American privateers.[28] When Lamb arrived at last in September, he brought with him a commission granting Adams and Jefferson full power to appoint agents to negotiate with the Barbary states; the two ministers would sign any treaties.[29]

Having appointed Barclay to Morocco, Jefferson suggested Algeria for Lamb. "I have not seen enough of him to judge of his abilities," Jefferson admitted to Adams, but "he seems not deficient as far as I can see, and the footing on which he comes must furnish a presumption

[25]O'Brien to Jefferson, August 24, 1785, ibid., pp. 440–41; Jefferson to Nathaniel Tracy, September 26, 1785, ibid., p. 555; Jefferson to Nathanael Greene, January 12, 1786, in Boyd, *Papers of Jefferson* (Princeton, 1954), 9:168.

[26]Jefferson to William Carmichael, August 18, 1785, ibid., 8:410; Jefferson to Monroe, November 11, 1784, ibid., 7:511–12.

[27]Jefferson to Adams, July 7, 1785, ibid., 8:266; Adams to Jefferson, July 18, 1785, ibid., p. 301; Jefferson to Adams, August 6, 1785, ibid., p. 347.

[28]Jefferson to Adams, September 4, 1785, ibid., p. 473; Adams to Jefferson, September 15, 1785, ibid., p. 521.

[29]Jefferson to Adams, September 19, 1785, ibid., p. 526.

for what we do not see."[30] Still, finding Lamb less than promising in manner and appearance, Adams and Jefferson appointed John Randall of New York, in whom they had great confidence, to accompany him. Actually Congress, after Lamb's departure, had rejected the committee report that recommended Lamb for the North African negotiation; nothing in his background or experience suggested to members of Congress that he was worthy of the trust. In dispatching Lamb to Algeria, therefore, Jefferson and Adams responded to necessity and not to anticipation of success. Adams suggested that Barclay and Lamb seek the support of foreign consuls. Without orders to the contrary, these European officials would have no choice but to aid the negotiations.[31] Adams assumed correctly that no European court would seek to embarrass or obstruct American negotiations with the Barbary states, but he wondered additionally whether even the cooperation of the foreign consuls would help the American negotiations. Only naval power sufficient to threaten Algeria with bombardment or capture, he wrote to Jefferson, would encourage the dey to sue for peace. Still the United States had no apparent choice but to pursue its diplomacy with the Barbary states under the assumption that it might prove successful. As Monroe reminded Jefferson early in 1786, "These pirates have already made a great impression upon our trade and unless these negotiations prove successful will materially injure it."[32]

With both Barclay and Lamb in Spain en route to North Africa, Adams learned in mid-February 1786 that Abdurrahman, the roving ambassador from Tripoli, was in London and wanted to see him. Adams judged a call necessary and, after a tour of other visits, stopped at his door, intending only to leave a calling card, but the ambassador was announced at home and ready to receive the American minister. Adams reported to Jefferson that soon his excellency was asking many questions about the United States:

> The soil Climate Heat and Cold, etc. and said it was a very great Country. But 'Tripoli is at War with it.' I was 'Sorry to hear that.' 'America had done no Injury to Tripoli, committed no Hostility; nor had Tripoli done America any Injury or committed any Hostility against her, that I had heard of.' True said His Excellency 'but there must be a Treaty of Peace. There could be no Peace without a Treaty. The Turks and Africans were the sovereigns of the Mediterranean, and there could be no navigation there nor

[30] Jefferson to Adams, September 24, 1785, ibid., p. 543.
[31] Jefferson to Carmichael, November 4, 1785, ibid., 9:14; Adams to Jefferson, October 2, 1785, ibid., 8:572; Monroe to Jefferson, January 19, 1786, ibid., 9:187.
[32] Adams to Jefferson, October 2, 1785, ibid., 8:571–72; Monroe to Jefferson, January 19, 1786, ibid., 9:187.

Peace without Treaties of Peace. . . . America must treat with Tripoli and then with Constantinople and then with Algiers and Morocco.'

The ambassador showed Adams his full powers to negotiate what treaties he pleased; he was ready to hear and propose terms of a peace with the United States. Adams wanted Jefferson's advice. "The Relation of my Visit," he wrote to Jefferson, "is to be sure very inconsistent with the Dignity of your Character and mine, but the Ridicule of it was real and the Drollery inevitable. How can We preserve our Dignity in negotiating with Such Nations?"[33]

Three days later the Tripolitan ambassador returned the call, arriving at Adams's residence at noon. "He 'called God to Witness,' that is to say, he swore by his beard," said Adams, "that his motive to this earnestness for peace, although it might be of some benefit to himself, was the desire of doing good." Time was short, however, and the sooner peace were made, the better. When Adams asked about terms, the ambassador recommended a perpetual treaty, requiring a sum of 30,000 guineas. This was only half of what Spain had paid; moreover, he would permit the United States to pay only 12,500 guineas the first year and 3,000 each year thereafter. Adams responded that he could not pay such sums until he had special permission from Congress. In his report to Jay, he estimated the total cost of negotiating treaties with the four Barbary states at about £200,000, an amount that could be borrowed only in Holland. A war with the pirates would cost even more. Adams urged Jefferson to join him in London to pursue the negotiations as far as conditions would permit.[34]

IV

Jefferson replied quickly to Adams's summons of February 1786 to treat with both the ambassador of Tripoli and the Portuguese minister in London. Early in March he set off from Paris with his secretary, arriving in London six days later amid disagreeable weather. For the moment the Chevalier de Pinto, Portugal's minister, was ill, but eventually Jefferson and Adams negotiated a commercial treaty with him. It granted the United States no special privileges but removed some

---

[33]Adams to Jefferson, February 17, 1786, ibid., pp. 284–87.
[34]Adams to Jay, February 20, 22, 1786, in *Works of John Adams*, 8:374–79.

existing obstacles to American trade. The effort came to naught, for the Portuguese government refused to accept the treaty.[35]

Shortly after Jefferson's arrival the two commissioners visited the ambassador of Tripoli. Since the United States had sent no agents either to Tripoli or Tunis, Jefferson explained to Jay, he and Adams might make an arrangement in London in less time and at less expense. At their meeting the ambassador again advised a perpetual peace to avoid the need of annual payments. Tripoli, the Americans learned, still wanted 30,000 guineas; Tunis would want a like sum. He could not speak for Morocco or Algeria, but they would demand more. To make peace with the four Barbary states would cost between 200,000 and 300,000 guineas, many times what Adams and Jefferson had available. The American commissioners asked the ambassador why the Barbary states made such demands on nations that had done them no injury. To their question he answered that

> it was founded on the Laws of their Prophet, that it was written in their Koran, that all nations who should not have acknowledged their authority were sinners, that it was their right and duty to make war upon them wherever they could be found, and to make slaves of all they could take as Prisoners, and that every Mussel-man who should be slain in battle was sure to go to Paradise. . . .
> It was the Practice of their Corsairs to bear down upon a ship, for each sailor to take a dagger in each hand and another in his mouth, and leap on board, which so terrified their Enemies that very few stood against them.

Congress, Adams and Jefferson agreed, could obtain the necessary funds to make peace with the Barbary states only by seeking another loan in Holland. But Jay had informed them that Congress would appropriate no additional funds and would authorize no new loans in Holland to ransom the captives until it had some prospect of paying the interest on the old ones.[36]

When Jefferson returned to Paris he learned that Lamb's mission to Algeria had failed totally. Lamb clearly was unsuited for the negotiation; among other deficiencies he could speak none of the local languages. Later O'Brien wrote to William Carmichael, the American

---

[35]For a review of the negotiations with the Portuguese minister in London see ibid., pp. 410–11; Adams to Jefferson, February 21, 1786, in Boyd, *Papers of Jefferson*, 9:295; Jefferson to Jay, March 12, 1786, ibid., p. 325; Jefferson to David Humphreys, May 7, 1786, ibid., p. 469.

[36]Jefferson to Jay, March 12, 1786, ibid., p. 325; Adams and Jefferson to Jay, March 28, 1786, ibid., pp. 358–59.

chargé d'affaires at Madrid, that Lamb "could speak nothing but English; that the French consul and the Conde d'Espilly, the Spanish ambassador, would not take the trouble to explain Mr. Lamb's propositions, as the terms of the peace would be advantageous to the Algerines; and that the French and Spaniards advised Mr. Lamb to return to America, that the Algerines would not make peace with the United States of America." Subsequently one Algerine official advised O'Brien that, "if the Americans sent an American to Algiers to make the peace, they should send a man who could speak the Spanish or Italian language. He ridiculed much their sending a man that no one could understand what he had to say."[37] Jefferson understood the impossible odds which Lamb had faced in Algeria. In August he wrote to Monroe: "I am persuaded that an Angel sent on this business, and so much limited in his terms, could have done nothing. But should Congress propose to try the line of negotiation again, I think they will perceive that Lamb is not a proper agent." Later Jefferson suggested that they might have made a better selection, but Adams assured him that the responsibility for Lamb's failure was not theirs. "We found him ready appointed on our hands," wrote Adams. "I never saw him nor heard of him. He ever was and still is as indifferent to me as a Mohawk Indian. But as he came from Congress with their Dispatches of such importance, I supposed it was expected We should appoint him."[38] No one sent by Congress, he added, could have succeeded in Algeria.

From the outset the negotiations in Morocco were more promising. Barclay reached that country in June 1786, and within one month he had concluded a treaty of amity and commerce with the emperor for $30,000. This was the first treaty with a Barbary power that did not stipulate tribute or presents; Barclay submitted it to Jefferson, who transmitted it to Congress. The treaty was to remain in force for fifty years, but unfortunately the emperor died soon after the signing. To relieve the burden of renegotiating the treaty with his successor, Congress appropriated $20,000 for presents and finally approved the treaty on July 18, 1787.[39] Except for the treaty with Prussia, that with Morocco was the only success at treaty-making that Adams and Jefferson achieved, and even that had resulted largely from Spanish support.

[37]Quoted in Eugene Schuyler, *American Diplomacy and the Furtherance of Commerce* (New York, 1886), pp. 205–06.

[38]Jefferson to Monroe, August 11, 1786, in Boyd, *Papers of Jefferson* (Princeton, 1954), 10:224; Adams to Jefferson, January 25, 1787, ibid. (Princeton, 1955), 11:66.

[39]Barclay to the American commissioners, June 26, July 16, September 18, and October 2, 1786, ibid., 10:71, 141, 389, 418–26; Jefferson to Adams, August 27, 1786, in *Works of John Adams*, 8:412–13; Adams to Jay, January 24, 1787, ibid., p. 422; commissioners to Jay, January 27, 1787, ibid., pp. 425–26.

As relations with the Barbary powers drifted on, Adams and Jefferson agreed that the ultimate American defense of its Mediterranean trade lay in the mutually objectionable alternatives of tribute or war. There would be little American commerce in the Mediterranean until Congress came to terms with the Barbary states, especially Algeria. Adams reminded Jefferson in May 1786 that the Algerines would never make peace with the United States until it had treaties with Turkey, Tunis, Tripoli, and Morocco; the Algerines always resisted negotiations to the last. Vergennes assured Jefferson one week later that a treaty with Constantinople would not protect American ships in the Mediterranean from the Algerian pirates.[40] Clearly the choices confronting the United States were narrow, and Adams noted what it would pay for not negotiating a peace with the North African states: a heavy insurance on all exports, the loss of much of its trade with Spain and Portugal, and the total loss of the Mediterranean and Levant trade. Those losses, wrote Adams in June 1786, would exceed £500,000 per year, and to fight the pirates would cost an equal amount without protecting the trade. Certainly, he concluded, war would cost far more than interest on a loan sufficient to pay the tribute.[41] Adams argued further, in a letter to Jefferson in early July, that the United States lacked the power to punish the Barbary states and therefore had no choice but to bribe them. America could not have peace in the Mediterranean unless it paid tribute; that tribute, feared Adams, would increase the longer the delay in negotiating. "From these premises," he wrote, "I conclude it to be the wisest for us to negotiate and pay the necessary sum without loss of time. . . . The policy of Christendom has made cowards of all their sailors before the standard of Mahomet. It would be heroical and glorious in us to restore courage to ours. I doubt not we could accomplish it, if we should set about it in earnest; but the difficulty of bringing our people to agree upon it, has ever discouraged me."[42]

Jefferson, in his reply, doubted that the price of negotiation necessarily would increase with the passage of time; that would depend on the value of any future captures. If the United States would have peace through negotiation, he could see no reason for delay. But Jefferson preferred war; to him, it would have the defense of honor, procure some respect in Europe, and strengthen the government at home. He argued additionally that war would cost less than tribute and that a

[40]Adams to Jefferson, May 23, 1786, ibid., 8:393; Jefferson to Adams, May 30, 1786, in Boyd, *Papers of Jefferson*, 9:595.

[41]Adams to Jefferson, June 6, 1786, ibid., pp. 611–12.

[42]Adams to Jefferson, July 3, 1786, ibid., 10:86–87.

peace not enforced with adequate power at sea could be of short duration. No agreement, moreover, would extend beyond the life of the dey who signed it.

Jefferson was equally convinced that the United States, in a war against the pirates, would have the support of Naples and perhaps Portugal. In time other powers would enter the confederacy to ensure the peace of the Mediterranean. Jefferson embodied his preferences for the use of force in a plan for concerted action against the pirates, one that would secure perpetual peace in the Mediterranean without tribute. He proposed a convention that called for cruising along the North African coast by a multinational naval force directed by a council of ambassadors, perhaps at Versailles. Lafayette found the proposal fascinating, as did some of the smaller European powers. What terminated the project was the financial hopelessness of Congress; this eliminated any decision.[43] Adams replied graciously in late July that, whereas he wanted a navy whether it be applied to the Algerines or not, he still favored negotiation, believing that Jefferson had underestimated the force required to humble the Algerines. He concluded that, "tho I am glad we have exchanged a Letter on the subject, I perceive that neither Force nor Money will be applied. Our States are so backward that they will do nothing for some years. . . . It is their Concern, and We must submit, for your Plan of fighting will no more be adopted than mine of negotiating. This is more humiliating to me, than giving the Presents would be."[44]

V

Early in December 1785, Adams had stated that the United States simply could not achieve a satisfactory arrangement with the present British ministry. He admitted to Jay that he no longer demanded Britain's evacuation of the posts because London always tied the issue of debts to the evacuation. He had insisted on the withdrawal in conversation but had made no formal requisition in the name of the United States. "If I had done it," he wrote, "I should have compromised my sovereign, and should certainly have had no answer. Whenever this is done, it should be followed up. I shall certainly do it, if I should see a moment when it can possibly prevail." Convinced that he would continue to meet a blank response, Adams would no longer press the British for a resolution of any of the issues. "In short, sir, I am like to

[43]Jefferson to Adams, July 11, 1786, ibid., pp. 123–25; Jefferson's proposed convention against the Barbary states [before July 4, 1786], ibid., pp. 566–68.

[44]Adams to Jefferson, July 31, 1786, ibid., pp. 177–78.

be as insignificant here as you can imagine. I shall be treated, as I have been, with all the civility that is shown to other foreign ministers, but shall do nothing."[45] Congress would need to share his patience. "It is most certain, that what is called high language," he observed realistically, "would be misplaced here at this time. It would not be answered with high language, but with what would be more disagreeable and perplexing,—with a contemptuous silence." With nothing to be done, he would await the next session of Parliament when the British design would become more apparent. "Thus, I find myself at a full stop," he acknowledged; "I shall not neglect any opportunity, to say or do whatever may have the least tendency to do any good; but it would be lessening the United States, if I were to tease ministers with applications, which would be answered only by neglect and silence." If the London government did not give him an answer in the spring, he wrote, then Congress could not avoid instructing him to demand an answer, to take his leave and return to America.[46]

On November 30, Adams had presented to Carmarthen a memorial demanding that the British withdraw their garrisons from the territories of the United States. He explained to Jay his reluctant decision: "I do not expect an answer till next summer. But I thought it safest for the United States to have it presented, because, without it, some excuses or pretences might have been set up, that the evacuations had not yet been formally demanded." Carmarthen informed Adams in January that he was preparing an answer to the memorial on the posts; in response he would cite the complaints of creditors to the ministry. "I am glad to have an answer," wrote Adams, "for, whatever conditions they may tack to the surrender of the posts, we shall find out what is boiling in their hearts, and by degrees come together."[47] In his reply Carmarthen justified the British detention of the posts by pointing to the laws of certain states which impeded the recovery of the old British debts. Another memorial on compensation for the Negroes, Adams predicted, would receive the same answer. For Adams the choices were clear: the United States either would await in vain the evacuation of the posts, the payment for the Negroes, a treaty of commerce, restoration of the prizes, or any other kind of relief, or the states would repeal their laws. The old creditors in Britain, added Adams, had formed themselves into a society and would not permit Parliament to

[45]Adams to Jay, October 15, 1785, in *Works of John Adams*, 8:320; Adams to Jay, December 3, 1785, ibid., p. 355.
      [46]Ibid.; Adams to Jay, November 5, 1785, ibid., pp. 336–37; Adams to Jay, December 6, 1785, ibid., p. 356.
      [47]Adams to Jay, December 9, 1785, ibid., pp. 359–60; Adams to Jefferson, January 19, 1786, ibid., p. 368.

forget them. "The States, it may be said, will not repeal their laws. If they do not, then let them give up all expectation from this Court and country," he warned Jay, "unless you can force them to . . . [invest] congress with full power to regulate trade."[48]

Driven by necessity and a sense of fairness, Adams now pressed the British case on Jay and Congress, reminding his official and private correspondents in America that there would be no progress in London until the states repealed their acts impeding payments to British creditors and terminated their mistreatment of Loyalists. He informed Congress in May 1786 "that it was unquestionably true, that by the seventh article the posts should have been evacuated; but that by the fourth and ninth it was also stipulated that there should be no legal impediment in the way of recovery of British debts; that these articles had been violated by almost every state in the confederacy."[49] When the United States complied with the provisions of the treaty, Adams promised, the king would also. "It will appear to all the world with an ill grace," he pleaded, "if we complain of breaches of the treaty, when the British Court have it in their power to prove upon us breaches of the same treaty, of greater importance. My advice, then if it is not impertinent to give it, is, that every law of every State which concerns either debts or royalists, which can be impartially construed contrary to the spirit of the treaty of peace, be immediately repealed, and the debtors left to settle with creditors, or dispute the point of interest at law." He observed to Samuel Adams in June 1786 that "when We have done equity We may with good Grace, demand Equity."[50]

If British compliance with the treaty provisions demanded a diplomatic recognition of the London government's case, British attitudes and commercial policy toward the United States did not. Adams's complaints of British behavior and the nature of American policies which would improve it continued to dominate his correspondence in 1786 and thereafter. For him the ministry in London continued to view the United States as a rival, and in the British lexicon that meant an enemy to be reduced by every possible means. Adams had complained in March 1786 that he had met very few Englishmen—much fewer than he expected when he arrived—who favored commercial reciprocity with the United States. "I have long informed congress," he wrote in May, "that nothing is to be expected from this country but poverty, weakness, and ruin." Again the answer for Adams lay in congressional

[48]Adams to Jay, May 25, 1786, ibid., pp. 394–95.
[49]Adams quoted in Monroe to Richard Henry Lee, May 24, 1786, in Stanislaus Murray Hamilton, ed., *The Writings of James Monroe* (New York, 1969), 1:130.
[50]Adams to Jay, May 25, 1786, in *Works of John Adams*, 8:395; Butterfield, *Diary and Autobiography of John Adams*, 3:201.

action. "The United States must repel monopolies by monopolies, and answer prohibitions by prohibitions," he advised; if Congress could agree to regulate the commerce of the United States, England would seek a treaty.[51] On the eve of the final adoption of the Constitution in February 1788, Adams assured Jay that, "as soon as there shall be one [a national government], the British Court will vouchsafe to treat with it."[52]

For Adams his negotiations in London had long ceased to have a future. In August and September 1786 he traveled to the Netherlands to exchange ratifications of the Prussian treaty with the Prussian minister. The trip offered him the opportunity to pay his respects to officials in Holland, a country to which he was still accredited and one which Mrs. Adams, who accompanied him, had never seen. Soon thereafter Adams pressed Congress for permission to return to the United States. During the early months of 1787 his routine office duties no longer involved any diplomatic business with the British government. On February 3 he reported to Jay that "Parliament opened with uncommon gloom and has been sitting in mournful silence." He noted that "a dead taciturnity prevails about America," but what troubled him even more was his discovery that Britain spent many times the profits of the fur trade to maintain its frontier posts in America. Adams acknowledged his dejection: "A life so useless to the public, and so insipid to myself, as mine is in Europe, has become a burden to me, as well as to my countrymen." Still his diplomatic burdens continued. The Dutch bankers, Willink and Van Staphorst, informed him that they had insufficient funds on hand to pay the interest on the American loan. On Adams's advice they secured a new one at 8 percent, but insisted that Adams come to Holland to sign the obligations so that they could acquire the necessary guilders. In Amsterdam, Adams found 2,000 bonds awaiting his signature. He sat at a desk for two days, signing his name, he told Abigail, until his "hand could hardly hold the pen." With that task completed, he returned to London.[53]

After the spring of 1787 the Adams family awaited the opportunity to return to America. Abigail, like her husband, could not look back on their two-year residence in London with great satisfaction; she too shared a deep resentment of British officialdom. London society offered only limited recompense, and she confessed to Mercy Warren:

---

[51]Adams to Matthew Robinson, March 2, 1786, in *Works of John Adams*, 8:383–85; Adams to James Bowdoin, May 9, 1786, ibid., p. 389.

[52]Adams to Jay, February 14, 1788, ibid., pp. 475–76.

[53]Butterfield, *Diary and Autobiography of John Adams*, 3:201; Adams to Jay, January 25, 1787, in *Works of John Adams*, 8:424; Adams to Jay, February 3, 1787, ibid., pp. 428–29; Adams to Jay, May 8, 1787, ibid., pp. 438–39; Messrs. Willink and others to Adams, May 18, 1787, ibid., pp. 440–41; Adams to Jay, June 16, 1787, ibid., p. 441.

I have resided in this Country near two years and in that time, I have made some few acquaintance whom I esteem and shall leave with regret, but the customs and manners of a Metropolis are unfriendly to that social intercourse which I have ever been accustomed to. Amusement and diversion may always be purchased at the Theatres and places of public resort, so that little pains is taken to cultivate that benevolence and interchange of kindness which sweetens life, in lieu of which mere visits of form are substituted to keep up the union.[54]

In July, Jay agreed that Adams should return home where his prospects for additional service to the nation seemed promising enough. "You have, my good friend," wrote Jay, "deserved well of your country; and your services and character will be truly estimated, at least by posterity, for they will know more of you than the people of this day." Adams explained to Jefferson his desire to leave Britain, attributing it more to necessity than to choice: "Congress cannot, consistent with their own honour and Dignity, renew my Commission to this Court—and I assure you, I should hold it so inconsistent with my own honour and Dignity little as that may be, that if it were possible for Congress to forget theirs I would not forget mine, but send their Commission back to them, unless a Minister were sent from his Britannic Majesty to Congress."[55]

To the end Adams condemned the attitude of the British court. "In preparing for my departure," he confided to Jay, "I have been personally treated with the same uniform tenor of dry decency and cold civility which appears to have been the premeditated plan from the beginning; and opposition, as well as administration, appear to have adopted the same spirit."[56] On February 20, 1788, Adams had his final audience with the king. After he had assured the monarch of America's friendship and desire for more liberal commercial relations, the king replied: "Mr. Adams, you may, with great truth, assure the United States that, whenever they shall fulfil the treaty on their part, I, on my part, will fulfil it in all its particulars."[57]

What now remained for Adams was the unwelcome necessity of taking leave of the queen, the cabinet members, and members of the diplomatic corps. Congressional failure to send him formal letters of recall from both Britain and Holland troubled him during his final days in London. The British government did not require a letter; however, Adams wrote memorials addressed to the Prince of Orange and

[54]Abigail Adams to Mercy Warren, May 14, 1787, in *Warren-Adams Letters*, 2:287.
[55]Jay to Adams, July 25, 1787, in *Works of John Adams*, 8:445–46; Adams to Jefferson, March 1, 1787, in Boyd, *Papers of Jefferson*, 9:189.
[56]Adams to Jay, February 14, 1788, in *Works of John Adams*, 8:476.
[57]Adams to Jay, February 21, 1788, ibid., p. 480.

the States General, requesting their secretary to deliver them. This the secretary refused to do and returned the letters. Since Adams had presented a letter of credence from Congress on his arrival in Holland, the secretary explained, he required a letter of recall from Congress as well. Adams reluctantly decided to travel to Holland again and take leave in person. Late in March he returned to London to discover that his wife had moved to the Bath Hotel so that packers could prepare the furniture and books in the legation for shipment to the United States. Just as he was entering his carriage on March 30 for the journey to Portsmouth, he received his official letters of recall. He posted one to Lord Carmarthen and the other to the Dutch ambassador in London and then departed from London, arriving in Portsmouth the following evening for his long-awaited journey to America.[58]

---

[58]William Stephens Smith to Jefferson, February 22, 1788, in Boyd, *Papers of Jefferson* (Princeton, 1955), 12:620; Butterfield, *Diary and Autobiography of John Adams*, 3:212.

CHAPTER THREE

Jefferson in Paris*

FOR THOMAS JEFFERSON the appointment as America's first minister to the French court assured adventure but not necessarily success. His nine months in Paris as an associate of Benjamin Franklin and John Adams had produced a treaty with Prussia, nothing more. Diplomacy with France had sought little and gained less, but the discourse at least had remained cordial; this alone created some prospect for diplomatic progress in Paris. Even before Adams departed for London in May 1785, Jefferson had informed the foreign minister, the Comte de Vergennes, of his appointment and had delivered his letter of credence to King Louis XVI in private audience. At his formal reception by the royal family, the king and Queen Marie Antoinette welcomed him to France in his new role. As a full member of the diplomatic corps, Jefferson was now entitled to attend the king's levee every Tuesday and to join the whole diplomatic corps at dinner. So high was Franklin's reputation at the French court that Jefferson soon found the task of succeeding him an exercise in humility. "On being presented to any one as the Minister of America," he later recalled, "the common-place question, used in such cases, was 'it is you, Sir, who replace Doctor Franklin?' I generally answered 'no one can replace him, Sir; I am only his successor.' "[1]

Somehow the experience of attending court scarcely thrilled Jefferson. He was too introspective to be impressed with such outward displays of wealth and power, nor did he hold the diplomats in high

---

*Carroll Lecture, Mary Baldwin College, October 13, 1982. Published as "Jefferson in Paris," in *Adams and Jefferson in Europe, 1783–1789* (Mary Baldwin College, Staunton, Virginia, 1984). Reprinted by permission.
[1]Jefferson to the Reverend William Smith, February 19, 1791, in Julian P. Boyd et al., eds., *The Papers of Thomas Jefferson* (Princeton, 1974), 19:113.

esteem. With few exceptions, he later told Gouverneur Morris, they were not worth knowing.[2] Jefferson had little regard for Parisian society or the general extravagance of the rich and aristocratic; he was more at home in French intellectual circles. Before Franklin left Passy in July he introduced Jefferson to the salon of Madame Helvétius in Auteuil where men of literature and learning congregated. It was here that Jefferson met many of his later associates.[3]

As minister to France, Jefferson faced the immediate challenge of furthering American commercial interests. The *Arrêt* of August 1784 opened seven ports in the French West Indies to American ships and extended the list of approved imports. This decree appeared in the Philadelphia press in March 1785. By then, the Marquis de Lafayette reported, French indignation over such a relaxation of French mercantile policy again threatened to close the West Indies. What incited the pressures on the French government was the narrow and apparently successful conduct of Great Britain. In June, Jefferson added his own warning: "The merchants of this country continue as loud and furious as ever against the Arret of August 1784, permitting our commerce with their islands to a certain degree. . . . The ministry are disposed to be firm, but there is a point at which they will give way."[4] The continuing American failure to break the restraints of European mercantilism on the country's foreign commerce destroyed his interest in the projected system of commercial treaties.

For Jefferson, American commercial interests in the Atlantic required two specific changes in established policy. The first was broad, permanent access to the West Indies; this would require concessions from the colonial powers. "Yet how to gain it," he wrote to James Monroe in June, "when it is the established system of these nations to exclude all foreigners from their colonies. The only chance seems to be this. Our commerce to the mother countries is valuable to them. We must endeavor then to make this the price of an admission into their West Indies, and to those who refuse the admission we must refuse our commerce or load theirs by odious discriminations in our ports."[5] American policy failed, Jefferson reminded John Jay, not in its inability to negotiate treaties with continental Europe but in its ineffectiveness in dealing with the powers that possessed American territory. To coerce these colonial powers, he argued in his second point, required that

---

[2] Dumas Malone, *Jefferson and the Rights of Man* (Boston, 1951), p. 14.
[3] Ibid., pp. 15–16.
[4] Lafayette to Madison, March 16, 1785, in Robert A. Rutland and William M. E. Rachal, eds., *The Papers of James Madison* (Chicago, 1973), 8:246–47; Jefferson to Monroe, June 17, 1785, in Boyd, *Papers of Jefferson* (Princeton, 1953), 8:228.
[5] Jefferson to Monroe, June 17, 1785, ibid., p. 232.

Congress superintend the commerce of the United States as effectively as the present Constitution would permit. In 1785 several states were pushing their own navigation laws against Britain. Jefferson warned, however, that individual state action would merely antagonize the Europeans without coercing them. Recognizing the need for a national policy, he suggested to Adams in October that the states be compelled to strengthen the confederacy.[6]

Failing to further American commerce through treaties opening either the West Indies or Europe, Jefferson turned to the immediate task of developing the promised Franco-American commercial axis. His new focus on French commerce in 1785 resulted from his position as minister to France as well as from his conviction that trade with France could break the British monopoly. The anticipation that France would displace Britain in the American market continued to meet with disappointment, but Jefferson believed that France might still succeed if it would abolish its internal restraints and monopolies which prevented a free exchange of goods in its domestic market. Jefferson reminded Vergennes of the possibilities of a direct commerce between France and the United States:

> We can furnish to France (because we have heretofore furnished to England), of whale oil and spermaceti, of furs and peltry, of ships and naval stores,' and of potash to the amount of fifteen millions of livres; and the quantities will admit of increase. Of our tobacco, France consumes the value of ten millions more. Twenty-five millions of livres, then, mark the extent of that commerce of exchange, which is, at present, practicable between us. We want, in return, productions and manufactures, not money. If the duties on our produce are light, and the sale free, we shall undoubtedly bring it here, and lay out the proceeds on the spot in the productions and manufactures we want. . . . The conclusion is, that there are commodities which form a basis of exchange to the extent of a million of guineas annually; it is for the wisdom of those in power to contrive that the exchange shall be made.[7]

Lafayette, many of the French physiocrats and *philosophes*, and Vergennes himself sympathized with Jefferson's purpose of achieving the commercial goals of the American Revolution.

When Jefferson pressed Versailles for new commercial arrangements in the fall of 1785, the French economy was depressed and the

[6]Ibid., p. 231; Jefferson to Adams, October 3, 1785, ibid., pp. 579–80; Jefferson to Jay, January 27, 1786, ibid. (Princeton, 1954), 9:235.

[7]Patrick Henry to Jefferson, September 10, 1785, ibid., 8:509; Jefferson to Vergennes, December [20], 1785, ibid., 9:112.

government had difficulty in defending the limited concessions it had made to American trade in the West Indies. What reinforced French caution was the conviction that America had become addicted to British trade, although Jefferson reminded Vergennes that, if it were a matter of national prejudice, the trade would come to France. Unable to cut the bonds of credit that tied U.S. commerce to Britain, Jefferson launched an assault on the French commercial restrictions that gave the British their advantage. Much of his effort centered on tobacco, America's leading export. France imported large quantities of American tobacco but granted a monopoly for its acquisition to the Farmers-General, the giant company to which the government farmed out the collection of several indirect taxes and customs duties, including that on tobacco. Because the Farmers-General was tied to the entire French system of public finance, any assault on the tobacco monopoly would be hazardous for anyone who undertook it.[8] Jefferson's case against the monopoly was persuasive. Since the Farmers-General did not engage in commercial exchange but paid in coin, Americans who sold tobacco in France could not really enter the French market. As a result, they generally invaded the British market with their money, and Jefferson reminded Vergennes that French policy merely supported British industry. As he explained,

> By prohibiting all His Majesty's subjects from dealing in tobacco except with a single company, one third of the exports of the United States are rendered uncommercial here. . . . A relief from these shackles will form a memorable epoch in the commerce of the two nations. It will establish at once a great basis of exchange, serving like a point of union to draw to it other members of our commerce. . . . Each nation has exactly to spare the articles which the other wants. . . . The governments have nothing to do but *not to hinder* their merchants from making the exchange.[9]

To make matters worse for Jefferson, the French government earlier had given Robert Morris, the American financier, a three-year contract to supply France with all of its American tobacco. This second monopoly had an adverse effect on tobacco prices and eliminated many U.S. tobacco merchants from the French trade entirely. Jefferson, supported effectively by Lafayette, convinced Vergennes to appoint the so-called American Committee to study Franco-American trade and

---

[8]Jefferson's report on conversations with Vergennes [December 1785], ibid., p. 139; Merrill D. Peterson, "Thomas Jefferson and Commercial Policy, 1783–1793," *William and Mary Quarterly* 22 (October 1965): 596–97.

[9]Jefferson to the Comte de Montmorin, July 23, 1787, in Boyd, *Papers of Jefferson* (Princeton, 1955), 11:617.

make recommendations for its improvement. The committee managed to end the Morris monopoly but not that of the Farmers-General.[10] In October 1786 the French government announced a series of concessions to American commerce and navigation which freed U.S. exports, as well as imports, both in France and in the West Indies. Not until December 1787 did the French government enact these concessions into law.[11]

Jefferson devoted much of his effort to obtaining a French market for American whale oil. Britain, through heavy subsidies and duties on American whale oil, managed to build its own whaling industry. France followed the British example only to fail miserably, thus injuring the U.S. industry to the benefit of Britain. Jefferson, in a long report, noted that French whaling policy again enhanced British sea power at the expense of American strength in the Atlantic. France could serve both the American and its own interest, he argued, by excluding all European oil from France. In December 1788, Paris adopted Jefferson's formula and granted French and American whale oil a monopoly in the French market.[12] For U.S. rice the problem was different: rice growers had lost much of their world markets to Britain's carrying trade, permitting its merchants to dominate the European rice market. What additionally placed American rice at a disadvantage in the French market was the French preference for the Mediterranean variety. Finding it more promising to alter American produce than the French cuisine, Jefferson, on his tour of France's southern ports in 1787, crossed into Piedmont and smuggled rice seeds across the Apennines. His limited gains in creating a French market for American rice, however, came less from his smuggling efforts than from his capacity to induce some French firms to enter the Carolina rice trade.[13]

Jefferson's successes in building Franco-American trade never matched his efforts. Between 1785 and 1789 the total volume of that trade changed little; whatever the real advances they were more in the West Indies than with France itself. The French monopolies assured Americans an overwhelming advantage in trade balances. Thus Jefferson failed where it mattered: he could never establish a system of fair exchange in the French market. The Anglo-French commercial

[10]Calonne, the French comptroller general, to Jefferson, October 22, 1786, ibid. (Princeton, 1954), 10:474–78.
    [11]For the French concessions see ibid.; final decree, December 29, 1787, in ibid. (Princeton, 1955), 12:468–70.
    [12]The *Arrêt* of December 7, 1788, ibid. (Princeton, 1958), 14:268–69.
    [13]Jefferson to Izard, August 1, 1787, ibid., 11:659; Rutledge to Jefferson, October 23, 1787, ibid., 12:263–64; Brailsford and Morris to Jefferson, October 31, 1787, ibid., pp. 298–301; Brailsford and Morris to Jefferson, March 10, 1789, ibid., 14:632–33; Rutledge to Jefferson, April 1, 1789, ibid. (Princeton, 1958), 15:12–13.

accord of 1786 flooded the French market with British goods. The resulting depression in French production further negated his efforts to create the essential market for French goods in America. Still Jay lauded Jefferson for the commercial arrangements which he had made. "They bear Marks of Wisdom and Liberality," he wrote in April 1788, "and cannot fail of being very acceptable."[14] Congress revealed its general satisfaction with Jefferson when on October 12, 1787 it renewed, without a negative vote, his ministry to France for three more years.

Jefferson had found Vergennes a great minister in European affairs but with little knowledge of things American. His devotion to despotism rendered him less than sympathetic to the U.S. government, Jefferson admitted, but his fear of England made him generally cooperative. "He is cool, reserved in political conversation, free and familiar on other subjects, and a very attentive, agreeable person to do business with," Jefferson wrote to James Madison. "It is impossible to have a clearer, better organised head but age has chilled his heart." Vergennes died in mid-February 1787, and the king appointed the Comte de Montmorin as his successor. From the beginning Jefferson thought highly of the new minister. "I am extremely pleased with his modesty, the simplicity of his manners, and his dispositions toward us," he confided to Lafayette.[15] Whatever Jefferson's opinion of the diplomatic corps in Paris, his standing with French officials and other members of the corps remained high. Thomas L. Shippen, the nephew of Arthur Lee, spent several weeks in Paris during January 1788 and accompanied Jefferson to court. "I observed," Shippen recalled, "that although Mr. Jefferson was the plainest man in the room, and the most destitute of ribbands crosses and other insignia of rank that he was most courted and most attended to (even by the Courtiers themselves) of the whole Diplomatic corps."[16]

Jefferson's crowning diplomatic achievement of his last years in France was the consular convention of 1788, which he negotiated with Montmorin. What made the convention necessary was the danger to American security posed by the extraterritoriality provisions of the convention that Franklin had negotiated with Vergennes in 1784 but which Congress had rejected. Jay, in opposing the convention, argued that Franklin had defied every instruction he received. Having won the

[14]Jefferson to Jay, December 31, 1787, ibid., 12:479–82; Jay to Jefferson, April 24, 1788, ibid. (Princeton, 1956), 13:106.

[15]Jefferson to Madison, January 30, 1787, ibid., 11:95–96; Jefferson to Adams, February 14, 1787, ibid., p. 143; Jefferson to Lafayette, February 26, 1787, ibid., p. 186; Carmichael to Jefferson, March 25, 1787, ibid., p. 237.

[16]For Shippen's observations of Paris, January 9, 1788 see ibid., 12:502–04. The observation on Jefferson is on p. 504.

approval of Congress for a new agreement, Jay sent Jefferson instructions to negotiate a convention in accordance with the original plan. Jefferson informed Montmorin that Congress desired changes in the convention and described these as tactfully as he could. Since France wanted consuls in American ports, the United States was willing to have them, but, Jefferson insisted, they could not enjoy immunities, privileges, and powers that did not conform to American laws. The only feature of extraterritoriality that remained was the right of French consuls to try civil cases involving only French subjects, a right American consuls enjoyed in French ports. Jefferson limited the convention to twelve years. The new convention was an agreement between equals; Jay expressed delight with it.[17]

II

Through his extended efforts to enhance America's stature in Europe, Jefferson saw that the real threat to American dignity and independence lay in British policy. He no less than Franklin and Adams believed that Britain harbored a fundamental hostility toward the United States. Jefferson, like Adams, accused it of flooding Europe with adverse reports about America. He complained to Madison on September 1, 1785: "There was an enthusiasm towards us all over Europe at the moment of the peace. The torrent of lies published unremittingly in every day's London paper first made an impression and produced a coolness. The republication of those lies in most of the papers of Europe (done probably by authority of the governments to discourage emigrations) carried them home to the belief of every mind. They supposed every thing in America was anarchy, tumult, and civil war."[18] Jefferson sought to defend the United States against such accusations. Writing to his German friend, Baron Geismar, in September 1785, he said:

> From the London gazettes, and the papers copying them, you are led to suppose that all there is anarchy, discontent, and civil war. Nothing however is less true. There are not, on the face of the earth, more tranquil governments than ours, nor a happier and more contented people. Their commerce has not as yet found the channels which their new relations with the world will offer to best

[17]Jay to Jefferson, August 18, 1786, ibid., 10:271–72; Jay to Jefferson, March 9, 1789, ibid., 14:628. Jefferson to Jay, November 14, 1788, pp. 56–57. For a history of the consular convention of 1788 see ibid., pp. 66–92; and Jefferson to Montmorin, June 20, 1788, ibid., pp. 121–25.

[18]Jefferson to Madison, September 1, 1785, ibid., 8:461.

advantage, and the old ones remain as yet unopened by new conventions. This occasions a stagnation in the sale of their produce, *the only truth among all the circumstances published about them.*

Several weeks later Jefferson again vented his anger toward Britain when he wrote: "England seems not to permit our friendship to enter into her political calculations as an article of any value. Her endeavor is not how to recover our affections or to bind us to her by alliance, but by what new experiments she may keep up an existence without us."[19]

Jefferson agreed with Adams that coercion alone would advance American commercial interests in London. To protect the public interest in foreign commerce, Congress required the authority to issue threats of retaliation against European discriminations. Jefferson wrote Madison in September 1785 that only when Europe detected a growing disposition to invest Congress with the regulation of commerce could he discover "the smallest token of respect towards the United States in any part of Europe."[20] Because commercial rivalry could ultimately lead to personal insult and property violations on the high seas, Jefferson argued that the United States required greater naval strength to punish any aggression.

Jefferson would have preferred that there was no commerce to defend. "Were I to indulge my own theory," he wrote in October 1785, "I should wish them [the Americans] to practice neither commerce nor navigation, but to stand with respect to Europe precisely on the footing of China. We should thus avoid wars, and all our citizens would be husbandmen." Such choices, he admitted, lay in theory only, "and a theory which the servants of America are not at liberty to follow." He favored agriculture to commerce but recognized the importance of shipping to his constituents. "Our people," he said, "are decided in the opinion that it is necessary for us to take a share in the occupation of the ocean, and their established habits induce them to require that the sea be kept open for them, and that that line of policy be pursued which will render the use of that element as great as possible to them. I think it a duty in those entrusted with the administration of their affairs to conform themselves to the decided choice of their constituents."[21]

---

[19]Jefferson to Geismar, September 6, 1785, ibid., pp. 499–500; Jefferson to James Currie, September 27, 1785, ibid., p. 559.

[20]Jefferson to Madison, September 1, 1785, ibid., p. 461.

[21]Jefferson to G. K. van Hogendorp, October 13, 1785, ibid., p. 633; Jefferson to Jay, August 23, 1785, ibid., p. 426.

During his temporary residence in London in March and April 1786, Jefferson experienced the full measure of official British arrogance. At his formal presentation to Lord Carmarthen, the minister was not insulting but cold and evasive. Adams and Jefferson had left a draft treaty with him, but he did not reply. When they learned accidently that the draft asked too much, they submitted a modified version; this too Carmarthen ignored. The two diplomats then informed the British minister that their commissions were about to expire and that Jefferson needed to return to Paris. Carmarthen was not impressed, yet Jefferson maintained his politeness by asking Carmarthen if he could carry any messages for him. However, as he confessed to Jay, he again found British silence invincible: "With this country nothing is done and that nothing is intended to be done on their part admits not the smallest doubt. The nation is against any change of measures. The Ministers are against it, some from principle, others from subserviency, and the King more than all men is against it."

At this point, Jefferson complained to Madison that British merchants "sufficiently value our commerce; but they are quite persuaded they shall enjoy it on their own terms. This political speculation fosters the warmest feeling of the king's heart, that is, his hatred to us. If ever he should be forced to make any terms with us, it will be by events which he does not foresee. He takes no pains at present to hide his aversion."[22] When Adams and Jefferson appeared before the king, the reception was most ungracious. According to the Adams family records, his majesty turned his back on the two Americans in a manner that permitted all surrounding courtiers to take full notice.[23] Upon his return to Paris, Jefferson suggested to Abigail Adams that the British monarch remained one of America's great benefactors because he was still driving its people toward independence.[24]

By the summer of 1787, Jefferson and Adams faced the task of negotiating another loan with the country's Dutch bankers, Willink and Van Staphorst. Jefferson learned in June that his secretary, William Short, had recommended him for the money negotiations in Holland and balked at the thought of going. "On the contrary," he wrote to Madison, "it is a business which would be the most disagreeable to

---

[22]Jefferson to Madison, April 25, 1786, in Rutland and Rachal, *Papers of Madison* (Chicago, 1975), 9:26; Adams to Carmarthen, March 13, 1786, in Boyd, *Papers of Jefferson*, 9:327; American commissioners to Jay, April 25, 1786, ibid., p. 406; Jefferson to John Page, May 4, 1786, ibid., p. 446; Jefferson to C. W. F. Dumas, May 6, 1786, ibid., p. 462; Jefferson to David Humphreys, May 7, 1786, ibid., p. 469.

[23]Charles Francis Adams's life of John Adams, in *Works of John Adams* (Boston, 1856), 1:420.

[24]Jefferson to Abigail Adams, August 9, 1786, in Paul Leicester Ford, ed., *The Writings of Thomas Jefferson* (New York, 1894), 4:261.

me of all others, and for which I am the most unfit person living. I do not understand bargaining nor possess the dexterity requisite to make it."[25] Jefferson had long argued that the United States should pay off its French debt and transfer its entire indebtedness to Holland. With France on the verge of bankruptcy in 1787, Jefferson believed that this transfer was all the more necessary; the debt to France, he reported to Madison in August, was injuring the standing of the United States in that country. That month Jefferson learned that Adams had traveled to Amsterdam alone and had negotiated another large loan with Willink and Van Staphorst. Thereafter Jefferson, Adams informed the Dutch bankers, would conduct the negotiations for any additional American loans.[26]

Early in 1788 the commissioners of the Treasury in the United States informed Jefferson that Adams's recent loan required renegotiation. He quickly apprised Adams of this latest financial crisis and asked him to undertake one more negotiation in Holland to tide the country over until it could establish a more effective taxing and credit structure. Adams believed that the sale of the bonds he had signed in the early summer of 1787 should have been sufficient to support American credit, and he feared that the Dutch bankers wanted to renegotiate merely to acquire a higher rate of interest. Adams suggested that Jefferson call their bluff. "Depend upon it," he advised Jefferson in February, "the Amsterdamers love Money too well to execute their Threats. They expect to gain too much by American Credit to destroy it." When Jefferson discovered that Adams would shortly return to The Hague to take leave of the Dutch government, he decided to join him in Holland to avail himself of Adams's experience. Adams executed bonds for still another loan and departed for London and his return to America; Jefferson remained in Amsterdam twelve more days to follow the progress of the new loan.[27]

III

No less than Adams and Jefferson, members of Congress chafed at the hindrances to American trade embodied in European commercial practices. Not even commercial treaties were a guarantee of equal advantage. Compelled by the mercantilist practices of the age to retreat from the idea of free trade, Americans adopted the principle of the most

[25]Jefferson to Madison, June 20, 1787, in Boyd, *Papers of Jefferson*, 11:482.

[26]Jefferson to Madison, August 2, 1787, ibid., p. 664; Adams to Jefferson, August 25, 1787, ibid., 12:55.

[27]Jefferson to Adams, December 16, 1787, ibid., pp. 429–30; Adams to Jefferson, February 12, 1788, ibid., p. 582; Jefferson to Jay, March 16, 1788, ibid., p. 671; Jefferson to the commissioners of the Treasury, March 29, 1788, ibid., pp. 698–700.

favored nation. They discovered quickly enough that the most-favored-nation principle assured no privileges in the exchange of goods. Nations in the late eighteenth century generally treated all nations as equals; therefore, the most-favored-nation policy did not grant favored treatment but merely the right to trade under the same restrictions imposed on others, and all nations protected their own productions with heavy duties on trade. Americans hoped to avoid such unequal practices by insisting on complete reciprocity in all commercial relations. Indeed, the commercial treaties of the United States embodied the principle of reciprocity, but the nation had no power to force the Europeans to adopt arrangements that would open all ports to American commerce or relieve the trade of restrictive duties. "This favoured Nation System," Elbridge Gerry complained to Jefferson in February 1785, "appears to me a System of Cobwebs to catch Flies. Attend to it as it respects Restrictions, prohibitions, and the Carrying Trade, and it is equally distant from a Rule of Reciprocity, which is the only equable and beneficial Rule for forming Commercial Treaties." Gerry observed accurately that the United States could protect itself from unequal trade practices only if Congress had the power to deny other nations the advantages they enjoyed in American ports. "To obtain reciprocal advantages," Monroe agreed, "cannot possibly be the object with other powers in treating with us, for more than this they now possess." He wondered whether the United States might negotiate treaties with one or more European states whereby, in exchange for certain commercial advantages in those countries, it would agree to impose higher duties on competitors in the American trade. This would scarcely substitute for reciprocal trade arrangements, but it would enable the United States to respond effectively to some offending nations.[28]

What troubled members of Congress even more than the failure of reciprocity, however, was the loss of the British West Indian trade, the only prerevolutionary trade that yielded a favorable balance. Parliament had decreed, moreover, that American vessels could not carry rice, tobacco, pitch, tar, turpentine, oil, and other articles, formerly another major source of remittances, to British ports. British ships carried off full cargoes from all the northern ports, while American ships rotted at anchor. Parliament's prohibitive duty on whale oil, designed to reserve the industry for British ships and sailors, was ruining the New England whaling villages. Merchants excluded from Britain's trade resented those who managed to profit from it. Through two years of independence the United States failed to develop any new

---

[28]Madison to Monroe, June 21, 1786, in Rutland and Rachal, *Papers of Madison*, 9:82–85; Gerry to Jefferson, February 25, 1785, in Edmund C. Burnett, ed., *Letters of Members of the Continental Congress* (Washington, 1936), 8:44; Monroe to Jefferson, January 19, 1786, in Boyd, *Papers of Jefferson*, 9:188.

commercial channels to compensate for the loss of British markets. British vessels so filled the harbor of Charleston, concluded one South Carolina pamphleteer, that the British enjoyed as much control of the state's economy as they had before the revolution. "What makes the British Monopoly the more mortifying," wrote Madison, "is the abuse they make of it. . . . In every point of view indeed the trade of this Country is in a deplorable Condition."[29]

The American addiction to British goods not only sustained the adverse commercial relationship but also encouraged Americans to consume to the limits of their credit. It was this refusal of Americans to curtail their consumption of British goods, observed Charles Pettit of Pennsylvania, that invited the treatment they received. He complained that the British "severally shut the Door of commercial Hospitality against us, while ours being open they enter and partake with us at their pleasure."[30] London's capacity to legislate the Republic's commercial relations with Europe was, for some Americans, an unacceptable assault on the nation's sovereignty. The time had come, believed Madison, when the United States either had to meet the British challenge or renounce its claims to a fair profit.

Centralized government with the power to retaliate with commercial restrictions alone seemed capable of terminating Britain's unilateral impositions. Writing from New York in January 1785, Pierse Long had argued for nothing less than the congressional control of commerce: "And when it is done I hope it will effectually put a stop to the daring Conduct as Great Britain is pursuing. It is amazing to see the quantity of Vessels in this City from all parts of England now in this Harbour carrying our goods to market, and a delay has so long been made to draw an equitable line of proceeding, I hope very soon there will be an end put to so diabolical a trade."[31] For Madison, Congress alone could exercise effective power over commerce. He stated that, "if it be necessary to regulate trade at all, it surely is necessary to lodge the power, where trade can be regulated with effect, and experience has confirmed what reason foresaw, that it can never be so regulated by the States acting in their separate capacities. They can no more exercise this power separately, than they could separately carry on war, or separately form treaties of alliance or Commerce." John Langdon of Portsmouth observed to Jefferson on December 7, 1785:

---

[29]Madison to Richard Henry Lee, July 7, 1785, in Rutland and Rachal, *Papers of Madison*, 8:315.

[30]Madison to Jefferson, March 18, 1786, ibid., p. 502; Madison to Monroe, April 9, 1786, ibid., 9:25–26; Charles Pettit to Jeremiah Wadsworth, May 27, 1786, in Burnett, *Letters of Members of the Continental Congress*, 8:370.

[31]Pierse Long to John Langdon, January 31, 1785, ibid., p. 18.

"We have no body to blame, but ourselves, that our trade is in its present situation; vesting Congress with full powers, and exerting ourselves with a little spirit, would soon remove the embarrassements we now labour under."[32] Rufus King of Massachusetts believed that Britain's impositions on American commerce would in time arouse a spirit of resistance and "not only direct but drive America into a system more advantageous than treaties and alliances with all the world—a system which shall cause her to rely on her own ships and her own marines, and to exclude those of all other nations."[33]

Throughout 1785 Monroe and other members of Congress continued their earlier efforts to invest that body with the power to regulate the commerce of the United States. Delegates generally favored some obstruction to British shipping, but many still opposed any surrender of state sovereignty to the federal government. British mercantile policy produced its most direct distress in Boston, New York, and Philadelphia where shippers especially called for the augmentation of congressional power to bring them relief. Many southerners, however, feared that effective restraints on British shipping would grant New England carriers a virtual monopoly of American ocean-borne commerce. The tobacco states produced a valuable export commodity but purchased their manufactured goods elsewhere.

Under the assumption that competition for the American market would assure the highest price for southern exports and the lowest price for industrial imports, the South favored the opening of American ports to the world. The northern states, some southerners feared, would seek a high price for their manufactured articles through policies of exclusion. Richard Henry Lee of Virginia believed that the South, through a careful and limited restraint of trade, could avoid major injury to itself. "But it seems to me clearly beyond doubt," he wrote to Madison, "that the giving Congress a power to legislate over the Trade of the Union would be dangerous in the extreme to the five Southern or Staple States, whose want of ships & Seamen would expose their freightage & their produce to a most pernicious and destructive Monopoly. . . . In truth it demands most careful circumspection that the Remedy be not worse than the disease, bad as the last may be."[34] Similarly, Lee reported to Jay in September 1785 that he had little confidence in New England carriers who "might fix a ruinous Monopoly upon the trade

[32]Madison to Monroe, August 7, 1785, in Rutland and Rachal, *Papers of Madison*, 8:333; Langdon to Jefferson, December 7, 1785, in Boyd, *Papers of Jefferson*, 9:84.
[33]Rufus King to Adams, November 2, 1785, in Burnett, *Letters of Members of the Continental Congress*, 8:247–48.
[34]Lee to Madison, August 11, 1785, in Rutland and Rachal, *Papers of Madison*, 8:340.

& productions of the Staple States." Madison observed to Jefferson in January 1786 that the adversaries of centralized restrictions on British trade "were bitter and illiberal against Congress & the Northern States, beyond example." Some argued that the South might better encourage the British marine.[35]

For conservatives, centralized authority appeared essential not only to protect the nation's commercial interests but also to unify the full spectrum of its external relations. Jay demonstrated the latter necessity when he presented a detailed report to Congress on October 12, 1786, regarding the violations of the peace treaty. The secretary dwelt masterfully on the infractions of both sides but emphasized the justice of the British charges by citing a long catalogue of state acts which allegedly violated the terms of the treaty. However one might view the deviations from the treaty before ratification, he said, the American deviations preceded those of Great Britain; therefore, American violations, rather than being justified by British acts, afforded the British an excuse for their infractions. Jay explained further:

> As to the detention of our posts, your secretary thinks that Britain was not bound to surrender them until we had ratified the treaty. Congress ratified it 14th January, 1784, and Britain on the 9th April following. From that time to this, the fourth and sixth articles of the treaty have been constantly violated on our part by legislative acts then and still existing and operating. Under such circumstances, it is not a matter of surprise to your secretary that the posts are detained; nor in his opinion would Britain be to blame in continuing to hold them until America shall cease to impede her enjoying every essential right secured to her, and her people and adherents, by the treaty.[36]

Jay proposed that Congress declare treaties to be "part of the law of the land" and urge the states to repeal all laws "repugnant to the treaty of peace." Congress, in March 1787, adopted his report unanimously. Jay drafted a letter to the states which Congress approved on April 13; in it he repeated his earlier appeal to the states and included a statement asserting congressional sovereignty in foreign affairs. Madison agreed with Jay that the European powers would not forever tolerate state violations of American treaties. "As yet," he admitted in

[35]Lee to Jay, September 11, 1785, in James Curtis Ballagh, ed., *The Letters of Richard Henry Lee* (New York, 1914), 2:389; Debates on Resolutions Related to the Regulation of Commerce, in Rutland and Rachal, *Papers of Madison*, 8:407; Madison to Jefferson, January 22, 1786, ibid., p. 476.
[36]See A. L. Burt, *The United States, Great Britain and British North America from the Revolution to the Establishment of Peace After the War of 1812* (New Haven, CT, 1940), pp. 100–01.

April, "foreign powers have not been rigorous in animadverting on us. This moderation however cannot be mistaken for a permanent partiality to our faults, or a permanent security agst. those disputes with other nations, which being among the greatest of public calamities, it ought to be least in the power of any part of the Community to bring on the whole."[37]

IV

By 1786 the impotence of Congress to protect the general interests of the American people in their relations with other countries drove the nation's conservative leadership toward the demand for a new frame of government. "To be respectable abroad," Jay wrote to Jefferson in July, "it is necessary to be so at home; and that will not be the Case until our public Faith acquires more Confidence and our Government more Strength."[38] No longer for Jay did the answer lie in commercial regulation. George Washington also agreed that commercial regulation alone would never establish the United States as an equal among nations: "Experience has taught us that men will not adopt and carry into execution measures best calculated for their own good, without the intervention of a coercive power. I do not conceive that we can exist long as a nation without having lodged somewhere a power, which will pervade the whole Union in as energetic a manner as the authority of the State government extends over the several States."[39]

Madison had little faith in conventions, and he continued to seek whatever revision of the articles would enable Congress to regulate trade, despite the discouraging knowledge that any revision would require unanimous approval of the states. As late as January 1786 he had hoped that some miraculous development would bring the two most reluctant states, Rhode Island and Georgia, into some agreement that would save the Union from perishing from insolvency and commercial strangulation. Still, Madison reacted favorably to the proposed meeting of commercial commissioners from all the states, scheduled for Annapolis in early September 1786. "I am far from entertaining sanguine expectations for it, and am sensible that it may be viewed in one objectionable light," he admitted to Monroe. Madison was equally

---

[37]Editorial notes on Madison in Congress, February–May 1787, in Rutland and Rachal, *Papers of Madison*, 9:263; Madison to Edmund Randolph, March 25, 1787, ibid., p. 332; Notes on Debates, April 25, 1787, ibid., p. 406; Views of the Political System of the United States, April 1787, ibid., p. 349.

[38]Jay to Jefferson, July 14, 1786, in Boyd, *Papers of Jefferson*, 10:135.

[39]Washington to Jay, August 1, 1786, in Jared Sparks, ed., *The Writings of George Washington* (Boston, 1855), 9:187–88.

concerned that the states would not send sufficient numbers of delegates, that the delegates who attended would not agree on proposals, or that the states would not ratify the proposals with the required unanimity. "I admit despair of success," he wrote to Jefferson; "it is necessary however that something should be tried & if this be not the best possible expedient, it is the best that could possibly be carried thro' the legislature here. And if the present crisis cannot effect unanimity, from what future concurrences . . . is it to be expected?"[40] Only representatives from Virginia, Delaware, Pennsylvania, New Jersey, and New York reached Annapolis. In the official report of the convention, Hamilton acknowledged that several of the commissioners had come to Annapolis with the power to consider a uniform system of commercial relations that might serve the common interests of the states.[41]

Those present at Annapolis agreed that the defects in the government of the United States "merited a deliberate and candid discussion, in some mode, which will unite the Sentiments and Councils of all the States." The mode which the meeting adopted was the calling of a convention of delegates from all the states to investigate a plan for correcting the defects which it might discover. The commissioners, if the states concurred, were to meet at Philadelphia on the second Monday in May 1787. Jefferson expressed disappointment over the failure of the Annapolis convention because of poor representation, but, if the convention produced a full meeting at Philadelphia in May, it could still succeed. "To make us one nation as to foreign concerns, & to keep us distinct in Domestic ones," he instructed Madison, "gives the outline of the proper division of powers between the general & particular governments."[42]

For Adams the essential task of the forthcoming Philadelphia convention was that of restoring an equilibrium in the nation's governmental structure. His political philosophy, he stated simply, was that "power is always abused when unlimited and unbalanced." Unchecked government always would become despotic whether the ruling power lay in a monarch, an aristocracy, or the people. Any of these, unless limited by countering power, would become intolerant, oppressive, and tyrannical. Sound and durable government required a distribution of authority that would enable the ambition and power of

---

[40]Madison to Monroe, March 14, 1786, in Rutland and Rachal, *Papers of Madison*, 8:498; Madison to Jefferson, March 18, 1786, ibid., p. 503.

[41]Address to the Annapolis convention, September 14, 1786, in Harold C. Syrett, ed., *The Papers of Alexander Hamilton* (New York, 1962), 3:687.

[42]Ibid., pp. 688–89; Jefferson to Madison, December 16, 1786, in Rutland and Rachal, *Papers of Madison*, 9:210–11.

some to offset the ambition and power of others. In February 1787 Congress belatedly endorsed the calling of the Philadelphia convention; thereafter the selection of delegates gained momentum.[43]

For Jefferson and Adams, no less than for their associates in America, the Philadelphia convention loomed as a critical test for the new Republic. Franklin believed that the convention's success was essential simply because the price of failure would be unacceptable. "Indeed," he wrote to Jefferson in April 1787, "if it does not do Good it must do Harm, as it will show that we have not Wisdom enough among us to govern ourselves; and will strengthen the Opinion of some Political Writers, that popular Governments cannot long support themselves." Monroe expressed his anxieties to Jefferson in July: "The affairs of the federal government are, I believe, in the utmost confusion; the convention is an expedient that will produce a decisive effect. It will either recover us from our present embarrassments or complete our ruin."[44] What mattered in the crisis was the quality of those who would decide the country's future. Adams hoped that the forthcoming convention would "consist of members of such ability, weight, and experience that the result must be beneficial to the United States"; Franklin reported to Jefferson that the delegates were indeed men of prudence and of high character. Jefferson in August noted the convention's progress, although he objected to its decision to keep the deliberations secret. "Nothing can justify this example," he observed, "but the innocence of their intentions, and ignorance of the value of public discussions. I have no doubt that all of their other measures will be good and wise. It is really an assembly of demigods." In London, Adams followed the news from Philadelphia with equal pleasure. The convention, he wrote to Jay in September, comprised "heroes, sages and demigods to be sure, who want no assistance from me in forming the best possible plan." Should the framers require his support in rendering the new document acceptable to the public, he would volunteer his services for that task.[45]

The Philadelphia Constitutional Convention spent almost four months in drafting the U.S. Constitution; it spent scarcely three days on the provisions controlling foreign affairs. Still, it managed to embody in the document the accumulated experience of the young Republic.

[43]Discourses on Davila, in *Works of John Adams* (Boston, 1851), 6:280; Madison to Monroe, February 25, 1787, ibid., p. 298.

[44]Franklin to Jefferson, April 19, 1787, in Albert Henry Smyth, ed., *The Writings of Benjamin Franklin* (New York, 1907), 9:574; Monroe to Jefferson, July 27, 1787, in Boyd, *Papers of Jefferson*, 11:630–31.

[45]Jefferson to Adams, August 30, 1787, ibid., 12:69; Adams to Jay, September 22, 1787, in *Works of John Adams*, 8:451–52.

Article I answered the perennial pleas of those who advocated the centralized control of the nation's commerce. In granting Congress the power to regulate foreign commerce, it declared that no state, without the consent of Congress, could lay any imposts or duties on imports or exports, nor could it lay tonnage dues on foreign ships. At the same time, the new frame of government provided Congress with the necessary powers to retaliate against nations that might impose on the United States: the power to lay and collect taxes, to establish and maintain an army and navy, and to provide for the common defense. Next, the Constitution defended the nation against state laws which might embarrass its external relations. Article VI declared that "this Constitution and the laws of the United States which shall be made in pursuance thereof and all treaties made, or which shall be made, under the authority of the United States, shall be the supreme law of the land." It further provided that no state could keep troops or ships of war in time of peace, or enter into any agreement or compact with a foreign power. Finally, Article II sustained the traditional executive authority over the country's external relations. It declared the president commander in chief of the army and navy, with the added authority to make treaties with the advice and consent of the Senate, provided that two-thirds of the members present concurred. It also assigned to the president the responsibility to appoint and receive ambassadors and other public ministers. Adams lauded the new Constitution: "It appears to be admirably calculated to cement all America in affection and interest, as one great nation."[46]

For its proponents the Constitution at last elevated the nation's capacity to enter into mutually beneficial relations with the governments of Europe. Alexander Hamilton, arguing for the adoption of the Constitution, reminded readers of *The Federalist* of the country's persistent failures abroad: "We may indeed with propriety be said to have reached almost the last stage of national humiliation. . . . There is scarcely any thing that can wound the pride or degrade the character of an independent nation which we do not experience." The imbecility of the U.S. government simply prevented other nations from treating with it. "Our ambassadors abroad are the mere pageants of mimic sovereignty," ran his final judgment. Americans, Hamilton assumed, had witnessed the persistence of ambition and conflict in world affairs and the resultant requirement of national power to sustain adequate relations with other countries.[47]

---

[46]Adams to Jay, December 16, 1787, ibid., p. 467.
[47]Alexander Hamilton, John Jay, and James Madison, in *The Federalist*, ed. Edward Mead Earle (New York, n.d.), pp. 87–88.

Madison, also in *The Federalist*, defended the specific constitutional provisions that granted Congress the power to raise and maintain land and naval forces, as well as to regulate the nation's commerce. At the convention he had argued with delegates from the South that the disadvantages which a navigation act would place on that section would be countered by both the increase in southern shipping and the elimination of injurious retaliations among the states. In declaring treaties the supreme law of the land, the Constitution had eliminated the frustrations created by state laws and antiforeign practices. "If we are to be one nation in any respect," wrote Madison, "it clearly ought to be in respect to other nations."[48] For Adams too the Constitution seemed to provide the power required to permit the United States to establish solid and permanent relationships with the European states. In time of war it would reinforce the Republic's capacity to protect its neutral rights. "The United States now stand in an elevated situation," he confided to Jay, "and they must and will be respected and courted, not only by France and England, but by all other powers of Europe, while they keep themselves neutral."[49]

Jefferson complimented Madison on the acceptance of the new Constitution by the necessary nine states. "It is a good canvas, on which some strokes only want retouching," he wrote. However, Jefferson objected most fundamentally to two decisions made at Philadelphia: first, to the exclusion of a declaration of rights; and second, to the perpetual re-eligibility of the president. This provision, he feared, would create an office for life which eventually would become hereditary. "I was much an enemy of monarchy before I came to Europe," he wrote, "I am ten thousand times more so since I have seen what they are. There is scarcely an evil known in these countries which may not be traced to their king as its source."[50]

Adams, like Jefferson, viewed the Constitution as less than perfect, but his perceptions of danger differed. "You are afraid of the one—I, of the few," he told Jefferson, "you are Apprehensive of Monarchy; I, of aristocracy. I would therefore have given more Power to the President and less to the Senate. . . . You are apprehensive the President when once chosen, will be chosen again and again as long as he lives. So much the better as it appears to me. . . . Elections, my dear Sir, Elections to offices which are great objects of Ambition, I look at with terror. Experiments of this kind have been so often tryed, and so universally found productive of Horrors, that there is great

[48]*The Federalist No. 41*, January 19, 1788, in Rutland and Rachal, *Papers of Madison* (Charlottesville, 1977), 10:391–95; *The Federalist No. 42*, January 22, 1788, ibid., p. 403.
[49]Adams to Jay, December 16, 1787, in *Works of John Adams*, 8:467.
[50]Jefferson to Madison, August 9, 1788, in Boyd, *Papers of Jefferson*, 13:489–90.

Reason to dread them." At the end Jefferson contemplated the new government with confidence. Indeed, he wrote to William Carmichael on March 4, 1789: "The friends of the new constitution agree pretty generally to add a declaration of rights to it, and the opposition becomes daily weaker, so that the government, confided generally to friendly hands, and gaining on the esteem of the nation, begins *this very day*, under the most auspicious appearances."[51]

V

To the Founding Fathers the world offered markets. It was logical, therefore, that their early diplomatic efforts focused on the expansion of the nation's commerce, but this attention to immediate economic concerns did not eliminate the necessity of defining the young Republic's proper relationship to the changing currents of international life in the 1780s. For some Americans the achievement of independence merely symbolized the rejection of Europe and its entire system of power politics. The United States had gained that favorable condition among nations, a status that Thomas Paine had predicted in *Common Sense*, when he argued that America's attachment to Britain alone endangered its security. It was the British connection that tended "to involve this Continent in European wars and quarrels, and set us at variance with nations who would otherwise seek our friendship, and against whom we have neither anger nor complaint." More specifically, Paine predicted that France and Spain, both New World powers, would never be "our enemies as *Americans*, but as our being *subjects of Great Britain*." An independent United States would have no cause to defy other countries with demanding foreign policies. He assured his readers that "our plan is commerce, and that, well attended to, will secure us the peace and friendship of all Europe; because it is the interest of all Europe to have America a free port. Her trade will always be a protection, and her barrenness of gold and silver secure her from invaders."[52]

Because all Europe was a potential market for American trade, it was essential that the United States form no partial connection with any European state. "It is the true interest of America," declared Paine in asserting his isolationist creed, "to steer clear of European contentions, which she never can do, while, by her dependence on Britain, she is made the makeweight in the scale of British politics."[53] He

[51]Adams to Jefferson, December 6, 1787, ibid., 12:396; Jefferson to Carmichael, March 4, 1789, in Ford, *Writings of Jefferson* (New York, 1895), 5:73.
    [52]Moncure Daniel Conway, ed., *The Writings of Thomas Paine* (New York, 1894), 1:86, 88.
    [53]Ibid., pp. 88–89.

advocated a navy adequate to protect American shores. By limiting its naval action to its own coast, the United States could overmatch the British navy with one-twentieth of Britain's naval power. If Great Britain had the strength to check America's trade with Europe in time of war, the United States could restrain British trade with the West Indies with equal effectiveness.[54] For Paine, American naval power would reinforce a policy of military and political isolationism.

Freed of the contamination and the constraints of power politics, the young Republic appeared ideally constituted to create a new order in world affairs. The American Revolution, as a triumphant avowal of the principle of free government, seemed to its adherents as an auspicious event in the eternal quest for peace and human rights. "The cause of America," proclaimed Paine, "is in great measure the cause of mankind." How could the monarchies of Europe, he wondered, satisfy the needs of humanity when they excluded their rulers from the means of securing information, yet empowered them to act in matters that required the highest judgment? For him governments so uninformed, inhumane, and irrational would not survive the revolutionary pressures then being unleashed by events in America. Franklin too proclaimed such sentiments when in April 1782 he said: "Establishing the liberties of America will not only make that people happy, but will have some effect in diminishing the misery of those, who in other parts of the world groan under despotism, by rendering it more circumspect, and inducing it to govern with a lighter hand."[55]

For American idealists those moral principles, which allegedly maintained peaceful and just relations among individuals, would become the principles that would rule the behavior of nations. Some Americans identified the achievement of universal peace with the triumph of free trade; the movement of goods to all nations would underwrite the new internationalism by limiting agreements to simple rules and practices necessary to govern the flow of commerce. Unlike the secret diplomacy of Europe, designed to hide and further the nefarious purposes of the governments that practiced it, the new diplomacy would be open and frank. No longer driven by national rivalries and ambitions, the old accoutrements of power politics—alliances, balances of power, and large armies—would disappear from the international scene. For those who took this internationalistic idealism seriously, the promise of a new peaceful, cost-free world order was attractive indeed.

[54]Ibid., pp. 102–06.
[55]Ibid., pp. 68, 73; Franklin to the Chevalier de Chastellux, April 6, 1782, Smyth, *Writings of Franklin*, 8:416. Felix Gilbert attributes much of this idealism in American thought to the French *philosophes*; see his *To the Farewell Address: Ideas of Early American Foreign Policy* (Princeton, NJ, 1961), pp. 55–75.

Among American conservatives who determined the course of American external behavior the rejection of this isolationist-idealist approach to international politics was total. They knew that the United States could not project any internationalist crusade beyond the reach of American law and therefore not beyond the borders of the nation. What determined the behavior of republics was not the uniqueness of their political structures or the outlook of their people but the international environment, which they could neither control nor escape, and the demands that their own ambitions, as well as those of other countries, imposed on them. Thus Madison, no less than others, denied that the foreign policies of republics differed essentially from those of monarchies.[56] Hard experience had taught the Revolution's leaders that nations dealt with others solely on the basis of interests and the capacity to render them effective.

Hamilton questioned the assumption that commerce softened the manners of men and extinguished "those inflammable humors which have so often kindled into wars." He observed that nations responded more readily to immediate interests than to more general or humane considerations of policy and asked:

> Have republics in practice been less addicted to war than monarchies? Are not the former administered by men as well as the latter? Are there not aversions, predilections, rivalships, and desires of unjust acquisitions, that affect nations as well as kings? Are not popular assemblies frequently subject to the impulses of rage, resentment, jealousy, avarice, and of other irregular and violent propensities? . . . Has commerce hitherto done any thing more than change the objects of war? Is not the love of wealth as domineering and enterprising a passion as that of power or glory? . . . Let experience, the least fallible guide of human opinions, be appealed to for an answer to these inquiries.

Carthage, a commercial republic, was the aggressor in the very war that terminated its existence. Holland, another such republic, played a conspicuous role in the wars of modern Europe. Britain's marked addiction for commerce never prevented that country from engaging in war. "There have been . . . almost as many popular as royal wars," Hamilton concluded. "The cries of the nation and the importunities of their representatives have, upon various occasions, dragged their

---

[56]Madison to Jefferson, August 20, 1784, in Rutland and Rachal, *Papers of Madison,* 8:106.

monarchs into war, or continued them in it, contrary to their incli-
nations, and sometimes contrary to the real interests of the state."[57]
Some Americans, he warned, had been amused too long by theories
which promised them "an exemption from the imperfections, weak-
nesses, and evils incident to society in every shape." The nation would
better defend its interests if it assumed, as did other inhabitants of the
globe, that the happy empire of wisdom and virtue did not exist.

More fundamentally, the Founding Fathers understood that peace
was not the overriding interest of nations, that all empires rested on
the use, or threatened use, of force. Even nations without empires were
not peaceful by nature. "I have long been settled in my own opinion,"
Adams confided to Jefferson in October 1787, "that neither Philosophy,
nor Religion, nor Morality, nor Wisdom, nor Interest, will ever govern
nations or Parties, against their Vanity, their Pride, their Resentment
or Revenge, or their Avarice or Ambition. Nothing but Force and Power
and Strength can restrain them."[58] For Hamilton, no less than Adams,
competition and conflict were the normal conditions of international
life. "To look for a continuation of harmony between a number of
independent, unconnected sovereignties in the same neighborhood,"
he wrote in *The Federalist No. 6*, "would be to disregard the uniform
course of human events, and to set at defiance the accumulated experience of ages." To him the causes of hostility among nations were
innumerable:

> There are some which have a general and almost constant oper-
> ation upon the collective bodies of society. Of this description are
> the love of power or the desire of preeminence and dominion. . . .
> There are others which have a more circumscribed though an
> equally operative influence within their spheres. Such are the rival-
> ships and competitions of commerce between commercial nations.
> And there are others, not less numerous than either of the former,
> which take their origin entirely in private passions; in the attach-
> ments, enmities, interests, hopes, and fears of leading individuals
> in the communities of which they are members. Men of this class,
> whether the favorites of a king or of a people, have in too many
> instances abused the confidence they possessed; and assuming the
> pretext of some public motive, have not scrupled to sacrifice the
> national tranquillity to personal advantage or personal
> gratification.[59]

[57]Alexander Hamilton, John Jay, and James Madison, in *The Federalist*, ed. Edward
Mead Earle (New York, 1937), pp. 30–31.
[58]Adams to Jefferson, October 9, 1787, in Boyd, *Papers of Jefferson*, 12:221.
[59]Hamilton, Jay, and Madison, in *The Federalist*, p. 27.

What such a hostile world demanded of a nation seemed clear enough: the assumption of international conflict and the tenuous nature of peace; an appreciation of the limitations imposed on national behavior by the persistent quest for equilibrium; the accumulation and assimilation of the ascertainable facts of international life as well as the willingness to act on them; and the acceptance of the need to redefine national interests in response to changes in the international environment. Together these elements constituted the proper philosophical base for determining national policy. If nations had no choice but to define and pursue their own interests, they had to be equally cognizant of the interests of others.

In large measure a country's reputation and prestige, its capacity to influence the behavior of others, rested on both power and wisdom. When circumstances demanded it, American leaders, like those who governed the politics of Europe, would advocate a reliance on power. Jefferson reminded Jay in August 1785 that "weakness provokes insult and injury, while a condition to punish it prevents it."[60] Alliances as well often discouraged aggression and preserved the peace by reinforcing an equilibrium of power. Hamilton defended alliances in *The Federalist No. 15;* "there is nothing absurd or impracticable," he reminded his readers, "in the idea of a league or alliance between independent nations for certain defined purposes precisely stated in a treaty regulating all the details of time, place, circumstances, and quantity; leaving nothing to future discretion; and depending for its execution on the good faith of the parties." Yet he detected the limitations of alliances, noting that they were "subject to the usual vicissitudes of peace and war, of observance and non-observance, as the interests or passions of the contracting power dictate."[61] It was the search for adequate power to support the nation's diplomacy that led American conservatives toward the creation of a new constitution.

For Hamilton the Constitution of the United States promised to give the nation the strength to baffle Europe's continuing efforts to restrain American trade and navigation, and to maintain its neutrality in time of war. Prohibitory regulations, extending throughout the states, could now compel foreign countries to bid against each other for the privileges of American trade. Any national policy that excluded a country from the ports of the United States would compel that country to grant valuable and extensive commercial privileges or shift to a less advantageous trade elsewhere. The United States, furthermore, at last possessed the authority to build a navy which, if it could not vie with

---

[60]Jefferson to Jay, August 23, 1785, in Boyd, *Papers of Jefferson*, 8:427.
[61]Hamilton, Jay, and Madison, in *The Federalist*, p. 90.

those of Europe's maritime powers, could at least be respectable enough to affect the course of a maritime war. This would be especially true in the West Indies where a few naval vessels, sent to reinforce one side or the other, would often be sufficient to determine the fate of a campaign. This naval power would compel the European states to bid not only for American friendship but also for American neutrality. "The rights of neutrality," warned Hamilton, "will only be respected when they are defended by an adequate power. A nation, despicable by its weakness, forfeits even the privilege of being neutral."[62] Countries that had nothing to fear from the United States would not hesitate to prey on American commerce in time of war. Hamilton, however, foresaw the moment when U.S. naval strength would enable his country to restrain European policies in America in accordance with its own interests.

Regional concerns indeed demanded that the United States seek no less than an ascendant position in American affairs. Europe, with its predominant power, had extended its dominion over Africa, Asia, and America. Soon the United States, in command of the means to threaten Europe's possessions in the New World, would compel the capitals of Europe to recognize the power and influence of the United States in western hemispheric affairs. In facing the challenge of European expansionism, the United States could not vindicate the honor and independence of Africa and Asia, but it could at least teach the Europeans to be less assuming in America. "Let Americans disdain to be the instruments of European greatness!" Hamilton admonished the readers of *The Federalist No. 11*. "Let the thirteen States, bound together in a strict and indissoluble Union, concur in erecting one great American system, superior to the control of all transatlantic force or influence, and able to dictate the terms of connection between the old and the new world!"[63]

VI

Experience had taught Americans that New World security rested ultimately on the distribution of power among the great European states and on the capacity of the United States to exploit the divergences among them. As a member of the Atlantic community, the nation would judge its interests and manage its policies in accordance with the vicissitudes of the European equilibrium. "While there are powers in Europe which fear our views," Jefferson observed in December 1787, "we should

[62]Ibid., pp. 64–65.
[63]Ibid., p. 69.

keep an eye on them, their connections and oppositions, that in a moment of need we may avail ourselves of their weakness with respect to others as well as ourselves, and calculate their designs and movements on all the circumstances under which they exist." Adams's views toward Europe remained unchanged. For him, in the future as in the past, the balance that would guarantee the security of the American Republic required the continued rivalry between Britain and France, the two major poles in the European equilibrium. As long as these two powers remained on opposite sides in any European confrontation, the United States could well pursue a policy of neutrality toward Europe's wars. Adams's advice to Jay followed that assumption: "My system is a very simple one; let us preserve the friendship of France, Holland, and Spain, if we can, and in case of war between France and England, let us preserve our neutrality, if possible."[64] Jefferson shared Adams's conviction that a policy of neutrality would best preserve the interests of the United States. "Our system," he wrote, "should be to meddle not at all with European quarrels, but to cultivate peace within and without."[65]

Neutrality assumed that the great powers would respect any American attempt to escape foreign wars, but Adams saw that Britain and France would honor American neutrality only as long as they could detect no disadvantage in such a policy. "It is natural for England and France," he reminded Jay, "to be jealous of our neutrality, and apprehensive that, notwithstanding our professions, we may be induced to connect ourselves with one against the other. While such uncertainties and suspicions continue, we may find that each of these rival kingdoms will be disposed to stint our growth and diminish our power, from a fear that it will be employed against itself."[66] Limited by the European equilibrium, France and Britain might leave the United States alone. Any weakening of the restraints which the balance of power imposed, however, would prompt one or the other to war on American neutrality. To negate the special danger of British infringements in time of war, Adams argued, the United States must above all reassure London that it could trust the nation not to aid the enemy. Ultimately, to avoid trouble with Britain, the United States had no choice but to rely on France's predominant position in Continental affairs. Should France decline in the scale of power, Adams warned, the United States "instead

---

[64]Jefferson to Edward Carrington, December 21, 1787, in Boyd, *Papers of Jefferson*, 12:447; Adams to Jay, April 13, 1785, *Works of John Adams*, 8:234.

[65]Jefferson to David Rittenhouse, September 18, 1787, in Boyd, *Papers of Jefferson*, 12:145; Jefferson to Charles Lilburne Lewis, January 11, 1789, ibid., 14:428.

[66]Adams to Jay, October 17, 1785, in *Works of John Adams*, 8:322; Adams to Jay, September 23, 1787, ibid., p. 454.

of being courted by the English, . . . will rather be more neglected, perhaps treated cavalierly."[67]

Jefferson and Adams observed Europe's shifting balance of power and pondered its meaning for the United States. Throughout 1787 the Dutch Republic was torn by internal controversy. The Patriots, a middle-class party to which many of Adams's friends belonged, succeeded in limiting the power of the stadtholder. The strife continued, enabling the Patriots to seize control of the government. This offended the Dutch princess, sister of the king of Prussia. During September the Prussian ruler, to defend family honor, dispatched a large army under the Duke of Brunswick to reestablish the Orange dynasty to its former position. The Prussian forces and their Dutch allies caught and executed the leading Patriots. Adams grieved over his many friends who either sought refuge in France or continued to live in Holland in fear of their lives. He believed that they had erred in depending too confidently on the support of France. Britain began to arm and informed the courts of Europe that a French intervention would bring war. Despite America's known sympathy for Holland and France, Adams advised a policy of strict neutrality. The United States, after all, was at peace with all Europe. "That our country may act with dignity in all events, that she may not be obliged to join in any war without the clearest conviction of the justice of the cause, and her own honor and real interest," he wrote, "it is indispensably necessary that she act the part, in Holland, of perfect independence and honest impartiality between the different courts and nations which are now struggling for her friendship, and who are all, at present, our friends."[68]

For Jefferson the Dutch crisis was dangerous because it threatened the critical Franco-Prussian alliance which checked the ambitions of Austria and Russia, both of whom looked to Britain for support. London's acceptance of the new Dutch government placed Britain on the side of Prussia and constituted an outrageous insult to France which, Jefferson and Adams agreed, the French court could hardly ignore. Yet any French attempt to return the Dutch Patriots to power, Jefferson predicted, would set off a general war. Adams, no less than Jefferson, believed that Europe's peace was precarious. He warned Jay as early as September that "the philosophical visions of perpetual peace, and

[67]Adams to Jay, April 13, 1785, ibid., p. 235; Adams to Jay, September 23, 1787, ibid., p. 454.

[68]For a general survey of the relations between the United States and the Netherlands during the 1780s see Lawrence S. Kaplan, "The Founding Fathers and the Two Confederations: The United States of America and the United Provinces of the Netherlands, 1783–89," in J. W. Schulte Nordholt and Robert P. Swierenga, eds., *A Bilateral Bicentennial History of Dutch-American Relations, 1782–1982* (New York, 1983), pp. 33–48.

the religious reveries of a near approach of the millennium, in which all nations are to turn the weapons of war into implements of husbandry, will, in a few years, be dissipated. . . . In short, there is every appearance that the peace in Europe will be for years but an armed truce." What troubled Adams was the danger in the new configuration of power to the European equilibrium on which the United States relied for its security. Britain, Prussia, and Holland, he suspected, would defeat France in war. This might compel the United States to join the house of Bourbon in self-defense because, he wrote, "after having humbled France, England would not scruple to attack the United States."[69]

France sympathized with the Dutch but refused to act. The decision of the Prussian king to return his brother-in-law to the throne of Holland, and the encouragement he received from London, forced the two empires, Austria and Russia, to seek an alliance with France. The French court, however, had no greater interest in committing itself to an active role in Eastern Europe than in Holland. Meanwhile, Britain encouraged the ongoing conflict between Russia and Turkey, with the hope that France's support of its traditional ally, Turkey, would bring the Paris government into direct conflict with Russia, but France chose to abandon the Turks. Thus Jefferson wrote in May 1788 that "you see that the old system is unhinged, and no new one hung in its place. Probabilities are rather in favour of a connection between the two empires, France and Spain." The dominant antagonisms, he believed, pitted Britain against France and Russia. "But to real hostilities," he concluded, "this country [France] would with difficulty be drawn. Her finances are too deranged, her internal income too much dissolved, to hazard a war."[70]

If neutrality dictated an adequate policy for the United States toward a land war in Europe, it was less certain that neutrality would protect American interests in a war that ventured onto the Atlantic. For the nation's early leaders, the combination of potentially high profits in the carrying trade and the country's naval weakness in wartime would elevate neutral rights to the level of primary concern. Unfortunately, neutral trade, if profitable, would undermine the interests of the belligerents. The American Treaty Plan of 1776 proposed to defend the nation's wartime commerce by establishing the principle that "free ships make free goods." When privateering assigned some American vessels the role of seizing, rather than defending, cargoes on the high seas, the United States modified its principles to include the removal of enemy goods from neutral ships.

---

[69]Adams to Jay, September 23, 1787, in *Works of John Adams*, 8:454; Adams to Jay, November 15, 1787, ibid., p. 461.
[70]Jefferson to Washington, May 2, 1788, in Boyd, *Papers of Jefferson*, 13:124–25.

In its treaties with Holland, Sweden, and Prussia, the United States insisted on the doctrine that free bottoms make free goods and enemy bottoms make enemy goods. Adams and Jefferson understood that, in a war between Britain and France, neutral rights, if recognized by both belligerents, would open unprecedented opportunities for American commerce and navigation. "If we remain neutral," Jefferson predicted in September 1787, "our commerce must become consider-able; and particularly the carrying business must fall principally into our hands. The West Indian islands of all the powers must be opened to us."[71] Unfortunately, the principle of free ships–free goods was unen-forcible in a world based on mercantilism, power balances, large armies and navies, and the acceptance of war as an instrument of policy. Perhaps the possibilities for commercial retaliation which the American Constitution provided would enable the United States to reinforce its neutral rights on the high seas. But Jefferson recalled that Britain, with its powerful navy, had never acceded to the principle of neutral rights in wartime, although it had acquiesced during the Revolutionary War to avoid trouble with the Continental powers. He doubted that Britain would accept again the maritime interests of neutrals; rather, he feared, that country would harass American shipping even at the price of war. Such a direct challenge to America's wartime profits, Jefferson con-fessed to Adams, would force Britain into an expensive war on land as well as on the sea. "Common sense dictates therefore," he continued, "that they should let us remain neuter: ergo they will not let us remain neuter."[72] Clearly the United States faced the inescapable choice of foregoing a profitable maritime commerce in some future European war or running the risk of conflict on the high seas.

Even as Jefferson joined Adams in contemplating the proper rela-tionship of the United States to a world of power politics, he anticipated a return to America. As early as November 1788 he broached the subject of a leave of absence from his ministerial duties to settle various per-sonal matters in Virginia and elsewhere. During the spring of 1789 he received permission to return and began his preparations, but not until the following fall was he ready to leave. He reported to Carmichael on September 12 that his baggage had been forwarded to the coast; he and his family would leave shortly.[73] On September 30 he arrived at Le Havre and booked passage on a ship from London which would

---

[71] Adams to Jefferson, October 28, 1787, ibid., 12:292; Jefferson to Alexander Donald, September 17, 1787, ibid., pp. 132–33.

[72] Jefferson to Carmichael, September 25, 1787, ibid., p. 174; Jefferson to Adams, September 28, 1787, ibid., p. 190.

[73] Jefferson to Washington, May 10, 1789, in Ford, *Writings of Jefferson*, 5:95; Jef-ferson to Carmichael, September 12, 1789, ibid., p. 126.

take him directly to Virginia. The trip was fast and pleasant, twenty-six days from land to land, bringing him to Norfolk on November 23. Upon his arrival, he informed Jay that he would proceed to Charlottesville to arrange his affairs and then continue on to New York for his return voyage to France.[74] That simple it was not to be, for the Norfolk newspapers that day carried the story that President Washington had nominated him to the new office of secretary of state. Whatever his choice between accepting the offer or returning to France, his public career had scarcely begun.

[74]Jefferson to Jay, September 30, 1789, ibid., pp. 128–29; Jefferson to William Short, December 14, 1789, ibid., p. 139.

CHAPTER FOUR

A Neutral in a World at War*

GEORGE WASHINGTON'S America, armed with its new Constitution and led by a remarkable group of men, seemed well prepared to face the external world, yet the unanswered challenges confronting the nation were profound: Britain continued to monopolize its commerce without granting a formal commercial treaty that distributed the benefits with reasonable equity; British troops still occupied the posts along the Great Lakes; and London refused to send a minister to New York, preferring to communicate with the U.S. government through its representatives in Quebec. When Washington dispatched Gouverneur Morris to London as an informal agent, the British scarcely acknowledged his presence.[1] Furthermore, Spain continued to bar American traffic on the Mississippi from easy access to the Gulf of Mexico. Europe's leading powers, with interests in North America, again hovered on the brink of war. To compel the European capitals to recognize its concerns, at least in matters of commerce, the United States possessed the power to regulate its foreign trade and thus the means to retaliate; however, it faced the question of retaliation with seriously divided counsels. The disagreement centered in the opposing views of Thomas Jefferson, the new secretary of state, and Alexander Hamilton, secretary of the treasury. Their differences, lodged in long contemplation and deeply conflicting perceptions of government, were irreconcilable.

---

*This essay was prepared specifically for this volume.
[1]Washington to Morris, October 13, 1789, John C. Fitzpatrick, ed., *The Writings of George Washington from the Original Manuscript Sources*, 39 vols. (Washington, 1931–1944), 30:440–42.

For Jefferson two immediate questions required the attention of his ministry: the conflicts with Great Britain and Spain over the Northwest posts and the Mississippi, and the defense of the nation's commercial interests.[2] To deal effectively with London and Madrid, he needed some base in European politics; this he found in the French alliance. America's potential commerce with Spain was not sufficient, Jefferson believed, to bid for it at the price of abandoning the American claim to free navigation on the Mississippi. After the failure of the Jay-Gardoqui negotiations in 1786, he agreed with his Virginia friends that western commerce required free access to the Gulf of Mexico.[3] For the moment Jefferson knew that he lacked the leverage to force a settlement of the Mississippi question. On the matter of the western posts and commercial relations with Britain, however, the secretary was prepared to exert force by both threatening closer relations with France and imposing commercial restrictions. Jefferson believed that Britain needed the American market far more than Americans needed British exports. Surely the United States possessed the power to wring concessions from London if Congress chose to use it.[4]

In the summer of 1789, James Madison introduced a commercial program, based on retaliation, into the first session of Congress by advocating, in the debate on the tonnage bill, discrimination between vessels of countries that had or did not have a commercial treaty with the United States. Congress had no desire to tangle with Britain and voted to place all nations on the same commercial footing. Madison, backed by Jefferson, reopened his assault on British commercial policy in the new session of Congress, demanding that it simply enforce the country's established policy of reciprocity against England. The contemplated impositions on that country would decline as the British eased their own restrictions. Again a coalition of planters requiring British ships and credit, Northeast shippers accustomed to existing conditions, Anglophiles, and Treasury spokesmen delighted at the revenues collected on British tonnage and imports, defeated Madison's measure.[5]

---

[2]See Merrill D. Peterson, "Thomas Jefferson and Commercial Policy, 1783–1793," *William and Mary Quarterly*, 3d ser. 22 (October 1965): 602.

[3]Jefferson's Report on Matters of Negotiations with Spain, March 7, 1792, in Paul L. Ford, ed., *The Writings of Thomas Jefferson*, 12 vols. (New York, 1892–1899), 5:441–49.

[4]The notion that the United States, with commercial restrictions, could force concessions from Britain was fundamental to Jefferson's entire commercial policy. See Peterson, "Thomas Jefferson and Commercial Policy," pp. 602–10.

[5]Monroe to Madison, July 19, 1789, in Stanislaus Murray Hamilton, ed., *The Writings of James Monroe* (New York, 1969), 1:203–04; Jefferson to Edward Rutledge, July 4, 1790, in Ford, *Writings of Jefferson*, 5:195–96.

Pro-British forces commanded the Congress, and behind them stood Hamilton. That he would devote his future efforts to the identification, if not the subordination, of American interests to those of Britain became clear during the Nootka Sound controversy of 1790. In June word reached the U.S. government that Spaniards had seized two British ships at anchor in Nootka Sound, on the western coast of Vancouver Island, and claimed exclusive rights to the entire Pacific coast. Britain demanded an indemnity and threatened war. President Washington faced the prospect that Britain might ask for permission to transport troops from Canada through American territory to attack Spanish New Orleans. Jefferson wanted no redistribution of British and Spanish territory along the American frontiers, but he also wanted no war to prevent it.

To avoid a decision on this issue, Jefferson advanced a policy of delay and strict neutrality.[6] At the same time, he believed that the Nootka case offered an opportunity to approach the Count of Floridablanca, the Spanish minister, on the issue of Mississippi navigation. He informed William Carmichael in Madrid, however, that he had no desire to resume negotiations unless the Spanish court was prepared to yield on the issue of Mississippi navigation and a port near the mouth of the river to support that navigation.[7] Jefferson suggested that Spain cede to the United States all territory east of the Mississippi on consideration that the United States would guarantee to Spain "all her possessions on the Western waters of that river. . . . Should Great Britain possess herself of the Floridas and Louisiana," he added, "she will establish powerful colonies in them. These can be poured into the Gulf of Mexico for any sudden enterprise there, or invade Mexico . . . and proceed successively from colony to colony." It would be safer for Spain to have the United States as its neighbor because it was not in the interest of the United States "to cross the Mississippi for ages." Should an Anglo-Spanish war occur, Jefferson reminded Madrid, it would add to the number of its enemies if it did not "yield our right to the common use of the Mississippi, and the means of using and securing it."[8]

Convinced that war over the Nootka Sound was imminent and that the war might spread into the Mississippi Valley, Washington, on August 27, asked each cabinet member what his response should be if

[6]Jefferson to Thomas Mann Randolph, June 20, 1790, ibid., 5:186–87; Opinion on War Between Great Britain and Spain, July 12, 1790, ibid., pp. 200–03. For a detailed study of the Nootka Sound controversy see William Ray Manning, "The Nootka Sound Controversy," *Annual Report of the American Historical Association, 1904* (Washington, 1905), pp. 286–471.

[7]Jefferson to Carmichael, August 22, 1790, in Ford, *Writings of Jefferson*, 5:228–29.

[8]Ibid., pp. 229–30.

Lord Dorchester, the governor of Quebec, should ask permission to march troops through American territory from Detroit to the Mississippi.[9] Jefferson, in a brief letter, believed it preferable for the country to join Spain in war than to permit Britain to seize Florida and Louisiana, but he advised a policy of neutrality as long as possible "because war is full of chances, which may relieve us from the necessity of interfering." If the British asked permission to cross American territory, Jefferson suggested that the president give no answer. If the British entered the United States without permission, he would express America's dissatisfaction to the British court and sustain the option of accepting British apologies or going to war.[10]

Vice-President John Adams advocated a policy of strict neutrality because "the People of these States would not willingly support a war, and the present government has not strength to command, nor enough of the general confidence of the nation to draw, the men or money necessary, until the grounds, causes, and necessity of it should become generally known and universally approved."[11] Neutrality demanded that the United States deny the British the right to cross American territory. If the British marched troops to the Mississippi without leave, the United States faced the choice of war or negotiation. He preferred the latter, a response rendered difficult by the absence of an American minister in London.

Hamilton consumed two weeks in preparing his long pro-British treatise in which he argued that American interests ruled out taking sides with either France or Spain. He acknowledged a danger in the British possession of Louisiana and the Floridas: to refuse permission to the British to cross American territory, he warned, would bring disgrace unless the United States could prevent it. If the British made the request, Hamilton favored consent; if Britain moved without asking permission, he advocated remonstrance "but in a tone that would not commit us to the necessity of going to war." It was essential, Hamilton believed, that the United States avoid a conflict with Britain. He would defend that nation's interests by giving it the right to cross American territory and by offering neutrality in war should Britain guarantee U.S. navigation on the Mississippi to the Gulf. This quid pro quo might

---

[9]Washington to Adams, August 27, 1790, in *The Works of John Adams* (Boston, 1853), 8:496–97; Washington to the heads of departments, August 27, 1790, in Fitzpatrick, *Writings of Washington*, 31:102–03.

[10]Opinion on Course of United States Towards Great Britain and Spain, August 28, 1790, in Ford, *Writings of Jefferson*, 5:238–39.

[11]Adams to Washington, August 29, 1790, in *Works of John Adams*, 8:498.

demonstrate at last that his pro-British policy was achieving results.[12]
The Nootka Sound controversy reinforced the American interest in
neutrality and articulated the principle that the United States would
oppose the transfer of American territory from one European power to
another. Spain capitulated when France refused to enter the conflict.

With the Nootka Sound no longer an issue, the Jefferson-Hamilton
conflict turned to American commercial policy. France entered the
debate when it protested the congressional decision on tonnage, arguing
discrimination. France had granted special commercial favors to the
United States in its decrees of 1787 and 1788. Jefferson, in his report
on the tonnage law in January 1791, hesitated to recommend the tonnage exemption which the French demanded; other countries under
the most-favored-nation principle would demand the same. Jefferson
sought to escape his dilemma by asking Congress to assign to French
vessels the advantages in American ports enjoyed by U.S. ships. No
other country would gain such privileges unless it matched the French
concessions.[13] In this Jefferson faced the full opposition of Hamilton.
To the Treasury secretary, France did not merit the proposed concession; Britain, moreover, would resent it. The United States, Hamilton
reminded Jefferson, required the revenue from British trade and therefore could not afford a commercial war with that country. Britain was
the nation's most important supplier, its best market, its only source
of credit. Washington supported Jefferson's new tonnage law, but the
Senate defeated it and compelled the secretary to deal with the French
as best he could as Franco-American commerce continued to stagnate.

On matters of commercial and financial policy, Hamilton confronted Jefferson with a body of assumptions and purposes totally at
odds with his own. Hamilton's acquiescence in Britain's maritime dominance denied Jefferson's contention that the United States had the
power to coerce England. For Hamilton the United States was weak
and Britain was strong. Recognizing such realities, he accepted the
need of a subordinate British connection. If America's economic and
security interests required close British-American relations, he was
willing to pay the price that British friendship demanded. His financial
program, designed to build national power on credit rather than commerce, was, for Jefferson, a dangerous system that would overextend

[12]Hamilton to Washington, September 15, 1790, in Julian P. Boyd, ed., *The Papers
of Thomas Jefferson* (Princeton, 1950), 17:143–60. In this long letter to Washington, Hamilton made many references to Puffendorf, Grotius, and Vattel, indicating his reliance
on the noted European writers for his views on foreign affairs.
[13]Jefferson's Report on Tonnage Law, January 8, 1791, in Ford, *Writings of Jefferson*,
5:267–73.

the power of government, enrich eastern merchants and speculators, offer little to southern planters who needed foreign markets, and restrain the expansion of American agriculture.[14] Jefferson found Hamilton's determination to bind the United States to British policy especially objectionable because it threatened to duplicate in America the English model of government and society. He complained to James Monroe in April 1791 that, despite Britain's further attacks on American commerce, the Treasury accepted the need of "passive obedience and nonresistance, lest any misunderstanding with them should *affect our credit, or the prices of our public paper.*"[15]

Jefferson, disappointed over his failure to expand Franco-American trade in the face of continuing French discriminatory duties, especially on tobacco, redoubled his war on British commercial policy. On February 1, 1791, he submitted his Report on the Cod and Whale Fisheries to Congress. Applying what he had learned of the whaling trade while in France, he attempted to prove that British bounties and restrictions were injuring the fishing industry of the United States. The French, as fellow victims of British policy, Jefferson noted, were cooperating with the United States. In building his case for France, he added: "Nor is it the interest of the fisherman alone, which calls for the cultivation of friendly arrangements with that nation; besides five-eighths of our whale oil, and two-thirds of our salted fish, they take from us one-fourth of our tobacco, three-fourths of our livestock . . . a considerable and growing portion of our rice, great supplies, occasionally, of other grain."[16] Jefferson's report produced a House bill to bar the importation of non-British goods in British bottoms. Congress rejected that measure, but on February 23 it asked Jefferson to study the whole question of commercial policy and make recommendations.

Both Hamilton and Jefferson recognized, in the views of the other, disturbing threats to the nation's welfare and security. In May 1792, Hamilton wrote to Edward Carrington that Jefferson and Madison consistently had attempted to turn the United States against Britain:

> In respect to our foreign politics the views of these Gentlemen are in my judgment equally unsound & dangerous. They have a *womanish attachment to France and a womanish resentment against Great Britain.* They would draw us into the closest embrace of the former & involve us in all the consequences of her politics, & they would

[14]Peterson, "Thomas Jefferson and Commercial Policy," p. 604.
[15]Jefferson to Monroe, April 17, 1791, in Ford, *Writings of Jefferson*, 5:319–20.
[16]Report on the Cod and Whale Fisheries, February 1, 1791, in Andrew A. Lipscomb and Albert Ellery Bergh, eds., *The Writings of Thomas Jefferson*, 20 vols. (Washington, 1903–04); 3:140.

risk the peace of the country in their endeavors to keep us at the greatest possible distance from the latter. . . . If these Gentlemen were left to pursue their own course there would be in less than six months *an open War between the U States & Great Britain.*[17]

The Hamilton-Jefferson quarrel had long penetrated the nation's press and divided the country. Washington admonished Hamilton on August 26 that suspicions and charges were "tearing the machine asunder." The president hoped that there would be "mutual forbearance and temporizing yielding *on all sides.*"[18] Hamilton acknowledged that he had faced continuous opposition from Jefferson, admitting that in self defense he had engaged in some retaliation in the press.[19]

Jefferson, in response to a similar appeal for unity, accused Hamilton of interfering with the country's external relations, especially with France and England. "My system," Jefferson informed President Washington, "was to give some satisfactory distinctions to the former, of little cost to us, in return for the solid advantages yielded us by them; and to have met the English with some restrictions which might induce them to abate their severities against our commerce. I have always supposed this coincided with your sentiments." The secretary admitted that the issue of the public debt lay at the heart of his disagreement with Hamilton: "I would wish the debt paid tomorrow; he wishes it never to be paid, but always to be a thing wherewith to corrupt and manage the Legislature."[20] Washington, in his reply, insisted that he could detect no basic discordance between Jefferson's and Hamilton's views. "I have a great, a sincere esteem and regard for you both," he wrote on October 18, "and I ardently wish that some line may be marked out by which both of you could walk."[21]

II

Americans hailed the French Revolution as another chapter in the struggle of republican liberty against monarchical tyranny, a struggle inaugurated by their own glorious revolution. As the revolution within

[17]Hamilton to Carrington, May 26, 1792, in Harold C. Syrett and Jacob E. Cooke, eds., *The Papers of Alexander Hamilton*, 26 vols. (New York, 1961–1979), 11:439.

[18]Washington to Hamilton, August 26, 1792, in Fitzpatrick, *Writings of Washington*, 32:132–34.

[19]Hamilton to Washington, September 9, 1792, in Syrett and Cooke, *Papers of Hamilton*, 12:347–49.

[20]Jefferson to Washington, September 9, 1792, in Ford, *Writings of Jefferson*, 6:103–05.

[21]Washington to Jefferson, October 18, 1792, in Fitzpatrick, *Writings of Washington*, 32:186.

France became more destructive of tradition, life, and property, conservatives in England and the United States began to reconsider. Edmund Burke's *Reflections on the Revolution in France* (1790) challenged the easy optimism of the revolutionaries as they dismissed the hard lessons of the past. Burke declared that he would suspend his congratulations on France's newfound liberty until he discovered "how it had been combined with . . . the discipline and obedience of armies; with the collection of an effective and well-distributed revenue; with morality and religion; with the solidity of property; with peace and order; with civil and social manners. All these (in their way) are good things too." In France, Thomas Paine answered Burke with his *Rights of Man* (1791), emphasizing the rights of individuals against Burke's defense of tradition: "Every age and generation must be as free to act for itself . . . as the ages and generations which preceded it. The vanity and presumption of governing beyond the grave, is the most ridiculous . . . of all tyrannies." This classical debate between conservative and liberal thought soon engulfed the United States, reinforcing the division over external policy already troubling the president.

Jefferson's experience in witnessing the dramatic beginnings of the French Revolution during his final months in Paris merely reaffirmed his admiration of France and his dislike of Britain. In a letter to Madison in August 1789, he contrasted the past relationship of France and England to the United States: "When of two nations, the one has engaged herself in a ruinous war for us, has spent her blood and money to save us, has opened her bosom to us in peace . . . while the other has moved heaven, earth & hell to exterminate us in war, has insulted us in all her councils in peace, shut her doors to us in every part where her interests would admit . . .; to place these two nations on a footing, is to give a great deal more to one than to the other."[22] Jefferson's affinity for France was profound.

After reading a borrowed copy of *Rights of Man*, Jefferson, on request, sent it to a Philadelphia bookseller who had agreed to reprint the pamphlet. Jefferson added a brief observation, not meant for publication, that he was pleased to find "that something is at length to be publicly said against the *political heresies* which have sprung up among us."[23] In the *Columbian Centinel*, John Quincy Adams attacked the French

[22]Jefferson to Madison, August 28, 1789, in Ford, *Writings of Jefferson*, 5:111. See also Jefferson to Madison, January 30, 1787, in Boyd, *Papers of Jefferson*, 11:96. Washington in 1789 also was inclined to laud the French Revolution but, unlike Jefferson, he believed it too massive to be controlled and thus would go to extremes. See Washington to Morris, October 13, 1789, in Fitzpatrick, *Writings of Washington*, 30:443.

[23]Worthington Chauncey Ford, ed., *Writings of John Quincy Adams*, 7 vols. (New York, 1913–1917), 1:65–110; Jefferson is quoted on p. 67. John Quincy Adams's "Publicola" papers were largely attacks on Thomas Paine's pamphlet.

Revolution, and Jefferson's defense of it, as "Publicola." The younger Adams's writings set off a storm of controversy across the country. Jefferson's supporters, believing that John Adams was the author, abused the vice-president in the press. On July 17, 1791, Jefferson acknowledged his regret to John Adams that the "Publicola" controversy had thrown their names "on the public stage, as public antagonists," insisting that he had never meant for his brief endorsement of Paine's work to be published.[24] Adams, recounting the viciousness of the attacks on him, responded that the Philadelphia printer had "sown the seeds of more evils than he can ever atone for" and denied that the writer of "Publicola" had ever consulted him.[25] The efforts of the two old friends to remove themselves from the controversy had no effect on the pro-French frenzy that swept the country.

In time America's heavy emotional involvement in the French Revolution created a crisis for the Washington administration. In 1793 the revolutionary leaders in France executed the king, proclaimed a republic, instituted the Reign of Terror against their enemies, and finally went to war against England, thus locking Europe's greatest land and naval powers in a final struggle for dominance. The president feared that the United States might be drawn into the conflict, and in April he warned Jefferson that the state of war existing between France and Britain behooved "the Government of this Country to use every means in its power to prevent the citizens thereof from embroiling us with either of those powers, by endeavoring to maintain a strict neutrality."[26] What complicated the issue of American neutrality and encouraged the country's pro-French elements was the Franco-American alliance, which bound the United States to defend the French West Indies in the event of war; Britain's known disregard of neutral rights in wartime; and the continued British occupation of the Northwest posts.

Washington again exposed his divided counsels when he asked his cabinet for advice on the issue of the French alliance.[27] Hamilton and Jefferson agreed from the outset that the United States should remain neutral, but Hamilton's neutrality tilted toward Britain, while Jefferson's sought to keep the United States in the good graces of

[24]Jefferson to Adams, July 17, 1791, in *Works of John Adams*, 8:504–05. For a view that John Adams was indeed the author of "Publicola" see Monroe to Jefferson, July 25, 1791, in Hamilton, *Writings of Monroe*, 1:225–26.

[25]Adams to Jefferson, July 29, 1791, in *Works of John Adams*, 8:506–07.

[26]Washington to Jefferson, April 12, 1793, in Fitzpatrick, *Writings of Washington*, 32:415.

[27]Questions Submitted to the Cabinet by the President, April 18, 1793, ibid., pp. 419–20. In Question III, Washington asked whether he should recognize a minister from revolutionary France.

France. Hamilton argued that the French alliance was invalid because it was defensive in nature (France had declared war on Britain) and had been negotiated with the deposed French monarchy. Washington, wrote Hamilton, should formally suspend the alliance and proclaim American neutrality. For Jefferson the alliance was symbolic of the country's independence from Great Britain, and a French victory in the European war was essential for American security. He observed that the United States had negotiated its alliance with the French nation; therefore, it remained valid. Jefferson accepted neutrality as the proper policy for the United States, but, in deference to France, he advised the president to delay any formal announcement of such a policy. That delay, he believed, might encourage Britain to buy U.S. neutrality at the price of recognizing American rights on the high seas. Indeed, he instructed Thomas Pinckney, the American minister to London, to advise the British that the United States favored neutrality "*on condition* that the rights of neutral nations are respected in us, as they have been settled in *modern* times."[28]

Few Americans wanted war. Monroe observed accurately that the country was overwhelmingly pro-French in sentiment, "but general as this sentiment is I believe it is equally so in favor of our neutrality. And this seems to be dictated by the soundest policy even as it may respect the object in view, the success of the French Revolution."[29] Washington knew that any public support of France would invite war with Britain. In proclaiming American neutrality on April 22, the president adopted the logic of the moment, warning all citizens, under the threat of punishment, to behave impartially toward the European belligerents. He did not suspend the French alliance but did accept Jefferson's reasoning that the United States should recognize de facto governments and prepared to receive the new French minister.[30] At the same time, the French government, recognizing America's limited fighting capacity, refrained from asking the United States to defend the West Indies or enter the war against Great Britain. America's shipping, operating under a neutral flag, could serve France more effectively by carrying its West Indian trade.

---

[28]Vattel, to whom Hamilton turned, wrote that an alliance is indeed made with a state and not a specific king, yet any change in government that rendered an alliance "*useless, dangerous,* or *disagreeable,*" properly subjected it to renunciation. See Hamilton's answer to Washington's third question in Syrett and Cooke, *Papers of Hamilton,* 14:383. For Jefferson's letter to Thomas Pinckney, April 20, 1793 see Lipscomb and Bergh, *Writings of Jefferson,* 9:67.

[29]Monroe to Jefferson, May 28, 1793, in Hamilton, *Writings of Monroe,* 1:257.

[30]For a classic statement of American recognition policy see Jefferson to Morris, November 7, 1792, in Ford, *Writings of Jefferson,* 6:131.

However deep the country's desire to avoid war, Washington faced the near rebellion of the multitudes who lauded the French Revolution; for them the neutrality policy was fundamentally antirevolutionary. Madison complained that the president's proclamation wounded the popular feeling "by a seeming indifference to the cause of liberty."[31] John Adams later wrote that mobs by the thousands stormed through the streets of Philadelphia, the nation's new capital, threatening to drag Washington from his house and start a new revolution. Jacobin clubs, the active cells of pro-French activity, joined by members of the press, advocated the arming of privateers to engage the British on the high seas. John Quincy Adams rushed to the president's defense with his "Marcellus" papers. Beginning on April 24 in the *Columbian Centinel*, these writings argued that France's unjustifiable war on all the commercial nations of Europe eliminated any American obligations to fight in its defense; moreover, the United States had no power to do so. Adams concluded that "it may be laid down as a universal principle that no stipulation contained in a treaty can ever oblige one nation to adopt or support the folly or injustice of another."[32] Washington, totally disheartened by the attacks on his administration, revealed his feelings privately. He wrote to Governor Henry Lee of Virginia that his enemies sought not only to impede the measures of government but also, "more especially, . . . to destroy the confidence, which it is necessary for the people to place . . . in their public servants."[33]

Edmond Charles Genêt, the new minister appointed by revolutionary France to the United States, landed at Charleston amid the uproar over Washington's proclamation, determined to involve the United States in France's war. His instructions did not include the pursuit of full American belligerency, but they did advocate activities that would make the United States a base of French operations in the New World. Genêt was rash and naive enough to believe that his defense of the revolutionary cause justified his disregard of established rules of diplomatic behavior. Even before he left South Carolina he organized military and privateering expeditions against the British. His subsequent trip to Philadelphia seemed more a triumphal march than a diplomatic mission. Encouraged by Republican organizations and Jacobin societies along the way, Genêt made incendiary speeches to mobilize popular support for France. Washington received him coldly when he reached Philadelphia in May. Jefferson was cordial enough but reminded Genêt of the country's official neutrality.

[31]Madison to Jefferson, May 8, 1793, in Gaillard Hunt, ed., *The Writings of James Madison*, 9 vols. (New York, 1900–1910), 6:127.
[32]"Marcellus" papers in Ford, *Writings of John Quincy Adams*, 1:144–45.
[33]Washington to Lee, July 21, 1793, in Fitzpatrick, *Writings of Washington*, 33:23.

Genêt interpreted Jefferson's friendly observations on France and his indiscreet observations on American politics as evidence that President Washington had little public support, and he therefore continued to outfit privateers in American ports. The embarrassed Jefferson informed Genêt in June that, whereas the French treaty specifically denied a mutual enemy the privilege of engaging in unneutral activity in either French or American ports, it did not imply that an ally had that privilege.[34] Washington commented that the "best that can be said of this agent is, that he is entirely unfit for the Mission on which he is employed." Finally Genêt threatened to appeal directly to the American people over Washington's head; thereafter, his popularity crumbled and even Jefferson turned against him. Americans sympathetic to France resented Genêt's attacks on the president and his open defiance of their system of government. The administration requested his recall for improper behavior.[35] The Paris government accepted the request, but Genêt, fearing for his life if he returned to France, asked for asylum and spent the remainder of his days living quietly in New York. In 1794 Congress passed a neutrality act which outlawed Genêt's practices and adopted Washington's interpretation.

Amid Washington's trials over neutrality in the summer of 1793, Hamilton launched a personal campaign to defend the president's proclamation with a series of brilliant essays published under the name "Pacificus." These writings constituted the most pervading examination of the diplomatic principles guiding the young Republic to come from the pen of any of the nation's early leaders. The country's pro-French legions had anchored their demands for a strong national allegiance to France on the grounds that the United States must be faithful to its treaty obligations, show gratitude for previous assistance, and underscore its affinity for republican institutions in a monarchical world. Hamilton attacked these three notions head on. In "Pacificus" of July 6 he argued that the country's first obligation was to itself. Without sea power the United States had no obligation even to the French islands in the West Indies. There could be no acceptable balance between the damage that the United States would inflict on itself by opposing Britain, and the advantages that it might bring to France. "All contracts," he wrote, "are to receive a reasonable construction. Self-preservation is the first duty of a Nation; and though in the performance of stipulations relating to war, good faith requires that the *ordinary hazards* of war should be fairly encountered, . . . yet it does not require

---

[34]Jefferson to Genêt, June 17, 1793, in Ford, *Writings of Jefferson*, 7:301–02.
[35]Washington raised the question of Genêt's conduct and the need of taking action in Washington to Jefferson, July 25, 1793, in Fitzpatrick, *Writings of Washington*, 33:28–29. For the decision of August 2, 1793 to ask for Genêt's recall see ibid., p. 58n.

that *extraordinary* and *extreme* hazards should be run." From engaging in a naval war with Great Britain, without a navy or coastal fortifications, he concluded, "we are dissuaded by the most cogent motives of self-preservation, no less than of interest."[36]

Next Hamilton attacked the question of gratitude as a basis of external policy, noting simply that governments could not operate as individuals:

> Existing Millions, and for the most part future generations, are concerned in the present measures of a government: While the consequences of the private actions of an individual, for the most part, terminate with himself, or are circumscribed within a narrow compass. Whence it follows, that an individual may, on numerous occasions, meritoriously indulge the emotions of generosity and benevolence; not only without an eye to, but even at the expense of, his own interest. But a Nation can rarely be justified in pursuing [a similar] course; and, when it does so, ought to confine itself within much stricter bounds.[37]

He further reminded his readers that the defense of liberty rested not only on the merits of the cause but also on the interest of the United States in rendering support.[38]

The continuing excesses of the Reign of Terror in Paris prompted Hamilton, in his "Americanus" papers of early 1794, to challenge the notion that the cause of France was the cause of liberty or that the United States, by entering the European struggle, could serve that cause with sufficient success to compensate for the cost of attempting it. Americans had been told, he declared, "that our own Liberty is at stake upon the event of the war against France—that if she falls, we shall be the next victim. The combined powers, it is said, will never forgive in us the origination of those principles which were the germs of the French Revolution. They will endeavour to eradicate them from the world." To counter such fears he told Americans that Europe's monarchies would comprise a danger only if the United States voluntarily entered the war against them. The enemies of France, he insisted, did not attribute the same principles to America which they believed dangerous in France, simply because they were not the same.[39]

Hamilton's Republican opposition did not challenge his fundamental principles. His defense of Washington's policies was in large

[36]Hamilton's "Pacificus III," July 8, 1793, in Syrett and Cooke, *Papers of Hamilton*, 15:66.

[37]"Pacificus IV," July 10, 1793, ibid., p. 85.

[38]This was the theme of "Pacificus VI," July 17, 1793, ibid., pp. 100–06.

[39]"Americanus II," February 7, 1794, ibid., 16:14.

measure a commentary on Emmerich de Vattel's *The Law of Nations* (1758), a book to which Jefferson was fully devoted. What troubled Jefferson, Madison, and Monroe was Hamilton's assertion of Executive primacy in the making of treaties, even to the exclusion of congressional restraint.[40] Jefferson wrote to Madison in July 1793 that "nobody answers [Hamilton] and his doctrine will therefore be taken for confessed. . . . My dear sir, take up your pen, select the most striking heresies and cut him to pieces in the face of the public. There is nobody else who can and will enter the lists with him."[41] Madison reluctantly answered Hamilton in a series of essays under the name of "Helvidius." Defending the constitutional principle of separation of power, Madison was concerned less with policy toward France than with the nature of the government that should prevail in the United States. The president, he observed, could hardly execute laws that Congress had not provided. To regard treaties, which are laws, as the special property of the Executive was an absurdity; a declaration of war repealed laws operating in a state of peace so far as they were incompatible with a state of war. Similarly, a state of peace annulled laws that belonged to war. Thus, argued Madison, matters of peace as well as war belonged to Congress no less than to the Executive. Therefore, Washington had infringed on powers belonging to Congress when he proclaimed neutrality.[42]

With the outbreak of war in 1793, France had opened its West Indian ports to American ships with the intent that American bottoms would carry its commerce. Whether London would sanction this profitable carrying trade depended, as Adams and Jefferson had predicted, on its willingness to accept the American principle that "free ships make free goods." The British gave their initial answer as early as June 8, 1793, when an Order in Council commanded the capture of any ship carrying flour, corn, or meal to French ports. In November the British broadened their assault by declaring that they would seize all vessels carrying produce and other goods to and from a French colony. This order went beyond the so-called Rule of 1756, which declared that any trade closed to neutrals in time of peace could not be opened to them in time of war. British policy declared war on some trade which the United States had enjoyed in time of peace. The Admiralty neglected to inform Pinckney of the new order in time to warn American sea captains. Primed to enforce the November decree, British vessels quickly rounded up some three hundred neutral ships in the West Indies. Early in 1794 London adopted the Rule of 1756

---

[40]Monroe to Jefferson, July 23, 1793, in Hamilton, *Writings of Monroe*, 1:270.
[41]Jefferson to Madison, July 7, 1793, in Ford, *Writings of Jefferson*, 6:338.
[42]*Letters and Other Writings of James Madison* (Philadelphia, 1865), 1:646–54.

but added military and naval stores to the list of items subject to seizure. Not until March 1794 did Philadelphia discover the magnitude of the British sweep through the West Indies.[43] British captures imperiled American trade with France even as British trade with the United States continued to grow.

Before Washington could frame a defense against British maritime policy he faced a renewed British threat on the Northwest frontier. From the posts of Detroit and Mackinaw the British continued to supply and encourage the Indians residing south of the Great Lakes. An expedition of 1790, sent to quell the Indians of Ohio, failed miserably. With the expectation of trouble with the United States, the British strengthened their alliance with the Indians. In February 1794, Lord Dorchester addressed a gathering of Indians: "I shall not be surprised if we are at war with [the United States] in the course of the present year; and if so, a line must then be drawn by the Warriors."[44] Philadelphia learned of this speech and the British seizures in the West Indies at almost the same time. Washington's cabinet faced its new crisis without Jefferson; the Virginian had left the State Department in December 1793.

III

With general sentiment antagonistic toward Britain and some Republicans even calling for war, Jefferson and Madison believed the time propitious for pushing a program of commercial retaliation against that country. On December 16, 1793, shortly before he resigned from the cabinet, Jefferson submitted to Congress his Report on the Privileges and Restrictions on the Commerce of the United States in Foreign Countries[45]; over two years had passed since Congress had requested the report. Jefferson planned to present it in the fall of 1791, but he feared Hamilton's predictable opposition. Jefferson revised it for submission in February 1793 but hesitated to run the gauntlet of the Second Congress with its still powerful Federalist bloc. Moreover, he assumed that the new French minister would bring an attractive commercial offer that would undermine the pro-British sentiment in Congress. Genêt indeed brought a promising commercial treaty with him, but it became lost in the controversy which he created. Because Jefferson's

    [43]Hugh B. Hammett, "The Jay Treaty: Crisis Diplomacy in the New Nation," *Social Studies* 65 (January 1974): 11.
    [44]Lord Dorchester to the Seven Nations of Lower Canada, February 10, 1794, in Brigadier General E. A. Cruikshank, ed., *The Correspondence of Lieut. Governor John Graves Simcoe*, 5 vols. (Toronto, 1923–1931), 2:150.
    [45]Report on the Privileges and Restrictions on the Commerce of the United States in Foreign Countries, December 16, 1793, in Ford, *Writings of Jefferson*, 6:470–84.

report called for a discriminatory policy toward Britain, it hardly seemed compatible with an official policy of neutrality. Despite his doubts as to the timing, Jefferson submitted his report.[46]

Madison, on January 3, 1794, offered a series of resolutions to the House, based on Jefferson's report. These proposed additional duties on the goods and tonnage of countries which had no commercial treaties with the United States, and they provided additionally for retaliation against restrictions imposed by foreign countries on American commerce. The Federalists, however, opposed the resolutions as assaults on British interests. In early February, Madison's discriminatory proposal passed the House by a narrow majority, while the debate on his remaining resolutions continued into March. Monroe reported the determination of the opposition to Jefferson: "The steady zeal with which any thing like a systematic operation on the British commerce, or indeed any branch of her interest is opposed, you have long witnessed & can of course readily conceive upon the present occasion."[47] He noted as well that the Federalists had discussed as a remedy "to send an Envoy Exty. to Engld. to complain of these injuries & seek redress." Having lost control of the House, the Federalists, in command of the Executive and the Senate, could still determine U.S.-British relations by defining them in a treaty. So promising was the prospect that Hamilton spoke for the mission to London. Monroe was amazed. "I sho'd. think it more suitable," he wrote, "to employ John Dickinson, who I believe drew the last petition of Congress to the king, in the course of the late revolution." On April 8, he penned a note to President Washington to contest Hamilton's appointment as injurious to the public interest.[48]

Washington accepted the Federalist escape from the growing Anglo-American crisis. He agreed with Hamilton that the revenues received from British imports were essential for the government's financial system and required peace. Washington was willing to send Hamilton as the special envoy to London but, because of Jeffersonian protests, proposed instead Chief Justice John Jay to the Senate.[49] The Republicans were not pleased; eight voted against the confirmation. Jay was a high Federalist but also an experienced diplomat. His instructions covered all disputes between the United States and Britain: evacuation

---

[46]Peterson, "Thomas Jefferson and Commercial Policy," pp. 584–85.

[47]Monroe to Jefferson, March 3, 1794, in Hamilton, *Writings of Monroe*, 1:281–82; Monroe to Jefferson, March 16, 1794, ibid., p. 285.

[48]Monroe to Jefferson, March 16, 1794, ibid., p. 289; Monroe to Washington, April 8, 1794, ibid., pp. 291–92.

[49]Hamilton's report to Washington, April [14], 1794, in Syrett, *Papers of Hamilton*, 16:265, 266–79. This letter is a long argument on the need of peace with Great Britain. Hamilton recommended Jay for the mission to London.

of the Northwest posts, settlement of the Northeast boundary and claims arising from prerevolutionary debts, compensation both for slaves removed by the British during the Revolution and recent maritime losses, recognition of American neutral rights, and the question of British West Indian trade.

Jay arrived in London in mid-June and was greeted by a display of cordiality that continued throughout his five months of negotiations. Convinced that the British wanted to avoid trouble, especially after General Anthony Wayne's victory over the Indians at Fallen Timbers had strengthened the American position in the Northwest, Jay took the offensive. Still, he discovered in time that he possessed little leverage. In part his problem lay in Hamilton's indiscreet assurances to the British minister in Philadelphia, George Hammond, that the United States would never join the European neutrals in seeking the defense of its rights against Britain.[50] If the British were vulnerable in Canada, they were predominant on the high seas. Lord Grenville, who conducted the negotiations with Jay, was conscious, moreover, of the dependence of the United States on revenues from English trade. At the end Grenville made few concessions. Under the terms of the treaty, signed in November 1794, Britain promised to withdraw its troops from the Northwest posts by June 1, 1796.

The British, however, refused to recognize the neutral rights of the United States and agreed only to submit American claims arising from recent maritime seizures to joint arbitration. Jay gave up for ten years any American right to impose tonnage dues or other discriminations against British shipping. In exchange he gained the limited entry of small U.S. vessels into the British West Indies. Jay failed to maintain the jurisdiction of American courts in the settlement of debts owed to British citizens. The Northeast boundary as well as the debts were assigned to joint commissions. The treaty ignored the issues of impressment and slaves. In a letter to Edmund Randolph, the new secretary of state, Jay expressed satisfaction over the treaty: "I have no reason to believe or conjecture that one more favourable is attainable."[51]

To deflect the anticipated political storm that the Jay mission would unleash, Washington determined in late May 1794 to send "a republican character" to revolutionary France. When Madison refused

<hr>

[50]Samuel F. Bemis uncovered enough evidence on Hamilton's private assurances to the British to term the final product of Jay's negotiations "Hamilton's treaty." See Bemis, *Jay's Treaty* (rev. ed.; New Haven, CT, 1962), p. 373. For a detailed account of Hamilton's dealings with British agents in 1790 see Julian P. Boyd, *Number 7: Alexander Hamilton's Secret Attempts to Control American Foreign Policy* (Princeton, NJ, 1964).

[51]Jay to Edmund Randolph, November 19, 1794, in Henry P. Johnston, ed., *The Correspondence and Public Papers of John Jay*, 4 vols. (New York, 1890), 4:138.

the mission, the president turned to Monroe, who believed that he "was among the last men to whom it wod. be made."[52] Monroe received his commission as minister to the French Republic on May 31, and, during his first days in Paris, he revealed his pro-French sympathies. When he received no invitation to appear before the Committee of Public Safety, he wrote to the National Convention, which invited him to address it. In his brief speech Monroe defied all the traditional rules of diplomatic discourse by developing the theme of republican fraternity: "Republics should approach near to each other. . . . In many respects they all have the same interest. But this is more especially the case with the American and French Republics:—their governments are similar; they both cherish the same principles and rest on the same basis, the equal and inalienable rights of man." Then he defied America's official neutrality by expressing the hope that, while "the fortitude, magnanimity and heroic valor of [France's] troops command the admiration and applause of the astonished world, the wisdom and firmness of her councils unite equally in securing the happiest result." Insisting that the president, as well as the American people, endorsed his views with one voice, he promised to do everything in his power "to preserve and perpetuate the harmony so happily subsisting at present between the two Republics."[53]

Monroe's speech shocked Philadelphia, but it did not result in his official repudiation; he insisted that he was protecting the interests of the United States against the adverse effect of the Jay mission. Finally, Monroe's attacks on Jay, and his repeated advocacy of closer ties to France, rendered his behavior intolerable and produced his recall. Upon his return to Philadelphia in June 1797, he published a long, vigorous, and uncompromising defense of his mission, one endorsed by both Jefferson and Madison.[54] Monroe defended his excesses as a necessary counter to the anti-French attitudes in Philadelphia.

When Jay's treaty reached Philadelphia in March 1795, the vindictiveness of Republican partisans quickly reached a new high. After examining the treaty, President Washington hesitated to submit it to a sharply divided nation. He held the treaty until June and then submitted it to the Senate in confidence. His secrecy aroused suspicions of perfidy; Senate critics leaked copies to Republican leaders and the press. The Senate confirmed the treaty, after two weeks of debate, with

---

[52]Monroe to Jefferson, May 27, 1794, in Hamilton, *Writings of Monroe*, 1:299–300; Monroe to Washington, May 27, 1794, ibid., pp. 301–02.

[53]Monroe's speech before the French Convention, in Stuart Gerry Brown, *The First Republicans* (Syracuse, NY, 1954), pp. 109–10.

[54]Jefferson to Madison, January 3, 1798, in Lipscomb and Bergh, *Writings of Jefferson*, 9:433.

a bare two-thirds majority. As the treaty terms spread across the country, Jefferson's partisans launched a counterattack. Some fence graffiti summed up the popular sentiment: "Damn John Jay! Damn every one that won't damn John Jay! Damn every one that won't put lights in his windows and sit up all night damning John Jay!!!"[55] In Boston a mob destroyed a British vessel at anchor. In the South, where the Federalists had little support, the attacks on the president were most virulent. John Randolph charged Washington with "treachery unexampled since Tiberius." Less critical of Washington was Jefferson's letter of April 1796 to his friend Philip Mazzei which was soon made public: "Curse on his virtues; they have undone the country." John Quincy Adams recalled that Jay's Treaty "brought on the severest trial which the character of Washington and the fortunes of the country have ever passed through."[56]

Hamilton, retired from public life, assumed the defense of Jay's Treaty with his remarkable "Camillus" essays, which began on July 22, 1795. "Camillus," like "Pacificus," read like a primer on Vattel.[57] Hamilton made no effort to uphold the treaty's specific provisions and omissions; indeed, he was disappointed by the absence of any stipulation against British impressment. At the same time, he refused to defend neutral rights in wartime because the United States did not have the means to enforce such claims, nor would he defend the claims of the South to blacks carried away by the British. Rather, Hamilton argued that the treaty was the best available and that it protected the nation's interest in peace. "The more or less of commercial advantages which we may acquire by particular treaties," he wrote to Washington, "are of far less moment. With peace, the force of circumstances will enable us to make our way sufficiently fast in Trade. War, at this time, would give a serious wound to our growth and prosperity." Whatever the costs of Jay's Treaty, they were insignificant compared to a single campaign fought for American rights. "The calculation is therefore a

[55]See Hammett, "The Jay Treaty," p. 15.
[56]Jefferson to Mazzei, April 24, 1796, in Ford, *Writings of Jefferson*, 8:72–78. Adams is quoted in Hammett, "The Jay Treaty," p. 15. Obviously Jay's Treaty intensified the pro-French feeling in Congress. Writing from Philadelphia in February 1795, Fisher Ames, the Massachusetts Federalist, complained that "Congress is too inefficient to afford the stuff of a letter. No public body exists with less energy of character to do good, or stronger propensities to mischief. We are Frenchmen, democrats, *antifeds*; every thing but Americans, and men of business. . . . Jacobinism and Gallomania are stronger here than anywhere else." See Ames to Thomas Dwight, February 28, 1795, in Seth Ames, ed., *Works of Fisher Ames*, 2 vols. (Boston, 1854), 1:169–70.
[57]These thirty-eight articles were entitled "The Defense" and signed "Camillus." They comprised a wide-ranging examination not only of the political and economic situation in the Western World but also of the principles of international conduct. See the introductory notes in Syrett, *Papers of Hamilton*, 18:475–79.

simple and a plain one," he concluded; "the terms are in no way inconsistent with national honor."[58] Seldom in history, Hamilton noted, did national outrages upon others render negotiations dishonorable. Honor, he said, would not be wounded by counseling moderation: "Nations ought to calculate as well as individuals, to compare evils, and to prefer the lesser to the greater; to act otherwise, is to act unreasonably; those who advocate it are imposters and madmen."[59]

Hamilton admonished Americans to recall that the United States, no less than the powers of Europe, lived under the established modes of international behavior: "In national controversies, it is of real importance to conciliate the good opinion of mankind, and it is even useful to preserve or gain that of our enemy. The latter facilitates accommodation and peace—the former attracts good offices, friendly interventions, sometimes direct support, from others." The measures of war must always look forward to peace.[60] Against such appeals to tradition and common sense, Jefferson stood helpless. He confessed to Madison that Hamilton was "really a colossus to the anti-republican party. Without numbers, he is almost a host within himself. . . . In truth, when he comes forward, there is no one but yourself who can meet him." "For God's sake," he pleaded, "take up your pen, and give a fundamental reply to . . . Camillus."[61] This time Madison declined the challenge.

Convinced along with Hamilton that Jay's Treaty served the country's highest interests, the president signed it in August 1795. Because of British delays the treaty did not become official until February 29, 1796, at which time Washington immediately sent it to both houses of Congress with a request for the measures required for its implementation. If the House Republicans could not prevent the treaty, they could prevent the appropriation of funds to carry it out. New York Congressman Edward Livingston opened the House debate by introducing a resolution requiring the president to send over copies

[58]Washington on July 3, 1795 asked Hamilton to prepare a defense of Jay's Treaty. Hamilton responded with Remarks on the Treaty of Amity Commerce and Navigation Lately Made Between the United States and Great Britain [July 9–11, 1795], ibid., pp. 404–54. The quotation is on p. 452.

[59]"Camillus V," August 5, 1795, ibid., 19:91–92.

[60]"Camillus XXI," October 30, 1795, ibid., p. 372. Washington lauded the "Camillus" papers as a needed defense of Jay's Treaty. As he wrote to Hamilton, "The difference of conduct between the friends, and foes of order, and good government, is in nothg. more striking than that, the latter are always working, like bees, to distil their poison; while the former, depending, often times *too much*, and *too long* upon the sense, and good dispositions of the people to work conviction, neglect the means of effecting it." Washington to Hamilton, July 29, 1795, in Fitzpatrick, *Writings of Washington*, 34:264.

[61]Jefferson to Madison, September 21, 1795, in Ford, *Writings of Jefferson*, 7:31–33.

of Jay's instructions and other relevant documents regarding the negotiations. The Federalists rushed to Washington's defense by insisting
that the treaty-making power belonged exclusively to the president and
the Senate. House Republicans answered that treaties were laws and
that Congress made the nation's laws. Fundamentally, the Republicans
were determined to set the bounds of Executive power operating through
the treaty-making authority. They passed Livingston's resolution easily, but Washington refused to send the papers, denying that the House
possessed any authority to demand them.[62]

Madison now took up the Republican cause, arguing that, whereas
the House had no treaty-making powers, any treaty that required
congressional action indeed came under the power of Congress. This
gave the House the right to judge the expediency or inexpediency of
any treaty; to that end it could demand the diplomatic correspondence.
The House passed Madison's resolution, but again Washington stood
firm and eventually the House capitulated. Madison understood why
the Federalists had consolidated their ranks sufficiently to defend the
Jay treaty, explaining to Monroe that "acquiescence had been incul-
cated . . . by exaggerated pictures of the public prosperity, an appeal
to the popular feeling for the President, and the bugbear of war; still,
however, there is little doubt that the real sentiment of the mass of the
community is hostile to the treaty."[63] Jay's Treaty had divided the
country along predictable lines. This time the divisions held firm; indeed,
it was the treaty that had crystallized the conflicting approaches to
external affairs into a permanent two-party system.[64]

Meanwhile in 1795 the Washington administration achieved a
notable diplomatic success elsewhere. Until that year Spain successfully
had resisted the American demands for free navigation on the Mississippi as well as for a formal commercial treaty. The execution of the
French king in 1793 had severed the Family Compact between France
and Spain. The ensuing war placed Spain on the side of Britain, but
the war went badly for Spain as the French moved into Spanish territory. Spain opened negotiations with France which led to the Treaty
of Basel in June 1795. Having changed sides in the war, Spain now
faced the hostility of Britain with all its naval might. Thomas Pinckney,
the new American minister, arrived in Madrid on June 28. During
subsequent weeks the Spanish court, troubled by Jay's Treaty, suggested an alliance with the United States. This Pinckney declined. In

[62]Washington to House of Representatives, March 30, 1796, in Fitzpatrick, *Writings of Washington*, 35:2–5.
[63]Madison to Monroe, December 20, 1795, in Hunt, *Writings of Madison*, 6:260.
[64]That Jay's Treaty solidified the political divisions in the country is the central
theme of Joseph Charles, *The Origins of the American Party System* (New York, 1961).

August the Spanish government decided to avoid trouble with the United States by settling the Mississippi question.[65] It offered free navigation of the river, not as a right but as a concession; it also granted the right of deposit at New Orleans for three years, a right renewable at New Orleans or elsewhere. Spain recognized the 31st parallel as the boundary of West Florida, with both nations protecting the border against Indian raids. These arrangements were embodied in the Treaty of San Lorenzo, signed on October 27, 1795. By then the terms of Jay's Treaty had reached Madrid, eliminating the danger of an Anglo-American alliance, but this made little difference because Spain's troubles lay in the West. Spanish officials had failed not only to win favor among western settlers but also to keep American boatmen, merchants, and traders from moving down the Mississippi through Spanish territory.[66]

Washington's Farewell Address of September 17, 1796, was the culminating statement of Federalist thought on matters of external policy and reflected the views of Madison, Hamilton, and Jay. Hamilton, in revising it, made it largely his own. Washington's valedictory was a message for the times, but it was far more. He admonished the nation to behave in accordance with established principles, especially as they applied to international affairs. Throughout his second term he had been troubled by the dangerous attachments of too many Americans to the European belligerents. In October 1795, he had stressed the necessity of greater independence in a letter to Patrick Henry: "My ardent desire is . . . to see that [the United States] *may be* independent of *all*, and under the influence of *none*. In a word, I want an *American* character, that the powers of Europe may be convinced we act for *ourselves* and not for *others*."[67] In his Farewell Address, Washington explained why foreign attachments endangered the country's well-being: "The Nation, which indulges toward another an habitual hatred, or an habitual fondness, is in some degree a slave. It is a slave to its animosity or its affection, either of which is sufficient to lead it astray from its duty and its interest."[68] Sympathy for favored countries, he

[65]Older studies of the Spanish decision to seek a treaty with the United States attributed Spanish motivation to Jay's negotiations. See, for example, George L. Rives, "Spain and the United States in 1795," *American Historical Review* 4 (October 1898): 70–76; and Samuel Flagg Bemis, *Pinckney's Treaty* (Baltimore, 1926), pp. 305–30.

[66]The western interpretation of the Treaty of San Lorenzo has been emphasized in Arthur Preston Whitaker, "New Light on the Treaty of San Lorenzo: An Essay in Historical Criticism," *Mississippi Valley Historical Review* 15 (March 1929): 450–52.

[67]Washington to Patrick Henry, October 9, 1795, in Fitzpatrick, *Writings of Washington*, 34:335.

[68]Washington's Farewell Address, in James D. Richardson, ed., *A Compilation of the Messages and Papers of the Presidents*, 10 vols. (Washington, 1896–1899), 1:221–23.

warned, assumed common interests which seldom existed and enmeshed a people in the enmities of others without justification. Later Washington expressed the wish that Americans would advocate their own cause rather than that of other states, that "instead of being Frenchmen, or Englishmen, in Politics, they would be Americans."[69]

IV

John Adams, upon entering the presidency in March 1797, was appalled by the continuing partisanship of the country's political factions toward Britain and France. He complained to his wife: "At the next election England will set up Jay or Hamilton, and France, Jefferson, and all the corruption of Poland will be introduced; unless the American spirit should rise and say, we will have neither John Bull nor Louis Baboon."[70] Actually, Adams had inherited a collapsing American relationship with France. Paris had regarded Jay's Treaty as a threat to the French alliance; the French minister in Philadelphia, Pierre Auguste Adet, had enlisted in the Republican forces opposed to its ratification; his own open partisanship alienated him from the Washington administration; and Washington's recall of Monroe, followed by Jefferson's narrow defeat in the election of 1796, had seemed to eliminate pro-French counsels from the nation's foreign policy establishment. Furthermore, to reassure France, Washington, in January 1797, had instructed the secretary of state to inform Paris that "the conduct of the United States toward France has been . . . regulated by the strictest principles of Neutrality. There has been no attempt in the government . . . to withhold any friendship we could render consistent with the Neutrality we had adopted."[71] By 1797 French displeasure over the pro-British sentiments that seemed to dominate Philadelphia erupted in a series of retaliatory measures. The French Directory condemned all neutral ships carrying enemy goods to capture. Then it rejected the new American minister, Charles Cotesworth Pinckney of South Carolina, when he arrived at Paris in December.

President Adams wanted no further trouble with France, although he, like Washington, believed that France was unreasonable in its demands for a special relationship with the United States. He complained that Adet "had laid his demands of gratitude so high, and all

[69]Washington to William Heath, May 20, 1797, in Fitzpatrick, *Writings of Washington*, 35:449.

[70]Adams to Abigail Adams, March 17, 1797, in Charles Francis Adams, ed., *Letters of John Adams, Addressed to His Wife* (Boston, 1841), 2:251–52.

[71]Washington to secretary of state, January 9, 1797, in Fitzpatrick, *Writings of Washington*, 35:360–61.

his partisans were in the habit of deafening our people with such rude, extravagant, and arrogant pretensions to it, that it seems to have become necessary to be explicit upon the subject."[72] With the advice of Hamilton and other high Federalists, Adams decided to dispatch a special commission to France to negotiate a comprehensive treaty with the Directory, aiming at the settlement of all issues in controversy. To the commission Adams appointed Pinckney, John Marshall of Virginia, and Elbridge Gerry of Massachusetts. Specifically, the commission was instructed to press the Directory for compensation for French attacks on American shipping and some modification of the Franco-American alliance.[73] During the early years of independence, Jay had attempted to consign the alliance to history. He reminded the French minister, the Comte de Moustier, that the alliance no longer served any useful object. The French refused to negotiate a formal abrogation of the treaty, and thus it continued nominally in force. Adams wanted, as a minimum, the release of the United States from any obligation to defend the French West Indies.

When the American commissioners gathered in Paris during October 1797, the Directory refused to recognize them. Finally Talleyrand, the foreign minister, sent a number of shadowy emissaries to present outrageous demands, which included a huge gift—a bribe—for himself and the Directory as well as a loan to the French government of $12 million. There would be no negotiations until the commissioners had met these demands and had apologized for a recent speech which President Adams had delivered to Congress. The three Americans terminated the proceedings abruptly.[74] Marshall and Pinckney returned to the United States as heroes, while Gerry remained to prevent a total breakdown in Franco-American relations. Long before the French eased Gerry out in July 1798, the news of the XYZ Affair, as Adams described the French emissaries to Congress, had created a crisis in Philadelphia. For the Federalists the XYZ Affair came as salvation, demonstrating the corruption and incorrigibility of the French government. Republicans who refused to believe the charges faced ridicule when, on April 2, Adams released the correspondence of the failed negotiations in Paris.[75]

---

[72]Adams to Elbridge Gerry, February 13, 1797, in *Works of John Adams*, 8:522.

[73]Adams to the heads of departments, April 14, 1797, ibid., pp. 540–41; Adams to Gerry, June 20, and July 8, 17, 1797, ibid., pp. 546–47, 549.

[74]For Adams's reaction to the episode see Adams to the heads of departments, January 28, 1798, ibid., pp. 561–62.

[75]Adams to the heads of departments, March 13, 1798, ibid., pp. 568–69. Fisher Ames believed that the XYZ Affair finally gave the country some unity and thereby strengthened its resolve. See Ames to Timothy Pickering, June 4, 1798, in Ames, *Works of Fisher Ames*, 1:226.

In a series of public papers entitled "The Stand," Hamilton, in March and April 1798, warned his countrymen of the danger of both French attacks on American commerce and France's pretensions to universal empire.[76] He argued that American merchant vessels "ought to be permitted not only to arm themselves, but to sink or capture their assailants. . . . This course, it will be objected, implies a state of war. Let it be so." Congress declared the French alliance null and void and passed measures to create a navy department, establish a fighting marine, arm merchant vessels, and triple the size of the regular army. To defend the country from alleged internal French influences, Congress passed the Alien and Sedition acts which eased the task of deporting unwanted aliens and prosecuting Americans who attacked the U.S. government and its officials.

Adams's policy toward France was scarcely conciliatory. Not only did the war spirit in America grant the president a sudden burst of popularity but also a war with France had been fundamental to high Federalist policy; still, he refused to ask for a declaration of war. The result was an undeclared war in the Atlantic, especially in the West Indies. America's new frigates were more than a match for French warships and far more powerful than French privateers. Hundreds of privateers and armed merchant ships combed the West Indies in search of French armed vessels; they did not attack French merchant ships. Altogether American warships and privateers captured about eighty French vessels. Meanwhile, Hamilton and other high Federalists favored a full-scale war against France. During the summer and fall of 1798, Rufus King, Thomas Pinckney's successor as the American minister in London, urged the Federalists to accept the opportunity for a glorious campaign against the Spanish possessions in the New World. Britain, he wrote, would furnish the fleet. He admonished Hamilton in January 1799 that "our children will reproach us if we neglect our duty, and humanity will escape many scourges if we act with wisdom and decision."[77] Hamilton hoped to lead the American army in the combined British-American assault on the Spanish Empire, but Adams refused to sanction a declaration of war or to fill the ranks of the army.[78] Facing the bitter reaction to the Alien and Sedition acts as embodied in the

---

[76]For Hamilton's warnings against French power and ambition see especially "The Stand No. 1," March 30, 1798, and "The Stand No. 3," April 7, 1798, in Syrett, *Papers of Hamilton*, 21:382–87, 402–08. The quotation is found in "The Stand No. 6," April 19, 1798, ibid., p. 438.

[77]Ames to H. G. Otis, April 23, 1798, in Ames, *Works of Fisher Ames*, 1:225; Charles, *Origins of the American Party System*, pp. 133–34.

[78]Adams, anticipating no French invasion, saw no reason to build up the American army. See Adams to James McHenry, secretary of war, October 22, 1798, in *Works of John Adams*, 8:613.

Virginia and Kentucky resolutions, he refused to antagonize the Republicans further. By early 1799 the president was troubled by the adverse effect of the undeclared war on American commerce; moreover, he had learned that Talleyrand was now prepared to negotiate.

Amid the disintegration of Franco-American relations in 1798, British prestige soared to the highest point of the decade. Minister King reported that Great Britain contemplated the sharing of lucrative commercial monopolies, such as sugar and coffee, with the United States. Britain, it appeared, was prepared at last to admit the high Federalists into partnership. That the United States would be a junior partner, readily accepting British commercial predominance, did not seem to concern them. Even limited British concessions to American commerce would demand a price, and the price in 1798 was naval aid and joint operations against the French. In addition, Britain wanted American seamen to man ten or twelve of its warships.[79] Meanwhile, in the absence of any general concessions, British captures and impressments continued. High Federalists expressed dismay that London made no effort to fulfill the promises made to those who had spent so much political capital in defending Britain and its policies. Thomas Fitzsimmons, a Philadelphia Federalist, expressed the disillusionment of a party:

> To me it appears strange that the British ministry have never thought it their interest to try and conciliate this country; they cannot be uninformed of the state of parties here, or insensible to the advantages they derive from a good understanding with us. A very considerable portion of the commerce of this country is carried on with their manufacturers, and the payment for these insures them no small proportions of our exports. With all this their conduct is invariably cold and suspicious. . . . I am not without my apprehensions too, that their necessity as well as their monopolizing spirit will, when there is a peace, draw a circle round our commerce, that for a time at least, will narrow it down to a very small compass. . . . If the British restrict our trade, let us meet them with restrictions on our part.[80]

Britain, however, simply refused to tie its policies to the concerns of a political faction in America.

On February 18, 1799, President Adams announced his intention to reopen negotiations with France. He nominated William Vans Murray as the new minister to Paris, as Talleyrand had assured the president that the French government was prepared to receive an American

---

[79]Charles, *Origins of the American Party System*, pp. 131–34.
[80]Fitzsimmons is quoted in ibid., p. 136.

minister.[81] Hamilton, unlike some Federalist extremists, had no desire to prevent the mission, but he recommended that Adams increase it to three men; the Senate agreed. Adams added the names of Chief Justice Oliver Ellsworth and William R. Davie of North Carolina. The three negotiators carried instructions to demand large reparations for French spoliations of American commerce and a formal termination of the Franco-American alliance. First Consul Napoleon Bonaparte's France, strong and confident, recognized no need to grant both requests. The Americans at length dropped their demands for reparations in return for an abrogation of the alliance. The Treaty of Mortefontaine of October 1800 terminated the old treaties of 1778, but it reestablished most-favored-nation commercial relations and the principle of neutral rights as embodied in the original alliance treaty—a provision the United States did not secure in Jay's Treaty. To Adams the Convention of 1800 comprised the crowning achievement of his career, observing later: "I desire no other inscription over my gravestone than: 'Here lies John Adams, who took upon himself the responsibility of the peace with France in the year of 1800.' "

V

Twenty-five years separated Jefferson's Declaration of Independence from his First Inaugural of March 1801. Nothing in the assumptions or experience of that long postrevolutionary generation suggested that it sought to engage the country in the affairs of the world except by the rules embodied in modern European practice.[82] The Founding Fathers recognized no diplomatic principles except those proclaimed by the chief theoreticians of the European state system. They saw as clearly as their European counterparts that the major forces in international society tended simultaneously toward stability and change. Individual nations ranged themselves on one side or the other of this equation in accordance with their immediate or long-term interests, as they understood them. It was the uncertainty, the lack of precision, in the international system that rendered assessments difficult. Decisions,

---

[81]Adams to Washington, February 19, 1799, in *Works of John Adams*, 8:624–25. Many of the high Federalists were astonished at Adams's decision. Ames wrote from Boston in February that "the new embassy to France . . . disgusts most men here. Peace with France they think an evil, and holding out the hopes of it another, as it tends to chill the public fervor." He complained that Adams had not consulted members of Congress in advance. See Ames to Dwight, February 27, 1799, in Ames, *Works of Fisher Ames*, 1:252. Ames wrote to Pickering on March 12: "I hope the President will not doubt that the public is averse to all delusive negotiations." Ibid., p. 254.

[82]See Charles G. Fenwick, "The Authority of Vattel," *American Political Science Review* 7 (August 1913): 406–10.

once made, soon engaged the interests and preferences of other countries and created situations that often passed beyond the control of even the most powerful. What sustained some semblance of peace and order in this fundamentally anarchical international system of individual sovereignties was the recurring interest and capacity of dominant combinations of power to curtail the ambitions of the more aggressive states. The challenge to any government in this balancing system was that of discovering, supporting, or enticing those forces that favored its own preferences. The weaker the nation or the more ambitious its objectives, the more of necessity it would seek its gains in alliance with other powers.

Washington and Hamilton had established the principles that determined the nation's behavior toward the external world. For Hamilton there was no guide to national policy but interest, although he acknowledged that nations too often neglected their real interests in response to momentary considerations and passions. His "Pacificus" and "Americanus" papers comprised a single, massive plea that the United States weigh its interests carefully before it ventured abroad. Washington, as president, never departed from his earlier admonition that "it is a maxim, founded in the universal experience of mankind, that no nation is to be trusted further than it is bound by its interest."[83] Whatever his errors in judgment, he trusted that no one could doubt that he would be "actuated by any interests separate from those of [his] country." He wrote amid his trials of 1795: "In every act of my administration I have sought the happiness of my fellow citizens. My system for the attainment of this object has uniformly been to overlook all personal, local, and partial considerations; to contemplate the United States as one great whole; . . . and to consult only the substantial and permanent interest of our country."[84] Regarding as dangerous the intrusion of concerns other than interests in affairs among nations, the Federalists committed the United States to a genuinely flexible, amoral world view that would maximize the country's capacity to recognize and pursue its highest interests.

---

[83]Washington to Henry Laurens, November 14, 1778, in Fitzpatrick, *Writings of Washington*, 13:256.

[84]Washington expressed his views on leadership, the public interest, and the absence of any infallible standard to follow in his noted letter to Henry Knox, September 20, 1795, ibid., 34:310. See also Washington to Joseph Pierce, October 9, 1795, ibid., pp. 333–34. Washington insisted that he desired nothing more than to serve his constituents and to that end had attempted to "pursue steadily such measures (of an Executive nature) as appears to be most conducive to their interest and happiness." Again, he wrote to Patrick Henry on October 9, 1795 that "I can most religiously aver I have no wish, that is incompatible with the dignity, happiness and true interest of the people of this country." Ibid., p. 335.

To guarantee the nation's independence from issues purely European, the Founding Fathers expanded the concept of geographic isolation into a fundamental theory of national policy. Except for the French alliance, the United States would not have gained its independence, but after 1783 Adams and Jefferson agreed that the country should avoid any entanglements with the European powers. Their recurring admonitions became the keystone of America's external relations. "It is our true policy," Washington declared in his Farewell Address, "to steer clear of permanent alliances with any portion of the foreign world, so far, I mean, as we are now at liberty to do it."[85] The Adams administration disposed of the French alliance in the Treaty of Mortefontaine without substituting a new one with Britain. When the House of Representatives passed a resolution to entrust the country's security to its own resources and energy, Adams responded enthusiastically: "The genuine disdain which you so coolly and deliberately express, of a reliance on foreign protection, wanting no foreign guarantee of our liberties, resolving to maintain our national independence against every attempt to despoil us of this inestimable treasure, will meet the . . . exulting applauses from the heart of every faithful American." Jefferson, in carrying forward this policy of isolation from Europe's political and military affairs, phrased its essentials precisely when he wrote: "Peace, commerce, and honest friendship with all nations, entangling alliances with none."[86]

An essential adjunct of American isolationism was the principle of nonintervention in the affairs of other nations. This doctrine found expression in the writings of all the Founding Fathers, but its most consistent and outspoken advocate was John Quincy Adams. When the Jacobin societies demanded that the United States rescue, in the name of humanity, the French victims of war and repression, he gave the principle of abstention classic form in his letters of "Marcellus":

> As men, we must undoubtedly lament the effusion of human blood, and the mass of misery and distress which is preparing for the great part of the civilized world; but as the citizens of a nation at a vast distance from the continent of Europe; of a nation whose happiness consists in a real independence, disconnected from all European interests and European politics, it is our duty to remain, the peaceable and silent, though sorrowful spectators of the sanguinary scene.

[85]Richardson, *Messages and Papers of the Presidents*, 1:223.

[86]Adams quoted in Samuel Flagg Bemis, *John Quincy Adams and the Foundations of American Foreign Policy* (New York, 1949), p. 98. For Jefferson's views see Jefferson to Gerry, January 26, 1799, in Ford, *Writings of Jefferson*, 7:18; and Jefferson's inaugural in Richardson, *Messages and Papers of the Presidents*, 1:323.

To involve itself in the revolutions of Europe, declared Adams, would doom the country to inevitable destruction and ruin. "We are therefore," he admonished his readers, "commanded by . . . that uncontrollable law of nature, which is paramount to all human legislation, . . . to remain at peace, and to content ourselves with wishing that laureled Victory may sit upon the sword of justice, and that smooth success may always be strewed before the feet of virtuous Freedom."[87] Adams thus warned the nation against adopting external policies designed specifically to further the cause of justice and freedom; such causes of necessity would triumph on their own or not at all.

Toward Europe's wars the Founding Fathers advocated a policy of neutrality, the third element in American isolationism. No country, they knew, could be totally free that had bartered away its right to be neutral, nor could a nation be free that lacked the strength to enforce its neutrality. Washington, like Hamilton, recognized the relationship between national power and neutrality: "If we remain one people, under an efficient government, the period is not far off when we . . . may take such an attitude as will cause the neutrality we may at any time resolve upon to be scrupulously respected; when belligerent nations . . . will not lightly hazard the giving us provocation." What mattered for Washington was the country's freedom to judge its interests in Europe's wars, even to the making of alliances. "Taking care always to keep ourselves by suitable establishments on a respectable defensive posture," he declared, "we may safely trust to temporary alliances for extraordinary emergencies." Nowhere did the Farewell Address excuse the government of the United States from acting when the country's interests justified involvements abroad. By maintaining a close balance between its commitments and its power, the nation could choose, in Washington's words, "peace or war, as our interest, guided by justice, shall counsel."[88]

For the Founding Fathers isolationism was more than a response to geographic factors or the basis of a thoughtless preoccupation with internal concerns and self-sufficient pursuits. The United States never sought the solitude of such hermit nations as Japan or Korea; from its republican beginnings it created and maintained a commercial empire that blanketed much of the globe. American isolationism was always political and military, never commercial or intellectual. Policies grounded in political and military isolationism recognized the Atlantic as a source of power and security which overseas commitments, not required by the country's economic and security interests, would seriously diminish.

---

[87]"Marcellus," in Ford, *Writings of John Quincy Adams*, 1:140, 146.
[88]Richardson, *Messages and Papers of the Presidents*, 1:222–23.

For John Marshall the Atlantic was an effective obstacle to European invasion. He advised a Richmond audience in 1798 that the United States, if united and awake to any impending danger, could successfully defend its independence.[89] Prudent policy, therefore, would limit the political interests of the United States to the Western Hemisphere where the nation's geographic insulation would contribute to the defense of those interests.

In his Farewell Address, Washington acknowledged the diplomatic and military benefits that accrued from distance. "Why forego the advantages of so peculiar a situation?" he asked. "Why quit our own to stand on foreign ground? Why, by interweaving our destiny with that of any part of Europe, entangle our peace and prosperity in the toils of European ambition, rivalship, interest, humor, or caprice?" The dynastic and territorial ambitions that had driven the powers of Europe into war for centuries, Washington knew, were not the concern of the American people. "Europe has a set of primary interests which to us have none or very remote relation," he wrote; "hence she must be engaged in frequent controversies the causes of which are essentially foreign to our concerns." Washington's convictions reflected as well a realistic judgment of European power and the conclusion that the young Republic would only waste its energies if it engaged in struggles abroad that it could not control. "Our detached and distant situation," he rejoiced, "invites and enables us to pursue a different course."[90]

That balance of power, which had made independence possible, also would preserve it. As long as that balance remained, the United States could have no vital interest at stake in Europe's wars. The European equilibrium reinforced the Atlantic barrier by eliminating the possibility that any European state could generate the strength and ambition to cross the Atlantic with sufficient force to endanger the territories, much less the independence, of the United States. Such a nation soon would face an overwhelming coalition of countering power in Europe itself. If the United States maintained its freedom of action more successfully during the wars of the French Revolution than did the powers of Europe, it did so because the eighteenth-century European equilibrium seemed to guarantee the country's security. As Thomas Boylston Adams wrote with remarkable perception in October 1799, "It must always happen, so long as America is an independent Republic

[89]Marshall is quoted in Charles A. Beard, *The Open Door at Home: A Trial Philosophy of National Interest* (New York, 1935), p. 267. In this volume Beard defended the isolationism of the 1930s. He discarded the theory of national interest because he doubted that economic and class interests, added to nationalistic emotions, would ever permit a nation to determine its real interests with any clarity. Ibid., pp. 154–78.

[90]Richardson, *Messages and Papers of the Presidents*, 1:222–23.

or nation, that the balance of power in Europe will continue to be of the utmost importance to her welfare. The moment that France is victorious and Great Britain with her allies depressed, we have cause for alarm ourselves. The same is true when the reverse of this happens."[91] Such observers of the balance of power were not inclined to entrust America's security to the Atlantic alone.

Isolationism and noninterventionism, however logical and sensible for the young Republic, were not the only determinants in the evolution of American foreign policy. The United States would not and could not escape the forces for international involvement which sustained the perennial conflicts among the states of Europe. Fundamentally, three pressures would war on American isolationism. First, the country's commercial and trading interests would demand an ongoing search for formal commercial arrangements. Many Republicans, learning little from the experience of the 1790s, assumed that American commerce, because it served the interests of peoples that shared it, held the power to coerce the nations of Europe.[92] Some Jeffersonians actually believed that the United States could isolate itself from Europe's political and military strife while it involved itself deeply in European economic affairs, even in time of war. Second, democratic idealism, in defiance of Federalist advice, could assign to American diplomacy the task of promoting the cause of humanity in distant regions of the world. The country's reaction to the French Revolution demonstrated how profound could be the impact of revolutionary causes on American emotions. Third, the country's genuine interests in eliminating dangerous and competing centers of power and influence from the North American continent, or threats to the European balance of power, would compel it to enter the international arena. For a nation with broad and varied concerns, there could be little real isolation, whether in mind or in action, from the major trends and events in world affairs.

VI

For five years following the Treaty of San Lorenzo, settlers in Kentucky and Tennessee—two-thirds of the entire trans-Allegheny population— enjoyed the unimpeded navigation of the Mississippi and the right of deposit at New Orleans. Although the treaty provisions for the deposit had elapsed, boatmen faced no Spanish hindrances to the river traffic;

---

[91]Thomas Boylston Adams to Joseph Pitcairn, October 23, 1799, quoted in Bemis, *John Quincy Adams*, p. 86.
[92]Jefferson to Dr. George Logan, March 21, 1801, in Ford, *Writings of Jefferson*, 8:23.

the major impediments to western commerce lay in the difficulty of moving wagons across the mountains or propelling barges and keelboats northward from New Orleans against the river's currents. So excellent were American-Spanish relations that the future of the Southwest seemed propitious. Unknown in the United States, however, the French Directory had ordered its minister in Madrid to seek the transfer of Louisiana to France. "We alone," it argued, "can trace with strong hands the bounds for the power of the United States and the limits for their territory." French ambitions toward Louisiana languished until 1797 when Talleyrand, with his vision of empire, became the minister of foreign affairs. In Napoleon, who came to power as First Consul in the coup d'état of November 1799, Talleyrand found a leader who shared his vision. The two men planned a new French empire in America with Santo Domingo in the West Indies as its base. To acquire Louisiana, Napoleon dispatched a special mission to Madrid in July 1800. He demanded the two Floridas as well as Louisiana, and in return he promised to establish a principality in Italy for the Duke of Parma. The Spanish court balked on the question of the Floridas but ceded Louisiana in the Treaty of San Ildefonso in October 1800.[93] The French did not occupy New Orleans immediately and even denied that France had acquired the region.

Mere rumors of the retrocession of Louisiana to France were sufficient to trouble Jefferson and his secretary of state, James Madison. Rufus King reported from London in March 1801 that in all probability the rumors were true. "I am apprehensive," he added, "that this cession is intended to have, and may actually produce, effects injurious to the union and consequent happiness of the United States." Jefferson shared King's apprehensions. In May he complained to Monroe, then governor of Virginia, that the transfer of Louisiana "is a policy very unwise in both [Spain and France] and very ominous to us." In July the president explained his growing fears to the governor of the Mississippi Territory: "With respect to Spain our dispositions are sincerely amiable and even affectionate. We consider her possession of the adjacent country as most favorable to our interests, & should see, with extreme pain, any other nation substituted for them. . . . Should France get possession of that country, it will be more to be lamented than remedied by us."[94] During subsequent months Jefferson sought the terms of the treaty through Robert R. Livingston, his minister in Paris, cautioning him to

[93]Mildred Stahl Fletcher, "Louisiana as a Factor in French Diplomacy from 1763 to 1800," *Mississippi Valley Historical Review* 16 (March 1930): 373–75.

[94]King to Madison, March 29, 1801, in *American State Papers: Foreign Relations* (Washington, 1832), 2:509; Jefferson to Monroe, May 26, 1801, in Ford, *Writings of Jefferson*, 8:58; Jefferson to William C. C. Claiborne, July 13, 1801, in ibid., pp. 71–72.

do or say nothing that might "unnecessarily irritate our future neigh-bors."[95] Despite King's insistence that he had seen the treaty, Liv-ingston received only denials that the treaty existed.

Finally, in the spring of 1802, Livingston informed the admin-istration that the treaty transferring Louisiana did indeed exist. Jef-ferson's noted response of April 18 acknowledged that the United States had few interests in conflict with France, but he added: "There is on the globe one single spot, the possessor of which is our natural and habitual enemy. It is New Orleans, through which the produce of three-eighths of our territory must pass to market. . . . France, placing herself at that door, assumes to us the attitude of defiance." Spain, wrote Jefferson, might have retained Louisiana quietly for years. That coun-try's feeble state would induce it to increase American facilities there and perhaps in time cede it to the United States in exchange for some-thing of greater value. He wondered why France would want to hold a region so valueless in time of peace and so vulnerable in time of war. France, he reasoned, could best reconcile its interests with those of the United States by ceding New Orleans and the Floridas.[96] The ensuing summer months brought no relief from the growing tension. The pres-ident admitted to Livingston in October that his earlier assumptions regarding the generally mutual interests between the United States and France had proved to be erroneous.[97]

On October 18, 1802, the acting Spanish intendant at New Orleans published a proclamation closing the American depot. What rendered the measure especially ominous was the assumption that Napoleon had ordered it. The closing of the right of deposit released fears that France now endangered the entire American position in the Southwest. The excitement seemed justified; the Mississippi, wrote Madison, was "the Hudson, the Delaware, the Potomac and all the navigable rivers of the Atlantic States formed into one stream." The intendant's proclamation did not interfere with the American right to free navigation of the Mississippi, but the withdrawal of the deposit impaired the river's value. Jefferson saw immediately that the gravest impediment to a proper national response lay not in Paris or Madrid but in his Federalist opposition, which seemed determined to exploit the crisis by attributing the French problem to the alleged weakness of the Republican admin-istration. Caught between Napoleon on one side and the Federalists on the other, the president adopted a policy of procrastination. In his December message to Congress he made no reference at all to the closing

[95]Madison to Livingston, September 28, 1801, in *American State Papers: Foreign Relations*, 2:510–11.
[96]Jefferson to Livingston, April 18, 1802, in Ford, *Writings of Jefferson*, 8:144–47.
[97]Jefferson to Livingston, October 10, 1802, ibid., pp. 172–73.

of the depot. Jefferson saw clearly that the West would be the critical battleground in the coming struggle for power. In January 1803 the Federalists inaugurated their bid for western support by pushing a resolution through the House, demanding information from the president relating to the retrocession of Louisiana to France.[98] Hamilton, as "Pericles," continued the attack on Jefferson in the *New York Evening Post*, proposing that the president either negotiate for New Orleans and ask for a declaration of war should the negotiation fail, or seize New Orleans as a prelude to negotiation. Hamilton favored the second alternative, declaring the seizure of New Orleans a simple matter, especially if supported by negotiations with London. "If the President would adopt this course," he wrote, "he might yet retain his character, . . . exalt himself in the eyes of Europe, save the country, and secure a permanent fame. But for this, alas! Jefferson is not destined."[99]

Jefferson met the Federalist challenge by nominating Monroe for an extraordinary mission to France, and on January 12, 1803 the Senate confirmed the nomination. Jefferson then urged Monroe to accept: "Were you to decline, the chagrin would be universal. . . . I know nothing which would produce such a shock, for on the event of this mission depends the future destinies of this republic."[100] Monroe's appointment was especially reassuring to the West; no one in public life was more directly tied to western interests. Jefferson had no reason to believe that Monroe could resolve the Mississippi question. His purpose of acquiring New Orleans and the Floridas, he admitted, was a measure "liable to assume so many shapes, that no instructions could be squared to fit them." Jefferson instructed Monroe to go wherever he chose—to Paris, Madrid, or London—and to negotiate any arrangement he could, because he suspected that Monroe would achieve nothing.[101]

On February 3 the president explained to Livingston that the country's belligerent mood had forced him to seek a settlement even against hopeless odds. What the situation required was patience and

---

[98]Arthur Preston Whitaker, *The Mississippi Question, 1795–1803* (New York, 1934), p. 206; Jefferson's second annual message, December 15, 1802, in *Annals of Congress*, 12:12–15. Hamilton complained in late December that Jefferson's "last *lullaby* message, instead of inspiring contempt, attracts praise." Hamilton to Charles Cotesworth Pinckney, December 29, 1802, in Syrett, *Papers of Hamilton*, 26:71; Theodore Sedgwick to Hamilton, January 27, 1803, ibid., p. 80. Sedgwick declared that the country's interests were being sacrificed in Louisiana.

[99]"Pericles" appeared in the *New York Evening Post*, February 8, 1803, ibid., pp. 83–84. Quotation is found on p. 85.

[100]Jefferson to Monroe, January 12, 1803, quoted in Whitaker, *The Mississippi Question*, p. 207.

[101]Ibid., pp. 208–09.

the public's confidence in peaceful measures, but the opposition, Jefferson complained, had raised the cry of war, encouraged the western inhabitants to seize New Orleans on their own authority, and introduced a series of inflammatory resolutions for Congress's adoption. Monroe's official communications to Livingston would be full and detailed; the president would not repeat them. However, he added that "the future destinies of our country hang on the event of this negotiation, and I am sure they could not be placed in more able or more zealous hands. On our parts we shall be satisfied that what you do not effect, cannot be effected."[102] After Monroe's departure the nation's mood became more complacent; Hamilton and his congressional allies failed in their nationalistic assault on the western mind. The leaders of Kentucky and Tennessee doubted that they could capture New Orleans or hold it if they did.[103]

Jefferson's acquisition of Louisiana was no calculated maneuver to serve the interests of American farmers. It is true that the noted Virginian regarded farming as the true foundation of the Republic; he was, moreover, an expansionist. He anticipated the time when North America would be covered by people speaking the same language and governed by similar laws, but he had not anticipated the expansion of the Republic. For Jefferson the United States would comprise a parent nation, nothing more, scattering its people and institutions over the continent. Even after the purchase of Louisiana he did not assume that the far Northwest would be other than a separate nation.

Finally, Jefferson's interest in the Far West was less agricultural than commercial. From an early date he had sought a trade route across the continent to exploit the potential riches of the Orient. While serving in Paris, he had dispatched young John Ledyard, a Yankee sailor and explorer, to find a continental route by entering Nootka Sound from Kamchatka and eventually following the Missouri River to St. Louis. The Russian empress had ruined this mission by refusing Ledyard authority to cross Siberia, but Jefferson continued his search. What he asked of André Michaux in conducting his western explorations was that he "seek for and pursue that route which shall form the shortest and most convenient communication between the high parts of the Missouri and the Pacific Ocean." The president's instructions to Meriwether Lewis in 1803 showed commercial motivation in unmistakable terms. "The object of your mission," he charged the

---

[102]Jefferson to Livingston, February 3, 1803, in Ford, *Writings of Jefferson*, 8:209–10.

[103]For western views of the Mississippi question see Whitaker, *The Mississippi Question*, pp. 216–19, 228.

frontiersman, "is to explore the Missouri River, and such principal streams of it, as by its course and communication with the waters of the Pacific Ocean, may offer the most direct and practicable water communication across the continent for the purposes of commerce." For Jefferson the object of continental expansion was as much the acquisition of a passage through Oregon to the Pacific as it was the acquisition of land.

The Louisiana Purchase was a diplomatic windfall, neither anticipated nor pursued. Jefferson's communications to Livingston and others admitted a deep concern for the acquisition of New Orleans and the Floridas, but nothing more. In explaining the Monroe mission to Livingston, the president again pointed to New Orleans as the area of friction and the object of American diplomacy. While waiting for Monroe's arrival, Livingston seized upon the growing hostility between Britain and France to remind the French government of the advantages of parting with New Orleans and thereby preventing any alliance between Britain and the United States. On March 8 he wrote to King in London: "I am laboring to pave the way for Mr. Monroe and I think I have got every man about the court to think as I do on the subject of Louisiana but as you know there is but one head here—I have addressed a very strong letter to the consul himself."[104] Suddenly Napoleon's dream of a New World empire collapsed when yellow fever destroyed much of his army in Santo Domingo, permitting Negro slaves to overthrow French rule and gain control of the colony.

Despite Livingston's preachments, Napoleon continued to stall. Finally, in March reports of British mobilization convinced him that Louisiana had become a burden. The Marquis de Barbé-Marbois, Napoleon's minister of the treasury, reported the First Consul's reaction: "Irresolution and deliberation are no longer in season. I renounce Louisiana." Napoleon's ministers closed in on Livingston, offering to sell the whole of Louisiana, but Livingston argued that the United States wanted only New Orleans and the Floridas. When the French government insisted on selling all of Louisiana, he proceeded to haggle over the price. His reluctance placed Barbé-Marbois, the French negotiator, in the strange role of explaining the advantages that would accrue to the United States from the acquisition of all Louisiana.[105] Eventually Livingston and Monroe, on April 30, 1803, signed a treaty

---

[104]Livingston to King, March 8, 1803, in Edward Alexander Parsons, ed., "The Letters of Robert R. Livingston," *Proceedings of the American Antiquarian Society* 52 (1942): 389–90.
[105]François Barbé-Marbois, *The History of Louisiana*, ed. E. Wilson Lyon (Baton Rouge, LA, 1977), p. 274; Livingston to Madison, April 13, 1803, in *House Ex. Doc. No. 4531*, 57th Cong., 2d sess., 1902–03, pp. 159–63.

which transferred Louisiana to the United States at the bargain price of $15 million. That purchase not only assured the United States control of the Mississippi Valley, but also it gave the nation rights to frontage on the Pacific. Still, the United States acquired only the French claims to the North American continent; establishing the boundaries of Louisiana would require further negotiations with London and Madrid.

VII

When Jefferson entered the presidency, Britain continued to monopolize American trade with superior products and ample credit. France still barred the United States from much of its imperial trade. With the return of war in 1803 the struggle between France and Great Britain—one supreme on land, the other supreme on the oceans—again ventured onto the Atlantic. Lord Nelson's destruction of the French fleet at Trafalgar in 1805 symbolized Britain's unprecedented command of the seas. British maritime supremacy, however, counted for little if France, driven from the seas by the Royal Navy, consigned its imperial trade to neutral carriers. To deny France its West Indian colonial trade, the British government insisted that Americans obey the principle of the broken voyage by unloading, storing, and paying duties on all goods imported from the French colonies. When it became obvious that American officials often cleared untouched cargoes for the ports of continental Europe, the British, in the *Essex* prize case of 1805, reasserted the British doctrine of continuous voyage.[106]

The *Essex* ruling declared flatly that a cargo's ultimate destination determined its nationality. Defending the British decision in his pamphlet, *War in Disguise*, James Stephen accused the United States of taking advantage of the European war at Britain's expense. The decision reestablished the Rule of 1756, that trade prohibited in time of peace could not be opened in time of war. No longer would Britain permit neutrals to carry the goods of the enemy with impunity under the guns of the British navy. In 1806 the British government declared a blockade of much of the European coast, a blockade rendered legitimate, at least in Britain's eyes, by the strength and reach of its naval power.

Britain's navy, carrying the burden of that country's war against Napoleon, faced a problem of desertion that threatened its effectiveness. For sailors a British warship approximated a floating hell. The expanding U.S. merchant marine, demanding four or five thousand additional

---

[106]Burton Spivak, *Jefferson's English Crisis: Commerce, Embargo, and the Republican Revolution* (Charlottesville, VA, 1979), pp. 15–25.

personnel each year, offered better wages, food, and living conditions. Thus the American carrying trade emerged as a special challenge not only to the British economy but also to the navy itself. To preserve its naval power, the London government exerted the right to stop American vessels and search them for British deserters. British policy stopped at the line where American sovereignty barred the pursuit of fugitives, and London claimed no British right to search within the territorial waters of the United States or to stop U.S. war vessels. It insisted only on the right to search private vessels on the high seas.

The United States, on the other hand, claimed no immunity from search in English territorial waters, nor did it question the traditional right of British warships to search private vessels for contraband in time of war. Furthermore, it denied that it had any intention of covering British deserters with the American flag. What troubled Americans was the too frequent British impressment of American seamen, rendered easy and defensible by similarities in language and appearance.[107] Eventually impressed American seamen served an essential role in the Royal Navy.

Jefferson faced the choice of accepting the *Essex* decision as a legitimate expression of British interests or attempting to remove it with argument, economic coercion, or diplomacy. Earlier he had attacked foreign commerce that fed on war as dangerous. In 1787 he had warned Americans not to become, in their pursuit of wartime profits, "sea-robbers under French colours," but in 1805 he was prepared to claim commerce tied to a foreign war as a natural right. Responding to the clamor for profits, as well as his own Anglophobia, he would defend America's neutral rights with whatever legal and moral arguments were required. He was soon convinced that Great Britain benefited as much from American neutral trade as did France; the ports of the United States provided enormous markets for English manufactured goods.

Madison himself, in a long pamphlet of January 1806 entitled *An Examination of the British Doctrine*, attempted to refute the *Essex* ruling. Jefferson was delighted. "I send you a pamphlet," he informed a friend the following month, "in which the British doctrine that a commerce not open to neutrals in peace shall not be pursued by them in war is logically and unanswerably refuted."[108] Economic coercion, more dangerous than argument, had a more limited appeal. Southerners, engaged in a direct commodity trade with Britain, opposed any threat to exclude

[107]For a superb discussion of impressment see A. L. Burt, *The United States, Great Britain and British North America, from the Revolution to the Establishment of Peace After the War of 1812* (New Haven, CT, 1940), pp. 211–14.

[108]Jefferson to Pierre Samuel du Pont de Nemours, February 12, 1806, Thomas Jefferson Papers, Library of Congress. For this letter I am indebted to Burton Spivak.

British vessels from American ports; some wondered whether the carrying trade was worth the risk required to sustain it. The Non-Importation Act of April 1806 was a half-hearted congressional attempt at coercion, with the implementation date postponed until December. For conservative John Randolph of Virginia the measure was merely "a dose of chicken broth to be taken nine months hence."[109]

In April 1806, Jefferson dispatched William Pinkney of Maryland to join Monroe, the minister at London, to negotiate a treaty embodying a British acknowledgment of American neutral rights as well as an effectual remedy for the practice of impressment. The negotiators were to reestablish the principle of the broken voyage and to secure indemnity for illegal seizures under the *Essex* ruling. Jefferson hoped that Britain, by reducing its restraints, would enable the United States to become genuinely neutral and "truly useful to both belligerents."[110] Monroe and Pinkney raised the question of impressment; the British promised to moderate their practices but would not concede the right of impressment by treaty. When word reached the Capitol in Washington that Monroe and Pinkney intended to negotiate a treaty that did not eliminate impressment, Madison, on February 3, 1807, informed the American negotiators that the president would reject any such agreement.

Signed in December 1806, the treaty already was on its way across the Atlantic, arriving in Washington on March 3. Jefferson informed Congress, about to adjourn, that he would not recall the Senate to consider the treaty; the absence of a satisfactory article on impressment ruled that out. In addition, the president discovered that Monroe and Pinkney had agreed to make any withdrawal of British restrictions contingent on American resistance to French commercial policy. For Jefferson that provision would compel the United States to join Britain in a common cause against France.[111] Later Monroe explained that he and Pinkney violated their instructions for fear that the failure of their negotiations would bring a war for which the United States was not prepared.[112]

During 1807 American commerce became trapped in a massive commercial war between Britain and France. In November 1806, the

---

[109]Randolph quoted in Merrill D. Peterson, *Thomas Jefferson and the New Nation* (New York, 1970), p. 829.

[110]Jefferson to James Bowdoin, July 10, 1806, in Lipscomb and Bergh, *Writings of Jefferson*, 11:118–21.

[111]Madison to Monroe and Pinkney, February 3, 1807, in *American State Papers: Foreign Relations*, 3:153–56; John Quincy Adams's diary, March 3, 1807, in Allan Nevins, ed., *Diary of John Quincy Adams, 1794–1845* (New York, 1951), p. 45.

[112]Monroe to Theodore Lyman, Jr., April 1817, in Hamilton, *Writings of Monroe*, 6:19–21.

Emperor Napoleon responded to the British blockade with his Berlin Decree which proclaimed a paper blockade of the British Isles to prohibit all neutral commerce with Great Britain. By threatening to seize any vessel that stopped at a British port, Napoleon hoped to deprive Britain of its European markets. London responded with its Order in Council of January 7, 1807, which outlawed all neutral commerce between ports under French control. Any neutral vessel that proceeded from one such port to another, after a British warning not to do so, would be subject to capture and condemnation as a lawful prize.

On March 12, David M. Erskine, the British minister to Washington, delivered the January order to Madison. "Neutral nations," he explained, "cannot . . . expect that the King should suffer the commerce of his enemies to be carried on through them, whilst they submit to the prohibition which France has decreed against the commerce of His Majesty's subjects."[113] Madison observed that London had no way of knowing what effect Napoleon's decree would have on American shipping. Certainly the United States would not acquiesce in the infringement of its neutral rights by any belligerent. Then, on March 29, Madison reminded Erskine that the British Order in Council would interfere with America's "customary mode of trading with the continent of Europe." Seldom did American ship captains visit only one European port to dispose of or acquire cargo. To compel them to do so, Madison complained, would be "as ruinous to our commerce as contrary to our essential rights."[114]

These new restrictions on Europe's coastal trade, added to the British doctrine of continuous voyage, threatened all American commerce with the European continent. Together Britain and France subjected any neutral vessel in European waters to seizure—inside the harbors if they had stopped at a British port, outside the harbors if they had not. In theory London and Paris were equally oppressive; legally they were not. Except for occasional captures by French vessels, Napoleon's seizures were inside ports under his direct control. British seizures were at sea and thus violations of neutral rights as recognized by international law. Essentially, neither the British nor the Americans could detect any justice in the other's cause. Napoleon's assertions that Britain sought no less than a monopoly of world commerce merely exacerbated American bitterness toward British behavior on the high seas. Still, Jefferson was determined to avoid a crisis with Britain. Publicly he rejected the Monroe-Pinkney Treaty only because of its

---

[113]Lord Howick to Monroe, January 10, 1807, in *American State Papers: Foreign Relations*, 3:2; Erskine to Madison, March 12, 1807, ibid., p. 158.
[114]Madison to Erskine, March 20, 29, 1807, ibid., pp. 158–59.

failure to eliminate impressment; he refused to quarrel openly with the treaty's commercial clauses. In December 1806 the president had deferred the operation of the Non-Importation Act to await the results of the Monroe-Pinkney negotiations. In March 1807, out of deference to Britain, he again postponed the decision to enforce the act, at least until December.[115]

Amid the continuing quarrel with Britain over impressment and commercial policy, Jefferson faced the *Chesapeake* crisis. On June 22, 1807, the American warship *Chesapeake* sailed from Hampton Roads only to be stopped by the British frigate *Leopard* within American territorial waters. When the *Chesapeake*'s captain refused to permit a muster of his crew, insisting that he had no British subjects aboard, the *Leopard* opened fire on the U.S. vessel, took it captive, and removed four American sailors from the ship. The badly damaged *Chesapeake* then returned to port. Clearly the British had violated the established rules of maritime warfare. In seizing the *Chesapeake* they had denied the immunity of a national ship of war, had seized the ship in American waters, and had removed men ascertained to be U.S. citizens. Madison immediately ordered Monroe to demand a formal disavowal of the incident, a restoration of the four seamen, and the abolition of impressment from vessels under the flag of the United States. Should the British refuse satisfaction, the minister should prepare to return to the United States and suspend negotiations on all other subjects. On July 17, Madison complained to Monroe that the British continued their insolence by detaining and examining merchant vessels in American waters.[116]

In part Jefferson's judgment of America's interests in the European struggle against Napoleon reflected his perception of the ever changing distribution of power. When war returned to Europe in 1803, Jefferson followed the struggle with outward aloofness. Conscious of the protections afforded by the Atlantic, he wrote in October: "Tremendous times in Europe! How mighty this battle of lions & Tygers! With what sensations should the common herd of cattle look on it? With no partialities, certainly."[117] After Britain's naval triumph at Trafalgar and Napoleon's great victory at Austerlitz, European power became so polarized that the president could exert no leverage on either side. Napoleon's success, however, troubled Jefferson, forcing him to

[115]Jefferson to Congress, December 3, 1806, in Ford, *Writings of Jefferson*, 10:320–22.

[116]Report to the House of Representatives, November 17, 1807, in *American State Papers: Foreign Relations*, 3:6–7; Madison to Monroe, July 6, 17, 1807, in Gaillard Hunt, ed., *The Writings of James Madison* (New York, 1908), 7:454–58, 463.

[117]Jefferson to Benjamin Rush, October 4, 1803, in Ford, *Writings of Jefferson*, 8:265.

consider an alliance with Britain. Soon British insolence forced him back into a posture of neutrality, although he continued to believe that the emperor endangered the balance of power and thus the long-range security of the United States. In 1806, Jefferson still favored "an English ascendancy on the ocean [as being] safer for us than that of France." However, in the wake of the *Chesapeake* affair, he confessed that "I never expected to be under the necessity of wishing success to Buonaparte. But the English being equally tyrannical at sea as he is on land, & the tyranny bearing on us in every point of either honor or interest, I say 'down with England' and as for what Buonaparte is then to do to us, let us trust to the chapter of accidents. I cannot with the Anglomen, prefer a certain present evil to a future hypothetical one."[118]

Jefferson's troubles in Europe were only beginning. Following his great victories at Jena and Friedland, Napoleon believed that he had at last gained mastery of Europe, especially when he persuaded Czar Alexander to extend the Continental System to Russian ports. During the late summer of 1807, Napoleon began to enforce his Berlin Decree with numerous seizures in the ports of Europe. The British retaliated with their famous Order in Council of November 11, 1807, which declared a blockade of all countries in the Napoleonic system, as well as their colonies, and condemned their products as lawful prizes. Napoleon then tightened his restrictions on Britain with his Milan Decree of December 17, 1807. Now any neutral ship, whether sailing from a British port or subjected to British search, lost its neutral character and became vulnerable to seizure by the French. These profound pressures on American neutral rights, with their corresponding assaults on American emotions, compelled Jefferson to terminate the drift in U.S. policy toward Europe's warring powers. Five days after Napoleon's Milan Decree the president recommended to Congress an embargo on all American vessels departing for foreign ports. After a brief debate the Republican majorities in Congress committed the country to Jefferson's program. Despite the American vessels at sea, which continued to carry on a profitable commerce, and the smuggling along the Canadian border, American officials shut off the nation's foreign commerce with reasonable effectiveness.

Unfortunately, the embargo produced far more coercion at home than abroad. The more economic coercion failed in Europe, the more the president required special measures to restrain his fellow citizens who regarded the embargo as a needless and inconsistent infringement on their commercial interests. New England merchants, Federalists by political preference, resented the administration's enforcement policies.

[118] Jefferson to Thomas Leiper, August 21, 1807, ibid., 9:130.

Jefferson soon lost interest in the embargo; for him it was always a temporary measure to be continued or terminated as conditions demanded. Still, he knew that any abandonment of the embargo before the British repealed their Orders in Council would leave American policy nowhere to go.[119] Whatever the dangers in failure, however, the embargo was doomed. A long-term embargo would face an outraged public; a short-term one would have no effect on Europe whatever. Dissident Republicans and New England Federalists favored abandonment, convinced that the embargo's ineffectiveness, prolonging and aggravating the country's frustrations, would eventually trap it in war.

When the administration finally turned the embargo into a weapon of coercion, it sought the power to coerce, not in the embargo itself, but in the threat of war should the embargo fail. To determine what European power would be the victim, the administration informed London and Paris that the embargo would end by December 1808; thereafter, the United States would resume trade with the belligerent that removed its restrictions and declare war on the other. If both belligerents responded favorably, the United States would have its trade without the price of war; if neither did, the United States, in Jefferson's words, would take its choice of enemies. These warnings had a decidedly pro-French bias. Madison reminded Paris that the United States asked little of it because the enforcement of the Continental System against Britain was so completely in the hands of France's land power. Both Britain and France rejected the American offers, but Madison wondered why the French would refuse an arrangement that demanded so small a sacrifice. Had they obliged, would Jefferson have favored war with Great Britain? He had adopted a predictably futile policy because every alternative seemed worse.

Jefferson's approach to the question of neutral rights reflected the peculiar self-centeredness that had come to characterize the country's external relations. In 1808 his policies could no longer distinguish between actions that injured American interests by intent from those that rendered harm as the result of struggles that really had little to do with the United States. One Pennsylvanian observed in late 1807: "[England and France] are engaged in a conflict upon the point of extermination. The weapons they employ, though they wound us, are only meant for each other. Let us act on that idea, and we may preserve our peace without sacrificing either our honor or our property."[120] Jefferson could have accepted that idea only if he were free to measure

---

[119]On the relationship of the embargo to war see Spivak, *Jefferson's English Crisis*, pp. 103–36.

[120]Alexander Dallas to Albert Gallatin, December 23, 1807, Albert Gallatin Papers, New York University. For this quotation I am indebted to Burton Spivak.

the nation's self-interest by the interests of others. Rather than acknowledge the predominant concerns of the warring countries, however, he sought to elevate America's neutral rights, and the immense profits they assured, to a higher order of importance through legal and moral argument. Blinded by the conviction that they were defending the world's long-term interests in law and justice, the Jeffersonians refused to compromise with Britain on any issue. For them any reasonable agreement on impressment was unacceptable because it would have injured U.S. commerce; there were simply too many English seamen on American merchant vessels. Compromises were available on matters of commerce, but the Jeffersonians, determined to protect the lucrative French carrying trade, never acknowledged any legitimacy or relevance in Britain's interests, commitments, or objectives. Their refusal to see the maritime struggle between Britain and France as more than an annoying and unnecessary impediment to America's own commercial and agricultural development eventually extracted its price in an unwanted war.

CHAPTER
FIVE

James Madison, Neutral Rights, and the War of 1812*

JAMES MADISON inherited the presidency both as Thomas Jefferson's secretary of state and as an indefatigible laborer in the Republican cause. In the best of times he had never shared Jefferson's unique standing in American life. The younger Virginian merited the country's approbation, but the appreciation he enjoyed flowed less from his personal qualities of leadership than from his remarkable achievements of mind in various matters of public concern. Unfortunately, in March 1809 the times were not propitious. British and French defiance of Jefferson's coercive efforts in behalf of American neutral rights had divided the country into angry factions and undermined Jefferson's control of Congress. Madison understood well the difficulties which the country faced abroad, yet that knowledge alone offered no solutions. Dealing from weakness in the face of powerful, antagonistic interests, the United States would experience frustration and ignominy if it pressed its claims and continued impositions if it did not. Madison's inaugural address acknowledged the diminishing choices confronting the nation: "The present situation of the world is indeed without a parallel, and that of our own country full of difficulties."[1] Madison had intended to name the able Albert Gallatin as his secretary of state, but, out of

*This essay is based on an address delivered at the James Madison Conference, University of Virginia, March 1981.
[1]Madison's First Inaugural, March 4, 1809, in Gaillard Hunt, ed., *The Writings of James Madison* (New York, 1908), 8:47.

123

deference to senatorial pressure, he kept Gallatin at Treasury and placed Robert Smith, Jefferson's secretary of the navy, over the State Department. Under any circumstance Madison would have exerted direct control over his administration's foreign policies; Smith's incompetence merely rendered it necessary.[2]

Except for the short peace of Amiens, Britain and France had been struggling for the mastery of Europe for sixteen years, forcing the other powers to take sides as interests and opportunities permitted. Napoleon, dominant on the Continent, desired to bring down British naval supremacy by cutting off Britain's European trade and ruining its economy. London, however, would retain its control over the seas and simultaneously strike at Napoleon's Continental System by denying France the benefit of America's wartime carrying trade. Both governments gave U.S. leaders the choice of accepting massive infringements on the country's neutral rights as the price of peace, or of engaging its interests, emotions, and prestige by demanding satisfaction from the warring giants. In choosing the latter course they assumed the risk of elevating America's wartime claims to levels where continued European defiance could become intolerable. America's commerce in the Atlantic had totally outrun the country's power to defend it. This compelled the United States to rely solely on the strength of its arguments, forgetting that in time of war countries are not always guided by reason. The embargo had not been an insignificant weapon. To John Quincy Adams it had indeed affected Europe's interests, but nations, he wrote in December 1808, "which sacrifice men by the hundred thousands and treasure by the hundred millions in War, for *nothing*, or worse than nothing, pay little attention to their real interests."[3]

Despite the failure of American diplomacy throughout 1808 to secure the country's neutral rights, peace remained tolerable enough. Congress, with the Non-Intercourse Act of March 1809, embarked on a potentially more effective policy, which not only terminated all commerce with Britain and France but also promised to restore trade with either belligerent should it agree to recognize American rights on the seas. Madison had pressed Congress for passage of the latter provision. The new president issued a quiet assurance to both European powers that a favorable action by either would provoke American retaliation against the other. In practice, nonintercourse, with its exclusion of all British and French vessels from American ports, injured Britain more than France; the British navy long had driven most French ships off

[2]Irving Brant, *James Madison: The President, 1809–1812* (Indianapolis, 1956), p. 25.
[3]Adams is quoted in Bradford Perkins, *Prologue to War: England and the United States, 1805–1812* (Berkeley, CA, 1961), p. 151.

the seas; therefore, it was hoped that Britain would respond by repealing its hated Orders in Council, rather than imposing new forms of retaliation. Madison reminded British minister David M. Erskine that Britain faced dangerously degenerating relations with the United States unless it made adequate concessions and thereby directed American animosity toward France. "I continue to be firmly persuaded," Erskine informed Foreign Minister George Canning on February 10, "that Mr. Madison . . . would most willingly seize the first opportunity of recommending to the next Congress to assert the neutral rights of the United States against France, should his Majesty . . . cause his Orders in Council to be withdrawn."[4]

Canning responded favorably to the nonimportation system. In the event of a British-American trade agreement, however, Canning wondered how the United States intended to keep its vessels, cleared for Britain, from entering the ports of France. Would the United States object to the use of the British navy in preventing illegal trade with the Continent?[5] Canning informed Erskine that London would respond to American impartiality with the withdrawal of its orders of January and November 1807, if the United States would withdraw its trade restrictions regarding Britain, thus leaving them in force against France; renounce its wartime carrying trade with the French colonies; and permit Britain to capture U.S. vessels attempting to trade with Continental ports in violation of American law.[6] American leaders readily accepted the first of Canning's three conditions but rejected the second and third. For Gallatin the issue of colonial trade was unrelated to the revocation of the Orders in Council; permitting British warships to enforce American law on the seas would be degrading in the extreme.[7] Still, Erskine believed the area of agreement sufficient to permit an immediate accord with the United States.

II

During April 1809, Erskine informed Smith that new instructions from London authorized him to settle all outstanding issues with the United States. The two men quickly negotiated a partial resolution of the *Chesapeake* affair. Then, on April 18, Erskine brought the welcome news that the British king would withdraw his Orders in Council of January

[1]Brant, *James Madison*, p. 35.

[5]Conversations between Canning and Pinkney, January 18, 22, 1809, in *American State Papers: Foreign Relations* (Washington, 1832), 3:299–300.

[6]Canning to Erskine, January 23, 1809, ibid., pp. 300–01.

[7]Gallatin to Erskine, August 13, 1809, ibid., p. 307; Gallatin to Jackson, October 9, 1809, ibid., p. 308.

and November 1807, effective on June 10, if the president would issue a proclamation for the renewal of trade with Great Britain.[8] Madison accepted the offer without hesitation and on April 19 proclaimed that the British withdrawal of the Orders in Council, effective June 10, would renew the trade of the United States with Great Britain. He explained his apparent good fortune to Jefferson: "The B. Cabinet must have changed its course under the full conviction that an adjustment with this country had become essential." The president anticipated a full response from France as well, observing to Jefferson that, "if France be not bereft of common sense, or be not predetermined on war with us, she will certainly not play into the hand of her enemy."[9] What troubled the administration, however, was the British order of April 26, 1809, which opened neutral commerce in all European ports not actually French but failed to abrogate the Order in Council of January 1807. The new order left British policy fundamentally unchanged. Erskine assured Smith that the British government would fulfill all the terms of the recent agreement.[10]

During May, Canning received Erskine's proposed agreement and rejected it. Erskine, he informed Minister William Pinkney, had acted in direct contradiction to his instructions. Canning had insisted on the right of British cruisers to stop U.S. vessels violating American law. But Erskine, Pinkney reported,

> had obtained no pledge, express or implied, . . . that we would enforce our non-intercourse system against *France* and her dependencies; that our actual system would, if not re-enacted or continued as to France, terminate with the present session of Congress; that . . . the embargo and non-intercourse laws . . . might even be repealed immediately, notwithstanding the perseverance of France in her Berlin and other edicts; and that Mr. Erskine had in truth secured nothing more . . . than the renewal of American intercourse with Great Britain.[11]

On July 31, Erskine told Smith that the British government had rejected the provisional agreement. Unable to explain the discrepancy between his instructions and his actions, he assured Smith that he had no intention of practicing any deception toward the government of the United States. "The disavowal, by His Majesty," Erskine informed

[8] Erskine to Smith, April 18, 1809, quoted in Hunt, *Writings of Madison*, 8:51.

[9] Madison to Jefferson, April 24, 1809, ibid., pp. 52–53.

[10] Madison to Lafayette, May 1, 1809, ibid., p. 56; Madison to Jefferson, June 20, 1809, ibid., pp. 62–63; *American State Papers: Foreign Relations*, 3:297.

[11] Canning to Pinkney, May 27, 1809, ibid., p. 301; Pinkney to Smith, June 23, 1809, ibid., p. 303.

Smith, "is a painful proof to me that I had formed an erroneous judgment of His Majesty's views and the intention of my instructions."[12] The British disavowal had no influence on French policy. On August 9, Madison issued another proclamation, withdrawing all trade concessions that resulted from the suspension of the Non-Intercourse Act. The embarrassed president explained to Jefferson that he had acted hastily both to avoid delay in obtaining British trade and to bring pressure to bear on France to follow the British example.[13] For Madison, Canning's behavior was inexplicable.

Canning replaced Erskine with Francis J. Jackson, who arrived in Washington during September 1809 without instructions to explain the disavowal of Erskine's proposal, to propose financial compensation for the *Chesapeake* affair, or to offer any arrangement leading to a revocation of the British Orders in Council. The president was dismayed, Smith explained to Pinkney, "on finding that he [Jackson] had not been charged to make to this Government either the frank explanations or the liberal propositions which the occasion manifestly required."[14] Madison concluded by mid-September that Jackson would make no conciliatory overtures. To counter Britain's temporizing policy, he suggested to Smith that the United States compel Jackson to explain his mission. Smith then conveyed the president's anger to Jackson by restricting him to any written communications.[15] Without awaiting his government's response, Jackson accused the administration of violating his essential rights as British minister without charging him with any misconduct. The administration expected him to discard the second and third conditions, which London imposed on Erskine, as irrelevant and to offer a new arrangement based essentially on the principles of the Erskine proposal. Instead, Jackson reaffirmed his government's right to execute American laws on the high seas as part of any compact against France. He reminded Smith that Erskine had ignored his instructions and that the three conditions that London imposed were well known to the American government.[16]

When it became clear in November that Jackson would offer no further British initiatives, Smith informed the British minister that the administration would accept no more communications from him, even in writing. Jackson withdrew to New York to await instructions from

[12] Erskine to Smith, August 14, 1809, ibid., p. 306.

[13] Madison to Jefferson, August 16, 1809, in Hunt, *Writings of Madison*, 8:68–69.

[14] Smith to Pinkney, November 23, 1809, in *American State Papers: Foreign Relations*, 3:319.

[15] Madison to Smith, September 15, 1809, in Hunt, *Writings of Madison*, 8:74–75; Smith to Jackson, October 9, 1809, in *American State Papers: Foreign Relations*, 3:308.

[16] Jackson to Smith, October 11, 1809, ibid., p. 309; Smith to Pinkney, November 23, 1809, ibid., p. 320.

London. Madison explained the rejection in his first annual message to Congress on November 29, 1809:

> It could not be doubted that it [the new mission] would at least be charged with conciliatory explanations of the step which had been taken and with proposals to be substituted for the rejected arrangement. Reasonable and universal as this expectation was, it also has not been fulfilled. From the first official disclosures of the new minister it was found that he had received no authority to enter into explanations . . . nor any authority to substitute proposals.

Madison reported that the administration had carried out the acts of Congress for the equipping of American vessels of war; he recommended that Congress give serious attention to the strengthening of the militia.[17]

France acknowledged that its Continental System injured American commerce; it insisted that necessity created by Britain, not animosity, determined its policies. Unlike Britain, France accepted the principle that a merchant vessel was a floating colony; that to violate such a vessel by visit, search, and other acts of arbitrary authority violated colonial territory. "The seas," admitted the French foreign minister, the Duc de Cadore, in August 1809, "do not belong to any nation; they are the common property of mankind, and the dominion of all." When France acquired a marine equal to its coasts and population, it would practice these maxims and terminate Britain's practice of blockading rivers and coasts by proclamation. Because Britain had placed France in a state of blockade, Napoleon, by his Berlin Decree, had put the British Isles in a state of blockade. By the Orders in Council of November 1807, Britain laid a toll on neutral vessels, compelling them to pass through its ports before they could proceed to their destinations. By his decrees of December 1807, the emperor had declared that vessels violated by British action had become denationalized and subject to seizure in European ports. Britain, in short, had forced France into policies of reprisal. Should Britain revoke its blockade and its Orders in Council, the French decrees would vanish and the United States would regain its freedom on the seas. "But it is for the United States, by their firmness," cautioned the Duc de Cadore, "to bring on these happy results." A country that wished to remain free and sovereign, he admonished, could not permit its temporary interests to threaten its independence, honor, and dignity. In his message of

---

[17]Madison's First Annual Message, in Hunt, *Writings of Madison*, 8:80–83.

November 1809, Madison informed Congress that France, no more than Britain, was prepared to relinquish its pretensions.[18]

III

During January 1810, Madison authorized Pinkney to resume negotiations with London. Specifically, he instructed Pinkney to urge the British government to appoint a successor to Jackson, to settle the *Chesapeake* affair, and to negotiate a revocation of the Orders in Council. Whereas it was not clear what retaliatory measures Congress would adopt, the president would exercise any power granted him to terminate any acts of Congress which would not exist except for the Orders in Council.[19] In April, Pinkney apprised Lord Wellesley, the foreign minister, of his instructions to settle the *Chesapeake* affair, as well as the issues embodied in the Orders in Council. The French foreign minister, Pinkney reminded Wellesley on April 30, had declared that "the only condition required for the revocation by the French Government of the decree of Berlin, will be the previous revocation by the British Government, of her blockades of France . . . of a date anterior to the date of the aforesaid decree."[20] Would the British government, to repeal the Berlin Decree, announce that the chief blockade in question, that of May 1806, was no longer in force? Wellesley avoided the issue. On June 13, Pinkney complained to Smith that Wellesley had not answered his letter of April 30.[21] Two weeks later Pinkney reported again that Wellesley still had not responded. On August 8, Pinkney asked once more for a reply; he received none. Clearly, the London government no longer could be bothered by what it regarded as Washington's unreasonable demands.

During the early months of 1810, Congress searched for an effective substitute for the Non-Intercourse Act. Madison characterized the outlook of Congress in a letter to Pinkney: "Few are desirous of war; and few are reconciled to submission; yet the frustration of intermediate courses seems to have left scarce an escape from that dilemma." Madison feared that any resort to force on the high seas, using warships or armed merchant vessels, would provoke a war without the full approval

---

[18]Count Champagny [the Duc de Cadore] to Armstrong, August 22, 1809, in *American State Papers: Foreign Relations*, 3:325–26; Smith to Armstrong, December 1, 1809, ibid., p. 326.

[19]Smith to Pinkney, January 20, 1810, ibid., p. 349.

[20]Pinkney to Smith, April 8, 1810, ibid., p. 356; Pinkney to Wellesley, April 30, 1810, ibid., p. 357.

[21]Pinkney to Smith, June 13, 1810, ibid., p. 359.

of the American people.[22] Finally, on April 8, Nathaniel Macon of the House Committee on Foreign Relations introduced a bill that opened trade with Britain and France but provided that, if either country revoked its edicts before March 3, 1811 and if within three months thereafter the other nation did not repeal its decrees, the United States would make the nonintercourse regulations effective against that nation. Macon's Bill No. 2 went into effect on May 1, 1810. Two groups produced the congressional majorities, those who believed that Britain and France would respond properly and those who believed that the bill would teach the advocates of open trade in wartime the folly of their demands.[23]

Congress had instituted the embargo and the subsequent Non-Intercourse Act to enable the Jefferson and Madison administrations to negotiate a satisfactory arrangement with the European belligerents; in practice those measures had given American diplomats no leverage at all. As Congress moved on to Macon's Bill No. 2, some members concluded that the United States had been sending the wrong signals. Joseph Desha of Kentucky voiced such fears: "Sir, my anxious wish is to avert war; but, if we keep receding, we must calculate on additional encroachments; whereas, if we form a manly stand, act with firmness, show Britain that we will not abandon our pretensions, she will recede."[24] In February, Henry Clay warned Congress that the United States could no longer tolerate the ignominy of having the European powers ignore its repeated quests for peaceful commercial agreements:

> No man in the nation desires peace more than I. But I prefer the troubled ocean of war, demanded by the honor and independence of the country, with all of its calamities, and desolations, to the tranquil, putrescent pool of ignominious peace. If we can accommodate our differences with one of the belligerents only, I should prefer that one to be Great-Britain. But if with neither, and we are forced into a selection of our enemy, then am I for war with Britain; because I believe her prior in aggression.[25]

For its proponents Macon's Bill No. 2, comprising the ultimate offer available to Congress, short of absolute capitulation to European encroachments, was the final test of British and French sincerity. The failure of either country to respond to what seemed a reasonable offer

[22]Madison to Pinkney, January 20, 1810, in Hunt, *Writings of Madison*, 8:91–92.
[23]Madison to Pinkney, May 23, 1810, ibid., pp. 99–100.
[24]See Ronald L. Hatzenbuehler and Robert L. Ivie, *Congress Declares War: Rhetoric, Leadership, and Partisanship in the Early Republic* (Kent, OH, 1983), p. 117.
[25]Clay's address to Congress, February 22, 1810, in Frank F. Hopkins, ed., *The Papers of Henry Clay* (Lexington, KY, 1959), 1:449.

of permanent, mutually beneficial commercial relations would be a clear demonstration of a "fixed and determined hostility" toward the United States.

Madison was not convinced that the new policy would influence either London or Paris. "At the next meeting of Congress," he lamented in May 1810, "it will be found, according to present appearances, that instead of an adjustment with either of the belligerents, there is an increased obstinacy in both; and that the inconveniences of the embargo and non-intercourse have been exchanged for the greater sacrifices, as well as disgrace, resulting from a submission to the predatory systems of force." At the same time, he assumed correctly that the new congressional action would bear heavily on France. Neither Britain nor France could view the new law as coercive to itself, but only to the other power. Because Britain, with its control of the seas, now had full access to American trade, the act placed France in a decided position of inequality. This, Madison predicted, would compel Napoleon to revoke his decrees.[26]

Indeed, on August 5, the Duc de Cadore reminded the U.S. minister in Paris, John Armstrong, of Congress's decision to retaliate against the belligerent that refused to acknowledge American neutral rights. "In this new state of things," the French foreign minister continued, "I am authorized to declare to you . . . that the decrees of Berlin and Milan are revoked, and that after the 1st of November they will cease to have effect; it being understood that, in consequence of this declaration, the English shall revoke their orders in council . . . ; or that the United States, conformably to the act you have just communicated, shall cause their rights to be respected by the English."[27] In the interval American ships in Continental ports would be subject to the Berlin and Milan decrees. On November 2, 1810, President Madison proclaimed that France had met the requirements of Macon's Bill No. 2 and warned Britain that, unless it revoked or modified its edicts within three months, the United States would terminate all commerce between the two countries.

IV

In London, Pinkney, armed with the Cadore letter, pressed Wellesley for a response, convinced that the British government would not hesitate to repeal its commercial edicts. "I take it for granted," he addressed

---

[26]Madison to Pinkney, May 23, 1810, in Hunt, *Writings of Madison*, 8:98–100; Madison to Jefferson, May 25, 1810, ibid., p. 102.

[27]The Duc de Cadore to Armstrong, August 5, 1810, in *American State Papers: Foreign Relations*, 3:387; Cadore to Armstrong, September 7, 1810, ibid., p. 388.

the British minister on August 25, "that the revocation of the British orders in council of January and November, 1807, and April, 1809, . . . will follow in course; and I shall hope to be enabled by your lordship, with as little delay as possible, to announce to my Government that such revocation has taken place."[28] On August 31, Wellesley informed Pinkney that Britain would relinquish its system of commercial restrictions when the French had repealed their decrees.[29] During September, Pinkney returned to the question of the British blockade which he had raised in his letter of April 30. Britain, he declared, had no right to blockade an entire coast by decree. "It may now be hoped," he wrote, "that those decrees and orders are about to disappear forever." Months passed without a British answer to the revocation of the French edicts. On November 15, Pinkney complained that "I hear nothing from Lord Wellesley, and not much from any other quarter, concerning the orders in council." Finally, on December 4, Wellesley again asked Pinkney for authentic information regarding the actual repeal of the French decrees. Pinkney wondered why the British would permit their system of commercial restrictions to survive the public declarations of France.[30] If the British government distrusted French sincerity, it faced no sudden or formidable peril even if the French edicts still had some force.

Ending his long silence, Wellesley reminded Pinkney on December 29, 1810 that the French government had taken no action that could justify the repeal of the British Orders in Council. To secure the revocation of the French decrees, Britain would not hesitate to repeal the Orders in Council; it would not, however, renounce the principles of blockade, embodied in the British order of May 1806, to which the French government objected. Those principles of blockade, Wellesley asserted, reflected both established maritime practice and the deepest interests of the British nation. Britain would revoke its Orders in Council when it was clear that France had withdrawn its decrees. As yet London had no evidence.

In conclusion Wellesley added that "the justice of the American Government will not consider that France, by the repeal of her obnoxious decrees under such a condition, has placed the question in that state which can warrant America in enforcing the non-intercourse act against Great Britain and not against France."[31] Pinkney then complained to Smith: "My answer to Lord Wellesley's letter was written

---

[28]Pinkney to Wellesley, August 25, 1810, ibid., p. 365.
[29]Wellesley to Pinkney, August 31, 1810, ibid., p. 366.
[30]Pinkney to Wellesley, September 21, 1810, ibid., p. 368; Pinkney to Smith, November 15, 1810, ibid., p. 374; Wellesley to Pinkney, December 4, 1810, ibid., p. 376; Pinkney to Wellesley, December 10, 1810, ibid., pp. 376–79.
[31]Wellesley to Pinkney, December 29, 1810, ibid., pp. 408–09.

under the pressure of indisposition and the influence of more indignation than could well be supposed. His letter proves, which scarcely required proof, that if the present Government continues, we cannot be friends with England."[32] Admitting that he had failed in his effort at conciliation, Pinkney, in late February 1811, took leave of the British government. That month the United States terminated all commerce with Great Britain. Amid this growing crisis Madison reorganized his cabinet, naming James Monroe as the new secretary of state.

During subsequent months British officials, to avoid war with the United States, argued their case with extreme care. Augustus J. Foster, the new, young, and attractive British minister in Washington, assured the administration in July 1811 that his government desired "to cultivate a good understanding with the United States, by every means consistent with the preservation of the maritime rights and interests of the British empire." Until the French effectively repealed their decrees, however, London would not retreat from policies that defended the country's honor and safety. Foster argued that

> Great Britain has a right to complain that neutral nations should overlook the very worst features of those extraordinary acts, and should suffer their trade to be made a medium of an unprecedented, violent, and monstrous system of attack upon her resources. . . . Not only has America suffered her trade to be moulded into the means of annoyance to Great Britain, under the provisions of the French decrees, but, construing those decrees as extinct, upon a deceitful declaration of the French cabinet, she has enforced her non-importation act against Great Britain.[33]

He pressed the Madison administration to suspend the operation of the nonimportation act against Britain. "How desirable it would be, sir," he addressed Monroe, "if a stop could be put to any material progress in such a system of retaliation, which, from step to step, may lead to the most unfriendly situation between the two countries."[34] The blockade of May 1806 was legitimate, and so the United States regarded it, Foster recalled, until the French declared it illegal. "Why America took up the view the French Government chose to give of it, and could see in it grounds for the French decrees," he complained, "was always [a] matter of astonishment in England."[35]

[32]Pinkney to Smith, January 17, 1811, ibid., p. 408.
[33]Foster to Monroe, July 8, 1811, ibid., pp. 435, 437; Foster to Monroe, July 16, 1811, ibid., p. 439.
[34]Foster to Monroe, July 14, 1811, ibid., p. 438.
[35]Foster to Monroe, July 26, 1811, ibid., p. 443.

Foster reminded Monroe that Britain was not responsible for the gigantic war being waged in Europe. "The question between Great Britain and France," he wrote, "is that of a honorable struggle against the lawless efforts of an ambitious tyrant, and America can but have the wish of every independent nation as to its result." It was desirable, he admitted, that the United States have free and unrestricted trade with both belligerents, but, because Napoleon was determined to overthrow British maritime power, the British government was reasonable in distrusting ambiguous French declarations. "America, as not being at war, . . . may be less scrupulous as to the evidence necessary to prove the fact; but, sir," Foster added, "it surely cannot be expected that Great Britain, who is contending for every thing dear to her, should not require more proof on a point so material to her."[36] It was for Americans to judge the merit of French policy and the honesty of French professions. Britain, however, had the right to ask that the United States not treat it as an enemy.[37]

Monroe rejected the entire British argument: "It is impossible to see in [the conduct of the British government] any thing short of a spirit of determined hostility to the rights and interests of the United States." He did not deny Britain's right to retaliate against the French decrees, but to permit the effects of such policy to fall on a neutral was wrong. To enforce restrictions on the commerce of another subverted both its sovereignty and independence.[38] Belligerents, argued Monroe, had always carried on their trade through neutrals, giving nations suffering the calamities of war the advantages of a peaceful commerce. "To reverse that rule, and to extend to nations at peace the calamities of war," he charged, "is a change as novel and extraordinary as it is at variance with justice and public law." The mere revocations of the French decrees were sufficient to justify the American demand for corresponding British measures; the United States would continue to enforce its nonimportation law against Britain.[39] At the end Foster regretted that he could not reach an agreement with Madison and Monroe which would reconcile the honor, rights, and interests of their two countries. Had the United States, he recalled, resisted the French decrees, there would have been no quarrel, but, despite these decrees, America had carried on its trade with the Continent simply because the French government encouraged it with special concessions. Thus the British were compelled to retaliate with their Orders in Council.

---

[36]Foster to Monroe, October 22, 1811, ibid., p. 449.
[37]Foster to Monroe, May 30, 1812, ibid., p. 457.
[38]Monroe to Foster, January 14, 1812, ibid., p. 453.
[39]Monroe to Foster, July 23, 1811, ibid., pp. 440, 442.

What troubled Washington, however, was Foster's continuing insistence that Britain would not rescind its orders until France absolutely and unconditionally revoked its decrees. Monroe expressed amazement that the British still required proof.[40]

Privately, U.S. officials were deeply troubled by France's behavior; clearly, the success of its policy required as much a British rejection as an American acceptance of Napoleon's overtures. British demands for evidence that the French actually had revoked their decrees compelled Monroe to press Joel Barlow, the new American minister in Paris, to verify these arrangements. Monroe complained to Barlow in November 1811 of continued restrictions, including the activities of French privateers, that harassed American commerce with France. If such oppressions did not stop, he warned, Congress might impose restrictions on U.S. trade with France.[41] Barlow reminded the French government that the United States had deprived itself of much of its commerce by excluding British goods; therefore, it expected free access to all the ports of Europe. Madison expressed a similar dissatisfaction with French policy and admitted to Barlow: "Altho in our discussions with G.B. we have been justified in viewing the repeal of the Fr. Decrees as sufficiently substantiated to require a fulfillment of the pledge to repeal the Orders in Council; yet the manner in which the F. Govt. has managed the repeal of the decrees, and evaded a correction of other outrages, has mingled with the conciliatory tendency of the repeal, as much of irritation and disgust as possible." British accusations of French duplicity merely aggravated the president's embarrassment. "In fact," he complained, "without a systematic change from an appearance of crafty contrivance, and insatiate cupidity, for an open manly, & upright dealing with a nation whose example demands it, it is impossible that good will can exist."[42]

In St. Petersburg, Adams shared the administration's private disillusionment over France. He hoped that Washington would take no action against Britain before it discovered French intentions in revoking the Berlin and Milan decrees. "It is a trap to catch us into a war with England," he wrote in April 1811.[43] Four months later in August, Adams termed the Cadore letter a fair offer to Britain "combined with a contingent snare to the United States." If London rejected the offer, then France "had laid the trap which she concluded would

[40]Foster to Monroe, June 14, 1812, ibid., p. 470; Monroe to Foster, June 3, 1812, ibid., p. 460; Monroe to Foster, June 13, 1812, ibid., p. 469.

[41]Monroe to Barlow, November 21, 1811, ibid., p. 514.

[42]Madison to Barlow, November 17, 1811, in Hunt, *Writings of Madison*, 8:169.

[43]Adams to Thomas Boylston Adams, April 29, 1811, in Worthington Chauncey Ford, ed., *Writings of John Quincy Adams* (New York, 1914), 4:65.

catch us in an English war. Of the duplicity which prevailed in the French cabinet at that time," he continued, "I have had proofs that would give sight to the blind. . . . Even now France must studiously withhold all evidence of her having practically revoked the two decrees with regard to us, because the English government . . . have declared, that upon such evidence being given they will revoke the Orders in Council." Adams noted that Napoleon wanted war between the United States and Britain, as did the French ambassador in St. Petersburg. In November he urged the administration to apply the principle of nonimportation to France, convinced that Napoleon continued to enforce his Berlin and Milan decrees.[44]

V

Neither the rationality of Foster's arguments nor official doubts regarding the sincerity of French policy determined the outlook of the Twelfth Congress which convened in November 1811. The Foreign Relations Committee, with Peter B. Porter of New York as chairman, had among its members Desha, John C. Calhoun of South Carolina, Felix Grundy of Tennessee, John Smilie of Pennsylvania, and John A. Harper of New Hampshire. These men, along with Speaker of the House Clay, were the leading proponents of war in the new Congress. Still, these men were the catalysts, not the determinants, of policy; they were always a minority even in the Republican party. The elections of 1810 had swelled the number of War Hawks in Congress, but the issues of war and peace had not dominated those elections, and many powerful War Hawks had failed, as members of the previous Congress, to lead a generally apathetic country to war. Most who eventually favored war, including southerners who carried the war vote, had little interest in the older issues—Canada, western lands, Indians, or the profits of the Mississippi River trade—which historians traditionally have regarded as critical. The western issues in no way explain the crucial support for the war in the southern and Middle Atlantic states, nor was the trade of those states in agricultural products affected adversely by European commercial policy. Indeed, the South, like the New England shippers, had much to lose economically by going to war. The challenge that united Congress for war was not economic necessity or territorial expansionism but rather the conviction that the United States needed

---

[44]Adams to William Eustis, August 24, 1811, ibid., p. 188; Adams to Monroe, October 3, 1811, ibid., p. 233; Adams to Thomas Boylston Adams, November 6, 1811, ibid., p. 273.

to vindicate its national honor and rebuff Britain's unseemly arrogant disregard of American rights.[45]

Madison informed the new Congress in November 1811 that Britain still had not followed France in removing the obstructions to its commerce with the United States; instead, the British had executed even more rigorously their orders against neutral commerce. Britain's action, the president complained, was "evidence of hostile inflexibility" with the purpose of "trampling on rights which no independent nation can relinquish."[46] That month Madison predicted that only a change in British maritime policy could avert a war; Congress would measure its level of preparation by the reactions of the British government.[47] The president, leading a still divided country unprepared to fight, in good conscience could not recommend war. At the same time, Monroe, more openly committed to war, assured members of Congress that the administration would support a firm policy toward Great Britain. During the spring of 1812, Monroe encouraged congressional leaders in their efforts to build a war consensus. If the War Hawks could create a rationale that would justify a declaration of war, the Republican party, generally cohesive, would fall into line readily enough.

In the Twelfth Congress the anti-British forces set out to create a war mood by arguing that Britain aimed not at defeating Napoleon but at undermining the United States. The evidence for such motives lay in Britain's continuing refusal to respond properly to Macon's Bill No. 2.[48] As the Foreign Relations Committee of the House phrased it, "When all those circumstances are taken into consideration, it is impossible for your committee to doubt the motives which have governed the British Ministry in all its measures toward the United States since the year 1805. Equally it is impossible to doubt, longer, the course which the United States ought to pursue towards Great Britain."[49] Clay claimed proof that Britain "will do everything to destroy us." Porter added that, if the United States continued to submit to British indignities, it "might safely calculate to be kicked and cuffed for the whole of the remainder of [its] life." For some War Hawks, Britain

[45]Norman K. Risjord has developed the national honor theme in "1812: Conservatives, War Hawks, and the Nation's Honor," *William & Mary Quarterly*, 3d ser., 18 (April 1961): 196–210.

[46]Madison's Third Annual Message, November 5, 1811, in James D. Richardson, ed., *A Compilation of the Messages and Papers of the Presidents*, 10 vols. (Washington, 1896–1899), 1:494–95.

[47]Madison to Barlow, November 17, 1811, in Hunt, *Writings of Madison*, 8:168–69.

[48]For an analysis of Macon's Bill No. 2 as the key to the diabolism theme of 1812 see Hatzenbuehler and Ivie, *Congress Declares War*, pp. 114–26.

[49]*Annals of Congress*, 12th Cong., 1st sess., p. 1554.

desired no less than the recolonization of America. Harper charged that Britain's conduct "bespeaks a determination to rule us, and can only be answered by the appeal to the God of Battles." Similarly, Calhoun warned Congress that Britain was determined to reduce the United States to a colonial state: "The evil still grows and in each succeeding year swells in extent and pretension beyond the preceding."[50]

In the absence of any reassurances from London, congressmen concluded that only a declaration of war could prevent the subjugation of the United States. The House Foreign Relations Committee, in a report on Britain's continued defiance, advised Congress: "To wrongs so daring in character, and so disgraceful in their execution, it is impossible that the people of the United States should remain indifferent. . . . The occasion is now presented when the national character, misunderstood and traduced for a time by foreign and domestic enemies, should be vindicated."[51] Jefferson so argued in a letter of April 20, 1812 that "we are . . . , it seems, to have no intermission of wrongs from England but at the point of the bayonet. We have done our duty of exhausting all the peaceable means of obtaining justice, and must now leave the issue to the arbitration of force."[52]

The specific conditions in U.S.-British relations in 1812 differed little from what they had been during the previous seven years. The crisis came not from an accumulation of events making war inescapable but from an accumulation of fear and anger that elevated the British threat from the curtailment of American commerce to the destruction of U.S. independence, giving the nation the simple choice between national humiliation and war. By offering that choice Republican leaders molded a consensus that favored war with Great Britain. During April and May the War Hawks reminded Congress that it was too late to reconsider. For Congress to reverse direction, Clay warned, would cover it "with shame and indelible disgrace." Smilie added that the country's honor was at stake; to recede would render the United States "a reproach to all nations."[53]

John Randolph, Virginia's noted conservative, questioned the assumption that American honor or security required a war against Great Britain. He reminded Congress in December 1811 that the United

---

[50]Clay, Porter, Harper, and Calhoun are quoted in Hatzenbuehler and Ivie, *Congress Declares War*, pp. 48, 53.

[51]*Annals of Congress*, 12th Cong., 1st sess., pp. 374–77.

[52]Jefferson to Duane, April 20, 1812, quoted in Hatzenbuehler and Ivie, *Congress Declares War*, p. 53.

[53]Clay and Smilie quoted in Risjord, "1812: Conservatives, War Hawks, and the Nation's Honor," pp. 209–10.

States had no power to defeat England or any interest to be served by contributing to Napoleon's success. Marching into Canada, he cautioned, would not protect the country's seacoast; the foundations of British power did not lie "in the frozen deserts of Labrador." Why, he wondered, should the United States regard Britain as its special enemy? "If it were allowable to entertain partialities," he observed, "every consideration of blood, language, religion, and interest, would incline us toward England." Still, members of Congress insisted on binding the nation to France and Napoleon, seemingly unmindful of that decision's possible impact on America's future. "Suppose France is in possession of the British naval power . . . , what would be your condition?" he asked. "What would be the situation of your seaports and their seafaring inhabitants?" Randolph declared that he would never tie the United States to France, and he hoped that House leaders would reconsider before they transferred from Congress to Napoleon the power to make war. "But, sir," he concluded, "if you have sold yourselves into foreign bondage I pray you to show me the equivalent, the *quid pro quo*. What have you got in exchange from the tyrant of the earth? Where is the mess of pottage . . . for which you have bartered away your birthright; the birthright of a whole people; the right of self-government; the power over war and peace!"[51]

Whatever Napoleon's sincerity, his actions alone gave Republican leaders the needed justification for war. Langdon Cheves of South Carolina believed the emperor's declaration sufficient evidence "of what shall be considered as obligatory on that country. . . . If our rights are now violated, it is a violation independent of the decrees." It was left for Clay to brush aside any doubts that Britain, not France, was the real danger to America's future as an independent nation. He recognized the dilemma in fighting Britain because British valor allegedly prevented Napoleon from achieving universal dominion. However noble the British cause, Clay argued, that country had no right to trample on the rights of others. "We are invited—conjured to drink the potion of British poison actually presented to our lips," he cautioned, "that we may avoid the imperial dose prepared by perturbed imaginations. We are called upon to submit to debasement, dishonor, and disgrace— to bow the neck to royal insolence, as a course of preparation for manly resistance to gallic invasion! What nation, what individual was ever taught, in the schools of ignominious submission, the patriotic lessons of freedom and independence?" For Clay, American interests in a

[51]Randolph's remarks of December 10, 16, 1811, in *Annals of Congress*, 12th Cong., 1st sess., cols. 441, 445–49, 453–54, 529–30.

balanced Europe would not be served by Britain's destruction of its French rival.[55]

VI

Throughout the early months of 1812, Madison refused to confront the issue of war. He had failed to argue the British into a recognition of American neutral rights; on the other hand, Britain avoided any new and dramatic impositions on the United States which might become the occasion for an unwanted war. If the United States wanted to fight, it alone would make the decision. Madison was conscious of the country's accumulating animosity toward Britain and reported to Jefferson on April 3 that the Spencer Perceval government in London seemed to prefer war to a repeal of the Orders in Council; the United States, therefore, had no choice but to prepare for it. During May all Washington awaited the arrival of the *Hornet* from Europe. After a long delay the vessel docked on May 22. For Madison the long-awaited communications were disheartening; neither the British nor the French governments offered any changes in their established policies. The French, he believed, had not enforced the Berlin and Milan decrees but persisted in keeping the British in doubt. "The manner of the F. Govt.," he complained to Jefferson on May 25, "betrays the design of leaving G.B. a pretext for enforcing her O[rders] in C[ouncil]. And in all other respects, the grounds of our complaints remain the same. . . . The business is become more than ever puzzling. To go to war with Engd. and not with France arms the federalists with new matter. . . . To go to war against both, presents a thousand difficulties."[56]

Adams, in St. Petersburg, still hoped to the end that the United States would not risk its independence in a European war. For him it was clear that the British leaders hated the United States more than France; in their relations with France they at least had the satisfaction of dealing with a great power. "Their hatred of America," wrote Adams, "is mingled with the mortification of having in her an enemy whom they wish to despise, but cannot. As a commercial rival they dread America much more than France." A war against England, he feared, would involve the country "in a state of fivefold dependence upon the caprices, the insolence and the rapacity of France."[57] If the United

---

[55]Clay's address to Congress, December 31, 1811, in Hopkins, *Papers of Clay*, 1:607–08.

[56]Madison to Jefferson, April 3, 1812, in Hunt, *Writings of Madison*, 8:185; Madison to Jefferson, May 25, 1812, ibid., pp. 190–91.

[57]Adams to George William Erving, August 13, 1811, in Ford, *Writings of John Quincy Adams*, 4:175; Adams to Eustis, October 26, 1811, ibid., p. 262.

States could man the battleships and battalions necessary to redress the wrongs committed against it, he would favor war; but "what king," he recalled from the Gospel of St. John, "going to make war against another king, sitteth not down first and consulteth whether he be able with ten thousand to meet him that cometh against him with twenty thousand." The conditions confronting the United States, Adams reminded his mother Abigail, were even less favorable than that. The United States had no power to force its commerce upon Europe. What would save the United States, he predicted, was the fact that both Britain and France, in their grasping for commerce and power, were abusing too much of the world and fighting for objectives that neither could obtain. If the United States could avoid war, both European powers eventually would admit American participation in their commerce. "Their necessities," Adams concluded, "will do more for the restoration of our rights than we could do by any exertion of our own forces."[58]

Late in May Clay, with a congressional deputation, called on the president to inform him that a majority of Congress would vote for war if he chose to recommend it. Madison's war message of June 1, 1812 declared Britain's war against France in some measure a war against the United States; he did not recognize in America's wartime demands any infringement on British interests: "We behold on the side of Great Britain a state of war against the United States, and on the side of the United States a state of peace toward Great Britain." Madison quite properly condemned the British for impressing American seamen, but the U.S. government had long ceased to make impressment an issue of war and peace. It was, moreover, a continuing problem and not an immediate danger to American interests. Similarly, the president complained that British cruisers hovered off the American coast and interfered with U.S. commerce, but this also had never been listed as a cause of war. The president declared the British blockade of the European coast a hypocrisy because Britain did not have the naval forces to enforce it. This accusation was not new. Madison faced the ultimate task of making the British harassment of American commerce a cause of war. That commerce the British attacked, not because it aided England's enemies but because it threatened Britain's monopoly of trade and navigation. Such charges rendered London's maritime policies not only a gross violation of America's neutral rights but also a threat to the nation's commercial future. To avoid war and take its chances on the high seas, the United States had no choice but to accept British restrictions as legitimate, or at least tolerable. That choice, amid

[58]Adams to Abigail Adams, January 1, 1812, ibid., pp. 284–86.

the proclaimed dangers to the nation's very integrity, Madison would no longer accept.[59]

On June 3, Calhoun read the famous war manifesto. The time had arrived, he declared, "when the United States must support their character and status among the nations of the earth, or submit to the most shameful degradation. Forebearance has ceased to be a virtue."[60] The Senate acted with surprising deliberation. Not until June 19 did Madison sign the declaration of war. The United States, at peace for twenty-nine years, was scarcely prepared to fight. The Treasury was empty. "After the war is once commenced . . . ," Obadiah German of New York warned the Senate, "I presume gentlemen will find something more forcible than empty war speeches will be necessary." Having declared war, the country could not have peace until it had obtained the consent of the enemy. It was his purpose, said German, "to check the precipitate step of plunging [the] country prematurely into a war, without any of the means of making the war terrible to the enemy; and with the certainty that it will be terrible to ourselves."[61]

As late as June 29, Adams urged an unprepared nation to avoid war. The British Orders in Council were troublesome, but in almost five years they had not produced conflict. With Perceval's death in May, additional patience might eventually secure the revocation of the orders without war.[62] Actually the House of Commons in mid-June had extorted a revocation of the Orders in Council from the new British ministry. Britain had perpetuated its infamous system, observed Adams, "until the proofs that thousands upon thousands of their manufacturers were starving under its operation had been exhibited in the minutest detail."[63] Britain was in trouble; it was hoped that the United States would use its diplomatic leverage to gain its ends without armed hostility. However, London's decision reached Washington long after Congress had acted.

When Congress elected that the country would fight, amid the absence of adequate preparations, it unveiled failure of national policy. War had its justifications, yet these were so divorced from

[59]Madison's War Message, June 1, 1812, in Richardson, *Messages and Papers of the Presidents*, 1:499–505.

[60]Calhoun's report to the House of Representatives, June 3, 1812, in *American State Papers: Foreign Relations*, 3:567.

[61]Obadiah German's remarks in the Senate, June 13, 1812, in *Annals of Congress*, 12th Cong., 1st sess., cols. 272, 275–82.

[62]Adams to John Adams, June 29, 1812, in Ford, *Writings of John Quincy Adams*, 4:358.

[63]Adams to Abigail Adams, July 13, 1812, ibid., p. 368. For the royal proclamation of June 23, 1812, which ended the Orders in Council, see *American State Papers: Foreign Relations*, 3:433.

fundamental American interests that the nation could never prosecute the war with a determination commensurate with the fears that justified it. In 1813, Madison explained why he would carry the country into a conflict for which it was not and would not be prepared. "It had become impossible," he wrote, "to avoid or even to delay war, at a moment when we were not prepared for it, and when it was certain that effective preparedness would not take place, whilst the question of war was undecided."[61]

The genuine choices confronting the U.S. government were as clear as they were unacceptable: either it might have accepted the infringements on American neutral rights as a natural by-product of a giant war and permitted commerce to proceed by belligerent rules, making an effort in the process to disengage American prestige and honor from the conflict of interests; or it might have prepared the nation to fight openly and forthrightly for its asserted rights. For Madison and his advisers the first choice was both politically and morally unacceptable; the country could not ignore the attacks of the European powers on its property and profits. However futile the quarrel, Madison and Congress would push it to the point of diplomatic and emotional crisis. To contemplate war as a positive alternative entailed a higher military and financial cost than the administration cared to advocate or Congress to accept. Thus the nation drifted into a state of fright and outrage leading to war, even while the actual dangers posed by Great Britain remained for most Americans too remote, abstract, or nonexistent to require an adequate defense.

---

[61]Madison is quoted in Perkins, *Prologue to War*, p. 405.

CHAPTER SIX

John Quincy Adams and the Federalist Tradition*

ON MARCH 4, 1817, James Monroe entered the American presidency as the third member of the Virginia dynasty; two days later he invited John Quincy Adams to enter his cabinet as secretary of state.[1] Adams's long experience in diplomacy had begun in the 1790s when President George Washington sent him to the Netherlands and later his father, President John Adams, transferred him to Berlin. Following Thomas Jefferson's accession to the presidency in 1801, Adams had returned to the United States and shortly thereafter entered the Massachusetts Senate as a Federalist. After he lost a race for the U.S. House of Representatives, the Massachusetts legislature elected him to the U.S. Senate. During his years in the Senate from 1803 until 1808, Adams gradually broke from the Federalist ranks and in the latter year voted with the Republican caucus that nominated James Madison for the presidency. Soon thereafter Madison sent Adams to Russia. His residence in St. Petersburg during the closing years of the Napoleonic Wars made him a natural choice to represent the United States in the negotiations with Britain at Ghent following the War of 1812. With the establishment of peace in 1815, Madison assigned him to London where, like his father in 1785, he had assumed the task of negotiating issues left unresolved by war. When Monroe asked Adams to join his

---

*This essay is an expansion of "John Quincy Adams and the Federalist Tradition," in Norman A. Graebner, ed., *Traditions and Values: American Diplomacy, 1790–1865* (Lanham, MD, 1985). Reprinted by permission.
[1]Monroe to Adams, March 6, 1817, in Stanislaus Murray Hamilton, ed., *The Writings of James Monroe* (New York, 1969), 6:15.

administration, John Adams advised his son to accept: "You are now approaching fifty years of age. In my opinion you must return to [your country], or renounce it forever. I am well aware of the critical situation you will be in. I know you have not the . . . immutable taciturnity of Franklin and Washington. But you must risque all."[2]

Jefferson lauded Monroe's choice. "They were made for each other," ran his comment. "Adams has a pointed pen; Monroe has judgment enough for both and firmness enough to have *his* judgment control."[3] Jefferson's was a Republican view, recognizing differences in personality and not philosophy. Monroe and Adams had occupied opposite poles during the great debates of the Washington years. Like Jefferson and other Founding Fathers, Adams believed that the United States should set a republican example for the world, but he rejected the notion, entertained by Monroe, that the country had a special mission to the world. For Adams the means for leading the world on some democratic humanitarian crusade were nonexistent. His Federalist convictions in 1817 were as firm as ever. "The President, I am sure," he wrote to his mother, "will neither require nor expect from me any sacrifice of principles inconsistent with my sense of right."[4] That the two men functioned as an effective team measured not only the overwhelming conversion of the Republicans in power to the older Federalist notions of proper diplomatic behavior but also Adams's acceptance of his subordinate role in policymaking.[5]

Adams worked independently, often as a minority of one. Far more learned, energetic, and forceful than Monroe, he tended to dominate cabinet discussions when foreign policy was at issue. He alone among the nation's leaders knew Europe's leading statesmen personally, especially Czar Alexander I, Talleyrand, and Castlereagh. Whatever Adams's convictions that his perceptions were keener than those of his less experienced cabinet colleagues, members of Monroe's powerful cabinet opposed Adams on numerous occasions. Recognizing both the secretary's independence of mind and his refusal to accept views regarded as rash by the diplomatic corps, Baron Hyde de Neuville, the French minister, wrote of Adams in December 1817: "I know that he has dared to declare himself very strongly on many occasions against indiscreet and purely speculative ideas."[6]

[2]John Adams quoted in Samuel Flagg Bemis, *John Quincy Adams and the Foundations of American Foreign Policy* (New York, 1949), p. 243.

[3]Jefferson is quoted in ibid., pp. 260–61.

[4]Adams to Abigail Adams, April 23, 1817, in Worthington Chauncey Ford, ed., *Writings of John Quincy Adams* (New York, 1913–1917), 6:182.

[5]*Memoirs of John Quincy Adams*, ed., Charles Francis Adams (Philadelphia, 1874–1877), 6:171.

[6]Hyde de Neuville to Richelieu, December 11, 1817, in Edward H. Tatum, Jr., *The United States and Europe, 1815–1823* (Berkeley, CA, 1936), pp. 208–09.

For Adams partisanship was as dangerous as it was inexcusable. He believed that the United States would succeed only if it maintained unity at home as well as independence in its external relations. Like Washington before him, he feared that internal dissension would invite external interference and injure the country as it had Holland and Poland in the eighteenth century. Earlier he had lamented the Jeffersonian attacks on Washington's foreign policies as well as the opposition of the New England Federalists, his erstwhile allies, to Jefferson and Madison. Of all the recent wartime deformities in need of elimination, the most disgusting, wrote Adams, "is the rancorous spirit of faction which drove one part of the country headlong towards the dissolution of the union, and towards a treacherous and servile adherence to the enemies of the country. . . . It required little less than a special interposition of Providence to save us from utter disgrace and dismemberment."[7] Unrestrained partisanship, he held, was rooted in politics and personal ambition; to his critics, therefore, he would seldom attribute sincerity.

Adams desired his judgments to be measured by their recognized standards of propriety, accuracy in reflecting world conditions, and possible contribution to the country's welfare. Thus he rebuked his critics of the press far more savagely than he did those diplomats who sometimes appeared unnecessarily obdurate. He complained of editors generally on one occasion: "There is not one of them whose friendship is worth buying, nor one whose enmity is not formidable. They are a sort of assassins who sit with loaded blunderbusses at the corner of streets and fire them off for hire or for sport at any passenger whom they select."[8] More pointedly, Adams passed judgment in his diary on the editors of the *Aurora* and the *Democratic Press*, in Philadelphia: "They are both men of considerable talents and profligate principles, always for sale to the highest bidder, and always insupportable burdens, by their insatiable rapacity, to the parties they support."[9]

II

Physically, Adams was less impressive than his cabinet colleagues; he scarcely resembled the classical diplomatist—suave, even-tempered, and reassuring. He was short, fat, and bald, with a belligerent demeanor and a rheumy affliction that caused his eyes to run incessantly, but, if Adams at times antagonized his associates, he was scarcely more

[7]Adams to Alexander H. Everett, March 16, 1816, in Ford, *Writings of John Quincy Adams*, 5:538; Adams to William Eustis, March 29, 1816, ibid., p. 546.
[8]*Memoirs of John Quincy Adams*, 5:173.
[9]Ibid., p. 112.

charitable toward himself. Following a dinner at the home of the president of the Bank of the United States in October 1818, he confided in his diary:

> I am not satisfied with myself this day, having talked too much at dinner. . . . Yet, in the estimation of others, I pass off on the whole better when I talk freely than when silent and reserved. This sometimes stimulates me to talk more than is wise or proper. . . . Nor can I always (I did not this day) altogether avoid a dogmatical and peremptory tone and manner, always disgusting, and especially offensive in persons to whose age or situation others consider some deference due.[10]

On occasion his diary notes were even more pitiless: "I am a man of reserved, cold, austere, and forbidding manners; my political adversaries say, a gloomy misanthropist, and my personal enemies, an unsocial savage. With a knowledge of the actual defect in my character, I have not the pliability to reform it."[11]

Beyond his deep-seated convictions, which neither time nor circumstance would alter, Adams possessed every other quality essential for diplomatic distinction. His knowledge of Europe and its relationship to the New World was profound, and he understood with equal precision the limits of effective American diplomacy. For Adams, no less than for Washington and Alexander Hamilton, U.S. foreign policy had one major purpose: to serve the interests of the country, defined in commercial and geographic terms. He recognized, as had Hamilton in *The Federalist*, the natural separation of the New World from the old and the essential advantages that the United States enjoyed in its global relationships. Throughout his career Adams denied that a genuine foreign policy could pursue abstract objectives. If he favored liberty, he refused to anchor the nation's foreign policies to its achievement. The means of enforcement, he knew, were not within his control, nor could such an objective be the subject of fruitful negotiations. Thus European diplomats always deemed him direct, reliable, and realistic. Even when he refused to surrender any advantage, diplomats found him simple-mannered and courteous.

Adams managed the technical aspects of diplomacy with remarkable skill. His diligence compelled him to read all dispatches sent out and received by the State Department. Monroe, equally experienced

---

[10]Ibid., 4:131–32.

[11]Adams is quoted in Bemis, *John Quincy Adams*, p. 253. Adams complained that dinners and evening parties resulted in late hours and caused him to lose the mornings that followed as well as the evenings. See *Memoirs of John Quincy Adams*, 4:279–80.

in foreign affairs, maintained a close surveillance over Adams's correspondence. When on occasion Adams objected to presidential statements, or accepted them only after futile argument, it was because the president again had reacted to events abroad from the standard of simple republican virtue rather than from a clear recognition of the interests and genuine intentions of the United States. Ultimately, it was Adams and not Monroe who gave leadership and direction to American foreign relations during the eight years of their close association.

If Adams, as secretary, often faced opposition in the cabinet, Congress, and the press, he towered over the Washington diplomatic corps. Those compelled to negotiate with him never ceased to admire his intelligence and learning, his industry and self-discipline, and his unwavering pursuit of his country's interests, grasped more surely by him than by any other man of his age. Adversaries questioned only his doggedness and disposition. British envoy Stratford Canning, for instance, wrote of Adams in his memoirs: "He was . . . much above par in general ability, but having the air of a scholar rather than statesman, a very uneven temper, a disposition at times well-meaning, a manner somewhat too often domineering."[12]

Behind the respect that Adams enjoyed was the essential honesty of his policies. For him the path of virtue was not always clear, nor was virtue always crowned with success; however, he believed that a policy, otherwise sound, would be wiser and more enduring if it possessed this quality. Perhaps there were occasions, especially in time of war, when deception was justifiable, but fraud, he thought, was never excusable where force would not be equally justified. Fraud must be used sparingly, for "every instance of it . . . tends when discovered to impair the confidence of mankind in the sincerity and integrity of him who uses it."[13] Adams preferred that his country's policies be just, whether successful or not. Stephen Decatur had offered his famous toast: "Our country! In her intercourse with foreign nations, may she always be in the right; but our country, right or wrong," to which Adams disagreed. Writing to his father in August 1816, he said: "I cannot ask of heaven success, even for my country, in a cause where she should be in the wrong. . . . I disclaim as unsound all patriotism incompatible with the principles of eternal justice. But the truth is that the American union, while united, *may* be certain of success in every rightful cause, and may if it pleases never have any but a rightful cause

---

[12]Quoted in Stanley Lane-Poole, *Life of Stratford Canning* (London, 1888), 1:308.
[13]*Memoirs of John Quincy Adams*, 5:47–48.

to maintain."[14] He understood that in matters of international morality status quo nations had the advantage.

Adams recognized the limits of American power and influence in Europe. Toward the Continent, emerging from a quarter century of war, he urged a posture of strict neutrality. Europe, he had written in 1815, "consists only of victors and vanquished, between whom no permanent state of social repose can exist. May we persevere in the system of keeping aloof from all their broils, and in that of consolidating and perpetuating our own union."[15] Several years later, in his noted oration of July 4, 1821, Adams insisted that the United States had conducted its foreign relations in a spirit of friendliness and reciprocity; it had recognized the independence of other countries and maintained its own. America sympathized for the cause of liberty everywhere. "Wherever the standard of freedom and Independence has been or shall be unfurled," he said, "there will her heart, her benedictions and her prayers be. But she goes not abroad, in search of monsters to destroy. She is the well-wisher to the freedom and independence of all. She is the champion and vindicator only of her own. She will comment the general cause by . . . the benignant sympathy of her example."[16] Any shift from liberty to force, Adams warned, might make the United States dictatress of the world and no longer the ruler of its own spirit. To his principle of neutrality he added that of nonintervention.

Toward the North American continent Adams was an expansionist, but his expansionism looked to geography and not to war. For him the Continent seemed destined to be one nation in language, religion, society, and politics. During November 1819, Secretary of the Treasury William H. Crawford informed him that many British and French citizens regarded the United States as ambitious and encroaching. Adams replied that to argue otherwise would be useless:

> Nothing that we could say or do would remove this impression until the world shall be familiarized with the idea of considering our proper dominion to be the continent of North America. From the time when we became an independent people it was as much a law of nature that this should become our pretension as that the Mississippi should flow to the sea. Spain had possessions upon our southern and Great Britain upon our northern border. It was impossible that centuries should elapse without finding them annexed to the United States; not that any spirit of encroachment or ambition on our part renders it necessary, but because it is a

[14]Adams to John Adams, August 1, 1816, in Ford, *Writings of John Quincy Adams*, 6:60–62.
[15]Adams to Joseph Hall, September 9, 1815, ibid., 5:376–77.
[16]This speech can be found in Walter LaFeber, ed., *John Quincy Adams and American Continental Empire* (Chicago, 1965), pp. 42–46.

physical, moral, and political absurdity that such fragments of territory, with sovereigns at fifteen hundred miles beyond sea, worthless and burdensome to their owners, should exist permanently contiguous to a great, powerful, enterprising, and rapidly growing nation. . . . Until Europe shall find it a settled geographical element that the United States and North America are identical, any effort on our part to reason the world out of a belief that we are ambitious will have no other effect than to convince them that we add to our ambition hypocrisy.[17]

One year later, in a conversation with Canning over the future of Oregon, he declared that the London government had certainly come "to the conclusion that there would be neither policy nor profit in cavilling with us about territory on this North American continent." When Canning asked if the secretary included Canada in his claims, Adams responded: "No, there the boundary is marked, and we have no disposition to encroach upon it. Keep what is yours, but leave the rest of the continent to us."[18]

To underwrite his hopes for peace and security in a still challenging world, Adams looked to a stronger union based on centralized government and to a reasonable level of military preparedness. "No nation can enjoy freedom and independence," he wrote, "without being always prepared to defend them by force of arms." He had reminded Monroe in November 1814 that "we shall have no valuable friends in Europe until we have proved that we can defend ourselves without them."[19] But adequate power, which Adams doubted the country would ever create except in time of war, dared not encourage a mood of belligerency. He advised the nation to employ every means available to settle disputes amicably and never to enter a war "without a fair prospect of attaining its objects," nor should it remain in a war unless the gains were clearly commensurate with the costs.[20] Such principles and purposes guided Adams in every diplomatic confrontation of his secretarial years.

III

European statesmen recognized the importance of France to the restoration of the balance of power in Europe. As the Declaration of Frankfurt expressed it, the allies desired a great and powerful France

---

[17] *Memoirs of John Quincy Adams*, 4:437–39.
[18] Ibid., 5:252–53.
[19] Adams to Abigail Adams, January 17, 1814, in Ford, *Writings of John Quincy Adams*, 5:5; Adams to Monroe, November 20, 1814, ibid., 5:202.
[20] Adams to William Harris Crawford, September 14, 1814, ibid., pp. 140–41; Adams to Everett, March 16, 1816, ibid., p. 537; Adams to John Adams, February 17, 1814, ibid., p. 18.

"because French power . . . [was] one of the essential foundations of the social structure" of the Continent. The restoration of the Bourbons, even the British agreed, would serve the best interests of all nations in a stable Europe. Despite the later condemnation leveled at the Congress of Vienna for its free assignment of territory, the decisions of that notable international conference rather completely underwrote the principle of balance.[21] To prevent a revival of French aggression and to defend the peace settlement, the victors—Austria, Britain, Prussia, and Russia—formed the Quadruple Alliance in November 1815. By effectively managing the international system, the allies hoped to eliminate the cataclysms that had disturbed the peace of Europe during the preceding quarter century. In 1818 the powers brought France into the alliance.

Meanwhile in September 1815, Czar Alexander had formed his Holy Alliance of Austria, Prussia, and Russia. This eastern alliance was designed less to stabilize the European equilibrium than to form an effective coalition against liberalism, revolution, and undesirable territorial and political change. Alexander believed post-Napoleonic Europe was endangered by a revolutionary conspiracy determined to destroy Christianity and undermine Europe's monarchical institutions. At the later conferences of Troppau (1820), Laibach (1821), and Verona (1822), the Holy Alliance adopted interventionist policies toward Italy and Spain especially. In the process the Holy Alliance undermined the Quadruple Alliance by enlisting France and alienating Britain. British leaders could detect, in Europe's liberal uprisings, no threat to Continental stability. The British cabinet declared as early as May 1820 that the Quadruple Alliance was never "intended as a union . . . for the superintendance of the internal affairs of other states." Ultimately, the Holy Alliance's contribution to European stability rested in the mutual restraints that it placed on its three members: it permitted Russia, Austria, and Prussia to manage their intra-alliance rivalries in East-Central Europe so that they might avoid war.[22] Prince von Metternich, the Austrian chancellor, suspected that Alexander might use the Holy Alliance as a cover to expand his influence in Europe. To limit his ambitions, Metternich totally committed the alliance to its archconservative principles and used it to control Russian policy within

---

[21]Contemporary writers on international affairs lauded the efforts of the Congress of Vienna to reaffirm the principle of balance, especially by making France a part of the new European equilibrium.

[22]Europe's general peace continued to rest on the mutual restraints of the eastern alliance. Managing that alliance from within was the key to Bismarck's diplomacy from 1878 to 1890; thereafter, the collapse of the three-power arrangement in eastern Europe set the stage for war. See Chapter Twelve.

the eastern alliance. Alexander's fears rendered him vulnerable to Austrian leaders who played on them by exaggerating and fabricating the evidence of revolutionary movements across Europe.

Adams recognized the fundamental purpose of Europe's postwar state system: to prevent the rise again of preponderant power and to restrain threats to the region's stability. With time, however, Adams also became critical of the czar's Holy Alliance. Europe, he complained in April 1816, had cast off Napoleon only to return to Divine Right. For American observers generally Europe appeared unstable, harboring ideals far different from those of the United States, and filled with combustible materials that any spark could reignite into the flames of war.[23] *Niles' Register* (Baltimore) in August 1817 warned its readers that the United States could scarcely trust the friendship of countries governed by kings. Adams expressed such fears when he said that "there is already in all governments of Europe a strong prejudice against us as Republicans, and as the primary causes of the propagation of those political principles, which still make the throne of every European monarch rock under him as with the throes of an earthquake. . . . There is a vague and general sentiment of speculative and fomenting jealousy against us prevailing all over Europe."[24]

If the great powers desisted, because of predictable costs, from imposing on one another, they scarcely seemed capable of imposing on the New World. Europe's balance served the American interest in achieving a stable and independent hemisphere, but it did not necessarily equalize the capacity of the European powers to influence American affairs, or even their intention of doing so. Toward France both the administration and the press expressed indifference; they regarded that power as neither a friend nor an enemy. As the *National Intelligencer* (Washington) noted on May 4, 1815, "France is the same to us, whether ruled by Napoleon or Louis, by a King or an Emperor.—We owed no enmity to Louis; we owe no debt of gratitude to Napoleon." The French government, fearful of British influence in Washington, anticipated considerable benefit from maintaining close and friendly ties with the United States. Shortly after the Congress of Vienna Adams reminded Monroe that such Continental powers as France would attempt to separate the United States from England.[25] France itself posed no threat.

[23]For U.S. attitudes see Tatum, *United States and Europe*, pp. 29–38.
[24]Adams to William Plumer, January 17, 1817, in Ford, *Writings of John Quincy Adams*, 6:141.
[25]Adams to Monroe, September 5, 1815, ibid., 5:370.

Russia, like France, seemed to lack the power or the intention to challenge American interest in the New World. Observant Americans recognized the contrast between the government and society of Russia and that of the United States, but they harbored no feeling of fear or distrust. Adams admitted that he trusted Czar Alexander more than any other monarch in Europe.[26] As a Continental power with a large army, Russia wielded major influence in Europe and the Middle East; elsewhere Britain exerted a moderating influence on Russian ambition. Indeed, many Americans hoped—and Adams among them—that Anglo-Russian rivalry would restrict the power of both countries outside the Eastern Hemisphere.

Such complacency did not exist toward England, as it had the power, and seemingly the interest, to interfere in American affairs. Adams had taken hope in Napoleon's retention of power in France as a counterweight to British might.[27] There was little conviction in the United States that England, having shaken off the restraints of France, would accept the Treaty of Ghent as an instrument of peace. Members of the press freely forecast renewed war, although not necessarily in the immediate future. As the *National Intelligencer* explained in April 1816, "It has been predicted by our most perspicacious statesmen, that future wars of a sanguinary character are to take place between Great Britain and the U. States.—These are events which, though perhaps as certain as mortality to man, it is agreeable to be enabled to believe are placed at a remote distance from us." Adams shared this postwar distrust of Britain when he wrote that, although British ascendancy in Europe would decline, that country would continue to seek the possible ruin of the United States. British animosity toward France had been satiated by the British victory, but, Adams warned, "[British] feelings against America are keener, more jealous, more envious, more angry than ever."[28] Furthermore, "we must not disguise from ourselves that the national feeling [in Britain] against the United States is more strong and universal than it has ever been."[29] Such fears did not govern U.S. policy toward Britain.

IV

For Adams peace with England was essential for American security and well-being. Britain alone of Europe's leading states had the power to injure the United States. "My special duty at present," Adams noted

[26] Adams to Abigail Adams, May 12, 1814, ibid., p. 43.
[27] Adams to John Adams, April 24, 1815, ibid., p. 309.
[28] Adams to Abigail Adams, December 27, 1815, ibid., p. 454.
[29] Quoted in Arthur P. Whitaker, *The United States and the Independence of Latin America, 1800–1830* (Baltimore, 1941), p. 206.

in May 1816, "is to preach peace. . . . I am deeply convinced that peace is the state best adapted to the interest and happiness of both nations."[30] As secretary one year later he resumed negotiations on those issues, still unsettled since Ghent, which he had begun in London. As early as the peace negotiations of 1782, his father had sought the dismantling of all fortifications along the Canadian-American frontier. At Ghent in 1814 the younger Adams had pressed the British for such an agreement but again without success. Undaunted, Adams repeated the offer in London during March 1816. The British government, hoping to avoid a naval race with the United States on the Great Lakes, accepted his overture. The result was the Rush-Bagot Agreement, signed in Washington during April 1817, which limited British and American naval arsenals on the lakes to those required for the enforcement of customs regulations. This treaty was the first reciprocal naval disarmament agreement in modern history. In removing a potential source of friction and expense, the treaty admirably served the interests of both Britain and the United States.

During the following year Adams achieved the long-standing quest of the United States for fishing rights off the Labrador and Newfoundland coasts. While in London he insisted that Britain had granted the inshore fisheries on the northern coasts to the United States in the original division of the empire. The British agreed to American fishing on the high seas and suspended trespass proceedings against New England fishermen. In Washington, Adams resumed his conversations on the fisheries question, determined to eliminate the English reference to "liberty" when referring to American access to both the Grand Banks and the high seas. Privately, he was opposed to compromise, preferring that the United States demand full fishing rights along the northern coasts and establish them by force if necessary. Overruled by Monroe, Adams proposed that the United States forfeit the right of drying and curing on the shore and reserve full rights to fishing. Ultimately, Albert Gallatin, who managed the final negotiations in 1818, achieved more extensive inshore fishing rights than Adams's instructions had demanded. The new treaty granted American fishermen permission not only to catch fish along extensive sections of the northern coasts but also to dry and cure fish on any of the unsettled coasts of Labrador. The British resisted the U.S. effort to guarantee these rights even in time of war, but, as a compromise, they granted Americans liberty "for ever" to take fish along the northern coasts.[31]

As late as 1815 the United States and Britain had conducted a flourishing trade without benefit of any formal commercial treaty. On

---

[30]Adams to John Adams, May 29, 1816, ibid., 6:38.
[31]See Bemis, *John Quincy Adams*, pp. 279–80, 290–91.

July 3 of that year Adams signed a commercial convention in London which, except for the prohibition of discriminatory duties, merely reaffirmed existing practice. The convention provided for reciprocal consulates and freedom of commerce between the United States and British territories in Europe, as well as equality of treatment of the products, ships, citizens, and subjects of each country in the ports of the other. The convention also permitted American ships to trade in the British ports of Calcutta, Madras, Bombay, and Penang in south Asia.[32]

Unfortunately, the Anglo-American convention failed to gain full reciprocal arrangements, for Britain refused to permit U.S. ships in the saltwater ports of British North America and the British West Indies. These restrictions, by permitting English traders to engage in a triangle traffic denied to Americans, canceled the advantages of full reciprocity in direct U.S.-British commerce. For Adams this policy was totally objectionable: "Being an interchange of commodities . . . [commerce] is just in itself. . . . The regulation of it should be by arrangements to which both parties consent and in which due regard is paid to the interests of both."[33]

Adams confronted the uncompromising London government with a series of congressional acts in 1817, 1818, and 1820 which imposed special tonnage dues on British ships entering the United States from ports denied to American vessels. Finally, Congress eliminated all British West Indian goods except those brought directly from the colony where they were grown. These restrictions injured the West Indian economy and prompted Parliament in 1822 to open some colonial ports to U.S. ships. At the same time, it enumerated American products that might compete with those of Canada. In March 1823, Congress, under Adams's direction, opened U.S. ports to British ships coming from colonial ports, but only from those to which American ships were admitted. Simultaneously, Congress authorized the president to impose a 10 percent discriminatory tariff on colonial goods imported in British vessels until London eliminated all colonial preferences. By 1826 the British again had cut off American trade with their West Indian islands. Adams had failed to negotiate conditions of greater reciprocity than those which existed in 1822.[34]

Adams pursued the principle of equal advantage for American merchants in France as well. That country was a special problem because of its discriminatory tariffs which favored goods shipped in French vessels over those arriving in foreign ships. What troubled

[32]Ibid., pp. 224–25, 227.

[33]Memorandum to Hyde de Neuville, April 26, 1821, in Ford, *Writings of John Quincy Adams*, 7:101–02.

[34]Bemis, *John Quincy Adams*, pp. 457–59, 465.

Adams was not the legality of France's acts but its refusal to amend its restrictions reciprocally. In July 1820, Congress inaugurated a trade war when it levied special duties on French bottoms. In Paris, Gallatin favored American acceptance of some French compromise proposal, convinced that U.S. vessels could compete favorably with the French against even the offered differential of $2.30 per ton. Monroe seemed to agree. Adams, however, insisted that the principle of reciprocity be maintained universally; Monroe rejected the French proposal. To terminate the quarrel, Paris dispatched its skilled diplomat, Hyde de Neuville, to negotiate with Adams in Washington. He offered to remove half the French discriminatory duties if the United States removed its retaliatory tonnage dues. Adams opposed this compromise, but Monroe, under Gallatin's influence, relented. During subsequent months Gallatin secured further reductions of French discriminations. Finally, in a treaty accepted by the Senate in June 1822, the two countries agreed to Adams's proposal of balanced discriminatory duties.[35] Although for a time he compromised his commercial principles, Adams ultimately managed to obtain better reciprocal arrangements with France than he did with England. The *National Intelligencer* of June 29, 1822 passed judgment on the new treaty: "It re-establishes relations of perfect amity with France, our old friend and ally, which have been somewhat disturbed by the recent collisions of the commercial regulations of the two countries." The French were equally pleased.

V

Even more spectacular was Adams's success in defining the boundaries of the Louisiana Purchase. In the Convention of 1818 with England, he negotiated the boundary line from the Lake of the Woods westward along the 49th parallel to the Rocky Mountains. West of the Rockies, however, British fur-trading interests were centered south of that parallel, largely along the valley of the Columbia River. London, therefore, demanded the Columbia as the boundary between the mountains and the Pacific. Adams, who would settle for no less than a usable port along the Oregon shore, had been convinced by New England seamen that the Columbia River would never meet that need, largely because of the dangers of the bar that blocked its entrance. He understood also that the Strait of Juan de Fuca and Puget Sound, both north of the Columbia but south of 49°, constituted one of the world's best inland waterways. For these reasons Adams demanded the extension of the 49th parallel to the Pacific. When British negotiators proved intractable

[35]Ibid., pp. 450–53, 455–56.

on this point, he agreed to a policy of joint occupancy with Britain in the Oregon country west of the Rockies for a period of ten years, an arrangement that either country could terminate on one year's notice. Thus Adams delayed the final Oregon settlement until that time when the diplomatic advantage would pass to the United States.

Adams's subsequent diplomatic achievement, perhaps his greatest, came in 1819 when, in the Adams-Onís Treaty, he not only acquired Florida for the United States but also defined the southern boundary of the Louisiana Purchase from the Gulf of Mexico to the Pacific Ocean. Florida in 1817 was still under Spanish rule, but that region had become a problem for the U.S. government—and for the citizens of Georgia— simply because the Madrid regime was too plagued with political and military disorders elsewhere to maintain order in its colony. British adventurers in Florida perennially armed and incited the local Indians to raid north of the Florida boundary. Monroe dispatched General Andrew Jackson to punish the Indians for their destruction of American lives and property. Carrying out his instructions with considerable vigor, Jackson in 1818 pursued a band of marauding Indians into Florida where he captured and executed two British agents as well as two Indian chiefs. Spain protested the action, and Jackson's enemies in Congress demanded the general's dismissal.

President Monroe and all members of the cabinet, except Adams, agreed that Jackson had exceeded his instructions and committed war against Spain, an act that required an official disavowal.[36] Adams reminded the cabinet that the general's actions were defensive and that he had entered Florida, not to war on Spain but to terminate the Indian depredations. Jackson had discretionary powers; to disavow them, Adams believed, was unthinkable. He admitted in his diary that he had pushed his case to the limit, but he added: "If the question was dubious, it was better to err on the side of vigor than of weakness— on the side of our own officer . . . than on the side of our bitterest enemies."[37] Adams's argument carried. On July 23, 1818, the secretary reminded the complaining Spanish minister, Don Luis de Onís, that Spain had an obligation, under treaty, to keep order in Florida. According to Adams, the fort at St. Mark would be restored only to a Spanish force strong enough to hold it against an Indian attack. Peace between the United States and Spain, he warned, "required that henceforth the

---

[36]In a long letter to Jackson, Monroe acknowledged the legitimacy of Jackson's action under the circumstances. He took the view that it probably would induce Spain to cede territory, provided that the United States did not incite Spain to declare war by holding the posts in Florida. See Monroe to Jackson, July 19, 1818, in Hamilton, *Writings of Monroe*, 6:54–59.

[37]*Memoirs of John Quincy Adams*, 4:113.

stipulations by Spain to restrain by force her Indians from all hostilities against the United States should be faithfully and effectually fulfilled."[38] If Spain could not control the Indians, then it had no choice but to cede Florida to the United States.

Jackson's forays into Florida troubled Spanish officials in Madrid; Adams's masterful defense of the general seemed to underscore the U.S. government's determination to settle the Florida matter. On July 10, 1818, the French minister in Washington, Hyde de Neuville, informed Adams that Spain, recognizing its weakness, would cede Florida to the United States, provided that Washington assumed the claims of American citizens against Spain, estimated at some $5 million. Onís immediately took up the negotiations, raising the issue of the still undefined southern boundary of the Louisiana Purchase. Spain hoped to push the line eastward and northward as far as possible, while Adams sought a boundary that would bring as much of Texas and the Southwest as possible into the United States. Onís, on July 11, proposed a western boundary that would separate the United States from Spanish Mexico at a line moving northward between Adeas and Natchitoches to the Red River and from there to the Missouri. Adams rejected this outright.[39] So uncompromising was Madrid that in October he threatened to break off the negotiations. Then on October 31 the secretary presented a note to Onís, outlining what he termed the final U.S. offer:

> Beginning at the mouth of the River Sabine, on the Gulf of Mexico, following the course of said river to the thirty-second degree of latitude; the eastern bank and all the islands in said river to belong to the United States, and the western bank to Spain; thence, due north, to the northern-most part of the thirty-third degree of north latitude, and until it strikes the Rio Roxo, or Red River, thence, following the course of the said river, to its source, touching the chain of the Snow mountains, in latitude thirty-seven degrees twenty-five minutes north, longitude one hundred and six degrees fifteen minutes west, or thereabouts, as marked on Melish's map, thence to the summit of the said mountains, and following the chain of the same to the forty-first parallel of latitude; thence, following the said parallel of latitude forty-one degrees, to the South Sea. The northern bank of the said Red River, and all islands therein, to belong to the United States, and the southern bank of the same to Spain.[40]

[38]*American State Papers: Foreign Relations*, 4:497–99.
[39]July 10, 11, 1818, *Memoirs of John Quincy Adams*, 4:106–07.
[40]October 26, 1818, ibid., p. 144; Adams to Onís, October 31, 1818, in Ford, *Writings of John Quincy Adams*, 6:457–58.

Through subsequent weeks the negotiations remained dead-locked. Then on January 3, 1819, Hyde de Neuville informed Adams that Onís had received new instructions which indicated a line extending to the Pacific at the 43rd parallel but required a larger barrier for Santa Fe than Adams's Red River line would permit. Onís, however, demanded a line from the Missouri River to the mouth of the Columbia on the Pacific, sufficient, he said, to enable the United States to construct a system of internal communications from the Atlantic to the Pacific.[41] This line Adams also rejected but responded favorably to Madrid's request regarding Santa Fe. He altered his proposal of October 31, substituting for the Red River (to its mouth) a line to run due north from the Pawnee bend of the Red to the Arkansas, following that river to its source in the Rockies. From that point the line would run due north to 42°. When Adams, to his chagrin, discovered that the Pawnee bend was four or five degrees west of his initial readings of 97° west longitude, he informed Hyde de Neuville that he preferred the 100th meridian. He then asked the French minister why Spain would demand four or five degrees of wilderness along the Pacific which would never be of value to it.

Thereafter Onís's counterproposals began to approach the American demands. On February 4 the French minister relayed Onís's acceptance of Adams's modified proposal along the Red, with the substitution of the 43rd parallel for the 42nd along the Pacific. So close was the agreement that Monroe was inclined to concede all remaining points of conflict. Adams observed that, "if Onís intends to conclude at all, we can obtain better." On February 12, he noted in his diary: "I am so constantly occupied and absorbed by this negotiation with Onís that almost all other business runs in arrear, and in a most especial manner this journal. I rode to the President's, and the adjourned Cabinet meeting was held. . . . I was finally authorized to accept the longitude one hundred from the Red to the Arkansas, and the latitude forty-three to the South Sea, if better cannot be obtained."[42]

By February 15, Onís had agreed to Adams's boundary, including the 42nd parallel, but insisted that the river lines follow the middle, rather than the south, bank of the streams. Adams countered that Spain would have no settlements near those rivers and that the middle of streams never lent themselves to precise lines of demarcation. He insisted before the cabinet that the United States adhere to the principle of owning the rivers and islands in them. Five days later Onís capitulated,

[41] January 3, 15, 1819, *Memoirs of John Quincy Adams*, 4:208–10, 218–19.
[42] February 4, 11, 12, 1819, ibid., pp. 244, 249–53.

observing that Adams had given him more trouble than had the president. The Spanish minister recalled the words a suitor once addressed to Philip IV: "Sire, your Majesty has no influence with the Minister of Grace and Justice, for he refuses me what you have granted."[43]

On February 22, 1819, Onís and Adams signed the Trans-Continental Treaty. For Adams it was the capstone of his diplomatic career: "It was, perhaps, the most important day of my life. . . . May no disappointment embitter the hope which this event warrants us in cherishing, and may its future influence on the destinies of my country be as extensive and as favorable as our warmest anticipations can paint!"[44] Later members of Congress urged Adams to put the treaty aside and claim the Rio Grande. The secretary reminded one congressman who came to criticize that he and Henry Clay were excellent negotiators in theory. Then he leveled a strong rebuke:

> They were for obtaining all and granting nothing. They played a game between their own right and left hands, and could allot with admirable management the whole stake to one hand and total discomfiture to the other. In the negotiations with Spain we had a just claim to the Mississippi and its waters, and our citizens had a fair though very precarious claim to indemnities. We had a mere color of claim to the Rio del Norte, no claim to a line beyond the Rocky Mountains, and none to Florida, which we very much wanted. The treaty . . . barely gives up to Spain the colorable claim from the Sabine to the Rio del Norte. Now, negotiation implies some concession upon both sides. If after obtaining every object of your pursuit but one, and that one weak in principle and of no present value, what would you have offered to Spain to yield that also?[45]

VI

Spain's challenge to the United States lay not only in that nation's weakness in Florida but also in its precarious position throughout the Western Hemisphere. Napoleon's invasion of Spain in 1808 had terminated Madrid's effective control of Spanish America. Provisional juntas maintained by Spain's ruling classes continued to claim jurisdiction over the empire, but by 1812 their New World influence was purely nominal. Freed of Spain's commercial restrictions, the various

[43]February 15, 18, 19, 20, 1819, ibid., pp. 255, 264, 267–68, 270.
[44]February 22, 1819, ibid., pp. 276–77.
[45]Ibid., 5:68–69.

regions of Latin America opened their commerce to the world. British and Yankee shippers entered South American ports in large numbers. When war broke out between the restored Spanish monarchy and the now rebellious colonies, the struggling South Americans looked to the United States especially for economic, military, and moral support.

Within the United States editors, congressmen, and administration officials favored Latin American independence with almost total unanimity. On the proper national response to Latin America's plight there was no agreement at all. The Abbé de Pradt, the prolific French writer, emphasized both the importance of Latin America to Europe and the possibility that, inasmuch as Spanish control was doomed, the great European powers might establish the region's independence on terms that would keep the new nations attached to the Continent. Determined to sever Europe's ties with the New World, editors led by William Duane of Philadelphia's *Aurora* demanded U.S. guardianship of Latin American independence. He argued that this nation would find in Latin America "the corrective of European jealousy, and the resources with which to defeat and counterplace the intolerant and malignant selfishness of European nations."[46] In Congress the powerful Clay denounced the administration for neglecting American interests and the cause of liberty.

Monroe and Adams would not be stampeded. They recognized the overwhelming preference of U.S. citizens for Latin American independence, but they refused to commit the United States before the European powers had revealed their intentions or the patriots of South America had demonstrated their capacity to establish their independence and maintain a semblance of order. Adams was appalled at the open congressional support for Latin America. "There seemed to me," he complained in June 1816, "too much of the warlike humor in the debates of Congress—propositions even to take up the cause of the South Americans; predictions of wars with this country to the end of time, as cool and as causeless, as if they were talking of the expense of building a light house."[47]

As the public pressure for involvement continued, Adams reminded his father in December 1817 that Latin America had replaced the French Revolution as the great source of discord in the United States: "The republican spirit of our country not only sympathizes with people struggling in a cause, . . . but it is working into indignation against the relapse of Europe into the opposite principle of monkery and despotism. And now, as at the early stage of the French Revolution, we have

[46]See Whitaker, *United States and the Independence of Latin America*, pp. 104–12.

[47]Adams to George William Erving, June 10, 1816, in Ford, *Writings of John Quincy Adams*, 6:45.

ardent spirits who are for rushing into the conflict, without looking to the consequences."[48] He doubted that the people of South America were capable of self-government; thus, he viewed the revolutions with little sympathy. Monroe, somewhat more sympathetic, argued that the United States could render Latin Americans no service more useful than to refrain from any action that might provoke direct European intervention. He explained his views in a letter to Jackson in December 1818, although later he omitted the key passage: "By this policy we have lost nothing, as *by keeping the Allies out of the quarrel*, Florida must soon be ours, and *the Colonies must be independent, for if they cannot beat Spain, they do not deserve to be free.*"[49]

During 1818 the ultimate course of U.S. policy toward Latin America began to emerge. In March, Monroe requested a congressional appropriation to defray the expenses of a commission of inquiry to South America. Clay attached an amendment appropriating $18,000 for a U.S. legation in Buenos Aires, thereby compelling the administration to recognize the independence of the Argentine. Clay stepped down from the speaker's rostrum to enter a strong plea for his measure, but the House remained unconvinced and voted down the amendment, 115 to 45. Shortly thereafter Adams expressed his contempt for Congress in his diary: "The present session will stand remarkable in the annals of the Union for showing how a legislature can keep itself employed when having nothing to do. . . . The proposal appropriation for a minister to Buenos Ayres has gone the way of other things lost upon earth, like the purchase of oil for light houses in the western country." In July the president's fact-finding commission returned to Washington, hopelessly divided.[50] Still, the administration continued to respond to changing conditions both in Europe and in Latin America. By the summer of 1818, Monroe and Adams concluded that the great European states would never agree on measures to restore Spanish sovereignty in South America, especially since Britain clearly favored independence. At the Conference of Aix-la-Chapelle, which opened in September 1818, England opposed the use of force against the Latin Americans, but Lord Castlereagh's rejection of Adams's suggestion for a concerted British-American policy encouraged further caution in Washington.

Through 1819 and 1820 Adams moved slowly and deliberately, proclaiming official U.S. neutrality toward the struggles of Latin America. He reminded Monroe that any successful revolution reaches a stage when those fighting for independence merit recognition, and when

---

[48]Adams to John Adams, December 21, 1817, ibid., pp. 275–76.
[49]Quoted in Whitaker, *United States and the Independence of Latin America*, pp. 210–11.
[50]*Memoirs of John Quincy Adams*, 4:155–56.

recognition is no longer a departure from the obligations of neutrality. Still, Adams continued, "the justice of a cause . . . is not sufficient to justify third parties in siding with it."[51] Finally, in February 1821 ratified copies of the Trans-Continental Treaty were exchanged in Washington, thereby eliminating the one remaining international argument against recognition of Latin American independence. That year the striking victories of the revolutionary forces all but destroyed Spain's remaining authority in South America. Clay secured passage of two resolutions in the House, one expressing interest in South American independence, the other encouraging the president to recognize the independence of the new nations whenever he believed it expedient. Shortly thereafter, in March 1821, Clay and Adams discussed Latin America at length, each regretting their years of deep disagreement. Adams again argued the administration's case for delay:

> That the final issue of their present struggle would be their entire independence of Spain I have never doubted. That it was our true policy and duty to take no part in the contest I was equally clear. . . . So far as they were contending for independence, I wished well to their cause; but I had seen and yet see no prospect that they would establish free or liberal institutions of government. They are not likely to promote the spirit either of freedom or order by their example. They have not the first elements of good or free government. Arbitrary power, military and ecclesiastical, was stamped upon their education, upon their habits, and upon all their institutions. Civil dissension was infused into all their seminal principles. War and mutual destruction was in every member of their organization, moral, political, and physical. I had little expectation of any beneficial result to this country from any future connection with them, political or commercial. We should derive no improvement to our own institutions by any communion with theirs. Nor was there any appearance of a disposition in them to take any political lesson from us. As to the commercial connection, I agreed with him that little weight should be allowed to arguments of mere pecuniary interest; but there was no basis for much traffic between us. They want none of our productions, and we could afford to purchase very few of theirs.[52]

In a special message to Congress on March 8, 1822, Monroe recognized the changing conditions, declaring that Chile, the United Provinces of the Plata (Argentina), Peru, Colombia, and Mexico were

---

[51]Adams to Erving, April 20, 1818, in Ford, *Writings of John Quincy Adams*, 6:309; Adams to Monroe, August 24, 1818, ibid., pp. 442–43.

[52]*Memoirs of John Quincy Adams*, 5:324–25.

fully independent and thus could rightfully claim recognition by other nations.[53] Congress responded by appropriating funds to meet the expense of "such missions to the independent nations on the American continent as the President might deem proper." Following formal recognition of the five new states, Latin American representatives added both numbers and variety to the Washington diplomatic corps. Adams assured the Spanish government that recognition in no way indicated preference for the former colonies over Spain and "is neither intended to invalidate any right of Spain, nor to affect the employment of any means she may yet be disposed or enabled to use, with the view of reuniting those provinces to the rest of her dominions. It is the mere acknowledgement of existing facts."

Further delay, Monroe explained to Madison, would have produced deep resentment in Latin America and opened the way for renewed European encroachments. Even as Monroe sought the exclusion of European influence from the Western Hemisphere, he reassured the Continental powers that the United States had no intention to control the new governments or to create a separate American system. Neither Monroe nor Adams revealed much concern for the nature of the Latin American regimes, nor did they favor the immediate assignment of ministers to the new capitals. No commercial treaties, based on reciprocity, could possibly affect Britain's dominance of Latin America's foreign trade. "As to running a race with England to snatch from these new nations some special privilege or monopoly," wrote Adams, "I thought it neither a wise nor an honest policy."[54]

VII

For the British, Spain was a special problem. Out of deference to that country London refused to follow the American lead in recognizing the independence of the new Latin American states. For many years, however, pirates and marauders had plundered British commerce in American waters; for these assaults the Spanish government offered no redress.[55] What complicated Britain's troubles was Spain's internal anarchy. Spanish revolutionaries had captured King Ferdinand VII and proclaimed a constitutional monarchy. To make matters worse, the members of the Holy Alliance—Russia, Austria, and Prussia— denounced Spanish liberalism and at the Congress of Verona in 1822

[53]Monroe's message to Congress, March 8, 1822, in Hamilton, *Writings of Monroe*, 6:207–11.

[54]*Memoirs of John Quincy Adams*, 6:24–25.

[55]Memorandum for the cabinet, November 15, 1822, in Edward J. Stapleton, ed., *Some Official Correspondence of George Canning* (London, 1887), 1:49, 58–59.

encouraged France to dispatch an army into Spain to restore the king. British Foreign Minister Lord Castlereagh had no interest in republicanism but opposed interventionism in Spain as a matter of policy. Distressed by his failure to nullify Europe's reactionary policies, he broke down and took his own life in August 1822. George Canning, his brilliant successor, exemplifying Britain's antipathy toward the repressive behavior of the Continental powers, withdrew British cooperation from the affairs of the Quadruple Alliance. British leaders regarded the Spanish revolution as legitimate. "Between King Ferdinand and the Cortes," wrote Canning, "there is not a feather of preponderance. The King is as bad a king and the Cortes as bad a Government as one can conceive."[56] Canning warned the French on February 1, 1823 that they were underestimating the magnitude of the enterprise which they were entering, as Spain in the past had shown immense powers of resistance. He reminded Paris that France's war with Spain which had begun in 1793 lasted for twenty-two years.[57]

Still, Canning understood that the French invasion, if regrettable, was not directed at the Spanish nation itself. Indeed, the Spanish people viewed the invasion more as a police action than as a conquest, and they accepted, even welcomed, the French presence.[58] Thus Canning was obliged to watch while France concluded an enterprise that enhanced its reputation and confirmed the predominance of the Holy Alliance in European affairs. There British forebearance stopped. Canning suspected that France might attempt to restore the Spanish Empire or, more unacceptable, use its influence in Spain to lay the foundation for another French empire in America.[59] In addition, Alexander's fears aggravated the threat. The czar viewed the revolutions of Latin America as mere extensions of Europe's revolutionary fervor and therefore dangerous to the Continent's political stability. Understandably, St. Petersburg was troubled by Washington's recognition of the Latin American republics; it admonished the governments of Europe not to follow the U.S. precedent. Clearly, Alexander was not opposed to European intervention in the Americas, provided that France assumed the initiative. With good reason French policy in Spain continued to cause unease in London well into the summer of 1823. Canning commented

[56]Canning to Charles Bagot, July 14, 1823, in Josceline Bagot, ed., *George Canning and His Friends* (New York, 1909), 2:181.

[57]Canning to Monsieur of France, February 1, 1823, in Stapleton, *Some Official Correspondence of Canning*, 1:72–73.

[58]Memorandum on the Policy of Great Britain in the Event of a War Between France and Spain, February 1823, ibid., p. 84.

[59]Canning's view of French policy in Spain can be found in his memorandum of February 1823, in Stapleton, *Some Official Correspondence of Canning*, 1:86–88. For a good discussion of Alexander's fears of Latin American revolution see Ernest R. May, *The Making of the Monroe Doctrine* (Cambridge, MA, 1975), pp. 71–72.

to Charles Bagot on August 20: "How shall matters be settled in Spain, and who shall settle them—France, Russia, Austria, England, Ferdinand, Cortes, Occupation, Guarantee? . . . Add Portugal, Brazil, Spanish America, and add thereto again United States, and see how matters grow into complication! As yet we are out of the whole affair."[60]

Several days earlier Canning, in a conversation with Richard Rush, the American minister in London, acknowledged the British decision to counter any French move to lay hands on the Spanish colonies. He then asked what attitude the U.S. government would have toward making a public declaration that it also opposed a European invasion of Spanish America. Canning did not anticipate any need for concerted action; he believed simply that the knowledge that Great Britain and the United States shared the same intention toward Latin America would be sufficient to restrain France. Rush agreed only to forward Canning's thoughts to the government in Washington.[61]

In a letter of August 20, Canning spelled out British policy toward Latin America. He agreed that Spain could not conceivably recover its New World colonies; still, England would await the proper time and circumstances for recognizing the independent states of Latin America. Britain would not place any impediment in the way of a Spanish arrangement with its former colonies, but it neither wanted any portion of the Spanish colonies nor would see the transfer of any of them to another power with indifference. Convinced that American purpose in Latin America conformed to that of Great Britain, Canning suggested that the United States and Britain issue a joint declaration, warning France and other Continental powers, while reassuring Spain, that neither country had any designs on the Spanish Empire.[62] Rush forwarded Canning's letter, which he received on August 22, to Adams with a note explaining his hesitancy in committing the U.S. government to a course of action with which it might disagree. During subsequent days Rush was flattered by Canning's continuing attentiveness. Finally, on August 28, Rush suggested that, if Britain made the conformity of policy complete by recognizing the new republics he would, without specific instructions, sign the declaration that Canning proposed.[63] The British foreign minister remained firm on the question of recognition. When he returned to London in mid-September, after a country excursion, he again refused to pledge his government to an immediate recognition of the South American states.

Suddenly in early October Canning dropped the subject of a joint British-American declaration from his conversations with Rush. "The

[60]Canning to Bagot, August 20, 1823, in Bagot, *Canning and His Friends*, 2:199.
[61]Rush to Adams, August 19, 1823, in Hamilton, *Writings of Monroe*, 6:361–64.
[62]Canning to Rush, August 20, 1823, ibid., pp. 365–66.
[63]Rush to Adams, August 28, 1823, ibid., p. 371.

termination of the discussion between us," Rush reported on October 10, "may be thought somewhat sudden, not to say abrupt, considering how zealously as well as spontaneously it was started on his side. As I did not commence it, it is not my intention to revive it." Two weeks later Rush privately informed Monroe that "the Spanish American topic has been dropped by Mr. Canning in a most extraordinary manner."[64] Not until November 24 did Rush discover the reason, when Canning informed him that their final discussion of the joint declaration on September 26 had convinced him that he could accomplish nothing with the United States. Determined to lose no more time, Canning, in a series of conferences with the Prince de Polignac, French ambassador in London, had delivered a warning directly to Paris.[65] France had interests to defend in the New World, especially in the Caribbean and on the Guiana coast, and French officials regarded the revolutionary movements in Latin America as in some measure threats to the French Empire in America. On the other hand, the French had no desire to injure their country's future trade with Latin America by appearing to oppose the region's independence from Spanish rule. From the beginning France's interests in Latin America's future were ambiguous; any firm resistance in either the United States or Britain would divide French counsels and encourage caution. The Paris government responded to Canning's ultimatum with the secret "Polignac Memorandum," which assured the British that it had no intention of dispatching an expedition to the New World. Thus Canning, through unilateral action, had resolved the immediate challenge to British policy.

VIII

In Washington, France's unopposed invasion of Spain troubled President Monroe. Unlike British leaders he viewed the Spanish revolt as an issue of human rights and wondered why England played into the hands of France and the Holy Alliance through its policy of inaction. Russia, he assumed, was too involved in Turkish affairs to concern itself directly in the problems of southwest Europe. Monroe wondered what American policy toward Spain should be. "Such is the state of Europe," he wrote Jefferson, "& our relation to it is pretty much the same, as it was, in the commencement of the French revolution. Can we, in any form, take a bolder atttitude in regard to it, in favor of

---

[64]Rush to Adams, October 10, 1823, ibid., p. 389; Rush to Monroe, October 22, 1823, ibid., p. 390.
[65]Rush to Adams, November 26, 1823, ibid., pp. 401–02.

liberty, than we then did?"[66] Shortly thereafter Adams made it clear that Monroe's liberal sentiments did not govern U.S. policy toward Europe:

> From the first war of the French Revolution, to the recent invasion of Spain, there has been a succession of wars, national and civil, in almost every one of which *one* of the parties was contending for liberty, or for independence. To the first revolutionary war a strong impulse of feeling urged the people of the United States to take side with the party which, at the commencement, was contending apparently at least, for both. Had the policy of the United States not been essentially pacific a stronger case to claim their interference would scarcely have been presented. They, nevertheless, declared themselves neutral; and the principle then deliberately settled has been invariably adhered to ever since.[67]

Rush's long communications of late August reached Washington on October 9, 1823. Canning's offer confronted the Monroe administration with a fundamental question: Did the nation's hemispheric interests require this projection of American influence into European politics, or could the United States entrust the independence of the Western Hemisphere to the protections afforded by the Atlantic, British power, and Latin American resistance? Members of the American press assumed that France, in placing its army and navy at the disposal of the Spanish king, intended to help Spain recover its lost New World colonies.[68] This Monroe wanted to prevent, but he harbored a profound distrust of English monarchy and continued to regard it as fundamentally hostile to the United States. Still, he believed that genuine British interests were driving that nation toward a new promising relationship with the United States. "Has not the epoch arriv'd," he asked Jefferson, "when G. Britain must take her stand, either on the side of the monarchs of Europe, or of the U States, & in consequence, either in favor of Despotism or of liberty & may it not be presum'd that, aware of that necessity, her government has seiz'd on the present occurrence, as that, which it deems the most suitable, to announce & mark the commenc'ment of that career?"[69]

Before accepting the British offer Monroe sought the advice of Jefferson and Madison. Jefferson, in quiet retirement at Monticello,

[66]Monroe to Jefferson, June 2, 1823, ibid., pp. 309–10.

[67]Adams to Rush, August 16, 1823, ibid., p. 361.

[68]See Harry Ammon, "The Monroe Doctrine: Domestic Politics or National Decision?" *Diplomatic History* 5 (Winter 1981):59.

[69]Monroe to Jefferson, October 17, 1823, in Hamilton, *Writings of Monroe*, 6:324.

responded with a classic reiteration of his concept of the two spheres; he urged Monroe to accept the British overture:

> The question presented by the letters you have sent me is the most momentous which has been offered to my contemplation since that of Independence. *That* made us a nation; *this* sets the compass and points the course which we are to steer through the ocean of time opening to us. . . . Our first and fundamental maxim should be never to entangle ourselves in the broils of Europe; our second, never to suffer Europe to intermeddle in cisatlantic affairs. America, North and South, has a set of interests distinct from those of Europe and peculiarly her own; she should have a system of her own, separate and apart from that of Europe.[70]

For Jefferson it was imperative that this country, if it desired to maintain the status quo in the Western Hemisphere, not take a stand against the existing order in Europe. Only one nation—Britain—could challenge American interests in the New World; it was the part of wisdom, therefore, to enlist that great power in the cause of emancipating the American continents from European influence. Madison likewise endorsed Canning's proposal.[71]

Meanwhile, Adams had responded to the French invasion of Spain by reasserting the doctrine of *no transfer*. France's policy in that country was not his major concern. What troubled him was the possibility that Spain might cede Cuba to Britain as the price of an Anglo-Spanish alliance. In April 1823, Adams sent a long note to Hugh Nelson, the American minister in Madrid, warning the Spanish government that the United States would oppose the transfer of Cuba to any European power. Such a transfer would not only affect Spanish-American relations but also subvert the rights of the Cuban people and justify the United States in supporting any resulting independence movement.[72] When Canning assured Washington that London had no intention of acquiring the island, Monroe suggested to the cabinet that the United States also issue a statement of self-denial. Adams objected; for him there was no reason for the United States to bind itself permanently against the possibility that Cuba might one day solicit union with the United States.[73] Monroe assured London informally that the United States had no designs on Cuba.

---

[70]Jefferson to Monroe, October 24, 1823, ibid., pp. 391–93.
[71]Madison to Monroe, October 30, 1823, ibid., p. 394.
[72]Adams to Hugh Nelson, April 28, 1823, in Ford, *Writings of John Quincy Adams*, 7:381.
[73]Ibid., p. 373.

Russia also had posed a threat to U.S. interests in the Western Hemisphere and provoked another historic response from Adams. Before the 1820s rumors of Russian encroachment along the Pacific coast of North America, as far south as California, had produced only indifference in Washington. To Adams, Russia lacked both the navy and the merchant marine to establish distant colonies.[74] In 1821, however, the Russian czar issued a ukase which excluded foreigners from trading, fishing, or navigating within one hundred Roman miles of the northwest coast from Bering Strait to the 51st parallel of north latitude. Both Britain and the United States objected. At a cabinet meeting on June 28, 1823, Adams introduced the question of Russian claims. These, he believed, America should contest, especially since that country had no settlements in the disputed region. On July 17, he informed Baron de Tuyll, the Russian minister, that the United States would contest the right of Russia to any territorial establishment on this continent, and that this nation assumed the principle that "the American continents are no longer subjects for *any* new European colonial establishments."[75] On July 22, Adams penned a note to Henry Middleton, the American minister in St. Petersburg:

> There can, perhaps, be no better time for saying, frankly and explicitly, to the Russian Government that the future peace of the world, and the interest of Russia herself, can not be promoted by Russian settlements upon any part of the American continent. With the exception of the British establishments north of the United States, the remainder of both the American continents must henceforth be left to the management of American hands.[76]

Thus Adams asserted the principle of *noncolonization*.

When Monroe returned to Washington with the opinions of Jefferson and Madison corroborating his own, Russia had created another crisis. Tuyll warned Adams that the czar would not recognize the new governments of Latin America and that, unless the United States remained neutral, Russia might support a European invasion of the former Spanish Empire. This threat merely confirmed those convictions in Washington that Canning's proposal should be accepted, but Adams refused to be frightened. He doubted that France intended armed intervention in Latin America; moreover, the British navy was powerful enough to prevent it. The secretary suspected that Canning's overture

---

[74]Adams to George Washington Campbell, June 28, 1818, ibid., 6:372.
[75]*Memoirs of John Quincy Adams*, 6:163.
[76]*American State Papers: Foreign Relations*, 5:443, 445.

was aimed less at obtaining unnecessary U.S. support than in preventing, through a self-denying agreement, future American expansion into Texas and the Caribbean. When the cabinet met on November 7, Adams proposed that the United States decline the British overture and take its stand against the Holy Alliance unilaterally. "It would be more candid, as well as more dignified," he said, "to avow our principles explicitly to Russia and France, than to come in as a cock-boat in the wake of the British man-of-war."[77]

Adams favored an overall American policy that would combine a letter to Russia with one to France in a single statement of national intent. To this Monroe agreed. Still, the president hesitated to reject the British proposal. The news that France had captured Cadiz caused him to despair for the future of South America. John C. Calhoun, equally fearful of Europe, proposed that Rush be given discretionary power to accept Canning's overture, if necessary. Adams argued that Spain had no more power to restore its control in the Western Hemisphere than had Chimborazo to sink to the bottom of the sea. He warned that, "if the South Americans were really in a state to be so easily subdued, it would be but a more forcible motive for us to beware of involving ourselves in their fate."[78]

One week later Adams delivered his note to the Russian minister, explaining that the United States was a republic and thus was attracted to the Latin American states by those very principles that repelled the czar. He hoped that Russia would maintain its policy of neutrality. Instead, it quickly created further alarm when another note reminded the United States of the Holy Alliance's success in putting down revolutions in Europe and its obligation to guarantee tranquility everywhere, including Latin America. As gloom settled over the Potomac, Adams told the cabinet:

> My purpose would be in a moderate and conciliatory manner, but with a firm and determined spirit, to declare our dissent from the principles avowed in those communications; to assert those upon which our own Government is founded, and while disclaiming all . . . interference with the political affairs of Europe, to declare our expectation and hope that the European powers will equally abstain from the attempt to spread their principles in the American hemisphere, or to subjugate by force any part of these continents to their will.

[77] *Memoirs of John Quincy Adams*, 6:177, 180–81.

[78] November 13, 1823, ibid., pp. 185–86. Chimborazo is an extinct volcano in Ecuador; until 1827 it was thought to be the highest mountain in the Andes.

Adams thus formulated the principle of *hands-off*; Monroe accepted it and, in his December message to Congress, decided to proclaim this new American purpose toward the Western Hemisphere.

On November 21, Monroe read to the cabinet a preliminary draft of his forthcoming message. Adams was shocked and recorded that "its introduction was in a tone of deep solemnity and of high alarm, intimating that this country is menaced by imminent and formidable dangers, such as would probably soon call for their most vigorous energies and the closest union." What distressed him especially was Monroe's reversion to his old republican innocence in taking up the cause of revolution in Spain and Greece, two areas in which he had no intention of acting. He asked the president to reconsider the entire subject:

> This message would be a summons to arms—to arms against all Europe, and for objects of policy exclusively European—Greece and Spain. It would be as new, too, in our policy as it would be surprising. . . . This message would at once buckle on the harness and throw down the gauntlet. It would have the air of open defiance to all Europe, and I should not be surprised if the first answer to it from Spain and France, and even Russia, should be to break off their diplomatic intercourse with us. I did not expect that the quiet which we had enjoyed for six or seven years would last much longer. The aspect of things was portentous; but if we must come to an issue with Europe, let us keep it off as long as possible. Let us use all possible means to carry the opinion of the nation with us, and the opinion of the world.[79]

Adams was especially disturbed at Monroe's open endorsement of the Greek independence movement, for he had long argued against U.S. involvement in that cause. The Greek revolutionary movement had slowly gathered strength until by 1821 it posed an immediate threat to Ottoman rule. Sultan Mahmud II retaliated with such violence and destruction that he aroused anti-Turkish sentiment throughout western Europe and the United States. In 1822, *Niles' Register*, dwelling on Turkish barbarities, chided the country for not taking up the cause of Greek liberty and independence. In his annual message of December 1822, Monroe expressed regret that a country which had contributed so much to civilization should live under a gloomy despotism. Still, concern for the Greek cause languished. Then in 1823 Edward Everett, professor of Greek literature at Harvard and editor of the *North American Review*, championed Greek independence in a long article appearing in

[79]November 21, 1823, ibid., pp. 194–95.

that journal.[80] Adams was not impressed and argued strongly against any American meddling in the affairs of Greece and Turkey, especially since the country was not prepared financially or militarily to intervene. When Crawford and Calhoun in the cabinet expressed great enthusiasm for the Greeks, Adams recorded his disgust:

> Mr. Gallatin had proposed in one of his last dispatches, as if he was serious, that we should assist the Greeks with our naval force in the Mediterranean—one frigate, one corvette, and one schooner. Mr. Crawford and Mr. Calhoun inclined to countenance this project. . . . Their enthusiasm for the Greeks is all sentiment, and the standard of this is the prevailing popular feeling. As for action, they are seldom agreed; and after two hours of discussion this day the subject was dismissed, leaving it precisely where it was— nothing determined, and nothing practicable proposed by either of them.[81]

Amid the critical cabinet debates on the president's message during late November, Adams again passed judgment on the Greek issue and the motives of those who favored it:

> I called at the President's, and found Mr. Gallatin with him. He still adhered to his idea of sending a naval force and a loan of money to the Greeks; and as he is neither an enthusiast nor a fool, and knows perfectly well that no such thing will be done, I look for the motives of this strange proposal, and find them not very deeply laid. Mr. Gallatin still builds castles in the air of popularity and, being under no responsibility for consequences, patronizes the Greek cause for the sake of raising his reputation. His measure will not succeed, and even if it should, all the burden and danger of it will not bear upon him, but upon the Administration, and he will be the great champion of Grecian liberty.[82]

He considered it essential that Monroe not antagonize the Holy Alliance needlessly. If the European powers chose to challenge the United States, Washington should meet the issue but not create it. If the Holy Alliance really intended to restore the colonies to Spain, which Adams doubted, the United States had perhaps been too hasty in acknowledging South American independence. Earlier the administration had not even thought

---

[80]Edward Everett, "Affairs of Greece," *North American Review* 17 (October 1823): 417–24. For an excellent survey of U.S. reaction to the Greek revolution see Myrtle A. Cline, *American Attitudes Toward the Greek War of Independence, 1821–1828* (Atlanta, GA, 1930), pp. 9–35.
[81]*Memoirs of John Quincy Adams*, 6:172–73.
[82]November 24, 1823, ibid., pp. 198–99.

of interfering in the affairs of Europe. "If they intend now to interpose by force," he warned, "we shall have as much as we can do to prevent them, without going to bid them defiance in the heart of Europe." Arguing steadily against any American involvement in European affairs, the secretary summarized his views before the cabinet: "The ground that I wish to take is that of earnest remonstrance against the interference of the European powers by force with South America, but to disclaim all interference on our part with Europe; to make an American cause, and adhere inflexibly to that." Adams had added to hands-off his principle of *abstention*.

This concept of two worlds Monroe embodied in his celebrated message to Congress on December 2, 1823. The so-called Monroe Doctrine declared specifically that the American continents were no longer open to European colonization and that the United States would regard any effort of the European powers to extend their government to any portion of the Western Hemisphere as a threat to its peace and safety. On the other hand, he assured the nations of the Old World that the United States would not interfere with their dependencies in the New World or involve itself in matters purely European.[83] On the day after delivering his message to Congress, newspapers from England reported that an expedition of 12,000 men was assembling in Cadiz to restore Colombia to the Spanish crown. Monroe and much of Washington responded with the customary alarm. The president prepared instructions to Rush, advising him to offer U.S. cooperation in preventing any European interference in the affairs of South America. Again it was Adams who argued that European intervention was unlikely. Rush's new instructions did not contemplate any action but emphasized, largely to impress Canning, the American commitment to the principle of Monroe's message.[84]

IX

During subsequent days Adams prepared documents for Britain and Russia, assuring Canning that the United States intended to pursue separate but parallel policies in Latin America. Together Adams and Monroe had wedded American policies to the status quo in the Atlantic, a status quo which, if threatened, would have the defense of the British navy, as the United States had only one warship on active duty in the Atlantic. Adams's communication to Russia concluded with a strong

[83]For Monroe's message of December 2, 1823 see Hamilton, *Writings of Monroe*, 6:325–42.
[84]See Ammon, "The Monroe Doctrine," pp. 59–61.

warning against European interference in the affairs of the Western Hemisphere. The secretary regarded this dispatch of November 27, 1823 as the most important state paper of his career.[85]

Some Continental diplomatists found the Monroe Doctrine especially distasteful because of its assumption that the political institutions of the New World were in some measure superior to those of the old. For Austria's Prince Metternich such claims to political virtue were nothing less than arrogant. His condemnation of America's attitudes toward the upheavals in Latin America and elsewhere was profound: "The United States of America . . . have cast blame and scorn on the institutions of Europe most worthy of respect. . . . In permitting themselves these unprovoked attacks, in fostering revolutions wherever they show themselves, in regretting those which have failed, in extending a helping hand to those which seem to prosper, they lend new strength to the apostles of sedition and reanimate the courage of every conspirator." Baron de Tuyll passed similar judgment on the Monroe Doctrine when he said that "the document in question enunciates views and pretensions so exaggerated, it establishes principles so contrary to the rights of the European powers that it merits only the most profound contempt."

To Canning, Monroe's principle of noncolonization was extravagant. He assumed with Rush that the doctrine was directed principally, if not specifically, against the equally extravagant claim of the Russian ukase of 1821. As he wrote to Bagot on January 9, 1824,

> Where one Power proclaims as a *Mare Clausum* an Ocean of 4,000 miles across, the other may have thought it a fair set off to prohibit colonization over the whole coasts of the Continent, with a view to which the *Mare Clausum* was attempted to be established. If this indeed be the meaning and the limit of the American pretension, it is to be hoped that the negotiation now pending between Russia and the United States may terminate in withdrawing both that pretension and the one in which it originated.[86]

During the spring of 1824, Adams resolved the far Northwest conflict with Russia. When New England traders demanded access to the fur seals and sea otters in the Aleutians far north of 51°, he reminded Stratford Canning in Washington that the United States had no territorial claims as far north as the 51st parallel and assumed that British interests would be sufficient to counter the Russians' demands. To

[85]*Memoirs of John Quincy Adams*, 6:211–12.
[86]Canning to Bagot, January 9, 1824, in Bagot, *Canning and His Friends*, 2:209–10.

them Adams suggested a boundary at 55° north latitude. In St. Petersburg the government accepted his noncolonization principle as well as the American right to unsettled regions north of the line of division. To keep all of Prince of Wales Island under their control, the Russians proposed the boundary of 54°40'. In the Convention of April 1824, Russia gained its preferred boundary but gave up all pretensions to a mare clausum in the north Pacific.[87]

Even as the April convention disposed of the Russian threat in the far Northwest, Adams's allies in Congress laid the Greek issue to rest. Among Everett's converts was Daniel Webster, then congressman from Massachusetts. A spokesman for New England's business interests, he had been cautious in public statements because the Smyrna trade of the Turkish Empire was one of the most lucrative in the world for Boston merchants. Indeed, the nation's tangible interests in Turkish trade far outweighed its abstract interest in Greek independence. Nevertheless, Webster introduced a resolution into the House in December 1823, which provided "that provision ought to be made by law, for defraying the expense incident to the appointment of an Agent or Commissioner to Greece, whenever the President shall deem it expedient to make such appointment."[88] On January 19, 1824, on this seemingly noncommittal text, he launched into a celebrated and eloquent appeal to American humanitarian sentiment. He asked nothing of Congress; courage and spirit, properly expressed by the passage of the resolution, would achieve more than money. The Greeks, he declared, looked to

> the great Republic of the earth—and they ask us by our common faith, whether we can forget that they are struggling, as we once struggled, for what we now so happily enjoy? I cannot say, sir, that they will succeed: that rests with Heaven. But for myself, sir, if I should tomorrow hear that they have failed . . ., I should still reflect, with the most heartfelt satisfaction, that I have asked you, in the name of seven millions of freemen, that you would give them at least the cheering of one friendly voice.[89]

John Randolph's reply to Webster on January 24 revealed the conservatism that the nation had learned to expect of him. He attacked

---

[87]For Monroe's view of the agreement see Monroe to Madison, August 2, 1824, in Hamilton, *Writings of Monroe*, 7:31–33. See also Bemis, *John Quincy Adams*, pp. 514–15, 523–24.

[88]Norman A. Graebner, *Ideas and Diplomacy: Readings in the Intellectual Tradition of American Foreign Policy* (New York, 1964), p. 148.

[89]Webster's address of January 19, 1824, in *Annals of Congress*, 18th Cong., 1st sess., cols. 1085–99.

especially Webster's effort, through the employment of sentimental appeals, to commit the nation abroad to what it could not accomplish except at enormous cost to its own interests. Why, he wondered, would Webster launch a crusade against slavery in the eastern Mediterranean when slavery existed by law within the United States itself? Randolph also asked why he would fix on Turkey as the enemy of America's democratic doctrines. For a century Turkey's behavior toward its neighbors had been preferable to that of the Christian nations of Europe. How would the United States operate effectively in a country distant by eighty degrees of latitude? "Do gentlemen seriously reflect," he asked, "on the work they have cut out for us? Why, sir, these projects of ambition surpass those of Bonaparte himself." Britain, he was sure, would gladly transfer to the United States major responsibility for preserving the balance of power, a balance that required Britain to fight constantly. Better, Randolph believed, for the nation to abide by Washington's principles of commerce and friendship with all nations, entangling alliances with none. Finally, he attacked the resolution itself:

> We are absolutely combatting shadows. The gentleman would have us to believe his resolution is all but nothing; yet again it is to prove omnipotent, and fills the whole globe with its influence. Either it is nothing, or it is something. If it is nothing, let us lay it on the table, and have done with it at once; but, if it is that something which it has been on the other hand represented to be, let us beware how we touch it. For my part, I would sooner put the shirt of Nessus on my back, than sanction these doctrines— doctrines such as I never heard from my boyhood till now. They go the whole length. If they prevail, there are no longer any Pyrenees—every bulwark and barrier of the Constitution is broken down; it is become *tabula rasa*—a *carte blanche*, for every one to scribble on it what he pleases.[90]

Such argumentation, much to Adams's delight, eliminated the issue of Greek independence from the nation's consideration.

These triumphs for the concept of the two worlds as embodied in the Monroe Doctrine were the last of Adams's secretarial years. Throughout his eight-year term it was his recognition of geographic factors as the foundation of national interests and diplomatic advantage that underlay his varied goals and successes. He detected more assuredly than his contemporaries that European influence in the Western Hemisphere was declining. This assumption encouraged his anticipation of Latin American independence, his vision of an expanding republic on

---

[90]Randolph's speech of January 24, 1824, ibid., cols. 1182–90.

the North American continent, and his disinclination to compromise on issues purely American. Recognizing the limits of U.S. power outside the Western Hemisphere, he argued against all verbal commitments that transcended easily demonstrable national interests or any intention of the government to act. Adams understood that such involvements served no national requirements and ultimately disappointed everyone who took the rhetoric seriously. Rejecting the need of threats or war, he settled for what diplomacy could accomplish. Where he possessed the diplomatic advantage, as in the Rush-Bagot and Adams-Onís treaties, he pursued the American interest as he defined it. Where the nation's advantage was doubtful, as on the questions of Oregon and commercial reciprocity, he either postponed the settlement until the superior interests and advantages of the United States became apparent or simply accepted less than he desired. Where the issue was revolution in Latin America, Greece, or Spain, he abstained from involvement totally. The essence of Adams's statesmanship was his ability to define a clear hierarchy of national interests to be pursued. He never permitted his objectives to outrun the means available to him.

Manifest Destiny: A Realist Critique*

"MANIFEST DESTINY,"a phrase used by contemporaries and historians to describe and explain the continental expansion of the United States in the 1840s, expressed merely a national mood. The belief in a national destiny was neither new nor strange; no nation or empire in history has ever been totally without it. For its proponents of the 1840s, however, the meaning conveyed by the phrase was clearly understood and peculiarly American. It implied that the United States was destined by the will of Heaven to become a country of political and territorial eminence. It attributed the probability and even the necessity of this growth to a homogeneous process created by certain unique qualities in American civilization—the energy and vigor of its people, their idealism and faith in their democratic institutions, and their sense of mission now endowed with a new vitality. It assigned to the American people the obligation to extend the area of freedom to their less fortunate neighbors, but only to those trained for self-government and genuinely desirous of entering the American Union. Expansionists of the 1840s saw this self-imposed limitation on forceful annexation as no serious barrier to the Republic's growth. It was inconceivable to them that any neighboring population would decline an invitation to enter the realm of the United States. Eventually editors and politicians transformed the idea of manifest destiny into a significant expression of American nationalism.

Such convictions of destiny came easily to the American people in the mid-forties, for they logically emerged from the sheer size and

*Published in Norman A. Graebner, ed., *Manifest Destiny* (New York: Macmillan, 1968). Reprinted by permission.

dramatic achievements of the young Republic. From New England and Pennsylvania, reaching on into the Ohio Valley and the Great Lakes region, an industrial revolution was multiplying the productive resources of the United States. New forms of transportation made possible by the efficient application of steam rendered the national economy greater than the sum of its parts. Steamboats transformed the Mississippi and Ohio rivers, with their many tributaries, into a mighty inland system of commercial and human traffic. Railroads long since had left the Atlantic seaboard and, by the 1840s, were creeping toward the burgeoning cities of the Middle West. Asa Whitney already had projected a railroad line from Lake Michigan to the Pacific Northwest. Samuel F. B. Morse's successful demonstration of the magnetic telegraph in 1844 ensured almost instantaneous communication across the entire continent. "What mighty distances have been overcome by railroads," exclaimed the *Southern Quarterly Review* in October 1844, "and, stranger than all, is the transmission of intelligence with the speed and with the aid of lightning!"

The purchase of Louisiana forty years earlier had enabled the United States to leap the Mississippi and extended its territorial claims westward to the shores of the Pacific. But in the 1840s the land resources of the nation no longer appeared as boundless as they once did to Thomas Jefferson. Augmented by Europe's ceaseless outpouring of humanity, the population of the United States had quadrupled in less than fifty years. Immigrants from Ireland and northern Europe flowed into the little settlements dotting the Mississippi Valley, and from these centers of trade they fanned out across the countryside, creating new markets and stimulating the region's industrial and agricultural expansion. Settlements extended as far west as the lower Missouri; beyond them stretched the treeless prairies inhabited by Indians and buffalo. Restless farmers, always reaching for the farthest frontiers, had started the grand overland trek to the inland valleys of Oregon and California. The easy identification of sufficient land with opportunity and the absence of oppression quickly converted manifest destiny into a major reform movement. Through territorial expansion the Republic would guarantee humanity's future. "Long may our country prove itself the asylum of the oppressed," pleaded Congressman James Belser of Alabama in January 1845. "Let its institutions and its people be extended far and wide, and when the waters of despotism shall have inundated other portions of the globe, and the votary of liberty be compelled to betake himself to his ark, let this government be the Ararat on which it shall rest."[1]

___
[1]*Congressional Globe*, 28th Cong., 2d sess., 1845, Appendix, p. 43.

This evidence of the nation's expanding power contrasted markedly with the relative absence of such progress elsewhere on the North American continent and assured the Republic that one day it would surpass in strength and grandeur the great nations of Europe. As one British traveler warned his countrymen in the late forties:

> We cannot conceal from ourselves that in many of the most important points of national capabilities they beat us; they are more energetic, more enterprising, less embarrassed with class interests, less burthened by the legacy of debt. This country, as a field for increase of power, is in every respect so infinitely beyond ours that comparison would be absurd. . . . They only wait for material power, to apply the incendiary torch of Republicanism to the nations of Europe.

However, manifest destiny's existence as an organized body of thought required more than a recognition and appreciation of national power and energy. It demanded above all a sense of mission, one anchored to political idealism. Americans of the early forties viewed their political system with a messianic consciousness, convinced that they held the future of republican government in their hands. Andrew Jackson asserted in his Farewell Address that Providence had selected the American people to be "the guardians of freedom to preserve it for the benefit of the human race."[2] Even more grandiloquent was the phraseology of John L. O'Sullivan, editor of the *Democratic Review*, who reminded the American people in July 1840 that to them much had been given and much would be required:

> We have been placed in the forefront of the battle in the cause of Man against the powers of evil which have so long crushed him to the dust. The problem of his capacity for self-government is to be solved here . . . he [Man] should be left to the individual action of his own will and conscience. Let us but establish this, and the race will have made an advance from which nothing short of the hand of Omnipotence can force it to recede. To no other has been committed the ark of man's hopes. . . . Surely we cannot fail of success in such a cause! Surely we cannot falter when so much depends upon our perseverance to the end![3]

O'Sullivan, always in the vanguard of American expansionist thinking, had helped to found the *Review* in 1837 and remained its editor until

---

[2] James D. Richardson, ed., *Messages and Papers of the Presidents* (Washington, 1896), 3:308.

[3] "The Progress of Society," *United States Magazine and Democratic Review*, 8 (July 1840): 87.

1846. With Samuel J. Tilden he founded the *New York Morning News* in 1844, and for the following two years as editor filled its pages with expansionist sentiment. It was O'Sullivan who, during the summer of 1845, first used the phrase "manifest destiny."[4]

That the American creed, as embodied in the Declaration of Independence, would not fail appeared obvious enough, for its foundation lay in human reason. "Democracy must finally reign," promised the *Democratic Review* in March 1840. "There is in man an eternal principle of progress which no power on earth may resist. Every custom, law, science, or religion, which obstructs its course, will fall as leaves before the wind." Few Americans even in that ebullient age would have denied that the nation's economic superiority rested on elements unique to the North American environment—its raw materials and climate as well as a wide spectrum of productive and commercial advantages—which existed on only a small portion of the earth's surface. Perhaps its democratic and free institutions, reflecting as they did specific historic and environmental conditions, might be no less endemic. But the propagandists for national expansion seldom dwelt on the possible limitations to the universal extension of their notions of sound and humane government. "The march of the Anglo-Saxon race is onward," boasted the *Washington Union* (June 2, 1845). "They must . . . accomplish their destiny, spreading far and wide the great principles of self-government, and who shall say how far they will prosecute the work?"

America's mission to humanity was not new, but the generation of the 1840s was the first to attach it to territorial expansion. The Founding Fathers had limited the nation's democratic mission to the creation and perpetuation of a model republic which might be worthy of emulation. Expansion, they feared, might disturb the federal structure of government by dispersing political authority too widely. The outspoken southern conservative of the Jeffersonian era, John Randolph, once observed, "We are the first people that ever acquired provinces . . . not for us to govern, but that they might *govern us*—that we might be ruled to our ruin by people bound to us by no common tie of interest or sentiment."[5] With the passage of time, however, even conservative easterners accepted the inevitability of American expansion and ceased to regard the westward-moving center of political power a threat to their estate. "We look forward to that event without alarm," the noted Massachusetts scholar and orator, Edward Everett, could

[4]O'Sullivan's role in promulgating "manifest destiny" has been developed in Julius W. Pratt, "The Origins of 'Manifest Destiny,' " *American Historical Review* 32 (July 1927): 795–98.

[5]Quoted in Russell Kirk, *Randolph of Roanoke: A Study in Conservative Thought* (Chicago, 1951), p. 145.

assure a Tennessee audience in 1829, "as in the order of the natural growth of this great Republic. We have a firm faith that our interests are mutually consistent, that if you prosper, we shall prosper."[6]

By the 1840s the addition of new states from the Louisiana Purchase, all without subverting the American federal system, had dispelled completely such earlier fears of expansion. The reestablishment of the states-rights principle under Jacksonian rule destroyed what remained of the older institutional arguments against national growth. In January 1838 the *Democratic Review* affirmed the compatibility between expansion and the basic principles of American government: "The peculiar characteristic of our system—the distinctive evidence of its divine origin . . . is, that it may, if its theory is maintained pure in practice, be extended, with equal safety and efficiency, over any indefinite number of millions of population and territory." Similarly Stephen A. Douglas of Illinois asserted in January 1845 that "our federal system is admirably adapted to the whole continent."[7] Indeed, to states-rights Democrats there was no better guarantee against federal consolidation than the addition of new states.

In essence, then, manifest destiny suggested that the American people were destined to extend their democratic principles over the North American continent. This vision was not lost on Senator James Buchanan, the Pennsylvania Democrat, who declared in March 1844: "Providence has given to the American people a great and important mission, and that mission they were destined to fulfill—to spread the blessings of Christian liberty and laws from one end to the other of this immense continent." To talk of confining the American spirit of emigration within limits, he added, "was like talking of limiting the stars in their courses, or bridling the foaming torrent of Niagara."[8] Two years later Congressman John S. Chipman of Michigan predicted with equal assurance that "this continent will be our own; the gentlemen may say it is by manifest destiny, or by Adam's will, or by whatever else they will. That destiny was found written in every page of our history."[9]

Such rhetoric was more than an expression of purpose; it was a search for justification. Historically, national ambition demanded no vindication beyond the demonstration of interest and the possession of

---

[6]Edward Everett, *Orations and Speeches on Various Occasions* (Boston, 1870), 1:196.

[7]"The Texas Question," *Democratic Review* 14 (April 1844): 429; *Congressional Globe*, 28th Cong., 2d sess., 1844, Appendix, p. 68.

[8]Buchanan's speech on the mission of the United States, March 12, 1844, *Congressional Globe*, 28th Cong., 1st sess., 1844, p. 380.

[9]Chipman's address of January 14, 1846, *Congressional Globe*, 29th Cong., 1st sess., 1846, p. 207.

the strength to achieve the objective. But no nation had ever embarked on a career of expansion so completely at the price of its own national ideology as did the United States in the 1840s. Its sense of mission collided sharply with its democratic doctrine of self-determination as well as its ideals of amity and peace. Morality among individuals is a rationale for self-sacrifice; among nations it often serves as a cloak for self-aggrandizement. Democratic idealism is easily transformed into an agency of imperialism when it attempts to deny opposing governments— because of their alleged corruption or immorality—the right to terri- tories which they possess. It seeks to rationalize the removal of those who stand in the path of destiny by declaring them politically and morally inferior. Such an approach to the achievement of external ambitions may ensure popular support for specific foreign policies for- mulated by the national government; it can do no more. National sentiment, unsupported by force or the threatened use of force, can wield no measurable influence in affairs among nations.

II

Never in history could a people more readily accept and proclaim a sense of destiny, for never were a people more perfectly situated to transform their whims into realities. Expansion was rationalized so effectively at each point of conflict that it seemed to many Americans an unchallengeable franchise. Confronted by problems neither of con- science nor of extensive countering force, the American people could claim as a natural right boundaries that seemed to satisfy the require- ments of security and commerce. Expanding as they did into a vacuum— vast regions almost devoid of population—they could conclude that they were simply fulfilling the dictates of manifest destiny. For them the distinctions between sentiment and action, between individual pur- pose and national achievement, appeared inconsequential.

Historians emphasizing the expansive mood of the 1840s have tended to identify the westward extension of the United States to the Pacific with the concept of destiny itself. Such identifications are mis- leading, for they ignore all the genuine elements of successful policy. Those regions into which the nation threatened to expand were under the legal jurisdiction of other governments. Their acquisition required the formulation of policies which encompassed both the precise defi- nition of ends and the creation of adequate means. Manifest destiny doctrine—as a body of sentiment and nothing else—avoided completely the essential question of *means*, and it was only the absence of powerful opposition on the North American continent that permitted the fallacy that power and its employment were of little consequence. Occupying a wilderness created the illusion that power was less important than moral progress, and that expansion was indeed a civilizing, not a conquering, process.

Jeremy Bentham once termed the concept of natural right pure nonsense, for the claims of nations were natural only when supported by superior force. The natural right of the United States to a continental empire lay in its power of conquest, not in the uniqueness of its political institutions. American expansionism could triumph only when the nation could bring its diplomatic and military influence to bear on specific points of national concern. What created the easy victory of American expansion was not a sense of destiny, however widely and dramatically it was proclaimed, but the absence of powerful competitors which might have either prevented the expansion entirely or forced the country to pay an exorbitant price for its territorial gains. The advantages of geography and the political and military inefficiency of the Indian tribes or even of Mexican arms tended to obscure the elements of force which were no less real, only less obtrusive, than that employed by other nations in their efforts at empire building. It was no wonder that British and French critics concluded that the American conquest of the continent was by pick and shovel.

Concepts of manifest destiny were as totally negligent of *ends* as they were of means. Expansionists agreed that the nation was destined to reach its natural boundaries. But what were these natural frontiers? For Benjamin Franklin and John Adams they comprised the Mississippi River. But when the United States, through the purchase of Louisiana, crossed the Mississippi, there was no end in sight. Expansionists now regarded Florida as a natural appendage, belonging as naturally to the United States, declared one Kentucky newspaper, as Cornwall did to England. John Quincy Adams observed in his diary that the acquisition of Florida in 1819 "rendered it still more unavoidable that the remainder of the continent should ultimately be ours." Eventually Europe would discover, he predicted, that the United States and North America were identical. But President James Monroe revealed no more interest in building a state on the Pacific than had Jefferson. Equally convinced that the distances to Oregon were too great to be bridged by one empire, Thomas Hart Benton of Missouri in 1825 defined the natural boundary of the United States as "the ridge of the Rocky Mountains. . . . Along the back of this ridge, the Western limit of this republic should be drawn, and the statue of the fabled god, Terminus, should be raised upon its highest peak, never to be thrown down."[10] President John Tyler in his message of December 1843 perpetuated this limited view

---

[10]Benton's remarks of March 1, 1825, *Register of Debates in Congress*, 18th Cong., 2d sess., 1825, col. 711–12.

of the nation's future. And as late as 1845, Daniel Webster continued to refer to an independent republic along the distant Pacific coast. Meanwhile, expansionists could never agree on the natural boundaries of Texas. Representative C. J. Ingersoll of Pennsylvania found them in the vast deserts between the Rio Grande and the Nueces. For others, they comprised the Rio Grande itself, but James Gadsden discovered in the Sierra Madre mountains "a natural territorial boundary, imposing in its Mountain and Desert outlines."[11]

Geographical predestination alone seemed sufficient to assure the sweep of the nation to the Pacific. Lord Curzon had once written, "Of all natural frontiers the sea is the most uncompromising, the least alterable, and the most effective."[12] As early as 1823, Francis Baylies warned the nation not to terminate its westward march at the Rockies. "Sir, our natural boundary is the Pacific Ocean," he declared. "The swelling tide of our population must and will roll on until the mighty ocean interposes its waters, and limits our territorial empire."[13] By the mid-forties the true proponents of manifest destiny had become continentalists. Douglas voiced these sentiments when he declared in January 1845:

> He would blot out the lines on the map which now marked our national boundaries on this continent, and make the area of liberty as broad as the continent itself. He would not suffer petty rival republics to grow up here, engendering jealousy at each other, and interfering with each other's domestic affairs, and continually endangering their peace. He did not wish to go beyond the great ocean—beyond those boundaries which the God of nature had marked out.[14]

Similarly the *New York Herald* prophesied that the American Republic would, in due course, embrace all the land from the Isthmus of Panama to the polar regions and from the Atlantic to the Pacific. One Texas correspondent of that newspaper (August 9, 1845) wrote that "the fact must be no longer disguised, that we, the people of the United States, must hold, and govern, under free and harmonious institutions, the continent we inhabit."

[11]Gadsden quoted in Albert K. Weinberg, *Manifest Destiny: A Study of Nationalist Expansionism in American History* (Baltimore, 1935), p. 56.

[12]Quoted in Weinberg, *Manifest Destiny*, p. 64.

[13]Debate of January 24, 1823, *Annals of Congress*, 17th Cong., 2d sess., 1823, col. 682–83.

[14]Speech of January 31, 1845, *Congressional Globe*, 28th Cong., 2d sess., 1845, pp. 226–27.

If the ultimate vision of American destiny in the 1840s comprised a vast federal republic that boasted continental dimensions and a government based on the principle of states rights, the future boundaries of the United States, as determined by the standards of geographical predestination, never seemed to possess any ultimate logic. Boundaries that appeared natural to one generation were rejected as utterly inadequate by the next. It was left for Robert Winthrop, the conservative Massachusetts Whig, in January 1846 to reduce the doctrine of geographical predestination to an absurdity:

> It is not a little amusing to observe what different views are taken as to the indication of 'the hand of nature' and the pointings of 'the finger of God,' by the same gentlemen, under different circumstances and upon different subjects. In one quarter of the compass they can descry the hand of nature in a level desert and a second-rate river, beckoning us impatiently to march up to them. But when they turn their eyes to another part of the horizon the loftiest mountains in the universe are quite lost upon their gaze. There is no hand of nature there. The configuration of the earth has no longer any significance. The Rocky Mountains are mere molehills. Our destiny is onward.[15]

Democratic idealism was even less precise as a guide to national action than the doctrine of geographical predestination. By 1845 such goals of reaching the Pacific were far too limited for the more enthusiastic exponents of the new expansionism. As they interpreted the expression of democratic idealism, the dogma represented an ever expanding force. Indeed, for some it had no visible limit at all. It looked beyond the North American continent to South America, to the islands of the Pacific, and to the Old World itself. One editorial in the *New York Herald* (September 15, 1845) declared,

> American patriotism takes a wider and loftier range than heretofore. Its horizon is widening every day. No longer bounded by the limits of the confederacy, it looks abroad upon the whole earth, and into the mind of the republic daily sinks deeper and deeper the conviction that the civilization of the earth—the reform of the governments of the ancient world—the emancipation of the whole race, are dependent, in a great degree, on the United States.

This was a magnificent vision for a democratic purpose, but it hardly explains the sweep of the United States across the continent. It bears no relationship whatever to the actual goals which the Tyler and Polk

---

[15] *Congressional Globe*, 29th Cong., 1st sess., 1846, Appendix, p. 294.

administrations pursued in their diplomacy with Texas, Mexico, and England.

III

Texas provided the necessary catalyst which fused all the elements of manifest destiny into a single national movement. When the annexation issue suddenly exploded on the national scene in 1844, the expansionist front had been quiescent for a full generation. The 1820s and 1830s had been years of introspection, and the changing structure of American political and economic life had absorbed the people's energies and directed their thoughts inward. Yet the same inner-directed concerns which rendered the country generally oblivious to external affairs promoted both the sense of power and the democratic idealism which, under the impetus of expansionist oratory, could easily transform the nation's mood and forge a spirit of national destiny.

As a public issue, Texas's annexation could provoke a national response only as the occasion demanded. Yet as early as the 1820s American pioneers had decreed that one day the occasion for a national decision would arise. Responding to the Mexican government's generous offer of free land, American frontiersmen surged into Texas in such overwhelming numbers that soon they dominated much of the province. In 1828 the Tèran Commission, dispatched to Texas by the Mexican government, rendered an alarming report on the number and quality of Americans residing in the area. Thereupon, Lucas Alamán, secretary of foreign relations, warned the Mexican Congress that American settlers were simply the advance agents of imperialism. Their techniques, he charged, were well established:

> They commence by introducing themselves into the territory which they covet, upon pretence of commercial negotiations, or of the establishment of colonies, with or without the assent of the Government to which it belongs. These colonies grow, multiply, become the predominant party in the population; . . . These pioneers excite, by degrees, movements which disturb the political state of the country . . . and then follow discontents and dissatisfaction, calculated to fatigue the patience of the legitimate owner, and to diminish the usefulness of the administration and of the exercise of authority. When things have come to this pass, which is precisely the present state of things in Texas, the diplomatic management commences: . . . the desired end is attained of concluding an arrangement as onerous for one party as it is advantageous to the other. Sometimes more direct means are resorted to; and taking advantage of the enfeebled state, or domestic difficulties, of the possessor of the soil, they proceed, upon the most extraordinary

pretexts, to make themselves masters of the country, as was the case in the Floridas; leaving the question to be decided afterwards as to the legality of the possession, which force alone could take from them.[16]

In 1830 an aroused Mexican government attempted to prohibit further American migration into Texas, but to no avail. The resultant tension between the Americans and their Mexican rulers erupted into open warfare which culminated in 1836 with the establishment of the Republic of Texas and its immediate request for admission into the American Union. Such northerners as John Quincy Adams, however, viewing events in Texas as a southern conspiracy designed to extend the area of slavery, managed to prevent any action by Congress.

That Texas finally kindled the nation's expansionist tendencies resulted less from the pressure of pioneers or the simple urge to expand than from the scheming and ambition of politicians. President Tyler, urged on by such southern advisers as Duff Green, R. M. T. Hunter, and Thomas W. Gilmer, commenced his promotion of the Texas issue as early as 1843, convinced that it would grip the country's imagination and help to repair his battered political fences. Tyler believed the issue powerful enough, if properly handled, to unhinge Henry Clay as titular head of the Whig party and perhaps secure for himself a second term in the White House. Tyler's personal efforts to control the Texas question culminated in a treaty of annexation negotiated with the Lone Star Republic, which he submitted to the Senate in April 1844. Even before the Senate rejected the treaty, however, the annexation issue had passed into other hands.

For an influential group of Southern Democrats, Texas comprised a purely sectional challenge upon which hinged the very existence of the South's institutions. As secretary of state in 1844, John C. Calhoun, now approaching the end of his long career as the special defender of southern causes, promoted annexation with the sectional fervor expected of him. "I only ask the South to stand by me," he wrote in May 1844. "Now is the time to vindicate and save our institutions."[17] For Calhoun and his colleagues it was British abolitionism that rendered annexation so essential for southern security. Lord Aberdeen, the British foreign minister, had made clear the attitudes of his government toward slavery. Reassuring the United States in December 1843 of Britain's honorable intentions toward Texas, Aberdeen added the disturbing comment that "Great Britain desires and is constantly exerting herself to promote

---

[16]*House Ex. Doc. No. 351*, 25th Cong., 2d sess., 1838, Serial 332, pp. 313–14.

[17]Calhoun to James H. Hammond, May 17, 1844, in J. Franklin Jameson, ed., *The Correspondence of John C. Calhoun, Annual Report of the American Historical Association, 1899* (Washington, 1900), 2:589.

the general abolition of slavery thoughout the world." Whereas England would do nothing secretly or underhandedly, he continued, it hoped to see that institution abolished in the United States. In his reply Calhoun not only defended the right of the United States to annex Texas but also reminded the foreign minister that slavery was a southern question and beyond the jurisdiction of the federal government.[18] Indeed, Southern Democrats hoped that the Texas issue would upset the hegemony of Martin Van Buren over their party and secure the nomination of Calhoun.

Southern politicians soon discovered that they could control the Texas question with no greater success than could the president. Eventually it was the agrarian Democrats centered in the lower Midwest, with their allies in the Southwest and East, who captured the issue, nationalized it, carried expansionism to its highest pitch of the decade, and rode into power on its emotional impact. It was their control of the Baltimore Convention of 1844 that upset the hopes of Van Buren and secured the nomination of James K. Polk of Tennessee. This faction, led by Douglas, Lewis Cass of Michigan, and Robert J. Walker of Mississippi, had no interest in the expansion of slavery. These men emerged rather as the true proponents of manifest destiny and defended the westward extension of the United States on broad national grounds. Their oratory fused the American concept of mission, traditionally limited to the creation of a model republic, with expansion itself. Through annexation, not merely through exemplary government, they agreed, the United States was destined to extend the area of freedom over the North American continent.

What compelled the identification of freedom with expansion in the American mind was the dread of European encroachment. Continental expansionism in the 1840s was in large measure a defensive maneuver in which the superior claims of the United States to contested lands were rationalized in terms of manifest destiny. In his message of transmittal President Tyler warned the Senate that if it rejected the Texas treaty, Texas would seek the friendship of other nations. "In contemplating such a contingency," he continued, "it cannot be overlooked that the United States are already almost surrounded by the possessions of European powers. The Canadas, New Brunswick, and Nova Scotia, the islands in the American seas, with Texas trammeled by treaties of alliance or of a commercial character differing in policy from that of the United States, would complete the circle." Similarly

---

[18]See Calhoun to Richard Pakenham, April 18, 1844, in William R. Manning, ed., *Diplomatic Correspondence of the United States: Inter-American Affairs, 1831–1860* (Washington, 1936), 7:18–22.

Jackson, in his famous letter to Aaron V. Brown in 1843, advocated extending "the area of freedom" to Texas to terminate British ambition and intrigue along the southwestern frontier of the United States. Polk's inaugural address of March 4, 1845, reminded the nation that annexation alone would preserve American democracy from the encroachments of European monarchy.

Ultimately the proponents of manifest destiny justified the annexation of Texas in terms of its contribution to the American system of government. Annexation would perfect the Union and guarantee the blessings of liberty to the people. Gilmer declared that "our union has no danger to apprehend from those who believe that its genius is expansive and progressive, but from those who think that the limits of the United States are already too large and the principles of 1776 too old-fashioned for this fastidious age."[19] For states-rights Democrats expansion was the surest defense against the country's great internal enemy: a federal government that would encroach on the liberties of the states and the people. "The dangers that an American patriot ought to apprehend," warned the *Southern Quarterly Review* in October 1844, "do not find their source in the growth of our people, the increase of our territory, or the power of foreign competitors. They originate in the sordid, grasping and rapacious spirit of our legislation, . . . in the usurpations of power, the shortness of memory and laxity of conscience in our public men. . . . Such rulers as these have elevated the government above the Constitution they were sworn to defend, and above the people who entrusted it to them to preserve." Those who opposed annexation, the writer noted bitterly, were likewise the defenders of centralization in government. They cared nothing for the nation's destiny. For them, he concluded, nothing "can be well ordered and sure but the pitiful present that they can command."

What removed all taint of injustice and oppression from the Texas question was the knowledge that the vast majority of Texans themselves favored annexation to the United States. Indeed, the expansionists of the day denied any interest in annexing anyone but Anglo-Saxon peoples and questioned the capacity of others for self-government. Expansionist Levi Woodbury of New Hampshire opened fraternization to all who would willingly partake of American institutions. He had no interest in the forceful annexation of distant lands and alien peoples:

> When gentlemen talked about Patagonia and the Celestial Empire coming into the Union . . . let them look back into our constitutional history, and see if it is possible for this government

[19]*Niles' National Register*, July 1, 1843.

to embrace any nation, unless that nation be willing to come in and adopt our republican institutions, and are conquered not by our swords, but by our liberal example and systems of equal rights, ennobling liberties and well-regulated laws. We must thus affiliate together—they with us and we with them—before a single step for amalgamation is likely to be taken on either side, however much gentlemen may appear to apprehend so many kinds of heterogeneous mixtures.[20]

Whig leaders condemned expansionist oratory as a dangerous appeal to American nationalism, perpetrated as much to elevate Democrats to public office as to secure the annexation of Texas. These conservatives harbored no fears of British encroachment; they regarded the identification of freedom with expansion as revolutionary and unsound. Representative George P. Marsh of Vermont ridiculed the idea of extending freedom into Texas as "an argument addressed to the ear and not to the understanding—a mere jingle of words without meaning, or, if significant, false in the only sense which the words will fairly bear."[21] E. S. Hamlin of Ohio wondered how men could talk of extending the area of freedom when annexation was designed to prevent the abolition of slavery in Texas. "Were it not for perpetuating slavery in that country," he charged, "we should hear no more of this measure."[22]

For the Whig party and its abolitionist allies in the North, Texas annexation posed a dual challenge of major proportions. The first source of anxiety was the contest for political power. Would the agrarianism of the West and South or the industrialism of the East and the Great Lakes dominate national policy? Philip Hone, the New York merchant, detected clearly why the Texas issue was rocking the Republic to its foundations. Southern demagogues, he said, were promoting their personal objectives and those of the South by solidifying their power through the addition of four or five slave states. Antislavery Whigs maintained that the second challenge was inherent in the first—the expansion and strengthening of the hated institution of slavery. Joshua R. Giddings, the Ohio abolitionist and Whig, held forth both in and out of Congress on the dual nature of the struggle over Texas. In a noted address before the House of Representatives in May 1844, Giddings demanded to know why the New England and Pennsylvania Democrats would support annexation while the Texans in Congress

---

[20]Woodbury's speech in the Senate, February 17, 1845, *Congressional Globe*, 28th Cong., 2d sess., 1845, Appendix, p. 233.

[21]Speech of January 20, 1845, *Congressional Globe*, 28th Cong., 2d sess., 1845, Appendix, p. 316.

[22]Hamlin's speech in the House, January 9, 1845, *Congressional Globe*, 28th Cong., 2d sess., 1845, Appendix, p. 375.

voted down their system of tariffs. Would western Democrats, he added, willingly give up their harbor improvements and the dredging of their rivers merely to improve the southern slave trade and perpetuate slavery in Texas?[23] Thomas Corwin, the conservative Ohio Whig, saw two prospects as disturbing: a divided country and the demise of Whig ascendancy. Perhaps a combination of Whigs and Democrats, he wrote, might still "keep *in* the Tariff and keep *out* Texas."[24]

The annexation issue upset the calculations of its opponents. "It is the greatest question of the *age*," wrote the Alabama expansionist, Dixon H. Lewis, "and I predict will agitate the country more than all the other public questions ever have. Public opinion will boil and effervesce . . . more like a volcano than a cider barrel—but at last it will settle down with *unanimity* for annexation in the South and West and a large majority in the North."[25] To Andrew Davezac, the New York Democrat, the issue was equally productive of change. "It has been the entering wedge," he admitted in July 1844, "that has opened both the ears and throats of my auditors everywhere—from Baltimore to Buffalo."[26]

National expansionism ultimately tipped the political scales in favor of the Democrats and thus ensured the annexation of Texas. When Congress convened in December 1844, the Democratic leadership brought a joint resolution of annexation before both houses. Convinced that Mexico would react violently to annexation, Benton proposed negotiation with the Mexican government prior to annexation for the purpose of defining the boundary. By January 1845, however, Benton had agreed to immediate annexation, with the question of the boundary left to future diplomacy. The House passed the resolution for annexation late in January, and by the end of February, by a vote of 27 to 25, the Senate approved an amended resolution. Tyler, anxious to proceed under the authority granted by Congress, directed the American chargé in Texas on March 3 to invite Texas to join the Union. Polk, upon entering office the following day, upheld Tyler's action. Texas responded favorably to the American invitation and entered the Union when Congress approved its new constitution the following December.

[23]See Giddings's speech of May 21, 1844, *Congressional Globe*, 28th Cong., 1st sess., 1844, Appendix, pp. 704–07.

[24]Corwin to Oran Follett, February 22, 1845, March 7, 13, 1845, in L. Belle Hamlin, ed., "Selections from the Follett Papers, II," *Quarterly Publication of the Historical and Philosophical Society of Ohio* 9 (July–September 1814): 80–81, 84.

[25]Lewis to Richard Cralle, March 19, 1844, Cralle Papers, Manuscripts Division, Library of Congress.

[26]Davezac to Polk, July 11, 1844, Polk Papers, Manuscripts Division, Library of Congress.

Needless to say, the doctrine of manifest destiny as a powerful Democratic appeal in the 1844 campaign played a significant role in the annexation of Texas. However, this does not demonstrate the relevance of national sentiment to the successful conduct of external relations. The concept of manifest destiny, as a major assault on the nation's mind and emotions, never created a genuine national interest to be pursued through diplomacy or war. Its proponents were overwhelmingly members of the Democratic party; the arguments of manifest destiny were in large measure political appeals designed to expand the power of the party as much as that of the country. Texas, after all, confronted the United States with a purely internal political question. The Lone Star Republic was not only a free agent in complete control of its own destiny but also it was determined to enter the American Union at the first opportunity. Whatever barrier still existed in 1844 to Texas's annexation lay not in the opposing power and interest of another nation, but in the configuration of sectional and party alignments in Congress. To the extent that the concept of manifest destiny strengthened the proannexationist forces in that body, it also contributed to American expansion, for no one would deny the relevance of public opinion to the actions of Congress.

IV

Even as Texas, with its annexation assured, receded from its commanding position in national thought and politics, American expansionism shifted its focus beyond the summit of the Rockies to the regions of Oregon and California. "The Rio Grande has no more efficacy as a permanent barrier against the extension of Anglo-Saxon power than the Sabine possessed," predicted the *Baltimore American* in March 1845. "The process by which Texas was acquired may be repeated over and over again."[27] The *New York Sun* assured its readers that the United States, with its system of self-governing states and homogeneous civilization, would, unlike Rome, increase in strength and durability as it expanded. "Who shall say," observed the *Sun* (March 7, 1845), "there is not room at the family altar for another sister like Texas, and in the fullness of time for many daughters from the shores of the Pacific?"

Expansionism, focusing in 1845 on regions beyond Texas, reached a new level of rhetorical extravagance. The notion of a continental destiny was not new, but editors now proclaimed it with a sense of finality. By September 1845 the *New York Herald* no longer recognized any clear limitation to the nation's future growth:

---

[27]*Baltimore American* quoted in *Niles' National Register*, March 15, 1845.

The minds of men have been awakened to a clear conviction of the destiny of this great nation of freemen. No longer bounded by those limits which nature had in the eye of those of little faith [in] the last generation, assigned to the dominion of republicanism on this continent, the pioneers of Anglo-Saxon civilization and Anglo-Saxon free institutions, now seek distant territories, stretching even to the shores of the Pacific; and the arms of the republic, it is clear to all men of sober discernment, must soon embrace the whole hemisphere, from the icy wilderness of the North to the most prolific regions of the smiling and prolific South.[28]

How this destiny was to be achieved rested lightly on the shoulders of those who proclaimed it. Texas had established the pattern which in the course of time would annex what remained of the continent to the Union. American pioneers who had built a civilization in Texas and then applied for admission to the United States would repeat the process elsewhere. Already settlers in the Willamette Valley of Oregon were creating a mature society. At Champoeg in 1843 they adopted a frame of government; next they made it clear that they desired and anticipated the extension of U.S. law and institutions into the Oregon country. Other pioneers, entering Mexican California, had by 1845 converted the Sacramento Valley into an American settlement. Clearly even in California the processes of annexation were at work. "Once let the tide of emigration flow toward California," predicted Alfred Robinson, a long-time resident of that province, "and the American population will soon be sufficiently numerous to play the Texas game."[29]

By what process the United States would acquire the heavily peopled and politically backward regions of Mexico and Central America was less clear, for the doctrine of manifest destiny assumed that only qualified populations desiring admittance would enter the Republic. Woodbury had rationalized the anti-imperialist nature of U.S. policy toward Texas in such terms, and even the archexpansionist O'Sullivan would recognize no other principle. His *New York Morning News* stressed this limitation when it declared on October 13, 1845:

Public sentiment with us repudiates possession without use, and this sentiment is gradually acquiring the force of established public law. It has sent our adventurous pioneers to the plains of Texas, will carry them to the Rio del Norte, and even that boundary, purely nominal and conventional as it is, will not stay them on their march to the Pacific, the limit which nature has provided.

[28]*New York Herald*, September 25, 1845.
[29]Alfred Robinson to Thomas O. Larkin, May 29, 1845, in George P. Hammond, ed., *The Larkin Papers* (Berkeley, 1952), 3:205.

In like manner it will come to pass that the confederated democracies of the Anglo-American race will give this great continent as an inheritance to man. Rapacity and spoliation cannot be the features of this magnificent enterprise, not perhaps, because we are above and beyond the influence of such views, but because circumstances do not admit of their operation. We take from no man; the reverse rather—we give to man. This national policy, necessity or destiny, we know to be just and beneficent, and we can, therefore, afford to scorn the invective and imputations of rival nations.

Oregon, the immediate objective of expansionism after March 1845, challenged the easy assumptions that lands along the Pacific would succumb through osmosis to the centripetal force of American civilization. Texas was a political issue, and its resolution lay generally within the competence of Congress. Oregon by contrast was a diplomatic question to be resolved, if at all, through successful negotiations with the London government. England's legal claims demanded that American expansionists either admit the irrelevance of national sentiment when confronted by the will and claims of another nation, or support its pretensions with superior argumentation or force. Argumentation promised to be far less demanding or disagreeable than war. What placed such a tremendous burden on American rhetoric, however, was the determination of western expansionists, supported officially by the Baltimore platform of 1844, to achieve no less than the whole of Oregon up to the Alaska line of 54° 40'. The U.S. claims, based on discovery, settlement, and the Spanish treaty of 1819, were substantial enough as far north as the Columbia River and were recognized as such by London. North of the Columbia, where the British Hudson's Bay Company was completely dominant, the American claims were inconclusive or nonexistent.

Clearly the claims to Oregon, if only to prevent compromise negotiations by the U.S. government, required augmentation. Unable to sustain their demands through historic claims or diplomatic precedent, the proponents of 54–40 discovered the true title to Oregon in a higher law. O'Sullivan defined the American claim in his editorial of December 27, 1845: "Away, away with all these cobweb tissues of rights of discovery, exploration, settlement, contiguity. . . . [The American title] is by the right of our manifest destiny to overspread and to possess the whole of the Continent which Providence has given us." Edward D. Baker of Illinois informed the House of Representatives in January 1846 that he had little regard for "musty records and the voyages of old sea captains, or the Spanish treaties, because we had a higher and better title under the law of nature and of nations." Some members of Congress pushed the American title back to Adam's will. To William Sawyer of Ohio it was even older: "We received our rights from high Heaven, from destiny, if you please."[30]

Fundamentally the true title of the United States to all of Oregon lay in the doctrine of geographical predestination. Such higher law claims had been used to justify the abrogation of Indian titles to unoccupied lands. Cass had cited such claims when, as secretary of war under Jackson, he demanded the removal of the Georgia Indians to the West. "There can be no doubt . . . ," ran one observation which appeared in the January 1830 issue of the *North American Review*, "that the Creator intended that the earth should be reclaimed from a state of nature and cultivated; that the human race should spread over it, procuring from it the means of comfortable subsistence, and of increase and improvement." That the Indians of Georgia had attained a high level of cultivation and of culture mattered little; the land was destined for Anglo-American occupation.

America's higher law claims to Oregon lay in the proximity of the region to the United States, especially when contrasted to the vast distances that separated it from England. Several lines of poetry in the February 1846 issue of the *Democratic Review* summarized the American contention:

Why clamor in the question, 'whose the right
By conquest or discovery?—what eye,
Briton or Apalachian, had first sight
Of the great wastes that now disputed lie?'
The right depends on the propinquity,
The absolute sympathy of soil and place,
Needful against the foreign enemy,
And for the due expansion of our race;
And this expansion, certain as the light,
Makes the right sure, in progress of the might!

What gave the right of propinquity its essential force was the related question of land utilization. "There is . . . no such thing as title to the wild lands of the new world," declared the *New York Morning News* in November 1845, "except that which actual possession gives. They belong to whoever will redeem them from the Indian and the desert, and subjugate them to the use of man. Title by discovery is nothing unless sustained by occupancy. . . . And such a shadowless title is all that Great Britain makes to Oregon." In the House of Representatives John Quincy Adams called upon the clerk to read from Genesis: "Be fruitful,

[30]*Congressional Globe*, 29th Cong., 1st sess., 1846, pp. 136, 301.

and multiply, and replenish the earth, and subdue it."[31] To Adams this biblical command gave the American people better right to the region than the Hudson's Bay Company. England wanted Oregon merely for navigation and hunting, while the United States wished to carry out the behest of the Almighty.

Finally, Democratic expansionists based the American title to Oregon on the nation's right to guarantee the future welfare and security of its citizens. O'Sullivan in the *New York Morning News* of December 27, 1845, pointed to the "duty and the right of providing the necessary accommodation for all this stupendous future of the American destiny." Similarly Baker observed that the United States had a continent before it in which to "spread our free principles, our language, our literature, and power; and we had the present right to provide for the future progress. To do this was to secure our safety, in the widest and highest sense; and thus our destiny had become so manifest that it could not fail but by our own folly."[32] Herein lay the right of vital necessity.

Armed by such allegedly uncontestable claims to Oregon, the ultras in Congress condemned every tendency toward compromise with Britain at the 49th parallel. "Away with the siren cry of concession and compromise," cried John A. McClernand in January 1846, "inexorable *destiny* interposes her iron sceptre to forbid it. Shame! Why should we *recede* to the 49th parallel while Britain *advances* to the same line?"[33] Some Democrats openly declared that they preferred war to compromise. "Shall we pause in our career, or retrace our steps," demanded Andrew Kennedy of Indiana in January 1846, "because the British lion has chosen to place himself in our path? Has our blood already become so pale that we should tremble at the roar of the King of Beasts? We will not go out of our way to seek a conflict with him; but if he crosses our path, and refuses to move at a peaceful command, he will run his nose in the talons of the American eagle, and his blood will spout as from a harpooned whale."[34]

Whatever the American dreams of empire along the Pacific's shores, they would be fulfilled by President Polk or not at all. Polk's accession to the White House seemed to assure the force of executive leadership behind the nation's expansionist program. His professed adherence to both the Texas and the whole-of-Oregon issues in the 1844 campaign seemed to place him in the camp of the true believers

---

[31]For Adams's remarks see *Congressional Globe*, 29th Cong., 1st sess., 1846, p. 342.
[32]Baker's speech of January 3, 1846, *Congressional Globe*, 29th Cong., 1st sess., 1846, p. 136.
[33]*Congressional Globe*, 29th Cong., 1st sess., 1846, Appendix, p. 277.
[34]*Congressional Globe*, 29th Cong., 1st sess., 1846, p. 180.

in manifest destiny. Yet his expansionism was less clearly expressed and far less boisterous than that of such enthusiasts as Cass and Douglas. His natural reserve was accentuated after his election by the burden of responsibility. However, Polk entered the White House at least outwardly committed to the acquisition of Oregon up to the Alaska line. In his inaugural address he insisted that the American title was "clear and unquestionable."[35]

When Polk assumed command of America's external relations in the spring of 1845 the United States had uncontested claims on the Pacific only up to that commercially impractical, but undeniably beautiful, coast which lay between 42° and the Columbia River. North of the Columbia the United States was in conflict with an expanding British Empire, supported by the Hudson's Bay Company. As late as the 1840s Oregon remained in a state of equilibrium between two westward-moving empires struggling for mastery of the Northwest coast. Almost thirty years of diplomacy had produced no boundary settlement for the simple reason that no American diplomatist, beginning with John Quincy Adams, would accept the Columbia River line. The reason was clear: such a settlement would not achieve for the United States any of its essential interests in the Pacific Northwest.

California no less than Oregon demanded its own peculiar expansionist rationale, for its acquisition confronted the United States with a series of problems not present in either the Texas or Oregon issues. If the government in Mexico City lacked the energy to control, much less develop, this remote province, its title was still as clear as its hold was ephemeral. The annexation of this outpost required bargaining with its owner. Even that possibility seemed remote in 1845, for the Mexican government had carried out its threat to break diplomatic relations with the United States rather than condone the annexation of Texas. For a decade American citizens had drifted into the inland valleys and coastal villages of California, but in 1845 they still comprised an infinitesimal number, even when compared to the small Mexican and Indian populations.

Obviously the United States could not achieve its continental destiny without embracing California. Yet this Mexican province had never been an issue in American politics; its positive contribution to national civilization scarcely had been established. California, moreover, because of its alien population, was by the established principles of U.S. expansion less than acceptable as a territorial objective. American acquisitiveness toward Texas and Oregon had been ethnocentric; it rejected the notion of annexing allegedly inferior peoples. "There

---

[35]Richardson, ed., *Messages and Papers of the Presidents*, 4:381.

seems to be something in our laws and institutions," Alexander Duncan of Ohio reminded the House of Representatives early in 1845, "peculiarly adapted to our Anglo-Saxon-American race, under which they will thrive and prosper, but under which all others wilt and die."[36] He pointed to the decline of the French and Spanish on the North American continent when American laws had been extended to them. It was their unfitness for "liberal and equal laws, and equal institutions," he assumed, that accounted for this inability to prosper under the United States.

Such inhibitions toward the annexing of Mexican peoples gradually disintegrated under the pressure of events. The decision to annex Texas itself encouraged the process by weakening the respect which many Americans held for Mexico's territorial integrity and thus pointed the way to further acquisitions in the Southwest. Having passed its arm "down to the waist of the continent," observed the *Dublin Freeman*, the nation would certainly "not hesitate to pass it round."[37] That the United States was destined to annex additional portions of Mexican territory seemed apparent enough, but only when its population had been absorbed by the Anglo-Saxons now overspreading the continent. As early as 1845 the rapid migration of pioneers into California promised to render the province fit for eventual annexation. In July of that year the *Democratic Review* noted that Mexican influence there was nearing extinction, for the Anglo-Saxon foot was on its border.

California's immense potential as the seat of a rich empire, contrasted to its backwardness under Mexican rule, added a new dimension to the doctrine of manifest destiny—the regeneration of California's soil. As early as September 1845, the *Daily Missourian* (St. Louis) observed that, despite the wonders of the region, under its present government it was "doomed to desolation and a barren waste, instead of the garden of the world." In a sublime passage the editor noted the need for its acquisition by the United States:

> That Mexico shall domineer over it, merely for the sake of domineering, without calling forth its resources, to contribute to the comfort and happiness of man—that enterprise shall be prevented from entering, exploring and bringing forth the fruits of that rich field—that this delightful land should only be a theatre for robbery and plunder, instead of being devoted to the uses which nature and nature's God designed it, we cannot believe. But that it can become other than it now is, we cannot see, unless settled by our countrymen—which we believe, is inevitable, as it seems

[36] *Congressional Globe*, 28th Cong., 2d sess., 1845, Appendix, p. 178.

[37] *Dublin Freeman* quoted in Frederick Merk, *Manifest Destiny and Mission in American History: A Reinterpretation* (New York, 1963), p. 83.

to be a law of nature, as a western statesman has well remarked, 'that the children of Adam follow the sun'; or, as the poet has it, 'Westward the star of empire holds its way.'[38]

In its January 1846 issue the *American Review* expanded this theme. After three centuries of Spanish and Mexican rule, California, despite its natural advantages, possessed no commerce, little agriculture, and no industry. In every respect, the region was as devoid of wealth, cultivation, and power as when the Spaniards first sailed its coasts. But to the writer such conditions could not continue, for "no one who cherishes a faith in the wisdom of an overruling Providence, and who sees, in the national movements which convulse the world, the silent operation of an invisible but omnipotent hand, can believe it to be for the interest of humanity, for the well-being of the world, that this vast and magnificent region should continue forever in its present state." The assurance of expanding migration into California after the out-break of the Mexican War merely emphasized the burgeoning American role of regeneration. Queried the *Illinois State Register* on July 10, 1846: "Shall this garden of beauty be suffered to lie dormant in its wild and useless luxuriance?" As U.S. territory, "it would almost immediately be made to blossom like a rose; myriads of enterprising Americans would flock to its rich and inviting prairies; the hum of Anglo-American industry would be heard in its vales; cities would rise upon its plains and seacoast, and the resources and wealth of the nation be increased in an incalculable degree."

V

Such varied arguments for manifest destiny hardly explain the sweep of the United States across the North American continent. American acquisitiveness toward California, like that displayed toward Texas and Oregon, progressed at two levels—that of abstract rationalization and that of concrete national interest. Expansion to the Pacific was a precise and calculated movement, limited in its objectives. The American diplomatic and military policy that secured the acquisition of both Oregon and California was in the possession of men who never defined their expansionist purposes in terms of a democratic ideal. The vistas of these men from Jackson to Polk were maritime and were always anchored to specific waterways along the Pacific coast. Land was necessary to them merely as a right of way to ocean ports, a barrier to be spanned by improved avenues of commerce. Any interpretation of westward

---

[38](St. Louis) *Missouri Reporter*, September 1, 1845.

expansion beyond Texas is meaningless unless defined in terms of commerce and harbors.

Travelers during the decade before 1845 had created a precise vision of the western coasts of North America; it was a vision born of the sea. With the exception of John C. Frémont, every noted traveler who recorded his impressions of Oregon and California had approached these regions by way of the Pacific. Some traders had sailed these coasts directly from Boston; others had first traversed the broad Pacific world as captains of merchant vessels or as explorers. Whatever their mission on the great ocean, they were without exception struck by the excellent quality of Juan de Fuca Strait, San Francisco Bay, and the harbor of San Diego, as well as by the possible role of these ports in the development of Pacific commerce.

Charles Wilkes, as the commander of a U.S. exploring expedition to the Pacific between 1838 and 1842, studied minutely not only the islands and sea-lanes of the entire ocean, but also the important harbors and bays along the North American coast from Juan de Fuca Strait to San Francisco. Wilkes was not certain that these coastal regions, separated as they were from the settled portions of the Midwest by almost two thousand miles of wilderness, would become anything other than a prosperous and independent maritime republic. Eminently qualified to speculate on these western harbors as stations of Pacific commerce, however, he predicted a sizable stream of traffic emanating from them:

> These two regions have, in fact, within themselves every thing to make them increase, and keep up an intercourse with the whole of Polynesia, as well as the countries of South America on the one side, and China, the Philippines, New Holland, and New Zealand, on the other. Among the latter, before many years, may be included Japan. Such various climates will furnish the materials for a beneficial exchange of products, and an intercourse that must, in time, become immense.[39]

American officials and expansionists refused to accept Wilkes's prediction of a separate commercial nation across the mountains; the threat of European encroachment convinced them that the grandeur of the Pacific coast must accrue to the wealth, prosperity, and commercial eminence of the United States. By 1845 the nation's press accepted the dreams of expansionists who had anticipated an American Boston or New York situated on some distant harbor. For those who perpetuated the expansionist program after Polk's inaugural in March

[39]Charles Wilkes, *Narrative of the United States Exploring Expedition During the Years 1838, 1839, 1840, 1841, 1842* (Philadelphia, 1845), 5:182–83.

1845, ports of call in Oregon and California were as vital as had been land empires in Texas during the preceding year. Except for what remained of the whole-of-Oregon fever, expansionism had lost its broad nationalism and had become anchored to the mercantile interests of the United States. The final treaties, which marked the far northwest and southwest boundaries of the United States, encompassed the great harbors of Puget Sound and San Diego Bay. So completely did those harbors, along with San Francisco Bay, satisfy U.S. interests in the Far West that their acquisition terminated American expansion along the distant Pacific coastline.

CHAPTER EIGHT

Maritime Factors in the Oregon Compromise*

OF THOSE FACTORS in American expansionism which sought solution in the Oregon negotiations of 1846, none appeared of greater concern to the people of the United States than the disposition of Asiatic trade. Historians have detected a persistent commercial motivation in this nation's expansion to the Pacific. Foster Rhea Dulles, for example, developed the theme that Oregon and California were not ends in themselves, but rather a point of departure for an Asiatic commercial empire.[1] Richard Van Alstyne held that American expansion can be only partly explained in terms of a continental domain.[2] Frederick Jackson Turner also took the broader view of American acquisitions on the Pacific Ocean, the mastery of which "was to determine the future relations of Asiatic and European civilization."[3]

Mercantile interests in the Pacific, however, explain more than one powerful motive in expansionism. Maritime calculations augmented the strong inclination of American commercial interests to seek a peaceful solution of the Oregon controversy and actually defeated

---

*This paper was read at the meeting of the Mississippi Valley Historical Association at Cincinnati in April 1951. Published as "Maritime Factors in the Oregon Compromise," *Pacific Historical Review* 20 (November 1951): 331–45. Reprinted by permission.

[1]Foster Rhea Dulles, *America in the Pacific* (Boston, 1938), p. 4.

[2]Richard W. Van Alstyne, "The Significance of the Mississippi Valley in American Diplomatic History, 1686–1890," *Mississippi Valley Historical Review* 36 (1949): 230. This same theme is developed in Robert G. Cleland, "Asiatic Trade and the American Occupation of the Pacific Coast," *Annual Report of the American Historical Association* (1914), 1:283–89.

[3]Frederick Jackson Turner, *Rise of the New West* (New York, 1906), p. 113.

the movement for 54° 40′ quite as effectively as the threat of war with Great Britain or Mexico. This ardent quest for ports on the Pacific, moreover, fused Oregon and California into one irreducible issue in the minds of the commercial enthusiasts and thereby played an intensely persuasive role in the eventual delineation of the nation's western boundaries.

When the 29th Congress met in December 1845, there was still little indication that within six months the settlement of the disturbing Oregon question would be assured. Enthusiasm for the whole area, engendered by the president's message, rapidly translated U.S. claims to the Far Northwest into what Albert K. Weinberg has termed a "defiant anti-legalism." It no longer mattered that the American title to territory north of the Columbia was far from conclusive, and above the 49th parallel practically nonexistent. It had become, wrote John L. O'Sullivan of the *New York Morning News*, "our manifest destiny to . . . possess the whole of the Continent."[4] To 54° 40′ proponents that seemed to settle the issue.

It quickly becomes evident from a study of the great debate that this expanding outlook was doomed from the beginning by the patent interests of U.S. commercialism. Too many congressional eyes were narrowly trained on ports to permit the triumph of agrarian nationalism. For almost a half century the trading empire of Boston and New York had given to Oregon's waterways a peculiar significance in the country's future economic growth. Countless early spokesmen for Oregon from John Jacob Astor to Hall J. Kelley had viewed the region primarily as an American window on the Pacific.[5] A decade of attention to trappers, missionaries, and pioneers, furthermore, had not obscured to congressmen the strategic importance of Oregon to the trade of Asia. Samuel Gordon of New York phrased for the House in January 1846 his district's cogent evaluation of Oregon: "It is the key to the Pacific. It will command the trade of the isles of the Pacific, of the East, and of China." Similarly Washington Hunt, also of New York, stated this repetitious theme: "Its possession will ultimately secure to us an ascendency in the trade of the Pacific, thereby making 'the uttermost parts of the earth' tributary to our enterprise, and pouring into our lap 'the wealth of Ormus and of Ind.' "[6]

Salt spray also had conditioned New England's outlook toward Oregon. Even before the introduction in January 1846 of the resolution

---

[4] Albert K. Weinberg, *Manifest Destiny: A Study of Nationalist Expansionism in American History* (Baltimore, 1935), p. 145.

[5] See Dulles, *America in the Pacific*, pp. 19–39.

[6] *Congressional Globe*, 29th Cong., 1st sess., Appendix, pp. 117, 239.

to terminate the convention of 1827, Robert C. Winthrop of Massachusetts had defined clearly the objectives of commercial America. "We need ports on the Pacific," he argued. "As to land, we have millions of acres of better land still unoccupied on this side of the mountains."[7]

During the preceding year William Sturgis, the noted Boston merchant and pioneer in the Northwest fur trade, had popularized such particularistic notions in the Bay State. In his famous lecture to the citizens of Boston in January 1845, Sturgis admitted that the Willamette Valley was both attractive and productive, but he added that he had never seen or heard of any Oregon lands superior to millions of uncultivated acres east of the Rockies.[8] His three decades of intense commercial activity in the Pacific had channeled his attention to ports rather than to land. Sturgis indicated, moreover, which ports in Oregon the United States would require to assure fully her future position in oriental trade. The Columbia, he warned, was always dangerous for large ships and almost inaccessible for a considerable portion of each year. Instead, this nation's maritime greatness in the Pacific would derive from the possession of Juan de Fuca Strait and its numerous branches which were "easy of access, safe, and navigable at all seasons and in any weather."[9]

Writings of such leading authorities on Oregon as Robert Greenhow, Thomas J. Farnham, and Charles Wilkes merely affirmed Sturgis's conclusions. They likewise had convinced the representatives of commerce that the Columbia, although traditionally associated with the Northwest trade, was of questionable value as an ocean port. Their narratives had made axiomatic the dangers of the sand bar between Cape Disappointment and Point Adams. "Mere description," wrote Wilkes, "can give little idea of the terrors of the bar of the Columbia: all who have seen it have spoken of the wildness of the scene, and the incessant roar of the waters, representing it as one of the most fearful sights that can possibly meet the eye of the sailor."[10]

In sharp contrast was their description of the strait and the sea arms to the east of it. "No part of the world," wrote Farnham, "affords finer inland sounds or a greater number of harbours than can be found

[7]Ibid., p. 99.

[8]William Sturgis, *The Oregon Question: Substance of a Lecture Before the Mercantile Library Association, Delivered January 22, 1845* (Boston, 1845), p. 28.

[9]Ibid., p. 27.

[10]Charles Wilkes, *Narrative of the United States Exploring Expedition During the Years 1838, 1839, 1840, 1841, 1842* (Philadelphia, 1845), 4:293. See also Thomas J. Farnham, *Travels in the Great Western Prairies, October 21–December 4, 1839*, in Reuben Gold Thwaites, ed., *Early Western Travels 1748–1846* (Cleveland, 1906), 29:80; Robert Greenhow, *The History of Oregon and California* (Boston, 1844), p. 23.

here."[11] Wilkes's description was equally glowing: "Nothing can exceed the beauty of these waters, and their safety: not a shoal exists within the Straits of Juan de Fuca, Admiralty Inlet, Puget Sound, or Hood's Canal, that can in any way interrupt their navigation by a seventy-four gun ship. I venture nothing in saying, there is no country in the world that possesses waters equal to these."[12] Herein lay the primary objectives in Oregon of the commercial Northeast.

II

Agrarian spokesmen of the Middle West also debated the Oregon question in maritime terms, for Oregon held a special commercial significance for their constituents. The Juan de Fuca Strait, saw these ardent expansionists, was the future link between the Mississippi Valley, with its surplus of grain, and the teeming millions of the Orient who in exchange could enrich the great valley with cargoes of tea, porcelain, silks and satins, velvets, sugar, and spices.[13] Through possession of the strait, moreover, the United States would challenge the commercial supremacy of England in the Pacific. Andrew Kennedy of Indiana sought to erase all doubts as to the tangible value of Oregon to the Middle West:

> It is the inch of ground upon which we can place a fulcrum, giving us the lever by which to overturn the world of British commerce. It will give us a cluster of manufacturing and commercial states on the Pacific corresponding with our New England States upon the Atlantic. Then the inhabitants of the great Mississippi Valley, who have in their possession the garden of the world and the granary of the universe, will stretch out one hand to the East Indies through the Pacific chain, the other to Europe through the Atlantic channel, grasping the trade of the civilized earth, as we now hold in possession the means of subsistence of the whole human family.[14]

[11]Farnham, *Travels in the Great Western Prairies*, pp. 61–62, 84; Greenhow, *History of Oregon and California*, pp. 24–25.

[12]Wilkes, *Narrative of the United States Exploring Expedition*, p. 305.

[13]See speech of J. B. Bowlin of Missouri in the House on January 6, 1846, *Congressional Globe*, 29th Cong., 1st sess., Appendix, p. 80.

[14]Ibid., p. 212. O. B. Ficklin of Illinois stated his opinion of the value of Oregon's ports on February 6, 1846: "Thus having the Atlantic on the east and the Pacific on the west, our commerce would display its canvass on both oceans, and bear from every clime the rewards of its enterprise. Every sinew and artery of the nation would be quickened and invigorated by the new impulse given to its strength and activity, whilst agriculture would reap the golden fruits of the harvest, and manufactures learn to excel the best productions of other nations." Ibid., p. 176.

What alarmed these nationalists, however, was the fact that the constant reiteration of the commercial value of Oregon bespoke compromise at the 49th parallel, for that boundary would give the United States access to the Juan de Fuca Strait. Representatives of commerce who wished to settle the issue and secure permanent title to the magnificent inlet pointed out that the United States could acquire all the excellent harbors in Oregon and still proffer an olive branch to England. Sturgis, for example, had argued effectively that a settlement at 49°, with the granting of Vancouver Island to Great Britain, would secure the maritime objectives of the United States and still not deny to England the navigation of the strait, a right which it would not relinquish.[15] On the other hand, Wilkes had described the Pacific coast north of the 49th parallel as being devoid of good harbors or any extensive commercial inducements.[16] His writings simply substantiated the particularistic view that everything of value in Oregon lay to the south of that line. Bradford Wood of New York assured Congress that it "knew nothing of the country north of that parallel. All that had been said of its value and beauty were mere draughts on the imagination."[17]

Uncompromising Democrats were driven by the logic of the commercial argument to assume the task not only of proving the value of Oregon north of 49°, but actually of doing so in realistic commercial terms. The acquisition of the strait alone, they sought to illustrate, hardly touched the commercial possibilities of the Northwest coast. They reminded Congress that a compromise would lose the islands of Vancouver and Washington with their sturdy forests for American shipbuilding, their excellent harbors, their unparalleled fisheries, and their commanding position on the sea-lanes. With such a settlement would go also other valuable islands and the bays and harbors which indented the coast. They demanded to know why the United States would grant voluntarily such enormous commercial advantages to Great Britain. John A. McClernand of Illinois impressed upon the commercial spokesmen of the House the fatal error of compromise when he declared:

> Commercially, indeed, by such a concession, we voluntarily decapitate ourselves upon the Pacific seaboard; we lose that portion of Oregon which bears the same relation to the Pacific, in furnishing a commercial marine upon that ocean, which New England now bears upon the Atlantic. . . . The American or British marine,

[15]Sturgis, *Oregon Question*, p. 25.
[16]Quoted in Farnham, *Travels in the Great Western Prairies*, p. 76.
[17]*Congressional Globe*, 29th Cong., 1st sess., Appendix, p. 218.

which will whiten the Pacific, and carry direct trade to Asia, Polynesia, and South to the Atlantic capes, will be built, owned, and navigated by a similar people, who shall dwell north of the 49th parallel. This must naturally come to pass, because the harbors, bays, timber, and material, to give existence to a marine, exist there in combination; and there, too, are fisheries which nurse seamen.[18]

Similarly warned Edward A. Hannegan, the Indiana senator: "Let England possess Nootka Sound, the finest harbor in the world, commanding as it does the Straits of Fuca, and consequently the access to Puget's Sound, and she has all of Oregon worth possessing in a commercial and maritime point of view."[19] He turned his abuse on men dominated by narrow commercialism: "It is the opinion of six-sevenths of the American people that Oregon is ours—perhaps I should rather say five-sevenths, for I must leave out of the estimate the commercial and stockjobbing population of our great cities along the seaboard, a great portion of whom are English subjects, residing among us for the purpose of traffic."[20]

Because of the "Bargain of 1844" and the necessity of agrarian unity in achieving the whole of Oregon, Hannegan would not write off the South or its Democratic leadership so easily. He castigated that region for losing interest in free territory after it had acquired Texas.[21] There is more evidence, however, that southern low-tariff advocates, such as John C. Calhoun, wanted to compromise the Oregon issue not only to avoid war with England, but also to facilitate the repeal of the British Corn Laws and the passage of a lower tariff in the United States. The *Charleston Mercury* gave evidence of this southern preference for free trade to the acquisition of the whole of Oregon when it declared that southern statesmen would not maintain a clear and unquestioned title to 54° 40' at the price of two million bales of cotton per annum.[22]

Actually the South, like the Northeast, revealed its inclination to compromise in commercial terms. No American publication called the attention of its readers to the importance of Asiatic commerce in more ebullient terms than did *DeBow's Commercial Review* of New Orleans. Its editor declared in January 1846:

[18]Ibid., p. 277.
[19]Ibid., p. 309.
[20]Ibid., p. 310.
[21]*Congressional Globe*, 29th Cong., 1st sess., p. 110.
[22]Cited in Thomas P. Martin, "Free Trade and the Oregon Question, 1842–1846," *Facts and Factors in Economic History: Articles by Former Students of Edwin Francis Gay* (Cambridge, 1932), p. 488. For an excellent discussion of the southern free trade thesis by M. P. Gentry of Tennessee see *Congressional Globe*, 29th Cong., 1st sess., Appendix, p. 182.

The commerce of the East Indies has for ages been a glittering object in the eyes of trading nations. They have sought it, and grown up to power and influence under its support. What, for instance, were the Italian republics, until the bounteous products of the East were thrown into their lap; and where were Venice and Genoa and Pisa, when the Portuguese, by a shorter passage to the Indies, had cut off these rich resources? Britain, too, what has been her advance since she has enjoyed an almost monopoly of this invaluable trade? If possessions on the Pacific Ocean will facilitate such a commerce—if they be necessary to its existence—then, surely, we will not be neglectful of these possessions.[23]

Even those who believed that the trade of Oregon would accrue to the benefit of other sections insisted on the preservation of the strait. But they would court no conflict by demanding more than 49°. To Jefferson Davis this guaranteed American interests in Oregon: "Possessed, as by this line we should be, of the agricultural portion of the country, of the Straits of Fuca, and Admiralty Inlet, to American enterprise and American institutions we can, without a fear, intrust the future."[24]

III

Widening emphasis on the Juan de Fuca Strait developed public opinion for compromise in 1845 and 1846. Perhaps more significant was the role of Pacific commerce in diverting attention from Oregon to the harbors of California. Whereas the excellence of the strait as an ocean port was widely recognized, its northern position blinded many to its potential value. All agreed that harbors were of real consequence in the development of commerce in the Pacific, but the known quality of San Francisco and San Diego harbors to the south convinced many travelers, politicians, and members of the press that the commercial growth of the United States in the Pacific was contingent upon the acquisition of the California ports. When by 1845 this ardent quest for ports encompassed the question of both Oregon and California, it increasingly motivated compromise at 49° and actually determined the fate of the Pacific coast from Lower California to Alaska.

Numerous travelers had pictured the harbor of San Francisco as the veritable answer to America's commercial dreams. Wilkes, who had also sailed the Juan de Fuca Strait, believed that California could

[23]"Oregon and California," *DeBow's Commercial Review* 1 (January 1846): 69.
[24]*Congressional Globe*, 29th Cong., 1st sess., Appendix, p. 216. For Calhoun's views on the importance of preserving Oregon's ports for the United States see Cleland, "Asiatic Trade," pp. 285–86.

boast "one of the finest, if not the very best harbor in the world." It was so extensive, he added, that the "combined fleets of all the naval powers of Europe might moor in it."[25] Farmham called it "the largest and best harbor of the earth" and "the glory of the Western world."[26] New England's remarkable hide trade with California publicized the value not only of San Francisco but also of San Diego. Its bay, small and landlocked, free of surf, and sufficiently deep that vessels could lie within a cable's length of the smooth beach, was "tailor-made" for drying, curing, and loading hides.[27] These facts were well known to commercial America.

Several noted writers and travelers, when they ignored the Juan de Fuca Strait and recounted in detail the inadequacies of the Columbia, stimulated the intensive desire of Americans to acquire ports in California. Albert Gilliam warned that Oregon was so devoid of harbors that if the United States did not secure ports in California it would ultimately lack sea room.[28] Similarly, Waddy Thompson, seeing no hope for commercial greatness in Oregon's waterways, praised San Francisco Bay in words reminiscent of Farmham and Wilkes.[29]

It is not strange that many Americans were willing to trade off varying portions of Oregon for an opportunity to acquire California. That Daniel Webster had little interest in land empires but enormous enthusiasm for spacious ports for his Yankee constituents is well known. In 1843 he attempted to cede all of Oregon north of the Columbia in exchange for the acquisition of San Francisco from Mexico through British intercession.[30] By 1845 the tremendous burst of enthusiasm for California which followed the passage of the Texas resolution had convinced many commercial expansionists that America's real interests lay to the south of Oregon. In March, Webster revealed his true interests in the American West: "You know my opinion to have been, and it now is, that the port of San Francisco would be twenty times as valuable to us as all Texas."[31] In July, Thomas O. Larkin of Monterey in a letter to the *New York Journal of Commerce* found the solution of the

[25]Wilkes, *Narrative of the United States Exploring Expedition*, 5:157; see also Alfred Robinson, *Life in California* (New York, 1846), p. 225.

[26]Thomas J. Farnham, *Life and Adventures in California* (New York, 1846), p. 352; *Niles' Register*, October 31, 1846.

[27]Richard Henry Dana, *Two Years Before the Mast, a Personal Narrative of Life at Sea* (New York, 1840), pp. 150–51.

[28]Albert M. Gilliam, *Travels in Mexico, During the Years 1843 and 1844* (Aberdeen, 1847), pp. 268–70.

[29]Thompson quoted in *Niles' Register*, June 20, 1846.

[30]John Quincy Adams, *Memoirs*, ed. by Charles Francis Adams (Philadelphia, 1876), 11:355.

[31]Webster to Fletcher Webster, March 11, 1845, in Fletcher Webster, ed., *The Private Correspondence of Daniel Webster* (Boston, 1857), 2:204.

Oregon question in the expanding commercial interest in California. He wrote: "If the Oregon dispute continues, let England take eight degrees north of the Columbia, and purchase eight degrees south of forty-two from Mexico, and exchange."[32] The *Journal* concurred in the view that California was this nation's real objective and therefore the United States could well settle at the Columbia and still retain ten degrees of coast.[33] John Tyler never lost the vision of Webster's tripartite proposal. He wrote to his son in December 1845 regarding the Oregon question: "I never dreamed of conceding the country, unless for the greater equivalent of California, which I fancied Great Britain might be able to obtain for us through her influence in Mexico."[34]

Other California enthusiasts desired to compromise the Oregon controversy but were far more sanguine in their objectives. Increasingly the American dream of empire on the Pacific included the ports of both Oregon and California. Writing to President James K. Polk in July 1845, Charles Fletcher, the Pennsylvania railroad booster, pictured an American union expanding from the Atlantic to the Pacific and from the 30th to the 49th degree of north latitude.[35] The *Missourian* (St. Louis) demanded both the Juan de Fuca Strait and San Francisco harbor to fulfill the maritime destiny of the United States.[36] Quite typically William Field, a Texan, advised the president to accept the parallel of 49° and then purchase California for as much as $50 million if necessary. He wrote: "I will only remark that if you can settle the Oregon difficulty without war and obtain California of Mexico, to the Gulf of California and the river Gila for a boundary, you will have achieved enough to enroll your name *highest* among those of the benefactors of the American people."[37] By 1846 this unitary view of the Pacific coast had penetrated the halls of Congress where Meredith P. Gentry of Tennessee observed: "Oregon up to the 49th parallel of latitude, and the province of Upper California, when it can be fairly acquired, is the utmost limit to which this nation ought to go in the acquisition of territory."[38]

Even the British press saw the impact of American interest in California on the Oregon question. Before the news of the Mexican

[32]Larkin to *New York Journal of Commerce*, July 1845, Thomas O. Larkin Papers, Division of Manuscripts, University of California Library.

[33]*New York Journal of Commerce*, October 18, 30, 1845.

[34]See Lyon Gardiner Tyler, *Letters and Times of the Tylers* (Richmond, 1885), 2:448.

[35]Fletcher to Polk, July 8, 1845, Polk Papers, Division of Manuscripts, Library of Congress.

[36]*Missourian* (St. Louis), April 17, 1846; *Missouri Reporter*, September 1, 1845, February 12, 1846.

[37]Field to Polk, February 10, 1846, Polk Papers.

[38]*Congressional Globe*, 29th Cong., 1st sess., Appendix, p. 184.

War had reached Europe, the *Times* (London) insisted that "if any incident should lead to the declaration of war against Mexico, the seizure of Port St. Francis and of Upper California, would be considered all over the Union as a sufficient pretext for adjourning the discussion of the Oregon Convention."[39]

It was more than the desire for San Francisco Bay that caused the California issue to prompt compromise on Oregon. The pervading fear that England was negotiating for California had not only designated that province as an immediate objective of manifest destiny in 1845, but also it now convinced certain American observers that the United States might well compromise on Oregon to diminish British pressure in California. In urging Americans to settle the Oregon question the *Richmond Enquirer* warned: "It is clearly England which retreats. But it is too much to retreat at the same time in Oregon and California. The English annals present no example of such prudence."[40] In one terse observation the *New York Herald* summed up the entire issue: "We must surrender a slice of Oregon, if we would secure a slice of California."[41]

By early 1846 the metropolitan expansionist press was fostering compromise vigorously. Because of its addiction to California, the *New York Journal of Commerce* succumbed early to the desire for compromise at 49°. By January 1846, both the *New York Herald* and the *New York Sun* had joined the trend, as had also the *Washington Union* and the St. Louis and New Orleans press. The leading compromise editors stressed the maritime significance of the Pacific coast, denounced members of Congress who still favored the whole of Oregon even at the cost of war, and minimized the worth of Oregon's soil, especially as compared to that of California. The *North American Review*, quite characteristically, after citing Wilkes, Farnham, and Greenhow to prove that Oregon was an "arid and rugged waste" inhabited only by hunters and Indians, concluded in January that "it is hardly too much to say that what Siberia is to Russia, Oregon is to the United States."[42]

Even after the outbreak of the Mexican War, expansionist editors continued uninterrupted in their commercial outlook toward the Pacific. To them the settlement with England had been made particularly acceptable by the anticipation of adding certain Mexican ports to the American Union. As war broke out in May 1846, the *New York Herald* urged the United States to seize San Francisco so that men would forget

---

[39] *Times* (London), May 15, 1846. This article was widely quoted in the United States.

[40] *Richmond Enquirer*, June 25, 1846.

[41] *New York Herald*, February 3, 1846.

[42] "The Oregon Question," *North American Review* 62 (1846): 218–26.

the whole of Oregon. One California correspondent predicted the result of the speedy occupation of the Pacific ports by the American naval commander: "We shall have then a country, bounded at the North latitude by 49 degrees, to the Pacific—and the South on the same ocean by 32 degrees—and the western and eastern boundaries, being what Nature intended them, the Pacific, with China in the outline, and the Atlantic with Europe in the background."[43] Such prospects pleased the editor of the *New York Herald*, who noted that the proposed boundaries gave the United States 1,300 miles of coast on the Pacific, several magnificent harbors, and "squared off our South-Western possessions." One writer for the *New York Journal of Commerce* in December 1846 rejoiced that with the acquisition of New Mexico and California the territory of the United States would "spread out in one broad square belt from one ocean to the other, giving us nearly as much coast on the Pacific as we possess on the Atlantic."[44] Obviously the imaginary line of 42° meant little to the American commercial expansionists of a century ago.

IV

American historians have analyzed thoroughly the factors which compelled Great Britain to settle the Oregon question in 1846. In fact, in British rather than American policy is to be found the key to the several well-known interpretations of the Oregon compromise. England had long since quit its claim to the regions south of the Columbia, while the United States had traditionally offered to yield all territory north of 49°. As late as July 1845, Polk had offered to treat on that line. Viewed from diplomatic history, therefore, a compromise at 49° was a British surrender. Melvin Jacobs has stated clearly this widely accepted assumption:

> Taking into consideration the indefiniteness and weakness of claims to new territory on the basis of discovery and exploration, in contrast to occupation and settlement, instead of raising the question as to the reasons why America did not secure the whole of Oregon to fifty-four degrees and forty minutes, it appears to be more appropriate to raise the question as to why England lost the

[43]See *New York Herald*, September 3, November 19, December 30, 1846; *New York Sun*, August 1, 1846; *Washington Union*, April 15, 1847.
[44]*New York Journal of Commerce*, December 17, 1846.

territory between the Columbia River and the forty-ninth parallel
after she had both occupied and, apparently, possessed it.[45]

Despite the many domestic pressures that drove Great Britain toward
compromise, the British willingness to accept the 49th parallel, just as
the American, was largely motivated by maritime considerations.

Two important streams of British trade met in Oregon waters:
the commerce with the Orient and the northwest fur trade of the
Hudson's Bay Company. To British officials and traders the Columbia
River, therefore, presented a watercourse of peculiar significance, fur-
nishing an ocean port as well as an access to the interior fur-bearing
regions. For this reason the London government during the early Oregon negotiations held to the Columbia boundary. George Canning, the
foreign minister, giving evidence of his own commercial motivation
during the 1826 negotiations, wrote that he would not care to have his
"name affixed to an instrument by which England would have foregone
the advantage of our immense direct intercourse between China and
what may be, if we resolve not to yield them up, her boundless establishments on the N. W. Coast of America."[46] Canning attempted unsuc-
cessfully to quiet the early American demand for 49° by offering a
frontage of isolated territory on the strait.[47] For the next two decades
Britain continued to hold to the Columbia line; in 1846, however, only
an English surrender of territory made possible a peaceful settlement.

Several American students of the Oregon question have attributed British conciliation to the pressure of American pioneers. It is
unquestionably true that the British viewed their growing numbers
south of the Columbia with dismay, for they endangered the peace and
disrupted the fur trade. When in 1845 the Hudson's Bay Company
moved its main depot to Vancouver Island because of the decline in
the fur traffic and American immigrant pressure, it admitted that its
perennial sine qua non in any treaty, the Columbia, was no longer its
vital trade route. This surrender of the Columbia, according to Frederick Merk, was the key to the Oregon settlement.[48]

[45]Melvin Jacobs, *Winning Oregon* (Caldwell, Idaho, 1938), p. 242. For similar views
see Frederick Merk, "British Government Propaganda and the Oregon Treaty," *American
Historical Review* 40 (1934): 38; Joseph Schafer, "The British Attitude toward the Oregon
Question, 1815–1846," *American Historical Review* 16 (1911): 275; Ray Allen Billington,
Westward Expansion (New York, 1949), p. 507.

[46]Quoted in Schafer, "British Attitude Toward the Oregon Question," p. 291;
Jacobs, *Winning Oregon*, p. 95.

[47]Jacobs, *Winning Oregon*, pp. 226–27.

[48]Frederick Merk, "The Oregon Pioneers and the Boundary," *American Historical
Review* 29 (1924): 696. For similar conclusions see Jacobs, *Winning Oregon*, pp. 219–20;
Richard W. Van Alstyne, "International Rivalries in the Pacific Northwest," *Oregon
Historical Quarterly* 46 (1945): 209; and Leslie M. Scott, "Influence of American Settlement
upon the Oregon Boundary Treaty of 1846," *Oregon Historical Quarterly* 29 (1928): 1–19.

Lord Aberdeen, who as foreign minister led the British govern-ment toward compromise, analyzed cogently his inclination to retreat in terms of Pacific ports. He wrote to Sir Robert Peel in September 1844:

> I believe that if the line of the 49th degree were extended only to the water's edge, and should leave us possession of all of Van-couver's Island, with the northern side of the entrance to Puget's Sound; and if all the harbors within the Sound, and to the Colum-bia, inclusive, were made free to both countries; and further, if the river Columbia from the point at which it became navigable to its mouth, were also made free to both, this would be in reality a most advantageous settlement.[49]

A year later Aberdeen admitted that England could obtain everything worth contending for in acquiring Vancouver Island, the navigation of the Columbia, and free access to all ports between the Columbia and 49°.[50]

Aberdeen's purpose in 1845 and 1846 was to propagandize the British people into an acceptance of his views. His specific task was to convince them that British claims to Oregon were imperfect, that Ore-gon was not worth a dispute with the United States, that the British fur trade was dying, that the Columbia offered little security for heavy commerce, and that the United States had reasonable claims to good harbors on the Pacific.[51] Several major British journals, especially the *Edinburgh Review*, the *Illustrated London News*, the *Quarterly Review*, and the *Times*, spread these doctrines for him. Thus the British willingness to compromise in 1846 was in a sense a triumph for Aberdeen's mar-itime views.

Historians have attributed the British inclination to settle at 49° to two other factors. First, such students of the question as Thomas P. Martin and St. George Sioussat have concluded that the harvest short-age of 1845 and the corresponding need of American grain contributed to British pacificism.[52] Merk, however, has challenged this interpre-tation by citing evidence that the scarcity of food in the British Isles was not sufficient to alter prices or trade considerably.[53] Second, a

---

[49]Aberdeen to Peel, September 25, 1844, in Hunter Miller, ed., *Treaties and Other International Acts of the United States of America* (Washington, 1937), 5:25.

[50]Aberdeen to Peel, October 17, 1845, ibid., p. 48.

[51]Frederick Merk, "British Government Propaganda and the Oregon Treaty," *American Historical Review* 40 (1934): 40–41.

[52]See St. George L. Sioussat, "James Buchanan," in Samuel Flagg Bemis, ed., *The American Secretaries of State and Their Diplomacy* (New York, 1928), 5:260; Martin, "Free Trade and the Oregon Question," p. 485.

[53]Frederick Merk, "The British Corn Crisis of 1845–46 and the Oregon Treaty," *Agricultural History* 8 (1934): 98–103.

popular interpretation, the free trade analysis, rests primarily on a variety of British statements such as one of Peel: "The admission of Maize will I believe go far to promote the settlement of Oregon."[54] Apparently certain spokesmen believed that the opening of the British grain market would provide a market for the surplus wheat of the Old Northwest and reduce the persistent Anglophobia of the region in direct proportion.[55] Perhaps more agrarian tempers were aggravated than soothed by this British action, however, for it removed the advantage of easy entry into the empire trade through Canada.[56]

The real significance of the famous British Corn Law crisis in motivating compromise rested in its creation of a realignment of parties that brought into power in England a coalition that was willing to settle the Oregon issue for an equitable distribution of ports. The essential fact is that by May 1846 Aberdeen, upon the passage of the resolution by the U.S. Congress to terminate the joint convention of 1827, was permitted by both the British government and British public opinion to proffer to the United States an acceptable treaty.[57]

That Polk without hesitation presented this proposal to the Senate indicates that he had moved far from his December position. Historical analyses of this policy shift fall basically into two categories. Julius W. Pratt has developed the thesis that Polk was convinced by his minister to Great Britain, Louis McLane, early in 1846 that the British would fight and that thereafter the president was less inclined to look John Bull in the eye.[58] Other historians such as Weinberg attribute Polk's desire to compromise to the growing threat of war with Mexico.[59]

Although it is true that tremendous pressure was placed upon the president to avoid war with England, it must be remembered that long before Polk forced the Oregon issue upon Congress and the British ministry in his message of December 1845, his vision of America's future position in the West had been fashioned by the Pacific. It was largely his interest in ports that turned his attention to California in

[54]Quoted in Sioussat, "James Buchanan," p. 261. Aberdeen had written in December 1845: "The access of Indian corn to our markets would go far to pacify the warriors of the Western States." See Aberdeen to Pakenham, December 3, 1845, in Miller, *Treaties*, p. 48.

[55]This widely accepted thesis has been fully developed by Thomas P. Martin. See Martin, "Free Trade and the Oregon Question," pp. 490 ff. See also Thomas P. Martin, "Cotton and Wheat in Anglo-American Trade and Politics, 1846–52," *Journal of Southern History* 1 (1935): 315.

[56]Merk has discounted the free-trade argument. See Merk, "The British Corn Crisis of 1845–46 and the Oregon Treaty," pp. 106–19.

[57]Ibid., pp. 119–22.

[58]Julius W. Pratt, "James K. Polk and John Bull," *Canadian Historical Review* 24 (1943): 341–49.

[59]Weinberg, *Manifest Destiny*, p. 153.

1845.[60] He admitted to Senator Thomas Hart Benton in October that, in his desire to limit British encroachment in North America, he had California and the bay of San Francisco as much in mind as Oregon.[61] He demonstrated this interest when he attempted to purchase that port from Mexico in the Slidell mission of November 1845. Yet at no time did the president lose sight of the Juan de Fuca Strait. In his first message to Congress he declared that the United States could never accept a settlement that "would leave on the British side two-thirds of the whole Oregon territory, including the free navigation of the Columbia and all valuable harbors on the Pacific."[62] Finally, in late December 1845, Polk noted in his diary that he would submit to the Senate for its previous advice any British offer that would grant to the United States the strait and some free ports to the north.[63]

This brief analysis of the maritime objectives of the national leaders would indicate that the Oregon settlement was no compromise at all, for Polk and Aberdeen were essentially in agreement over an equitable distribution of Oregon waterways even before the great debate of 1846. For large portions of both the British and American people, however, the final settlement was viewed as a sacrifice. The task of leadership in the crisis consisted of bringing public opinion in both nations to an acceptance of the 49th parallel. Since the unequivocal language of Polk's message tied his hands, the movement for compromise in the United States had to come from Congress and the metropolitan press. For Aberdeen the task of securing support was more difficult, since Britain, unlike the United States, was forced to retreat from its traditional offer.

Both nations as a whole were content with the distribution of land and ports. During the closing argument on the Oregon treaty Benton passed final judgment on the 49th parallel: "With that boundary comes all that we want in that quarter, namely, all the waters of Puget's Sound, and the fertile Olympian district which borders upon them."[64] The Oregon treaty brought to the business community on both sides of the Atlantic relief from the evils of suspense and uncertainty. A brief

---

[60]Polk's commercial motivation is clearly indicated in his instructions to John Slidell. See Buchanan to Slidell, November 10, 1845, Instructions to Mexico, Department of State, National Archives, Vol. XVI.

[61]James K. Polk, *Diary of James K. Polk*, ed. by Milo Milton Quaife (Chicago, 1910), 1:71.

[62]*Congressional Globe*, 29th Cong., 1st sess., Appendix, p. 4.

[63]Polk, *Diary*, p. 135. Buchanan revealed this same inclination of the administration to compromise on the basis of the strait in a letter to Louis McLane in February 1846. See Miller, *Treaties*, p. 60.

[64]*Congressional Globe*, 29th Cong., 1st sess., Appendix, p. 867.

poem in America's leading expansionist newspaper, the *New York Herald*, summed up the attitude of the English-speaking world:

> Old Buck and Pack
> Are coming back
> And will soon together dine.
> And drink a toast
> Upon their roast
> To number forty-nine.[65]

CHAPTER
NINE

The Mexican War:
A Study in Causation*

ON MAY 11, 1846, President James K. Polk presented his war message
to Congress. After reviewing the skirmish between General Zachary
Taylor's dragoons and a body of Mexican soldiers along the Rio Grande,
the president asserted that Mexico "has passed the boundary of the
United States, has invaded our territory and shed American blood upon
the American soil. . . . War exists, and, notwithstanding all our efforts
to avoid it, exists by act of Mexico." No country could have had a
superior case for war. Democrats in large numbers (for it was largely
a partisan matter) responded with the patriotic fervor which Polk
expected of them. "Our government has permitted itself to be insulted
long enough," wrote one Georgian. "The blood of her citizens has been
spilt on her own soil. It appeals to us for vengeance." Still, some
members of Congress, recalling more accurately than the president the
circumstances of the conflict, soon rendered the Mexican War the most
reviled in American history—at least until the Vietnam War of the
1960s. One outraged Whig termed the war "illegal, unrighteous, and
damnable," and Whigs questioned both Polk's honesty and his sense
of geography. Congressman Joshua R. Giddings of Ohio accused the
president of "planting the standard of the United States on foreign
soil, and using the military forces of the United States to violate every
principle of international law and moral justice." To vote for the war,
admitted Senator John C. Calhoun, was "to plunge a dagger into his

*Published as "The Mexican War: A Study in Causation," *Pacific Historical Review*
49 (August 1980): 405-26. Reprinted by permission.

223

own heart, and more so." Indeed, some critics in Congress openly wished the Mexicans well.

For over a century such profound differences in perception have pervaded American writings on the Mexican War. Even in the past decade, historians have reached conclusions on the question of war guilt as disparate as those which separated Polk from his wartime conservative and abolitionist critics. Justin H. Smith's *The War with Mexico* stands at the core of the perennial debate. Few books of American history have such impressive scholarly credentials; the footnotes and bibliography alone seem worthy of the Pulitzer Prize which the book received in 1920. According to Smith, the war was "deliberately precipitated by the will and act of Mexico."[1] Consequently, for the past half century every judgment of the Mexican War has begun with the acceptance or rejection of that verdict. Bernard De Voto, in *The Year of Decision*, wondered how Smith could accept conclusions which denied the very facts he presented: "If there is a more consistently wrongheaded book in our history, or one which so freely cites facts in support of judgments which those facts controvert, I have not encountered it."[2] Similarly Glenn W. Price, in his *Origins of the War with Mexico*, concluded that "Smith's work, in all its argument that pertained to the origins of the War, was simply preposterous as history."[3] Yet as recently as 1971 Seymour V. Connor and Odie B. Faulk, in their *North America Divided: The Mexican War, 1846–1848*, while acknowledging that they did not follow Smith "slavishly," concluded that his study "remains today a monument of historical scholarship."[4] Although nationalistic biases will color the judgments of those who study war, it seems strange that historical agreement on a subject as remote and as well documented as the Mexican War should be that elusive. President Polk's diary, published in 1910, remains the last major addition to the historic record on the origins of that war.

In some measure the diversity of judgment on the Mexican War, as on other wars, is understandable. By basing their analyses on official rationalizations, historians often ignore the more universal causes of war which transcend individual conflicts and which can establish the bases for greater consensus. Neither the officials in Washington nor those in Mexico City ever acknowledged any alternatives to the actions which they took. But governments generally have more choices in any

---

[1] Justin H. Smith, *The War with Mexico* (New York, 1919), 1:155.

[2] Bernard De Voto, *The Year of Decision: 1846* (Boston, 1943), p. 510.

[3] Glenn W. Price, *Origins of the War with Mexico: The Polk-Stockton Intrigue* (Austin, 1967), p. 103.

[4] Seymour V. Connor and Odie B. Faulk, *North America Divided: The Mexican War 1846–1848* (New York, 1971), pp. 192–93.

controversy than they are prepared to admit. Circumstances determine their extent. The more powerful a nation, the more remote its dangers, the greater its options between action and inaction. Often for the weak, unfortunately, the alternative is capitulation or war. Certainly the choices available to Franklin D. Roosevelt and Cordell Hull in their relations with Japan in 1941 were far greater than either would acknowledge. Similarly, as James C. Thomson had noted so well, the Kennedy administration vigorously eliminated a multitude of available alternatives when it bound itself to a single course of action in Vietnam.[5] Polk and his advisers developed their Mexican policies on the dual assumption that Mexico was weak and that the acquisition of certain Mexican territories would satisfy admirably the long-range interests of the United States. Within that context, Polk's policies were direct, timely, and successful. But the president had choices. Mexico, whatever its internal condition, was no direct threat to the United States. Polk, had he so desired, could have avoided war; indeed, he could have ignored Mexico in 1845 with absolute impunity.

II

In explaining the Mexican War historians have dwelled on the causes of friction in American-Mexican relations. In part these lay in the disparate qualities of the two populations, in part in the vast discrepancies between the two countries in energy, efficiency, power, and national wealth. Through two decades of independence Mexico had experienced a continuous rise and fall of governments; by the 1840s survival had become the primary concern of every regime. Conscious of their weakness, the successive governments in Mexico City resented the superior power and effectiveness of the United States and feared American notions of destiny that anticipated the annexation of Mexico's northern provinces.[6] Having failed to prevent the formation of the Texas Republic, Mexico reacted to Andrew Jackson's recognition of Texan independence in March 1837 with deep indignation. Thereafter the Mexican raids into Texas, such as the one on San Antonio in 1842, aggravated the bitterness of Texans toward Mexico, for such forays had no purpose beyond terrorizing the frontier settlements.

Such mutual animosities, extensive as they were, do not account for the Mexican War. Governments as divided and chaotic as the

---

[5]For James C. Thomson's analysis of the efforts of the Kennedy administration to eliminate all alternatives to its single course of action, see "How Could Vietnam Happen? An Autopsy," *Atlantic* 221 (April 1968): 47–53.

[6]For an excellent review of Mexican attitudes toward the United States, see Gene M. Brack, *Mexico Views Manifest Destiny 1821–1846* (Albuquerque, 1975).

Mexican regimes of the 1840s usually have difficulty in maintaining positive and profitable relations with their neighbors; their behavior often produces annoyance, but seldom armed conflict. Belligerence toward other countries had flowed through U.S. history like a torrent without, in itself, setting off a war. Nations do not fight over cultural differences or verbal recriminations; they fight over perceived threats to their interests created by the ambitions or demands of others.

What increased the animosity between Mexico City and Washington was a series of specific issues over which the two countries perennially quarreled—claims, boundaries, and the future of Texas. Nations have made claims a pretext for intervention, but never a pretext for war.[7] Every nineteenth-century effort to collect debts through force assumed the absence of effective resistance, for no debt was worth the price of war. To collect its debt from Mexico in 1838, for example, France blockaded Mexico's gulf ports and bombarded Vera Cruz. The U.S. claims against Mexico created special problems which discounted their seriousness as a rationale for war. True, the Mexican government failed to protect the possessions and the safety of Americans in Mexico from robbery, theft, and other illegal actions, but U.S. citizens were under no obligation to do business in Mexico and should have understood the risk of transporting goods and money in that country. Minister Waddy Thompson wrote from Mexico City in 1842 that it would be "with somewhat of bad grace that we should war upon a country because it could not pay its debts when so many of our own states are in the same situation."[8] Even as the United States after 1842 attempted futilely to collect the $2 million awarded its citizens by a claims commission, it was far more deeply in debt to Britain over speculative losses. Minister Wilson Shannon reported in the summer of 1844 that the claims issue defied settlement in Mexico City and recommended that Washington take the needed action to compel Mexico to pay. If Polk would take up the challenge and sacrifice American human and material resources in a war against Mexico, he would do so for reasons other than the enforcement of claims. The president knew well that Mexico could not pay, yet as late as May 9, 1846, he was ready to ask Congress for a declaration of war on the question of unpaid claims alone.[9]

---

[7]Clayton Charles Kohl came to this general conclusion in his study, *Claims as a Cause of the Mexican War* (New York, 1914). Those who defend Polk quite logically recognize the legitimacy of all Polk's arguments for war, including claims. See, for example, Connor and Faulk, *North America Divided*, p. 234.

[8]Quoted in Kohl, *Claims as a Cause of the Mexican War*, p. 51.

[9]Milo Milton Quaife, ed., *The Diary of James K. Polk* (Chicago, 1910), 1:384–85.

Congress's joint resolution for Texas annexation in February 1845 raised the specter of war among editors and politicians alike. As early as 1843 the Mexican government had warned the American minister in Mexico City that annexation would render war inevitable; Mexican officials in Washington repeated that warning. To Mexico, therefore, the move to annex Texas was an unbearable affront. Within one month after Polk's inauguration on March 4, General Juan Almonte, the Mexican minister in Washington, boarded a packet in New York and sailed for Vera Cruz to sever his country's diplomatic relations with the United States. Even before the Texas Convention could meet on July 4 to vote annexation, rumors of a possible Mexican invasion of Texas prompted Polk to advance Taylor's forces from Fort Jesup in Louisiana down the Texas coast. Polk instructed Taylor to extend his protection to the Rio Grande but to avoid any areas to the north of that river occupied by Mexican troops.[10] Simultaneously the president reinforced the American squadron in the Gulf of Mexico. "The threatened invasion of Texas by a large Mexican army," Polk informed Andrew J. Donelson, the American chargé in Texas, on June 15, " is well calculated to excite great interest here and increases our solicitude concerning the final action by the Congress and the Convention of Texas."[11] Polk assured Donelson that he intended to defend Texas to the limit of his constitutional power. Donelson resisted the pressure of those Texans who wanted Taylor to advance to the Rio Grande; instead, he placed the general at Corpus Christi on the Nueces River. Taylor agreed that the line from the mouth of the Nueces to San Antonio covered the Texas settlements and afforded a favorable base from which to defend the frontier.[12]

Those who took the rumors of Mexican aggressiveness seriously lauded the president's action. With Texas virtually a part of the United States, argued the *Washington Union*, "We owe it to ourselves, to the proud and elevated character which America maintains among the nations of the earth, to guard our own territory from the invasion of the ruthless Mexicans." The *New York Morning News* observed that Polk's policy would, on the whole, "command a general concurrence of the public opinion of his country." Some Democratic leaders, fearful of a Mexican attack, urged the president to strengthen Taylor's forces

<hr>

[10]For Taylor's instructions, see George Bancroft to Taylor, June 15, 1845, *House Ex. Doc. 60*, 30th Cong., 1st sess., p. 81; William L. Marcy to Taylor, July 30, 1845, *Senate Ex. Doc. 18*, 30th Cong., 1st sess., p. 9.

[11]Polk to Donelson, June 15, 1845, Polk Papers, Manuscripts Division, Library of Congress.

[12]Taylor to Donelson, July 30, 1845, Donelson Papers, Manuscripts Division, Library of Congress.

and order them to take the offensive should Mexican soldiers cross the Rio Grande.[13] Others believed the reports from Mexico exaggerated, for there was no apparent relationship between that country's expressions of belligerence and its capacity to act. Secretary of War William L. Marcy admitted that his information was no better than that of other commentators. "I have at no time," he wrote in July, "felt that war with Mexico was probable—and do not now believe it is, yet it is in the range of possible occurrences. I have officially acted on the hypothesis that our peace may be temporarily disturbed without however believing it will be." Still convinced that the administration had no grounds for alarm, Marcy wrote on August 12: "The presence of a considerable force in Texas will do no hurt and possibly may be of great use."[14] In September William S. Parrott, Polk's special agent in Mexico, assured the president that there would be neither a Mexican declaration of war nor an invasion of Texas.[15]

Polk insisted that the administration's show of force in Texas would prevent rather than provoke war. "I do not anticipate that Mexico will be mad enough to declare war," he wrote in July, but "I think she would have done so but for the appearance of a strong naval force in the Gulf and our army moving in the direction of her frontier on land." Polk restated this judgment on July 28 in a letter to General Robert Armstrong, the U.S. consul at Liverpool: "I think there need be but little apprehension of war with Mexico. If however she shall be mad enough to make war we are prepared to meet her." The president assured Senator William H. Haywood of North Carolina that the American forces in Texas would never aggress against Mexico; however, they would prevent any Mexican forces from crossing the Rio Grande. In conversation with Senator William S. Archer of Virginia on September 1, the president added confidently that "the appearance of our land and naval forces on the borders of Mexico & in the Gulf would probably deter and prevent Mexico from either declaring war or invading Texas."[16] Polk's continuing conviction that Mexico would not attack suggests that his deployment of U.S. land and naval forces along Mexico's periphery was designed less to protect Texas than to support an aggressive diplomacy which might extract a satisfactory treaty from Mexico without war. For Anson Jones, the last president of the Texas Republic, Polk's deployments had precisely that purpose:

[13]Semi-Weekly Union (Washington), July 10 and August 11, 1845; C. J. Ingersoll to Polk, August 20, 1845, Polk Papers.

[14]Marcy to General P. M. Wetmore, July 5 and August 12, 1845, Marcy Papers, Manuscripts Division, Library of Congress.

[15]Quaife, Diary of James K. Polk, 1:33.

[16]Polk to A. O. J. Nicholson, July 28, 1845; Polk to General Robert Armstrong, July 28, 1845; Polk to William H. Haywood, August 9, 1845, Polk Papers; Quaife, Diary of James K. Polk, 1:13.

Texas never actually needed the protection of the United States after I came into office. . . . . There was no necessity for it after the 'preliminary Treaty,' as we were at peace with Mexico, and knew perfectly well that that Government, though she might bluster a little, had not the slightest idea of invading Texas either by land or water; and that nothing would provoke her to (active) hostilities, but the presence of troops in the immediate neighborhood of the Rio Grande, threatening her towns and settlements on the south-west side of that river. . . . But Donelson appeared so intent upon 'encumbering us with help,' that finally, to get rid of his annoyance, he was told he might give us as much protection as he pleased. . . . The protection asked for was only *prospective* and contingent; the *protection* he had in view was *immediate* and *aggressive*.[17]

For Polk the exertion of military and diplomatic pressure on a disorganized Mexico was not a prelude to war. Whig critics of annexation had predicted war; this alone compelled the administration to avoid a conflict over Texas. In his memoirs Jones recalled that in 1845 Commodore Robert F. Stockton, with either the approval or the connivance of Polk, attempted to convince him that he should place Texas "in an attitude of active hostility toward Mexico, so that, when Texas was finally brought into the Union, *she might bring war with her.*"[18] If Stockton engaged in such an intrigue, he apparently did so on his own initiative, for no evidence exists to implicate the administration.[19] Polk not only preferred to achieve his purposes by means other than war but also assumed that his military measures in Texas, limited as they were, would convince the Mexican government that it could not escape the necessity of coming to terms with the United States. Washington's policy toward Mexico during 1845 achieved the broad national purpose of Texas annexation. Beyond that it brought U.S. power to bear on Mexico in a manner calculated to further the processes of negotiation.[20] Whether the burgeoning tension would lead to a negotiated boundary settlement or to war hinged on two factors: the nature of Polk's demands

[17]Anson Jones, *Memoranda and Official Correspondence Relating to the Republic of Texas, Its History and Annexation* (New York, 1859), p. 53.

[18]Ibid., pp. 46–47.

[19]Some historians have accepted Jones's allegations. See Richard R. Stenberg, "The Failure of Polk's Mexican War Intrigue of 1845," *Pacific Historical Review* 4 (March 1935): 39–68; Richard W. Van Alstyne, *The Rising American Empire* (New York, 1960), p. 138; and Price, *Origins of the War with Mexico*, pp. 49–78, 105–52. Price's effort to perfect the case against Polk was laudable; his evidence remained circumstantial.

[20]For Polk's preference for peaceful negotiations see James Buchanan to John Black, September 17, 1845, *House Ex. Doc. 60*, 30th Cong., 1st sess., p. 12. Others agreed with Polk that the mere presence of American forces in Texas would compel the Mexicans to negotiate. For example, the *Missouri Reporter* (St. Louis) declared on July 29, 1845: "By displaying a competent military and naval force, we shall command respect, and secure the objects we have in view without delay. The Administration should, in the mean time, be looking forward to what may be accomplished by negotiation."

and Mexico's response to them. The president announced his objectives to Mexico's troubled officialdom through his instructions to John Slidell, his special emissary who departed for Mexico in November 1845 with the assurance that the government there was prepared to reestablish formal diplomatic relations with the United States and negotiate a territorial settlement.

III

No one grasped the limited choices confronting Mexico more clearly than Charles Bankhead, the British minister in Mexico City. This experienced diplomat recognized both the mounting U.S. pressures on Mexico and the despair which they created among Mexican officials. Bankhead, no less than the Mexicans, feared that Washington would use the occasion of Texas annexation to push its boundary claims on a weak and reluctant neighbor. The American squadrons off Vera Cruz and Mazatlán created consternation throughout the country. On May 30, 1845, Bankhead reported to Lord Aberdeen in London that the United States was seeking an excuse to attack.[21] Bankhead condemned the anti-Americanism in Mexico City, for it compelled the Mexican government to confront Washington with a bravado that eliminated any forthright negotiations and belied its apprehensions and doubts. "It is distressing," he wrote, "to see a country like Mexico, possessing so many elements of prosperity, torn to pieces by intestine broils, brought about in reality for purposes of the basest personal aggrandisement."[22]

Until the summer of 1845, British officials in both Mexico City and London urged the Mexicans to preserve, if possible, the one defense available to them—an independent Texas. Annexation, Aberdeen argued, would endanger no fundamental British interest, but Mexico, without a buffer state separating it from the United States, would not withstand the encroachments of American power. Indeed, he feared that the United States in possession of Texas would threaten the very independence of Mexico. Thus, Aberdeen advised the Mexicans to normalize their relations with Texas; without that, the friends of Mexico could offer little help. At the same time, Bankhead warned repeatedly that Mexico could not reconquer Texas; Mexican officials seemed to agree. This enabled him to assure Charles Elliot, the British chargé in Texas, that Mexico wanted to avoid trouble and had dispatched troops to the frontier for defense alone. As late as February 1845, Bankhead

---

[21]Bankhead to Aberdeen, April 29 and May 30, 1845, Foreign Office 50, vol. 185, Public Record Office, London (hereafter cited as PRO).

[22]Bankhead to Aberdeen, July 30, 1845, F.O. 50, vol. 186, PRO.

continued to warn the Mexicans that their security demanded an independent Texas. Finally in May Mexican officials acknowledged the independence of Texas, too late to prevent its annexation to the United States.[23] Within two months Mexico faced an American military presence on its exposed and still undefined border.

Mexico's troubles were not limited to the Rio Grande frontier. By 1845 Mexican officials had reminded Bankhead repeatedly of California's vulnerability to American encroachment. During July 1845, Bankhead reported that California had become the major topic of concern in the Mexican capital.[24] Informed residents could recall that President Jackson had attempted to purchase San Francisco Bay in 1835. Only one year later Mexico accused Americans of supporting a revolution in California which ousted the governor. José María Tornel, the Mexican minister of war, had predicted in 1837 that the loss of Texas, if accepted by Mexico, "will inevitably result in the loss of New Mexico and the Californias."[25] What disturbed Mexican leaders more profoundly was Commodore Thomas ap Catesby Jones's seizure of Monterey in 1842. Jones, as commander of the U.S. naval squadron in the Pacific, had acted under the rumor that his country and Mexico were at war.

When Californians launched a second revolution in 1844 to overthrow the Mexican regime, officials in Mexico City assumed that Americans were attempting to repeat the Texas drama in California. Captain John C. Frémont's defiance of local authorities at Monterey prompted Tornel to repeat his earlier warning:

> The passion of the Anglo-American people, their pronounced desire to acquire new lands, is a dynamic power which is enhanced and nourished by their own industry. An ill-defined line, the source of a yet unknown river, scientific explorations with the pretext of establishing monuments that shall *mark with perfect accuracy* the limits of both nations, all these have given a golden opportunity to the combined efforts of the people and government to promote their plans to acquire what belongs to their neighbors.

[23]Bankhead to Aberdeen, May 30 and 31, 1844 and February 3, 1845, F.O. 50, vols. 174, 183; Aberdeen to Bankhead, June 3, September 30, October 23, November 28, and December 31, 1844. F.O. 50, vols. 172, 183; Bankhead to Elliot, March 22, 1845, F.O. 50, vol. 184, PRO.

[24]Aberdeen to Bankhead, October 1 and December 31, 1844, F.O. 50, vols. 172, 183; Bankhead to Aberdeen, June 29, 1844, and July 30, 1845, F.O. 50, vols. 174, 186, PRO.

[25]Carlos E. Castaneda, trans. and ed., *The Mexican Side of the Texas Revolution by the Chief Mexican Participants* (Dallas, 1928), pp. 368, 370; quoted in Frank A. Knapp, Jr., "Mexican Fear of Manifest Destiny in California," in Thomas E. Cotner, ed., *Essays in Mexican History* (Austin, 1958), p. 195.

"California is entirely at the mercy of the North Americans," lamented *El Amigo del Pueblo* (Mexico City) in August 1845. "In regard to the United States," echoed *El Patriota Mexicano* (Mexico City) in November, "its designs [on California] are no longer a mystery." For *El Siglo Diez y Nueve* (Mexico City) the strongest evidence of American ambition was the "irritating insolence" which the newspapers of the United States displayed in advocating emigration and the annexation of California.[26]

Confronted with the loss of its borderlands, Mexico reached out to Britain for help. Earlier, Mexican officials had warned Bankhead that, without British guarantees, an independent Texas would not protect Mexico's northern border. Now they offered Britain a protectorate in California; some even suggested that Britain purchase the province. In September 1845 a distraught Mexico again sought a British commitment to the defense of its frontiers, but British diplomacy was not prepared to underwrite the Mexican cause. Aberdeen, hoping to keep California out of American hands, suggested that Mexico concentrate all its military power in California. Bankhead admitted that Mexico, standing alone, had little chance of success in its mounting crisis with the United States, but he refused to draw his country into the quarrel. He acknowledged a British interest in Mexico's welfare, nothing more.[27]

Unable to offer support, Bankhead could only advise the Mexicans to show greater restraint in their relations with the United States. Local writers, he complained, were too inflammatory; moreover, they created objectives which no Mexican government could achieve. Politicians and journalists aggravated the Mexican spirit of defiance by insisting that the United States was militarily weak, was divided over slavery and the justice of Polk's demands, and therefore would not fight. Mexico, they added, would benefit from the advantages that accrue to defensive power. Yet among the leaders there was always a sharp contrast between their public expressions of confidence and their private admissions of dread. Mexico, they knew, stood no chance in a war with the United States. If Mexico was too weak to fight, Bankhead warned, it had no choice but to negotiate. He advised the Herrera government in Mexico City to deal directly with Washington rather than risk a drift toward war. Yet that regime, even as it toppled in December 1845, denounced the United States to counter the appeals of its political opposition to Mexican nationalism. Such behavior distressed Bankhead. "The self conceit and weakness of the government here," he complained to Aberdeen, "preclude the possibility of my

---

[26]Ibid., pp. 196, 200, 203.
[27]Bankhead to Aberdeen, January 29 and July 30, 1845, F.O. 50, vols. 184, 186, PRO.

giving them any advice."[28] Bankhead had recognized Herrera's vulnerability; Paredes, he reported as early as August, could overthrow him whenever he chose. Yet Bankhead believed that Paredes would be an improvement over Herrera's Federalists. As the leader of the Centralists, Paredes appeared better able to give Mexico the strong, central administration that it required. Despite his deep disillusionment with Mexican politics, Bankhead believed Slidell's arrival unwisely premature, for it seemed no less than an American effort to impose an immediate boundary settlement on a chaotic Mexico under the threat of force.[29]

Actually, Slidell's presence in Mexico inaugurated a diplomatic crisis not unlike those which precede most wars. Fundamentally the Polk administration, in dispatching Slidell, gave the Mexicans the same two choices that the dominant power in any confrontation gives to the weaker: the acceptance of a body of concrete diplomatic demands or eventual war.[30] Slidell's instructions described U.S. territorial objectives with considerable clarity. If Mexico knew little of Polk's growing acquisitiveness toward California during the autumn of 1845, Slidell proclaimed the president's intentions with his proposals to purchase varying portions of California for as much as $25 million. Other countries such as England and Spain had consigned important areas of the New World through peaceful negotiations, but the United States, except in its Mexican relations, had never asked any country to part with a portion of its own territory. Yet Polk could not understand why Mexico should reveal any special reluctance to part with Texas, the Rio Grande, New Mexico, or California. What made the terms of Slidell's instructions appear fair to him was Mexico's military and financial helplessness. Polk's defenders noted that California was not a sine qua non of any settlement and that the president offered to settle the immediate controversy over the acquisition of the Rio Grande boundary alone in exchange for the cancellation of claims. Unfortunately, amid the passions of December 1845, such distinctions were lost. Furthermore, a settlement of the Texas boundary would not have resolved the California question at all.[31]

[28]Bankhead to Aberdeen, September 29 and November 29, 1845, F.O. 50, vols. 186, 187, PRO.

[29]Bankhead to Aberdeen, August 29, September 29, and November 29, 1845, F.O. 50, vols. 186, 187, PRO.

[30]The issues were different—the desire for California as opposed to the demand for an independent Cuba, the preference for a British victory, or the defense of China's integrity—but the limited choices which the United States gave its opponents in 1846, 1898, 1917, and 1941 were similar in quality and had the same effect.

[31]Historians who regard Polk's proposals as fair have scant respect for Mexico's belligerent rejection of them. Dwelling on Mexican behavior which followed Congress's completion of annexation and the arrival of Polk's emissary, Slidell, in Mexico during

Throughout the crisis months of 1845 and 1846, spokesmen of the Polk administration repeatedly warned the Mexican government that its choices were limited. In June 1845, Polk's mouthpiece, the *Washington Union*, had observed characteristically that, if Mexico resisted Washington's demands, "a corps of properly organized volunteers . . . would invade, overrun, and occupy Mexico. They would enable us not only to take California, but to keep it." American officials, in their contempt for Mexico, spoke privately of the need to chastize that country for its annoyances and insults. Parrott wrote to Secretary of State James Buchanan in October that he wished "to see this people well flogged by Uncle Sam's boys, ere we enter upon negotiations. . . . I know [the Mexicans] better, perhaps, than any other American citizen and I am fully persuaded, they can never love or respect us, as we should be loved and respected by them, until we shall have given them a positive proof of our superiority." Mexico's pretensions would continue, wrote Slidell in late December, "until the Mexican people shall be convinced by hostile demonstrations, that our differences must be settled promptly, either by negotiation or the sword." In January 1846 the *Union* publicly threatened Mexico with war if it rejected the just demands of the United States: "The result of such a course on her part may compel us to resort to more decisive measures . . . to obtain the settlement of our legitimate claims." As Slidell prepared to leave Mexico in March 1846, he again reminded the administration: "Depend upon it, we can never get along well with them, until we have given them a good drubbing."[32] In Washington on May 8, Slidell advised

---

December 1845, Connor and Faulk have rebuilt the classic case against Mexico. For them, Mexico's responsibility for the coming of war was unmistakable: the Mexicans simply translated their inexcusable animosity toward the United States into preparations for war and the final decision of April 1846 to attack. "Perhaps it was all foreordained," they wrote, "for there can be no question but that the annexation of Texas precipitated a reaction among patriotic zealots in Mexico which produced war—California, Polk, Manifest Destiny, claims, Nueces boundary notwithstanding." Connor and Faulk argue logically that California was no issue in the coming of the war. That province, they noted, "was peripheral to the main issue—the arousing of Mexican nationalism (by Herrera's opponents) over the annexation of Texas. By the time of Slidell's appointment in November 1845 Herrera's overthrow was imminent and war was virtually inevitable. It really matters little whether Polk was interested in California or not." Connor and Faulk, *North America Divided*, pp. 22, 27, 28, 32.

[32]Parrott to Buchanan, October 11, 1845, Slidell to Buchanan, December 27, 1845, and Slidell to Buchanan, March 18, 1846, all in William R. Manning, ed., *Diplomatic Correspondence of the United States: Inter-American Affairs 1831–1860* (Washington, 1937), 8:760, 803, 832. Slidell again revealed his lack of respect for Mexico and its power when he wrote on April 2, 1846: "The best security for the inaction of Paredes is his utter inability, to concentrate on the frontier, a sufficient force to cope with General Taylor, he cannot at present by any effort unite six thousand men for that object, and from what I have seen of the Mexican troops, I should have no apprehension of the result of any attack with that number." Slidell to Buchanan, April 2, 1846, ibid., p. 839.

the president "to take the redress of the wrongs and injuries which we had so long borne from Mexico into our own hands, and to act with promptness and energy."[33]

Mexico responded to Polk's challenge with an outward display of belligerence and an inward dread of war. Mexicans feared above all that the United States intended to overrun their country and seize much of their territory. Polk and his advisers assumed that Mexico, to avoid an American invasion, would give up its provinces peacefully. Obviously Mexico faced growing diplomatic and military pressures to negotiate away its territories; it faced no moral obligation to do so. Herrera and Paredes had the sovereign right to protect their regimes by avoiding any formal recognition of Slidell and by rejecting any of the boundary proposals embodied in his instructions, provided that in the process they did not endanger any legitimate interests of the American people. At least to some Mexicans, Slidell's terms demanded nothing less than Mexico's capitulation. By what standard was $2 million a proper payment for the Rio Grande boundary, or $25 million a fair price for California? No government would have accepted such terms. Having rejected negotiation in the face of superior force, Mexico would meet the challenge with a final gesture of defiance. In either case it was destined to lose, but historically nations have preferred to fight than to give away territory under diplomatic pressure alone. Gene M. Brack, in his long study of Mexico's deep-seated fear and resentment of the United States, explained Mexico's ultimate behavior in such terms:

> President Polk knew that Mexico could offer but feeble resistance militarily, and he knew that Mexico needed money. No proper American would exchange territory and the national honor for cash, but President Polk mistakenly believed that the application of military pressure would convince Mexicans to do so. They did not respond logically, but patriotically. Left with the choice of war or territorial concessions, the former course, however dim the prospects of success, could be the only one.[34]

IV

Mexico, in its resistance, gave Polk the three choices which every nation gives another in an uncompromisable confrontation: to withdraw his demands and permit the issues to drift, unresolved; to reduce his goals

---

[33]Quaife, *Diary of James K. Polk*, 1:382.
[34]Brack, *Mexico Views Manifest Destiny*, p. 179.

in the interest of an immediate settlement; or to escalate the pressures in the hope of securing an eventual settlement on his own terms. Normally when the internal conditions of a country undermine its relations with others, a diplomatic corps simply removes itself from the hostile environment and awaits a better day. Mexico, despite its animosity, did not endanger the security interests of the United States; it had not invaded Texas and did not contemplate doing so. Mexico had refused to pay the claims, but those claims were not equal to the price of a one-week war. Whether Mexico negotiated a boundary for Texas in 1846 mattered little; the United States had lived with unsettled boundaries for decades without considering war. Settlers, in time, would have forced a decision, but in 1846 the region between the Nueces and the Rio Grande was a vast, generally unoccupied wilderness. Thus there was nothing, other than Polk's ambitions, to prevent the United States from withdrawing its diplomats from Mexico City and permitting its relations to drift. But Polk, whatever the language of his instructions, did not send Slidell to Mexico to normalize relations with that government. He expected Slidell to negotiate an immediate boundary settlement favorable to the United States, and nothing less.

Recognizing no need to reduce his demands on Mexico, Polk, without hesitation, took the third course which Mexico offered. Congress bound the president to the annexation of Texas; thereafter the Polk administration was free to formulate its own policies toward Mexico. With the Slidell mission Polk embarked upon a program of gradual coercion to achieve a settlement, preferably without war. That program led logically from his dispatching an army to Texas and his denunciation of Mexico in his annual message of December 1845 to his new instructions of January 1846, which ordered General Taylor to the Rio Grande. Colonel Atocha, spokesman for the deposed Mexican leader, Antonio López de Santa Anna, encouraged Polk to pursue his policy of escalation. The president recorded Atocha's advice:

> He said our army should be marched at once from Corpus Christi to the Del Norte, and a strong Naval force assembled at Vera Cruz, that Mr. Slidell, the U.S. Minister, should withdraw from Jalappa, and go on board one of our ships of War at Vera Cruz, and in that position should demand the payment of [the] amount due our citizens; that it was well known the Mexican Government was unable to pay in money, and that when they saw a strong force ready to strike on their coasts and border, they would, he had no doubt, feel their danger and agree to the boundary suggested. He said that Paredes, Almonte, & Gen'l Santa Anna were all willing for such an arrangement, but that they dare not make it until it was made apparent to the Archbishop of Mexico & the

people generally that it was necessary to save their country from a war with the U. States.[35]

Thereafter Polk never questioned the efficacy of coercion. He asserted at a cabinet meeting on February 17 that "it would be necessary to take strong measures towards Mexico before our difficulties with that Government could be settled." Similarly on April 18 Polk told Calhoun that "our relations with Mexico had reached a point where we could not stand still but must treat all nations whether weak or strong alike, and that I saw no alternative but strong measures towards Mexico." A week later the president again brought the Mexican question before the cabinet. "I expressed my opinion," he noted in his diary, "that we must take redress for the injuries done us into our own hands, that we had attempted to conciliate Mexico in vain, and had forborne until forbearance was no longer either a virtue or patriotic."[36] Convinced that Paredes needed money, Polk suggested to leading senators that Congress appropriate $1 million both to encourage Paredes to negotiate and to sustain him in power until the United States could ratify the treaty. The president failed to secure Calhoun's required support.[37]

Polk's persistence led him and the country to war. Like all escalations in the exertion of force, his decision responded less to unwanted and unanticipated resistance than to the requirements of the clearly perceived and inflexible purposes which guided the administration.[38] What perpetuated the president's escalation to the point of war was his determination to pursue goals to the end whose achievement lay outside the possibilities of successful negotiations.[39] Senator Thomas Hart Benton of Missouri saw this situation when he wrote: "It is impossible to conceive of an administration less warlike, or more intriguing, than that of Mr. Polk. They were *men of peace, with objects to be accomplished by means of war*; so that war was a necessity and an indispensability to their purpose."[40]

Polk understood fully the state of Mexican opinion. In placing General Taylor on the Rio Grande he revealed again his contempt for

[35]Quaife, *Diary of James K. Polk*, 1:228–29.

[36]Ibid., pp. 233, 337, 354.

[37]Ibid., pp. 306–12, 317.

[38]During the spring of 1846 Polk made clear in his diary that the settlement he sought would include no less than the Rio Grande border and the transfer of San Francisco Bay to the United States. See ibid., p. 307.

[39]Such inflexibility of purpose underwrote the most classic of all escalations in U.S. history—that in Vietnam between 1965 and 1968.

[40]Thomas Hart Benton, *Thirty Years' View* (New York, 1856), 2:680. Italics are those of the writer.

Mexico. Under no national obligation to expose the country's armed forces, he would not have advanced Taylor in the face of a superior military force. Mexico had been undiplomatic; its denunciations of the United States were insulting and provocative. But if Mexico's behavior antagonized Polk, it did not antagonize the Whigs, the abolitionists, or even much of the Democratic party. Such groups did not regard Mexico as a threat; they warned the administration repeatedly that Taylor's presence on the Rio Grande would provoke war. But in the balance against peace was the pressure of American expansionism. Much of the Democratic and expansionist press, having accepted without restraint both the purposes of the Polk administration and its charges of Mexican perfidy, urged the president on to more vigorous action.[41]

During March 1846, Taylor established his headquarters on the northern bank of the Rio Grande opposite the Mexican village of Matamoros. He assured its citizens that the United States, in placing an army on the Rio Grande, harbored no hostility toward Mexico and would not disturb the Mexicans residing north of the river. His army, he added, would not in any case go beyond the river unless the Mexicans themselves commenced hostilities. Still Mexican officials reacted violently. "The civilized world," proclaimed the local commandant at Matamoros, "has already recognized in [the annexation of Texas] all the marks of injustice, iniquity and the most scandalous violation of the law of nations. . . . The cabinet of the United States does not, however, stop in its career of usurpation. Not only does it aspire to the possession of the department of Texas, but it covets also the regions on the left bank of the Rio Grande." What hope was there of treating with an enemy, continued the proclamation, that sent an army into territory which was not an issue in the pending negotiations? "The flame of patriotism which burns in our hearts will receive new fuel from the odious presence of these invaders for conquest."[42] On April 11, General Pedro Ampudia, backed by 3,000 Mexican troops, arrived at Matamoros and immediately ordered Taylor to return to Corpus Christi. Taylor refused to move, declaring that he had taken positions along the Rio Grande under presidential orders. He warned Ampudia that the side which fired the first shot would bear responsibility for the war.

Amid the pressures which Taylor's maneuvering exerted, Paredes visited Bankhead with another plea for help. The British minister reported that Paredes "did not exaggerate the difficulties in which this

---

[41]See Norman A. Graebner, *Empire on the Pacific: A Study in American Continental Expansion* (New York, 1955), pp. 151–53.

[42]For Taylor's communications, see the notes in the Trist Papers, 33, Manuscripts Division, Library of Congress.

country finds itself." Bankhead advised a prudent course and the avoid-ance of any show of aggression along the frontier. Paredes agreed to avoid a conflict and ordered his general to remain on the south bank of the Rio Grande. Late in March, Paredes in a final gesture urged Bankhead to place the Mexican dilemma before the government in London; Britain alone, he said, could save Mexico from its impending struggle with the United States. When Bankhead learned that Taylor had reached the left bank of the Rio Grande, he urged the Mexicans to remain on the defensive but suspected correctly that the Mexican officers would disobey orders and attack. Mexico's chances appeared dim. Because there would be no help, he concluded, "the extinction of this country as an independent state is near at hand." For too long Mexico's rulers had lacked the capacity and honesty to protect "what might, under other hands, have become one of the most flourishing countries in the world."[43]

Facing the certainty of a clash along the Rio Grande, Polk made no effort to avoid war. On May 5 the cabinet discussed the status of the American army along the river and the possibility of a brush with Mexican forces. On the following day the president noted in his diary that he had received dispatches from Taylor dated as late as April 15. "No actual collision had taken place," he wrote, "though the proba-bilities are that hostilities might take place soon." On May 9 the cabinet agreed that any Mexican attack on Taylor's forces would require an immediate message to Congress requesting a declaration of war.[44] Polk, in this crisis, wanted war with Mexico precisely as Roosevelt had wanted war with Germany amid his private operations in the Atlantic during the summer and autumn of 1941. There would be no war until Mexico committed the necessary act of open hostility; thereafter, that country would bear the responsibility alone. The United States, dealing from strength, could afford to wait. The Mexicans, facing a symbolic threat at the Rio Grande to their entire military and diplomatic position, revealed the impatience of those who find their strength disintegrating.

Confronted with the prospect of further decline which they could neither accept nor prevent, they lashed out with the intention of pro-tecting their self-esteem and compelling the United States, if it was determined to have the Rio Grande, New Mexico, and California, to pay for its prizes with something other than money.[45] On April 23,

[43]Bankhead to Aberdeen, March 10 and 30, April 6, 8, and 29, 1846, F.O. 50, vol. 196, PRO.
[44]Quaife, Diary of James K. Polk, 1:379, 380, 384.
[45]Mexico's behavior was symbolically identical to that of the South when it attacked Fort Sumter in 1861, to that of Spain in its resistance to American demands in 1898 (a variant because Spain did not order the destruction of the Maine although the effect of the destruction was the same), to that of Germany when it launched unrestricted

Paredes issued a proclamation declaring a defensive war against the United States. Predictably, one day later the Mexicans fired on a detachment of U.S. dragoons. Taylor's report of the attack reached Polk on Saturday evening, May 9. On Sunday the president drafted his war message and delivered it to Congress on the following day. Had Polk avoided the crisis, he might have gained the time required to permit the emigrants of 1845 and 1846 to settle the California issue without war.

What clouds the issue of the Mexican War's justification was the acquisition of New Mexico and California, for contemporaries and historians could not logically condemn the war and laud the Polk administration for its territorial achievements. Perhaps it is true that time would have permitted American pioneers to transform California into another Texas. But even then California's acquisition by the United States would have emanated from the use of force, for the elimination of Mexican sovereignty, whether through revolution or war, demanded the successful use of power. If the power employed in revolution would have been less obtrusive than that exerted in war, its role would have been no less essential. There simply was no way that the United States could acquire California peacefully. If the distraught Mexico of 1845 would not sell the distant province, no regime thereafter would have done so. Without forceful destruction of Mexico's sovereign power, California would have entered the twentieth century as an increasingly important region of another country.

Thus the Mexican War poses the dilemma of all international relations. Nations whose geographic and political status fails to coincide with their ambition and power can balance the two sets of factors in only one manner: through the employment of force. They succeed or fail according to circumstances; and for the United States, the conditions for achieving its empire in the Southwest and its desired frontage on the Pacific were so ideal that later generations could refer to the process as the mere fulfillment of destiny. "The Mexican Republic," lamented a Mexican writer in 1848, " . . . had among other misfortunes of less account, the great one of being in the vicinity of a strong and

---

submarine warfare in 1917, and to that of Japan when it attacked Pearl Harbor in 1941. In each case, the United States, as the more powerful antagonist and with its interests not directly engaged, could rest easily behind its uncompromising demands, while the weaker power, conscious of its slipping position and with its interests directly engaged, made the decision for war in the hope of salvaging what it could from an immediately threatening and ultimately hopeless situation. It is well to recall that General Tojo, in explaining the Japanese decision for war in 1941, remarked that "sometimes a man has to jump with his eyes closed, from the temple of Kiyomizu into the ravine below." The Mexican-American confrontation of 1846 presented a pattern of challenge and response not unlike those which brought the United States into most of its wars.

energetic people."[46] What the Mexican War revealed in equal measure is the simple fact that only those countries which have achieved their destiny, whatever that may be, can afford to extol the virtues of peaceful change.

---

[46]Quoted in Brack, *Mexico Views Manifest Destiny*, p. 1.

CHAPTER
TEN

Lessons of the
Mexican War*

FOR A NATION SURFEITED with victory and tired of its war with Mexico, the prospects of peace appeared immediate and bright in the early fall of 1847. During the previous year, the two invading American armies under Zachary Taylor and Winfield Scott had swept the Mexican forces before them. Scott's troops, having fought their way from Vera Cruz to Puebla, had entered the Valley of Mexico. There, in August 1847, they won notable victories at Contreras and Churubusco. When the Mexicans offered no acceptable armistice, Scott ordered a reconnaissance of the defenses before Mexico City. Thereafter, the Americans quickly stormed the fortresses of Molino del Rey and Chapultepec. By early September, Scott's army stood poised before the capital itself. Still, American conservatives, such as Daniel Webster, had wondered throughout that year of unbroken military triumphs whether the United States could as easily translate these victories against Mexico into a satisfactory peace as it had earlier converted less satisfactory wars into highly acceptable treaties with Great Britain.[1]

At the outbreak of the war with Mexico in May 1846, President James K. Polk had anticipated not only a series of military successes but also an accompanying diplomacy with the defeated enemy which would bring peace as well as his territorial war aims. Instead, he

---

*Published as "Lessons of the Mexican War," *Pacific Historical Review* 47 (August 1978): 325–42. Reprinted by permission.
[1]See Webster to D. Fletcher Webster, August 6, 1846, in C. H. Van Tyne, ed., *The Letters of Daniel Webster* (New York, 1902), p. 343. For a similar warning that victory would not necessarily lead to a satisfactory peace, see the *Times* (London), November 9, 1846.

discovered to his chagrin that for the United States—a nation over-whelmingly powerful when contrasted to the enemy of the moment—military policy was far less demanding than diplomacy. Somehow the easy military victories of the United States did not ensure a satisfactory conclusion of the war at all, for even in defeat the Mexican government balked at Polk's territorial demands.

Polk hesitated to desert the struggle until he had achieved some gains commensurate with the cost of the war, yet Mexican officials continued to avoid a diplomatic confrontation. Clearly the adminis-tration was in trouble. As the conflict dragged on, the beleaguered president requested of Congress larger military appropriations to esca-late the pressures on the ephemeral enemy that would not treat. Con-gress, it seemed, had no choice but to meet Polk's demands. As one Whig writer complained, Congress "would never refuse to grant any-thing and everything necessary or proper for the support and succor of our brave troops, placed, without any fault of theirs, in the heart of a distant country, and struggling with every peril, discomfort and difficulty."[2]

As Polk searched for a way out of his dilemma, war critics—and they were legion—reminded the nation that the president and his advis-ers alone were responsible for the decisions that had led to war and placed a modern army in a backward and politically chaotic country where it could no longer discover any significant strategic objectives. "The responsibility of the President and his administration in permit-ting the country to become involved in a war which could and should have been avoided," charged the *American Review*, official organ of the Whig opposition, "is fearfully great. Among a virtuous and wise people, this condemnation alone should be enough to overwhelm those who have been guilty of so great a crime. A civilized and Christian people engaged in an unnecessary war, in the middle of the nineteenth century, is a spectacle of backsliding and crime over which angels may weep." As the attack on the war mounted in intensity each succeeding week, Illinois Whig Congressman Abraham Lincoln demanded that the pres-ident show that the soil where the first blood was shed actually belonged to the United States. "But if he *can* not, or *will* not do this . . . ," warned Lincoln in speaking for much of his party, "then I shall be fully con-vinced, of what I more than suspect already, that he is deeply conscious of being in the wrong—that he feels the blood of this war, like the blood of Abel, is crying to Heaven against him."[3] Having involved the nation in the war, ran a further Whig complaint, the president had

[2]"The Whigs and the War," *American Review* 6 (October 1847): 343.

[3]Ibid., p. 331; Lincoln's speech in the House of Representatives, January 12, 1848, in Roy P. Basler, ed., *The Collected Works of Abraham Lincoln* (New Brunswick, 1953), 1:439.

proceeded to mismanage it without any reliance upon Congress other than his requests for a recognition of the war after it had begun and, thereafter, for the appropriation of the men and money required to pursue it.

Now that the United States had conquering forces in the heart of Mexico, it was no longer clear what ultimate intentions the administration had in mind. Polk had never admitted any wartime objective other than an honorable peace. If that were true, queried the *American Review*, why was there no peace? What terms was the United States government exacting that ruled out an acceptable diplomatic arrangement which might conclude the struggle? The explanation of the nation's dilemma seemed clear enough: the administration was seeking too vast an accession of Mexican territory. Even the Whigs, admitted the *Review*, were not averse to the acquisition of California, provided that the United States could achieve it by fair and just means. "But we are sure we are safe in saying," continued the writer, "that there is not a Whig in the United States who does not, with all honest and ingenuous minds, reject with scorn the very thought that his country should be engaged in war with a sister republic far below ourselves in every element of strength and greatness, for the real purpose . . . of effecting a forcible dismemberment of that republic, and of profiting ourselves by the spoils."[4]

Still, the Whigs understood clearly that wars, once begun, have a logic of their own, and that commitments to war, once made, cannot readily be withdrawn. They might abhor and ridicule the war as unnecessary and immoral, they might point the finger of accusation at the president for his failure to avoid it, but they refused to share the burden of its conduct. Realists that they were, the Whigs recognized the fact that a war leaves the executive few choices between the search for military victory and the search for a reasonable peace that reflects the experience of the battlefield. Whig behavior, therefore, was less than consistent, for while that party overwhelmingly rejected the war, it shared with the administration and the Democratic party the need for sustaining the military effort toward some reasonable goal. Thus, Whig attacks, especially from the party's congressional spokesmen, were always somewhat restrained; indeed, some Whig editors refused to criticize the war at all. They could offer no alternative to administration policy, and they feared that opposition to the war might prove to be politically dangerous. They could not be sure that the war was generally unpopular, for the Polk administration, ably supported by many congressional Democrats, had bombarded the country with a series of arguments, logical within themselves, which rationalized the necessity

[4]"The Whigs and the War," p. 332.

of the Mexican involvement. Millions of Americans—perhaps a majority of them—still accepted uncritically Polk's uncomplicated assertion that the Mexicans had spilled American blood on American soil and that his administration pursued victory only to achieve an honorable peace.

The Whig party, however, was prepared officially to utilize the failure of Polk's peace moves and the continued recalcitrance of Mexico for its own purposes. Following the elections of November 1847, the new Whig majority in the House agreed that party unity demanded opposition both to the war and to all territorial expansion. During the weeks before the opening of Congress in December, the Whig inclination to broaden its attacks on the war received an impetus from Webster's lengthy antiwar oration at Springfield, Henry Clay's widely heralded speech at Lexington, and the publication of Albert Gallatin's critical pamphlet, *Peace with Mexico*.[5] Whigs generally lauded these peace sentiments, but many editors questioned their courage. Would the critics actually assume responsibility commensurate with their oratory for changing national policy? One writer for the *New York Journal of Commerce* observed dryly that "the greatest debater I ever knew or heard was a prominent Whig, and when he had finished one of his magnificent and overpowering arguments, and convinced everyone but himself, he never knew which way to vote on the very question he had so luminously explained."[6]

II

Polk maintained control of national policy despite the opposition and ridicule that he faced. His initial purpose of acquiring his precise territorial goals through limited war had ended in miscalculation simply because no Mexican government would come forth to negotiate on America's terms with representatives of the U.S. government. For the president, the choices were narrowing. Either the United States would be obliged to subjugate and hold the entire country of Mexico or it would be forced to withdraw its forces without a formal peace simply to escape its political and diplomatic impasse. By the autumn of 1847, the growing conviction that the tenuous nature of the Mexican government might prolong an expensive war indefinitely convinced the expansionist press that the United States had no choice but to meet its destiny and annex the entire Mexican republic. General Scott's victories during the summer and early fall had brought initial demands

[5]Albert Gallatin, *Peace with Mexico* (New York, 1847).
[6]*New York Journal of Commerce*, February 5, 1848.

that Vera Cruz and other Mexican ports be acquired by the United States.[7] As early as June, a thoroughly frightened John C. Calhoun had observed that a party was growing in the United States bent on acquiring all of Mexico.[8]

Americans experienced no immediate elation at the prospect of absorbing multitudes of Mexican citizens. One correspondent of the *New York Herald* declared that the country "has no affinity to us, and cannot expect, for years to come, to be received into our Union."[9] Even the expansionist *Democratic Review* warned in June, "However we may *want* the land, we surely do not *need* the incorporation with us of such a people of inferior mixture as the Mexicans."[10] As late as October, that publication still opposed the permanent annexation of Mexico, for it believed that people as "proverbially indolent" and "dishonestly envious" as the Mexicans would make "unprofitable and dangerous inmates of our political family."[11] Mexico might better achieve its needed political reforms under a government of its own choice.

When the American occupation of Mexico City in September 1847 brought no capitulation, the all-of-Mexico movement brushed aside all scruples and gathered increased momentum. The *New York Globe* called attention to a new spirit in the land, "a spirit of progress, which will compel us, for the good of both nations and the world at large, TO DESTROY THE NATIONALITY *of that besotted people.* It would almost seem that they, like the Israelites of old, had brought upon themselves the vengeance of the *Almighty,* and we ourselves had been raised up to overthrow AND UTTERLY DESTROY THEM as a separate and distinct nation."[12] With little exaggeration, Calhoun reminded the Senate in December that almost every newspaper carried editorials on the subject of annexing Mexico. Clay admitted that he was "shocked and alarmed by the manifestation of it in various quarters."[13]

Nowhere was the new annexationist sentiment more apparent than at the numerous Democratic dinners, some honoring returned heroes of the Mexican campaign. At one banquet, Senator Daniel S. Dickinson of New York offered a toast, received with wild approbation,

---

[7]W. A. Scott to Polk, September 30, 1847; Charles Fletcher to Polk, October 9, 1847, Polk Papers, Manuscripts Division, Library of Congress.

[8]R. B. Rhett to Calhoun, June 21, 1847; F. W. Byrdsall to Calhoun, July 17, 1847, in J. Franklin Jameson, ed., "The Correspondence of John C. Calhoun," *Annual Report of the American Historical Association* (Washington, 1899), pp. 1120, 1127.

[9]*New York Herald,* April 22, 1847.

[10]*Democratic Review* 20 (June 1847): 486.

[11]Ibid., 21 (October 1847): 381.

[12]Quoted in the *National Intelligencer* (Washington), October 18, 1847.

[13]See Calhoun in the *Congressional Globe,* 30th Cong., 1st sess. (1848), p. 54; Calvin Colton, ed., *The Works of Henry Clay* (New York, 1857), 3:66.

to "*a more perfect Union:* embracing the entire North American continent." At another such dinner, the Democratic guests drank to "the Destiny of the United States Government—To overshadow the whole of North America; therefore we may as well begin with Mexico." Those gathered looked to the ultimate domination of the continent by the American republic and its extension to the Isthmus of Panama. Two lines of verse summed up the passions of the hour:

> No pent-up Utica contracts our powers,
> But the whole boundless continent is ours.[14]

This move to absorb Mexico had its reverberations in the 30th Congress, which met in December 1847. Senator R. M. T. Hunter of Virginia regretfully acknowledged the expansionist oratory which resounded through the chamber: "Schemes of ambition, vast enough to have tasked even a Roman imagination to conceive, present themselves suddenly as practical questions. . . . We already hear of public opinion forming for the absorption of all of Mexico and its annexation as a dependent province."[15] Lewis Cass, the Michigan expansionist, informed his colleagues in the Senate that "if the people will the annexation of Mexico, nothing in our power to do can prevent it, you may as well plant yourself upon the brink of the cataract of Niagara and bid the waters be still."[16] Such papers as the *New York Herald* predicted that the topic would play the same role in 1848 that Texas and Oregon had played in 1844.[17] During January 1848, both the New York Democratic convention and a great mass meeting at Tammany Hall heard speeches and passed resolutions that called for the annexation of Mexico. After the autumn of 1847, both James Buchanan and Robert J. Walker of the Polk cabinet, as well as Vice-president George M. Dallas, openly concurred in these annexationist views. Buchanan, as secretary of state, urged the president to inform the American people that if the war continued, the United States "must fulfill the destiny which Providence may have in store for both countries."[18]

What made the all-of-Mexico movement unique was not merely the magnitude of the contemplated acquisition, but also the nature of the national objective. At issue was not only the territorial goal of

---

[14]Quoted in the *Congressional Globe*, 30th Cong., 1st sess. (1848), Appendix, p. 446.

[15]Speech of R. M. T. Hunter in the Senate, February 7, 1848, Historical Pamphlets, Durrett Collection, University of Chicago Library.

[16]Speech of Lewis Cass in the Senate, January 3, 1848, Mexican War Pamphlets, Durrett Collection.

[17]*New York Herald*, January 25, 26, February 5, 19, and 23, 1848.

[18]Milo Milton Quaife, ed., *The Diary of James K. Polk* (Chicago, 1910), 3:226–27.

annexation, but also the political and moral purpose of Mexican regeneration. Perhaps no contemporary hero expressed this purpose more dramatically than did Commodore Robert F. Stockton at a Philadelphia dinner given in his honor late in December 1847:

> We have a duty before God which we cannot—we must not evade. The priceless bond of civil and religious liberty has been confided to us as trustees . . . [and] if the war were to be prolonged for fifty years, and cost money enough to demand from us each half of all that we possess, I would still insist that the inestimable blessings of civil and religious liberty should be guaranteed to Mexico. . . . We cannot lose sight of the great truth that nations are accountable as well as individuals, and that they too must meet the stern responsibilities of their moral character—they too must encounter the penalty of violated law in the more extended sphere adapted to their physical condition.[19]

Herschel V. Johnson of Georgia reminded the Senate that war long had been an instrumentality for achieving "the great end of human elevation and human happiness." The nation would be recreant to its duty, he argued, if it failed to acquiesce in "the high purpose of the wise Providence" and extend the "area of human liberty and happiness" by conquering all of Mexico.[20]

The annexationists agreed that the means for achieving the regeneration of Mexico would be costly. It would require, admitted Stockton, not only an American occupying force capable of both resisting any future assaults against it and maintaining open lines of communication, but also the search for native leaders who, with American support, could create a government that guaranteed to the Mexican people all the immunities and privileges enjoyed by Mexicans residing in the United States. Walt Whitman, the noted American poet and editor of the *Brooklyn Daily Eagle*, advocated, as did others, the necessary commitment of men and money to assure Mexico the political and commercial progress required to stabilize that country. His admonition was clear:

> Let fifty thousand fresh troops be raised and sent forward with all possible despatch. . . . This talk about a peace party is all moonshine, until we are able to protect them from their own military tyrants; and secure their property from military seizure, or the plunder of guerrilla robbers. We must make our authority respectable—we must make our possession of the country safe to

[19]*Niles' National Register*, January 22, 1848.
[20]*Congressional Globe*, 30th Cong., 1st sess. (1848), Appendix, p. 379.

the people, and give them security in the pursuit of their lawful occupations, and in their trade and traffic with our Army. It is idle to garrison a town with ten or twenty or five hundred men while as many thousand guerrillas . . . are sweeping around the place to pounce upon them, and having intercourse with them— whenever a dozen yards from the walls.[21]

Obviously, the power of the guerrillas could not be broken until American might had rendered the countryside secure. To those who pointed to the expense of such a venture, Whitman replied, "The miserable cry of expenses and running the country in debt is too late now. . . . God knows we have no love for this or any other kind of war; but we know that this temporising, delaying, negotiating, peace-begging policy with an ignorant, prejudiced, and perfectly faithless people, is not the way to end the contest. *There is no middle course—either we must back out of it entirely, or we must drive it through with a vigorous hand.*"[22] Clearly Mexico's diplomatic resistance was limiting Washington's choices drastically.

III

For conservative America, there was yet another alternative. Calhoun favored a plan that by late 1847 had gained widespread adherence not only among American editors and politicians but also among leading officers in Mexico who favored some retreat from the prospect of annihilating the political structure of their country.[23] To conquer and occupy Mexico, they feared, would require an army of 100,000 men which, in turn, would be subjected to endless guerrilla warfare; to withdraw the army from Mexico without a peace treaty would leave that nation elated with pride, embittered by defeat, and more intractable than it had been before the war. To meet the requirements of a limited, yet adequate, policy, this group advocated the establishment of an indemnity line across northern Mexico which the United States might maintain with a small force of 7,000 to 10,000 troops. Such a policy would render an immediate treaty unnecessary, yet it would remind the Mexicans that

---

[21]For Whitman's editorial, see Cleveland Rodgers and John Black, eds., *The Gathering of the Forces: Editorials, Essays, Literary and Dramatic Reviews and Other Material Written by Walt Whitman as Editor of the Brooklyn Daily Eagle in 1846 and 1847* (New York, 1920), 1:259–63.

[22]Ibid. Italics supplied.

[23]Elwood Fisher to Calhoun, December 4, 1847, in Jameson, ed., "Correspondence of John C. Calhoun," p. 1146.

they faced a permanent occupation by American forces until they offered a satisfactory peace.

Commodore Matthew C. Perry, General Persifor Smith, and General Taylor favored such a solution. Smith pressed the administration in Washington to order an immediate American withdrawal from Mexico City. He advised Secretary of War William L. Marcy: "Should the movement be delayed longer than will determine the peaceful dispositions of the Congress at Querétaro, we must inevitably grow weaker, more encumbered with sick, more annoyed on our communications and more subject to those chances which[,] so distant from our resources, would be fatal to us."[24] In December, Smith argued in a note to General Franklin Pierce that as soon as the United States had settled the matter of national honor, it should abandon the country rather than court further the evils of conquest and occupation.[25] One enthusiast for the indemnity line suggested to the president the permanent occupation of the cities of Matamoras, Monterrey, Saltillo, Durango, and Mazatlán, giving the United States a good highway to the Pacific.[26] A writer for the *New York Herald* summed up this solution to the Mexican problem: "Draw your line, proclaim it, hold it, hold the Mexican ports to pay the costs, and when she acknowledges the line, break up and open the blockade."[27] How many occupying troops such a policy would require to render it effective was not clear; equally troublesome was the problem of defense against enemies with the freedom to maneuver. But, at least in theory, the policy would compel Mexico to make peace before it would free itself of unwanted intruders.

Calhoun took command of that Senate minority which favored the indemnity line. He had no objection to the acquisition of California, provided that it be gained by means other than war. But the annexation of all Mexico he regarded as a thoughtless and potentially disastrous overcommitment. On December 15, 1847, he introduced resolutions into the Senate which asserted that the conquest and occupation of Mexico, either as a province or as part of the Union, would conflict with the character and genius of the American people and ultimately undermine its free and popular institutions. What disturbed Calhoun was the conviction that any Mexican government established by the United States would require the continued support of an American army—an endless and largely unremunerative obligation. Calhoun

---

[24]Smith to William L. Marcy, September 28, 1847, Marcy Papers, Manuscripts Division, Library of Congress.

[25]Smith to Franklin Pierce, December 13, 1847, Pierce Papers, Manuscripts Division, Library of Congress.

[26]Harvey Curtis to Polk, May 20, 1847, Polk Papers.

[27]*New York Herald*, October 22, 1847.

rejected the proposition that the United States could establish political stability in Mexico with military means. "I protest utterly," he declared, "against this Government undertaking to build up any government in Mexico with the pledge of protection. The party placed in power must be inevitably overthrown, and we will be under the solemn obligation to return and reinstate them in power; and that would occur again and again, till the country would fall into our hands precisely as Hindostan fell into the hands of the English."[28]

What Calhoun feared as well was the rising cost and complexity of the American involvement in Mexico. Any argument against withdrawing the U.S. army, he warned, would have double force after the nation had spent $60 million and had acquired possession of the whole of Mexico. The army itself would be larger and more influential. "Those who live by the war," he pointed out, "the numerous contractors, the sutlers, the merchants, the speculators in the lands and mines, of Mexico, and all engaged every way, directly and indirectly, in the progress of the war, and absorbing the whole expenditures—will be all adverse to retiring, and will swell the cry in favor of continuing and extending conquest."[29] By withdrawing to a defense line, Calhoun concluded, the United States would do more for liberty and mankind than it would by a thousand victories in Mexico.

Senator John Bell of Tennessee spoke for those conservative Whigs who found merit in Calhoun's proposal. Bell, no less than Calhoun, wondered how the administration could create a government for Mexico with which it might negotiate effectively and which would not thereafter require the permanent military and physical support of the United States. Indeed, Bell reminded the Senate in February 1848, the Mexican faction which the administration favored had no interest in a treaty of peace whatever; it preferred, because of its own weakness, that U.S. occupying forces remain indefinitely. For that reason, Bell warned, any involvement in the politics of Mexico would render future retreat difficult, if not impossible. "The subjugation of Mexico," he concluded, "will be a perpetual drain upon our resources, and reduce instead of adding to our present rank as a military power."[30] The Tennessean attacked the so-called Progressive Democrats—the expansionists—for their defiance of the conservative views of the founders of the Republic.

---

[28] *Congressional Globe*, 30th Cong., 1st sess. (1848), p. 97. Calhoun favored a line from the Pacific Ocean to El Paso on the Rio Grande, a line which he believed defensible with a few vessels and a regiment of soldiers. Ibid., p. 96.
[29] Ibid., p. 97.
[30] For Bell's conservative argument, see ibid., Appendix, pp. 189–201.

IV

Despite such pressures for changes in policy, President Polk refused to alter the course which he had established at the outset of the war: to pursue a limited war in the quest of a specific territorial indemnity. Having discovered, much to his embarrassment, that his limited war had not achieved a satisfactory peace, he agreed with his cabinet during October and November 1847 that Mexican pride must be thoroughly broken. As on previous occasions, Polk's frustration and disgust at Mexican rebuffs drove him toward a determination to increase the tempo of the war.

Still, in December 1847, Polk was unwilling to ask for more than the two Mexican provinces—New Mexico and California—which had been the objectives of his expansionism in the Southwest since 1845. Although visions of continental dominion were tempting, Polk clung to his more limited and realistic course. He understood correctly that his opponents would make political capital out of any extreme demands on Mexico. That the annexationists had wooed public opinion with some success was clear enough, but it was equally clear, in December 1847, that they still faced determined opposition among Whigs and Democrats alike. Polk was too astute a politician to favor any cause until public opinion had crystallized. After admitting at last, in his annual message, that he favored the retention of California and New Mexico, Polk reminded Congress that "the doctrine of no territory is the doctrine of no indemnity; and, if sanctioned, would be a public acknowledgment that our country was wrong, and that the war declared by Congress with extraordinary unanimity was unjust, and should be abandoned." Such an admission, declared the president, would be "unfounded in fact, and degrading in national character." He assured Congress that he had not entered the ranks of the all-of-Mexico annexationists when he added: "It has never been contemplated by me, as an object of war, to make a permanent conquest of the Republic of Mexico, or to annihilate her separate existence as an independent nation." He asked Congress for additional troops so that he might wage the war with increased energy. At the same time, he offered support to the friends of peace in Mexico.[31]

Polk's apparent moderation satisfied that important segment of editors, politicians, and the public which shrank from the prospect of a long-term involvement in Mexican affairs, but who agreed that the United States had no choice but to increase the military pressure on

[31]Ibid., pp. 2, 4.

Mexico in the absence of any satisfactory negotiations. The *Washington Union*, official organ of the Polk administration, expressed this notion well. "Our work of subjugation and conquest," it declared, "must go on rapidly and with augmented force, and, as far as possible, at the expense of Mexico herself. Henceforth, we must seek PEACE, and compel it by inflicting on our enemies all the evils of war."[32] Many leading Whig editors, such as Thurlow Weed of the *Albany Evening Journal*, refused to attack the president or the war, despite the growing disillusionment with the nation's Mexican policies. Much of the American public remained content to follow the lead of the president as the only genuine choice available to the country.

But no consensus existed to prevent the continued public attack on the war and the military policies which that war now required. As the antiwar sentiment became more embittered, the president's embarrassment became more profound. Week after week, Polk's so-called Ten Regiment Bill furnished the vehicle for Whig invectives against the administration and the unending war with Mexico. Horace Greeley's *New York Tribune* took the lead in attacking the war and demanding peace. It warned its readers that the rulers of the United States were precipitating the people "into a fathomless abyss of crime and calumny." The first act of this war, echoed the *Mount Carmel Register*, was "A GROSS OUTRAGE UPON MEXICO." It declared that Polk and his advisers could not whitewash "A CRIME SO UNPARDONABLE AS THIS MEXICAN WAR."[33] In January, the Whigs in the House heaped the last measure of condemnation on the administration when they attached the Ashmun amendment to a joint resolution of thanks to General Taylor for his services in a war which was "unnecessarily and unconstitutionally begun by the President of the United States."[34] Whig editors generally decried any further escalation of the war. As the *Haverhill* (Massachusetts) *Gazette* trumpeted, "TO VOLUNTEER OR VOTE A DOLLAR TO CARRY ON THE WAR IS MORAL TREASON AGAINST THE GOD OF HEAVEN, AND THE RIGHTS OF MANKIND."[35]

Eventually, the *National Intelligencer* (Washington, DC), the mouthpiece of Whig conservatism, entered the crusade against the war. On January 15, 1848, the editor chided such leading Whig newspapers as the *Albany Evening Journal* for their refusal to oppose the war. If those who believed a war foolish and terminable had no right to oppose it

---

[32]Quoted in William Jay, *A Review of the Mexican War* (Boston, 1849), p. 259.
[33]Quoted in speech by Sidney Breese on the Ten Regiment Bill, February 14, 1848, Historical Pamphlets, Durrett Collection.
[34]*Congressional Globe*, 30th Cong., 1st sess. (1848), Appendix, p. 95.
[35]Quoted in Sidney Breese's speech of February 14, 1848, Historical Pamphlets, Durrett Collection.

publicly, asked the *Intelligencer*, then what measures of an administration could they rightly and expediently oppose? Certainly, declared the writer, "a war being, at best, one of the greatest ills which a Government can inflict upon a people, and an unnecessary war being the greatest of all national crimes, what is [a newspaper] permitted to oppose, if not a war which, . . . in addition to visiting carnage and devastation on Mexico, visits upon ourselves so much that is mournful or guilty or suicidal?"

Ultimately, a minority of abolitionists and pacifists pursuing the antiwar arguments to their logical conclusion joined such conservatives as Gallatin in condemning the war as a moral outrage and demanded that the executive terminate the conflict by withdrawing all U.S. forces from Mexico immediately. William Jay, a spokesman for the American peace movement, condemned the congressional Whigs for voting men and supplies under the fiction that they thereby would rescue General Taylor and his army from the Mexicans. He attacked the clergy for joining in military pageants and giving sanction to the cause in which the soldiers had perished, but he reserved his major criticism for the administration. What disturbed him, he wrote, was the willingness of men in high office to use falsehood as an instrument of policy. "The falsehoods respecting the Mexican War, coined in Washington, became a circulating medium throughout the country," he charged. "They were found in almost every official despatch; they were uttered through the press; they were passed as genuine by Governors in their messages, and by Legislatures in their resolves. Who shall estimate the injury done to the morality of the nation by this widespread contempt for truth?"[36] To keep troops in Mexico was, for Jay, an inexcusable outrage.

Frederick Douglass, the noted black abolitionist and editor of the antislavery paper, the *North Star*, similarly centered his editorial criticism on those in positions of power and eminence who refused to hazard their popularity, their social or political position, through an unqualified disapprobation of the war. "None seem willing to take their stand for peace at all risks," complained Douglass, "and all seem willing that the war should be carried on, in some form or other."[37] Even the clergy by their silence seemed to give sanction to the crime. Meanwhile, the administration, facing only minority opposition, continued to prosecute the war. For Douglass there was only one answer. He concluded his editorial of January 1, 1848, with the following plea:

---

[36]Jay, *Review of the Mexican War*, pp. 245–66. The quotation appears on pp. 265–66.

[37]For Douglass's editorial, see Philip S. Foner, ed., *The Life and Writings of Frederick Douglass* (New York, 1950), 1:291–96.

Our nation seems resolved to rush on in her wicked career, though the road be ditched with human blood, and paved with human skulls. Well, be it so. But, humble as we are, and unavailing as our voice may be, we . . . beseech our countrymen to leave off this horrid conflict, abandon their murderous plans, and forsake the way of blood. Peradventure our country may yet be saved. Let the press, the pulpit, the church, the people at large, unite at once; and let petitions flood the halls of Congress by the millions, asking for the instant recall of our forces from Mexico. This may not save us, but it is our only hope.

Similarly, Gallatin not only rejected the administration's rationalization for the war, but also challenged the notion that the alleged U.S. effort to enlighten the Mexicans, to improve their social state, and to increase their happiness was more than a shallow attempt to disguise the administration's unbounded cupidity and ambition. American military success alone, he believed, should permit the nation to grant peace terms that would remove the imputation that it responded to any but the most elevated motives. Gallatin, like other critics, advised the administration to withdraw the nation's forces from Mexico. "A more truly glorious termination of the war, a more splendid spectacle, an example more highly useful to mankind at large," he wrote, "cannot well be conceived, than that of the victorious forces of the United States voluntarily abandoning all their conquests, without requiring anything else than that which was strictly due to our citizens."[38]

Obviously Polk faced a divided nation which he could not unite and troubles abroad which he could not resolve. Still, his policies in time brought not only a formal end to the war, but also a satisfactory peace which conveyed both California and New Mexico to the United States and permitted this nation to extricate its forces from Mexico. Nevertheless, the Treaty of Guadalupe Hidalgo, which terminated the war, was an unanticipated source of salvation. Until the treaty's arrival in Washington during February 1848, the president did not know where to turn in his efforts to rid himself of the burdensome involvement in Mexico. In lieu of a settlement, which few in February believed possible, Polk could discover no alternative to his pursuit of a satisfactory boundary settlement but continued military escalation against an enemy that already had been defeated by all the standards of civilized war. No member of Congress detected Polk's dilemma more precisely than did Lincoln, who declared in his noted address of January 12, 1848:

As to the mode of terminating the war and securing peace, the President is . . . wandering and indefinite. First, it is to be done

[38]Gallatin, "The Mission of the United States," *Peace with Mexico*, p. 30.

by a more vigorous prosecution of the war . . . ; and after apparently talking himself tired on this point, the President drops down into a half-despairing tone, and tells us that 'with a people distracted and divided by contending factions, and a government subject to constant changes by successive revolutions, the continued success of our arms may fail to secure a satisfactory peace.' Then he suggests the propriety of wheedling the Mexican people to desert the counsels of their own leaders, and, trusting in our protestations, to set up a government from which we can secure a satisfactory peace; telling us that 'this may become the only mode of obtaining such a peace.' But soon he falls into a doubt of this too; and then drops back onto the already half-abandoned ground of 'more vigorous prosecution.' All this shows that the President is in nowise satisfied with his own positions.[39]

Ultimately, the president's policies triumphed, so much so that historians have scarcely recognized the dilemma into which the Mexican War forced the administration. Peace seemed to follow the war so quickly and satisfactorily that for historians generally the process of coming to terms with the Mexican government has posed no problem at all. Several precise conditions saved the Polk administration from the accumulation of further embarrassments. One was the element of good fortune. At a time when Polk himself believed peace totally impossible, Mexican officials contacted his agent in Mexico, Nicholas P. Trist. Trist disobeyed his instructions to return to the United States and ignored some minor demands of the administration to negotiate the Treaty of Guadalupe Hidalgo. Polk disclaimed all responsibility for Trist's actions, but he accepted the treaty with both hands.

Still, behind Polk's unexpected success in terminating the Mexican War with a satisfactory peace lay more than simple good fortune. The president, after all, had maintained a reasonable balance between the means and the ends of his policy. Throughout the war, he had kept his war aims limited and specific; he maintained them in a form which demanded nothing of Mexico except a cession of territory. It was Polk's rejection of the goal of political and social regeneration for Mexico that made the American escape from further involvement possible. Thus, U.S. soldiers were never subject to the guerrilla warfare which Benito Juárez's Mexican forces inflicted on the French army in the 1860s when that army came to Mexico to uphold the monarchy of Archduke Maximilian of Austria. The Mexican War illustrated early the fact that military invasions of backward countries, with neither material achievements nor political traditions to defend, can be more easily productive

[39]Basler, *Collected Works of Abraham Lincoln*, 1:441.

of military than diplomatic success. That war demonstrated as well that the transition from war to peace can be rendered smooth and relatively permanent only by terms of peace that are limited, tangible, and precise.

CHAPTER
ELEVEN

Northern Diplomacy and European Neutrality*

MAJOR ROBERT ANDERSON's surrender of Fort Sumter in April 1861 placed an unprecedented burden on American diplomacy. Not since the American Revolution had the foreign relations of the United States been reduced to a defense of the Republic's very existence. Diplomacy, to be sure, was only one element in the vast arsenal of resources upon which Northern leadership could draw to frustrate the South's determination to sever the Union, but from the outset of the struggle it assumed a primary importance. Even limited European power, thrown effectively into the scale against the North, could have rendered the Southern cause successful. The nation's future, therefore, rested on the efficiency of its diplomatic as well as its military corps.

Europe's involvement in the American Civil War emerged as a danger to the Union simply because the Southern independence movement threatened all the fundamental power relationships between the Old World and the New. Despite its tradition of isolationism toward Europe, the United States had become by 1861 a potential force in world politics. Cassius Clay, President Abraham Lincoln's choice for the court at St. Petersburg, wrote in April 1862 that it was "useless to deceive ourselves with the idea that we can isolate ourselves from European interventions. We became in spite of ourselves—the Monroe Doctrine—Washington's farewell—and all that—a part of the 'balance

*Address delivered at the annual Civil War Conference, Gettysburg College, November 1958. Published as "Northern Diplomacy and European Neutrality," in David Donald, ed., *Why the North Won the Civil War* (Baton Rouge, LA, 1960). Reprinted by permission.

of power.' " To European leaders the United States was a major Atlantic power, but the relationship of American strength and traditions to the precise interests of Europe varied from country to country.

London promised to become the focal point of all wartime diplomatic maneuvering. Britain was the dominant power of Europe, and its control of Canada and the sea-lanes of the north Atlantic created extensive commitments in the New World. France was equally concerned over events in America but lacked the power to escape the British lead. Keeping such interested and calculating countries neutral became the chief task of Northern diplomacy. Fortunately for the North, Anglo-American relations had never been more cordial than they were in 1861. This, however, was no guarantee of British neutrality. Britain's powerful conservative classes, always cynical toward the democratic experiment in the United States, recognized the fundamental meaning of the Civil War. Democratic institutions were on trial. The United States as a nation had passed beyond the normal control of Old World power, but, if the American people were determined to destroy their national greatness and demonstrate the failure of their institutions, the least that reactionary Europe could do was to encourage them in their effort so that the work of destruction might succeed. British aristocrats long had regarded the American democratic example as a threat to their estate. For them the breakup of the Union would impede the expansion of democracy everywhere. In July 1861, *Blackwood's Edinburgh Magazine* declared that "it is precisely because we do not share the admiration of America for her own institutions and political tendencies that we do not now see in the impending change an event altogether to be deplored."[1]

British conservatives resented the growth of the United States into a formidable maritime rival no less than the progress of its democratic system. The Russian minister reported from London that Britain's ruling class "at the bottom of its heart, desires the separation of North America into two Republics. . . . Then England, on terms of peace and commerce with both, would have nothing to fear from either; for she would dominate them, restraining them by their rival ambitions."[2] Similarly, the Russian minister in Washington, Edouard de Stoeckl, predicted that England would benefit more than any other country from the disintegration of American power. The British cabinet,

[1]"The Disruption of the Union," *Blackwood's Edinburgh Magazine* 90 (July 1861): 126. For similar observations see Edward L. Pierce, ed., *Memoir and Letters of Charles Sumner* (Boston, 1883), 4:150–53; Charles Francis Adams to Charles Francis Adams, Jr., January 31, 1862, in Worthington Chauncey Ford, ed., *A Cycle of Adams Letters, 1861–1865* (Cambridge, MA, 1920), 1:107.

[2]Quoted in Ephraim D. Adams, *Great Britain and the American Civil War* (New York, 1925), 1:50–51.

he warned his government, "is watching attentively the internal dis-
sensions of the Union and awaits the result with an impatience which
it has difficulty in disguising."[3] From St. Petersburg, Clay advised
Lincoln that "I saw at a glance where the feeling of England was. They
hoped for our ruin! They are jealous of our power. They care neither
for the South nor the North. They hate both."

Even British liberal sentiment turned instinctively against the
North. In its burgeoning struggle against the South, the government
in Washington found itself in the unwanted position of employing force
to repress the will of a national minority which desired to establish its
independence. Clay once had declared that the United States was
fighting for nationality and liberty. The *Times* (London) retorted sar-
castically that it was difficult to understand how "a people fighting
. . . to force their fellow citizens to remain in a confederacy which they
repudiated, can be the champions of liberty and nationalism." Many
British liberals, moreover, had long been attracted to the South's free
trade principles. Disunion could enhance Britain's trade connections
with the Southern market and sources of supply. American slavery
placed British leaders and observers in a quandary. Overwhelmingly
they opposed slavery; they understood, however, that any Northern
effort to confiscate or emancipate the slaves would drive the South to
desperation and aggravate the savagery of the war. For British officials
especially the choices appeared tragic. Without emancipation the
restored Union would end in disgrace; with emancipation it would end
in physical and emotional disaster.[1]

Western Europe long had been indignant at the American effort
to keep the Western Hemisphere off limits to further European
encroachment. For the ambitious Louis Napoleon of France especially
events in the United States were encouraging, for they seemed to be
rendering the Monroe Doctrine inoperative. No American fleet would
block the contemplated movement of French troops to Vera Cruz or
demolish his unfolding dreams of establishing a vassal empire in Mexico. A strong and friendly Confederate States of America would create
a buffer between what remained of the United States and his new
Mexican possessions. Secession appeared so consequential to Europe
because it again exposed the Western World to European partition.

In Washington, Henri Mercier, the French minister, favored
immediate action. He informed his government that in recognizing the
Confederacy it would give the American conflict the character of a war

[3]Stoeckl is quoted in Albert A. Woldman, *Lincoln and the Russians* (Cleveland,
1952), p. 85.
[1]See Lord Lyons to Lord John Russell, March 10, 1862, in Foreign Office 5/826,
Public Record Office; Russell to Lyons, March 15, 1862, Russell Papers, 30/22/96, Public
Record Office; and Russell to Lyons, March 7, 1862, F.O. 5/818.

and thereby extend to French seamen the benefit of neutral rights. The United States could not complain, he added, because it had recognized the revolutionary governments of Spanish America. Certainly the American people could not be offended merely because other nations lauded their democratic principles of self-determination. Yet Mercier was a realist; he admonished the French foreign minister in Paris to formulate his American policy only in agreement with the other powers of Europe. What ultimately determined all official British and French policies toward the Confederate cause was the progress of the war itself. It was the dread of a long, indecisive, and destructive war with its necessary infringements on neutral rights that eventually prompted British and French leaders to extend offers of mediation and arbitration, if not to break the Union, at least to terminate a senseless war.

Russia alone of the European states made the preservation of the Union a matter of conscious policy. For Stoeckl the destruction of the Union threatened the equilibrium of world politics. The United States, he argued, had become Europe's best guarantee against British aggression and arrogance. Traditional Russo-American friendship had been based on a mutual rivalry toward Great Britain; it had been the case of the enemies of a rival becoming friends. After the outbreak of the Civil War the *Journal of St. Petersburg*, official organ of the czarist government, declared that "Russia entertains for the United States of America a lively sympathy founded on sentiments of mutual friendship and on common interests. She considers their prosperity necessary to the general equilibrium."[5] Nothing, the imperial cabinet agreed, should be permitted to weaken this powerful counterpoise to England. Prince Gortchakov, the Russian foreign minister, instructed Stoeckl in July 1861 to assure the American nation that it could assume "the most cordial sympathy on the part of our August Master, during the serious crisis which it is passing through at present."[6] This entente cordiale between the world's great despotism and its leading democracy was realpolitik at its diplomatic best, for, despite the incompatibility of political principles, it served the interests of both countries.

II

William H. Seward, Lincoln's secretary of state, assumed the essential task of preventing the introduction of European power into the American Civil War. His diplomacy had but one objective: the preservation of the Union. Lord John Russell, the British foreign secretary, addressed Lord Lyons, the British minister in Washington, in February 1861:

Journal of St. Petersburg quoted in Woldman, *Lincoln and the Russians*, p. 126.
"Prince Gortchakov is quoted in ibid., p. 129.

"The success or failure of Mr. Seward's plans to prevent the disruption of the North American Union is a matter of deep interest to Her Majesty's Government." Seward's devotion to the Union cause was so intense that early in April he recommended to Lincoln a foreign war, perhaps against Spain and France, to rally the seceded states around the American flag and thus reforge the Union.[7] The president tactfully ignored the proposal, but the Washington diplomatic corps was amazed. Lord Lyons warned the Foreign Office in London that Seward would be "a dangerous foreign minister." On April 8, several days before the Fort Sumter crisis, Seward invited William H. Russell, the noted war correspondent of the *Times*, to his home for a rubber of whist. After a while Seward left the room and returned with a paper. "The Secretary," Russell noted in his diary, "then lit his cigar, gave one to me, and proceeded to read slowly and with marked emphasis a very long, strong, and able despatch, which he told me was to be read by . . . the American minister in London to Lord John Russell. It struck me that the tone of the paper was hostile, that there was an undercurrent of menace through it, and that it contained insinuations that Great Britain would interfere to split up the Republic, if she could."[8] Should war come to America, Seward warned, the European powers would do well to ignore it.

What endangered the success of Seward's rigid position toward Europe was the rapid expansion of the conflict between North and South onto the Atlantic. It was fundamental in Lincoln's strategy to weaken and destroy the Southern economy by cutting off shipments of cotton to Europe through a blockade of the Southern ports. Shortly after the surrender at Fort Sumter the Confederate government issued a proclamation calling for privateers; thereupon, Lincoln announced his blockade. Seward warned Lyons that the North would tolerate no further European commerce with the South, but he denied that a formal blockade destroyed his claims that war did not exist. Lyons saw that the blockade, whatever its legality, gave Europe the choice of defying the North or submitting to the interruption of its valuable commerce with the South. He assured Seward that Britain would recognize the blockade as long as Washington conducted it with consideration for foreign interests.[9] When Mercier suggested that Britain and France

[7]John G. Nicolay and John Hay, *Abraham Lincoln: A History* (New York, 1890), 3:445–47.

[8]William H. Russell, *My Diary North and South*, ed. Fletcher Pratt (New York, 1954), pp. 41–42.

[9]On British policy toward the American war on the high seas see James P. Baxter, III, "The British Government and Neutral Rights, 1861–1865," *American Historical Review* 34 (October 1928): 9–29; and Sarah Agnes Wallace and Frances Elma Gillespie, eds., *Journal of Benjamin Moran, 1857–1865* (Chicago, 1948), 2:856.

break the blockade when the South had prepared its 1861 cotton crop for export, Lyons rejected the idea.

Britain, fearful of being trapped in a maritime war, took immediate steps to protect its commerce.[10] On May 13, 1861, without awaiting the arrival of the new American minister, Queen Victoria issued a declaration of neutrality, which called upon British subjects to avoid hostilities between the North and the South. Soon France, Spain, the Netherlands, and Brazil followed the British lead. This recognition of Southern belligerency granted to Southern ships the privileges of neutral ports accorded the ships of the North. Washington was shocked at the British decision, for it not only suggested collusion between Britain and France but also presaged the diplomatic recognition of the South. Charles Sumner, the Massachusetts senator, termed the queen's proclamation "the most hateful act of English history since the time of Charles 2nd." Seward's reaction was even more violent. "They have misunderstood things fearfully, in Europe," he wrote home in May. "Great Britain is in great danger of sympathizing so much with the South for the sake of peace and cotton as to drive us to make war against her, as the ally of the traitors."[11]

Late in April, Washington discovered that the Confederate government had dispatched commissioners to the European capitals. In Paris the French minister, Edouard-Antoine Thouvenel, informed American officials that he planned to receive the commissioners unofficially; only if the South established its de facto independence would the French government consider recognition. Through William L. Dayton, the American minister in Paris, Seward warned the French government that the United States would regard any communication between its minister and the Southern commissioners as "exceptional and injurious" to American dignity and honor. Even an unofficial reception of the emissaries of disunion, he complained, would give them encouragement to prosecute their effort to destroy the American Republic. Seward's major focus was on London where the commissioners arrived in May. When Lord Russell learned that William L. Yancey, the noted Southern secessionist and one of the commissioners, would seek recognition for his government, he wrote to Lyons: "If it can possibly be helped, Mr. Seward must not be allowed to get us into a quarrel. I shall see the southerners when they come, but unofficially and keep them at a proper distance." When Seward learned that Russell

---

[10] Ibid., 1:xxxiii–iv, 806.

[11] Even more threatening to the North was the London government's announcement in June 1861 that, to ensure British neutrality, it would not permit Northern warships or privateers to bring their prey into British ports, nor could privateers remain in any British port longer than twenty-four hours. See ibid., 2:825.

had received the Southern commissioners informally, he prepared a letter—his famed No. 10 of May 21—so menacing that Lincoln modified certain passages and removed others. Even in revised form the dispatch was little less than an ultimatum, suggesting that the American minister break off relations with the British government if Russell persisted in seeing any of the Southern emissaries.[12]

Charles Francis Adams, the new American minister, arrived in Britain on May 13, the day of the queen's proclamation. In an interview with Lord Russell a few days later, he protested the British action. Then, on June 10, Adams received Seward's dispatch of May 21. Henry Adams, the minister's son and secretary, termed it "so arrogant in tone and so extraordinary and unparalleled in its demands that it leaves no doubt in my mind that our Government wishes to face a war with all Europe. . . . I do not think I exaggerate the danger. I believe that our Government means to have a war with England; I believe that England knows it and is preparing for it."[13] Minister Adams regarded Seward's warning as little less than a declaration of war. Moderating the tone of Seward's dispatch, Adams informed Russell that the United States would regard any further relations between the British government and the Confederate commissioners, whether official or not, as a manifestation of hostility. Russell assured Adams that his unofficial conversations with the Southerners did not imply recognition. He had seen them twice, and he had no intention of seeing them again. Lord Palmerston, the prime minister, announced a hands-off policy, stating that England had not been involved in that contest and, if possible, he wanted to keep his country out of it.

Throughout the summer of 1861, Seward condemned the British and French governments for behaving as if a war existed in the United States. He admitted that their involvement in the American struggle might protract it and aggravate its evils; no external measures, he warned them, would alter the outcome. When Lord Lyons in June suggested British mediation to end the war, Seward wrote to Adams that the British government "will do wisely by leaving us to manage and settle this domestic controversy in our own way." The United States would not negotiate any abridgment of its sovereignty. "There is here, as there has always been," he reminded Paris on June 17, "one

[12]Seward to Adams, May 21, 1861, in George E. Baker, ed., *The Works of William H. Seward* (Boston, 1884), 5:245.

[13]For Adams's interview with Russell on May 20 see Wallace and Gillespie, *Journal of Benjamin Moran*, 2:816; Henry Adams to Charles Francis Adams, Jr., June 10, 1861, in Worthington Chauncey Ford, ed., *Letters of Henry Adams, 1858–1891* (Boston, 1930), p. 93; and Henry Adams to Charles Francis Adams, Jr., July 2, 1861, in Ford, *Cycle of Adams Letters*, 1:17.

political power, namely, the United States of America, competent to make war and peace, and conduct commerce and alliances with all foreign nations." What existed in the South, he explained, was an armed sedition seeking to overthrow the government. Seward admitted that international law permitted the recognition of established de facto governments; he merely denied that one existed in the South. "The United States," he concluded, "will not refine upon the question where and how new nations are born out of existing nations. They are well aware that the rights of the states involve their duties and their destinies, and they hold those rights to be absolute as against all foreign nations."[11] He advised Mercier that French recognition of the Confederacy would result in war with the United States. In a letter to Minister Dayton, Seward had warned Paris directly that "foreign intervention would oblige us to treat those who should yield it as allies of the insurrectionary party and to carry on the war against them as enemies. . . . The President and the people of the United States deem the Union, which would then be at stake, worth all the cost and all the sacrifices of a contest with the world at arms, if such a contest should prove inevitable."[15]

European interference meant war, but Seward reminded both Britain and France of their long tradition of friendship with the United States and assured them that his country had cherished that peace. The American Republic, he told Adams, was "anxious to avoid all causes of misunderstanding with Great Britain; to draw closer, instead of breaking, the existing bonds of amity and friendship. There is nothing good or great which both nations may not expect to attain or effect if they may remain friends. It would be a hazardous day for both branches of the British race when they should determine to test how much harm each could do the other."[16] The secretary also extended similar assurances to the French: "We have no hostile or interested designs against any other state or nation whatever, and, on the contrary, we seek peace, harmony, and commerce with them all."[17] Seward repeated ceaselessly his contention that the United States was one; that the countries of Europe should not view themselves as neutrals between two imaginary belligerents in America but as friends of the United States. The U.S. Constitution, he reminded the Europeans, provided

[11]Seward to Dayton, June 17, 1861, in Baker, *Works of William H. Seward*, 5:268–76.

[15]On Mercier's interview with Seward in June and Seward's response see Daniel B. Carroll, *Henri Mercier and the American Civil War* (Princeton, NJ, 1971), pp. 76–77; Seward to Dayton, April 22, 1861, in Baker, *Works of William H. Seward*, 5:230.

[16]Seward to Adams, June 19, 1861, ibid., pp. 278–79.

[17]Seward to Dayton, July 10, 1861, ibid., pp. 331–32.

all the required means for surmounting internal disorders. Arbitration would endanger the nation's integrity by substituting nonconstitutional devices for the normal functioning of the American system.[18]

The U.S. relations with Britain were disturbed unnecessarily in December 1861 when Captain Charles Wilkes of the federal warship *San Jacinto* stopped the British mail steamer *Trent* off the coast of Cuba; removed two Confederate agents, James M. Mason and John Slidell; and took them as prisoners to Fortress Monroe and finally to Fort Warren in Boston harbor. The Confederate government had dispatched these men, among the South's ablest, to London and Paris, respectively, to replace the earlier commissioners. To the zealous Wilkes their capture was an unprecedented coup. Members of the Lincoln administration and the Northern press seemed to agree. Gideon Welles, secretary of the navy, sent Wilkes a congratulatory telegram: "Your conduct in seizing these public enemies was marked by intelligence, ability, decision, and firmness, and has the emphatic approval of the department."[19] Welles regretted only that Wilkes had not taken the vessel as well. In the outburst of public commendation, editors seemed to lose their heads. The *New York Tribune* reported that "the faces of loyal Americans broadened into a universal grin." That the incident might generate a crisis with Britain did not seem to matter. "Speaking generally," Charles Francis Adams, Jr., recalled, "I think I do not remember in the whole course of a half-century's retrospect . . . any occurrence in which the American people were so completely swept off their feet, for the moment losing possession of their senses, as during the weeks which immediately followed the seizure of Mason and Slidell."[20]

Unfortunately Wilkes, in defying English neutral rights on the high seas, had broken the cherished maritime principle for which the United States supposedly fought the British in the War of 1812. In London, Henry Adams saw the issue clearly, writing to his brother in America: "Good God, what's got into you all? What do you mean by deserting now the great principles of our fathers, by returning to the vomit of that dog Great Britain? What do you mean by asserting now principles against which every Adams yet has protested and resisted?

---

[18]Seward stressed this theme in Seward to Dayton, May 30, 1861, ibid., pp. 259–60; Seward to Dayton, June 8, 1861, ibid., pp. 267–68; and Seward to Adams, June 19, 1861, ibid., pp. 276–80.

[19]*New York Daily Tribune*, December 9, 1861; Thomas L. Harris, *The Trent Affair* (Indianapolis, 1896), pp. 120–21.

[20]*New York Daily Tribune*, November 18, 1861; Charles Francis Adams, "The Trent Affair," *Proceedings of the Massachusetts Historical Society* 45 (1911–12): 37; Charles Francis Adams, Jr., to Adams, November 19, 1861, in Ford, *Cycle of Adams Letters*, 1:71.

. . . It's pitiable to see such idiocy in a nation."[21] Seward was embarrassed. He faced the necessity of satisfying the British who were wronged and at the same time of protecting American prestige abroad. "If I decide this case in favor of my own government," he admitted, "I must disavow its most cherished principles, and . . . forever abandon its essential policy. The country cannot afford the sacrifice. If I maintain those principles, and adhere to that policy, I must surrender the case itself." Seward soon decided on the latter course and conceded to the British with remarkable grace; nowhere did the *Trent* case challenge his Union policies. "In coming to my conclusion," he wrote to Lyons, "I have not forgotten that, if the safety of this Union required the detention of the captured persons, it would be the right and duty of this government to detain them. But the effectual check and waning proportions of the existing insurrection, as well as the comparative unimportance of the captured persons themselves, when dispassionately weighed, happily forbid me from resorting to that defense."[22] Federal officials released the two Confederates promptly and sent them on their way.

III

What gave the South its initial presumption of success in its quest for European recognition was the alleged economic power of cotton. Southern writers in 1861 assumed that Britain, in time, would break the Northern blockade to guarantee the flow of cotton into England. *De Bow's Review* predicted that a blockade of the Southern ports would be "swept away by the English fleets of observation hovering on the Southern coasts, to protect . . . the free flow of cotton to English and French factories." The *Charleston Mercury* noted that "cotton would bring England to her knees." Southern leaders argued that Britain logically could not condemn slavery when slave labor produced the raw cotton its industries required. The *Times*, as if to underscore the Southern contention, observed in June 1861 that "so nearly are our interests intertwined with America that civil war in the States means destruction in Lancashire." Acknowledging the British interest in cotton, Palmerston wrote in October that, if the war continued into 1862, Britain might "be obliged either singly or conjointly with France to tell the Northerners that we cannot allow some millions of our people to perish to

---

[21]Henry Adams to Charles Francis Adams, Jr., November 30, December 13, 1861, ibid., pp. 75, 83; Adams to Charles Francis Adams, Jr., December 12, 1861, ibid., p. 81; Adams, "The Trent Affair," p. 128.

[22]Seward to Lyons, December 26, 1861, in Baker, *Works of William H. Seward*, 5:295–309.

please the Northern States, and that the blockade of the South must be so far relaxed as to allow cotton loaded ships to come out." Lord Lyons warned Seward that, "if the United States determined to stop by force so important a commerce as that of Great Britain with the cotton-growing States, [he] could not answer for what might happen." Even Richard Cobden wondered how long the British would tolerate the blockade after the new cotton crop was ready. If cotton was king, as Southern and English observers seemed to agree, the South had only to place an embargo on that commodity to compel Britain to destroy the blockade. The Confederate Congress refused to establish an embargo, but Committees of Public Safety in the Southern seaport towns effectively halted the export of cotton to Europe. The South, playing for high stakes, needed European recognition, not immediate profits from cotton.

By the spring of 1862 King Cotton had compelled neither Britain nor France to recognize Southern independence or break the blockade. Confederate efforts to force action in London by depriving Lancashire of raw cotton through embargo and crop destruction expected too much of economic coercion. As one British leader observed, "I wonder the South do not see that our recognition *because* they keep cotton from us would be ignominious beyond measure, & that no English Parlt could do so base a thing." Mason complained in March 1862 that cotton had no effect on British policy, concluding that "even in Lancashire and other manufacturing districts no open demonstration has been made against the blockade." British officials had provided some alternative sources of supply, especially in India, Australia, and Egypt, but still the British and French need for cotton seemed insatiable. "The suffering among the people of Lancashire . . . ," Henry Adams reported in May, "is already very great and is increasing enormously every day without any prospect of relief for months to come."[23] In Washington, Lyons, urged on by the London government, pressed Seward for a federal policy to reestablish the cotton trade, at least through Southern ports in control of the North. Seward could not ensure the delivery of cotton to Southern wharves. Even Russell noted correctly that the Union capture of any Southern port merely guaranteed the destruction of cotton in the surrounding countryside. Additionally, any successful marketing of cotton would serve the financial interests of the South; under no circumstance would Seward promote it. Only a Northern triumph, he assured Lyons and Mercier, would reopen that trade.

[23]Henry Adams to Charles Francis Adams, Jr., May 8, 1862, in Ford, *Cycle of Adams Letters*, 1:139; Adams to Charles Francis Adams, Jr., June 27, 1862, ibid., p. 159.

Britain and France could pursue their interests in cotton most effectively by curtailing their scarcely disguised sympathy for the Confederate cause.[21]

IV

If industrial capacity and financial resources were the major sinews of war, British analysts in the spring of 1861 doubted that the South, even in a defensive war, could sustain an extended struggle against the more powerful North. But the rout of the Union forces at Bull Run in July 1861 dispelled the illusion of an easy Northern victory and presaged a long, costly, and destructive war. "This defeat," lamented Benjamin Moran, assistant secretary of the American legation in London, "will have a bad effect for the North in Europe, & will raise the hopes of the rebels. English inherent hatred of us is being expressed unmistakably to-day, in sneers and chuckling over our misfortune."[25] Following Bull Run, Henry Adams issued a warning of his own: "If this happens again, farewell to our country for many a day. Bull's Run will be a byword of ridicule for all time. Our honor will be utterly gone." Britain would deal summarily with the United States were it not for European complications that limited its action. "Every day," Adams complained in late October, "our authority, prestige and influence sink lower in this country, and we have the mournful task of trying to bolster up a failing cause."[26] During the autumn months British journals and leaders in Parliament agreed that the North could not win the war; therefore, it should permit the South to depart without further destruction. William Russell concluded, after talking to many Americans—North and South—that "it's all up with U.S."[27]

So apparent was the lack of energy and direction in the Northern war effort that foreign observers questioned the capacity of the Union forces to subdue the Confederacy at all. In January 1862, Charles Francis Adams reported from London that the assumption of Northern

---

[21] Lyons to Russell, February 11, 17, and 21, 1862, F.O. 5/825; Lyons to Russell, March 31, 1862, F.O. 5/827; Lyons to Russell, May 16, 1862, F.O. 5/830.

[25] Wallace and Gillespie, *Journal of Benjamin Moran*, 2:858, 903. Surveying the opening months of the war on December 31, 1861, Moran concluded that "the conduct of the British people toward the Federal Government has been of covert malicious foes, who have illy-concealed their delight at the seeming success of the Slavocracy in their efforts to break up the Union." Ibid., p. 933.

[26] Henry Adams to Charles Francis Adams, Jr., August 25, and October 25, 1861, in Ford, *Cycle of Adams Letters*, 1:26, 62. Adams reported that no government in Europe would offer the Union any sympathy: "They all hate us and fear us, even the most liberal." Henry Adams to Charles Francis Adams, Jr., November 7, 1861, ibid., p. 66.

[27] See Russell, *My Diary North and South*, pp. 36–40, 172–76.

weakness "prevails so much here that it will undoubtedly become the basis of a movement for recognition [of the South] before long." Later that month Henry Adams wrote to his brother in America: "The truth is, we are now in a corner. There is but one way out of it and that is by a decisive victory."[28] Perhaps a major Northern triumph in six weeks would prevent Britain and France from raising the blockade, but Seward's repeated assertions that the United States would never accept separation presaged only an endless and unprofitable war. The Northern capture of Fort Henry and Fort Donelson in February failed to impress the British. "All the successes of the North," Lord Russell observed, "do not persuade me they can conquer the South."[29] British neutrality still appeared stable enough, but how long would the English people tolerate a war at once so pointless and so potentially destructive of neutral rights? The closing of mills in every direction, warned Henry Adams, "will soon produce fresh agitation for mediation or intervention . . . if no progress is made by our armies."[30]

General George B. McClellan's retreat from Richmond in June 1862 merely confirmed the general European conviction that the American Union was doomed. "It is plain," declared the *Times*, "that the time is approaching when Europe will have to think seriously of its relations to the two belligerents in the American War. . . . That North and South must now choose between separation and ruin, material and political, is the opinion of nearly every one who, looking impartially and from a distance on the conflict, sees what is hidden from the frenzied eyes of the Northern politicians." Much of the English press clamored for intervention; recognition of a successful cause could be safe, legitimate, and effective. So dominant was the pro-South trend in British opinion that Henry Adams wrote from London: "There is no doubt that the idea here is as strong as ever that we must ultimately fail, and unless a very few weeks show some great military result we shall have our hands full in this quarter." Public hostility, he further reported in July, was "rising every hour and running harder against us than at any time since the Trent affair." There was nothing to do but retreat.

---

[28]Charles Francis Adams to Charles Francis Adams, Jr., January 10, 1862, in Ford, *Cycle of Adams Letters*, 1:99; Henry Adams to Charles Francis Adams, Jr., January 22, 1862, ibid., p. 105.

[29]Russell to Lyons, April 26, 1862, in Russell Papers, PRO 20/22/96. Early in February 1862, Lyons complained of the injury to neutral rights resulting from the war. He urged Washington to adopt "immediate measures to relieve the present evils which the civil war in this country brings to neutral nations." Lyons to Russell, February 11, 1862, F.O. 5/825. The British diplomatic correspondence is replete with complaints of wartime infringements on the rights and interests of British citizens.

[30]Henry Adams to Charles Francis Adams, Jr., July 4, 1862, in Ford, *Cycle of Adams Letters*, 1:164.

"I shut myself up," he complained, "went to no more parties and avoided contact with everyone except friends."[31]

Reports in the British press of McClellan's alleged capitulation seemed designed to carry the House of Commons as it commenced debate on William Schaw Lindsay's resolution calling for recognition of the Confederacy. In defense of his resolution, he pointed to the inevitability of separation between North and South. Lancashire was in distress. Lindsay quoted from a letter written by a mill hand: "We think it high time to give the Southern States the recognition they so richly deserve." The British ministry had assured friends of the North that it would not be influenced by the parliamentary debate; thereafter, the Union sympathizers adopted the strategy of permitting the pro-Confederates to wear themselves out against a stone wall of silence. As the debate continued into the evening of July 18, Lindsay and his forces retreated to simple mediation. At the end Lord Palmerston warned Parliament that mediation meant war, and Lindsay withdrew his motion.[32]

Throughout the summer of 1862 the Civil War was the all-absorbing subject of conversation in England. As the London correspondent of the *New York Times* reported: "John Bull even departs from his customary unsocial habits, and talks with his neighbor in the railway carriage or omnibus, on this dreadful war. And he likes it less and less. He grows more and more impatient. He thinks that something ought to be done." Despite the British preference for a negotiated settlement of the war, the public and private pressures against intervention were intense. Any effective mediation, warned the *Birmingham Daily Post*, would require forceful intervention. "Mediation, unless in the form of armed and active intervention," argued the *London Daily News*, "is the vainest of dreams."[33] Conservative leaders like Benjamin Disraeli and the Earl of Derby opposed mediation and recognition of the Confederacy as an overextension of British purpose. Derby reminded Disraeli as early as mid-July that

> You cannot even get at [the Confederacy]. The whole coast is in federal hands. It can hardly be argued that a country which has not a port, not a means of ingress or egress, is in a position to claim recognition of its independence. Mediation is impossible.

[31] Henry Adams to Charles Francis Adams, Jr., July 19, 1862, ibid., pp. 166–68; Wallace and Gillespie, *Journal of Benjamin Moran*, 2:1020, 1040–44.

[32] For an excellent account of Lindsay's activities on behalf of the South see Frank L. Owsley, *King Cotton Diplomacy: Foreign Relations of the Confederate States of America* (Chicago, 1931), pp. 240–49.

[33] *New York Times*, July 15, 1862; *Birmingham Daily Post*, June 13, 1862; *London Daily News*, June 16, 1862.

The offer of it useless, unless you want to provoke insult from the North. If you intervene, you must prepare to enforce the acceptance of your proposal. . . . If the autumn campaign ends without decisive result, the South will have held its own for two complete years; debt, taxes, failure of trade, will have begun to tell on the North, which they have not yet done. . . . By the beginning of next session, the position will have become intelligible.[31]

Few conservatives favored more than the continued recognition of Britain's limited capacity to end the war.

In London, Mason, misled by the public evidence of British interventionism and unmindful of the disturbing doubts in and out of the Foreign Office, moved to drive home his apparent advantage. He dispatched a brief note to Lord Russell, requesting an interview. This Russell refused, assuring Mason that nothing could result from it. In a second dispatch the Confederate commissioner phrased his position in great detail, but again Russell replied that the moment for recognition had not arrived.[35] For Mason the official British position suddenly became clear: the ministry in London would not alter its policies until the South revealed its ability to gain and maintain its independence, and reports from America indicated that the South was faltering at New Orleans, Memphis, and Shiloh. From Vienna, Minister John Lothrop Motley observed with accuracy that diplomacy would continue to reflect the course of the war in America.

In Paris, Slidell's quest for recognition produced only anxiety and frustration. Foreign Minister Thouvenel had little interest in the Confederate cause.[36] He doubted that the French public favored intervention or that the South would ever establish its independence. Without British and Russian support, France's intervention would overcommit its power and expose that country to Northern retaliation. Russia, he surmised correctly, would reject any proposal for joint action. Prince Gortchakov made it clear that his government would regard the dissolution of the Union as a catastrophe. In an interview with Bayard Taylor of the American embassy in October 1862 he explained:

You know that the government of the United States has few friends among the Powers. England rejoices over what is happening to

[31]Edward Stanley [the Earl of Derby] to Disraeli, July 15, 1862, Disraeli Papers, Hughenden Manor, B/XX/S/708; Lord Henry Lennox to Disraeli, September 23, 1862, Disraeli Papers, B/XX/LX/163.

[35]For Mason's communications with Russell see Adams, *Great Britain and the American Civil War*, 2:25–27.

[36]Louis Martin Sears, "A Confederate Diplomat at the Court of Napoleon III," *American Historical Review* 26 (January 1921): 260.

you; she longs and prays for your overthrow. France is less actively hostile; her interests would be less affected by the result; but she is not unwilling to see it. She is not your friend. . . . Russia, alone, has stood by you from the first, and will continue to stand by you. We are very, *very* anxious that some means should be adopted— that *any* course should be pursued—which will prevent the division which now seems inevitable.

For the ambitious Napoleon III the secessionist movement appeared so consequential because it again exposed the New World to European partition. During the months following Bull Run, Napoleon assured London that he would recognize Southern independence whenever Britain was prepared to do so. Slidell analyzed the South's dilemma in a letter to Mason dated February 12, 1862: "The Emperor's sympathies are with us—that he would immediately raise the blockade and very soon recognize us, if England would only make the first step, however small, in that direction, but for the present at least he is decided that she shall take the initiative."[37] As the weeks passed the French press clamored for independent action. By April the feeling was so intense that Slidell informed Mason: "I am not without hope that the Emperor may act alone";[38] still, France avoided any open commitment to the Southern cause. Thouvenel explained that France was too involved in Italy, but Slidell recognized the real cause for French hesitancy. Addressing the Confederate government on August 24, he said that "you will find by my official correspondence that we are still hard and fast aground here. Nothing will float us off but a strong and continued current of important successes in the field."[39]

V

Throughout the autumn of 1862, European diplomacy continued to reflect the experience of the battlefield. In Washington, William Stuart, who replaced the vacationing Lyons, and Mercier carefully followed the military maneuvering, searching for the victory that might resolve Europe's diplomatic dilemma. Early in September, Robert E. Lee's Confederate army crossed the Potomac into Maryland. There on September 17 it met McClellan's Union forces outside Sharpsburg in the famed battle of Antietam. The Confederates left the scene of battle but recrossed the Potomac with baggage and artillery intact. Battles so destructive, yet so indecisive, convinced Stuart that the American war

[37]Sidell to Mason, February 12, 1862, ibid., p. 257.
[38]Ibid., p. 259; Owsley, *King Cotton Diplomacy*, p. 306.
[39]Ibid., p. 350.

had reached a critical stage. Without foreign intervention, he believed, the war would never end. "I can only add," he admonished Russell, "that a crisis is approaching, and that some risk will have to be incurred sooner or later. The result will depend upon the fitness of the moment chosen, unless we wait for complete exhaustion." The British and French ministers in Washington believed that London and Paris, relying on the judgments of their representatives in America, should watch for the opportune moment for intervention. On September 22, five days after Antietam, Mercier argued that the time had come for Britain and France to offer their good services in search for peace *without reference to separation.*[10] Stuart endorsed Mercier's proposal and forwarded it to London.

Even before that advice reached London, the British ministry, encouraged by Southern successes at Richmond and the second battle of Bull Run, had taken up the question of mediation. Upon reading of General T. J. "Stonewall" Jackson's exploits in Virginia, Lord Russell, on September 14, informed Palmerston that "it really looks as if he might end the war." Palmerston, noting especially Lee's victory at Bull Run (Manassas), penned a note to Russell that same day: "The Federals . . . got a very complete smashing. . . . Even Washington and Baltimore may fall into the hands of the Confederates. If this should happen, would it not be time for us to consider whether in such a state of things England and France might not address the contending parties and recommend an arrangement upon the basis of separation?"[11] Palmerston and Russell turned for support to both the British cabinet and the French government. Russell asked Paris for Mercier's latest views on the proper timing for a British-French offer of mediation. Should Washington reject any reasonable proposal, Russell informed the French, he would recommend a joint recognition of the Confederacy by Britain, France, Russia, Austria, and Italy.[12]

Before Napoleon could commit France to intervention, the British cabinet passed the moment of decision. On September 22 the wise and respected Lord Granville expressed to Russell his conviction that Britain should avail itself of a proper occasion for some form of intervention, but he warned Russell that recognition of the South just before a Northern victory would be disastrous. "In any case," wrote Granville,

[10]Stuart to Russell, September 9, 23, and October 17, 1862, Russell Papers, PRO 30/22/36.

[11]Russell to Palmerston, September 14, 1862, Palmerston Papers, GC/RU/726/1 (by permission of the Trustees of the Broadlands Archives, presently housed in the Historical Manuscripts Commission, London); Palmerston to Russell, September 14, 1862, Russell Papers, PRO 30/22/14D.

[12]Russell to Lord Cowley, September 13, 26, 1862, Russell Papers, PRO 30/22/105.

"I doubt, if the war continues long after the recognition of the South, whether it will be possible for us to avoid drifting into it."[13] By early October Palmerston had begun to reflect Granville's caution. The prime minister's earlier support of Russell's position had assumed a successful Southern invasion of Maryland. News of Antietam and Lee's retreat across the Potomac had reached London by late September. On October 2, Palmerston reminded Russell that mediation based on separation would favor the South; Northern acceptance of mediation therefore hinged on Southern triumphs on the battlefield. "The whole matter is full of difficulty," he concluded, "& can only be cleared up by some more decided events between the contending parties."

William E. Gladstone, chancellor of the exchequer, ignored Palmerston's new mood of caution, and on October 7 he declared in a speech at Newcastle: "Jefferson Davis and the other leaders have made an army, and are making, it appears, a navy, and they have made what is more than either, they have made a nation." Faced with newspaper accusations that he had departed from official British policy, Gladstone acknowledged that his Newcastle speech had gone too far. To Russell he admitted that he had argued that the Confederacy had the power and the will to defend its independence; he had even suggested that under conceivable circumstances the powers of Europe might take action without facing insult or war. He had not, he reminded Russell, recommended any specific policy for Britain.[14]

By mid-October Russell had embarked on a course designed to commit the cabinet to mediation. He instructed Lord Cowley, the British ambassador to France, to press Napoleon on the matter of a joint offer of mediation. Then he prepared a memorandum for the cabinet that advocated the adoption of his mediation plan. Gladstone alone of the cabinet members supported Russell's program; the rest urged restraint. The Duke of Argyll warned the foreign secretary that British recognition of the Confederacy before the North accepted separation "would be either nugatory, or would be a measure, to be followed up by other measures, and in this case, would probably involve us in war." The Duke of Newcastle agreed with others that in time the North would quit the war. Until then, however, European intervention would be premature and merely would strengthen Northern resolve to continue the war. Sir George Cornewall Lewis opposed intervention

[13]Granville to Russell, September 29, 1862, Russell Papers, PRO 30/22/25.

[14]Palmerston to Russell, October 2, 1862, Palmerston Papers, Letter Book for 1862; Palmerston to Russell, October 8, 1862, Russell Papers, PRO 30/22/14D. On Gladstone's speech at Newcastle and the reaction to it see Wallace and Gillespie, *Journal of Benjamin Moran*, 2:1078; Pierce, *Memoir and Letters of Charles Sumner*, 4:155–58; Gladstone to Russell, October 17, 21, 1862, Russell Papers, PRO 30/22/19.

completely, advising Russell that any action that failed to involve Britain in some form of coercion would be ineffectual.[15] In a note to Russell, Sir George Grey argued that recognition of the Confederacy would produce deep resentment in Washington and probably a break in diplomatic relations; moreover, it would commit Britain to a gratuitous sanction of slavery in America and would neither shorten the war nor bring larger shipments of cotton. "Unless therefore you have reason to think that an offer of mediation would be well received," he cautioned Russell, "I think our clear course is to adhere to the line of strict neutrality."[16]

Facing a divided cabinet, Palmerston sought the advice of Derby, who reiterated the fundamental conviction of British Conservatives that mediation or recognition merely would irritate the North without advancing the cause of the South or procuring a single bale of cotton. Mediation, Derby continued, would gain its apparent objectives—peace and separation—only if England were prepared to sweep away the blockade and invite a declaration of war from Washington. There was simply no way whereby England could influence events in America short of a direct military involvement. Palmerston's ultimate decision to oppose mediation reflected that fundamental reality. The North, he reminded Russell, demanded no less than a restoration of the Union; the South, independence. To offer mediation merely would pledge each party in the conflict to its uncompromisable objective. "I am therefore inclined to change the opinion on which I wrote to you when the Confederates seemed to carry all before them," he informed Russell on October 22, "and I am very much come back to our original view of the matter, that we must continue to be lookers on till the war shall have taken a more decided turn."[17]

During the critical months of September and October 1862, Napoleon had not disguised his sympathy for the Confederate cause; still, he balked at involvement in the American conflict. He complained to Slidell of troubles in Italy and Greece, and he acknowledged his fear that if he acted alone Britain would desert him or attempt to embroil him in a war with the United States. Slidell assured Napoleon that the North would not regard recognition as a casus belli, and that with his powerful navy he could defend French interests on the seas without difficulty. To Slidell joint mediation was worthless, as he shared Napoleon's distrust of both England and Russia. Early in November the

[15]Russell to Cowley, October 11, 1862, Russell Papers, PRO 30/22/105; Duke of Argyll to Russell, October 11, 1862, Duke of Newcastle to Russell, October 14, 1862, and Lewis to Russell, October 25, 1862, Russell Papers, PRO 30/22/25.
[16]Sir George Grey to Russell, October 27, 1862, Russell Papers, PRO 30/22/25.
[17]Palmerston to Russell, October 22, 1862, Russell Papers, PRO 30/22/14D.

new French minister, Edouard Drouyn de Lhuys, in response to Russell's appeal, offered Britain and Russia a tripartite proposal for a renewable six-month armistice in the American Civil War. British Conservatives were not impressed. The Earl of Malmesbury wrote a brief note to Disraeli, stating that "I can't suppose the North will accept it." What disturbed Derby was Russell's role in extracting the offer from the French government. Palmerston was equally displeased; he no longer had any interest in European intervention. At issue in the final cabinet decision was the attitude of Russia. As early as November 8, St. Petersburg had informed the Foreign Office that the Russian government had rejected Napoleon's proposal. Prince Gortchakov advised the French that it was "essential to avoid the appearance of any pressure of a nature to offend American public opinion, and to excite susceptibilities very easily roused at the bare idea of intervention." Russell attempted to define terms upon which the warring parties in America could agree; he conceded the futility of the effort at a cabinet meeting on November 11.[18] After two days of deliberation the British cabinet, on November 12, rejected the French offer.

VI

Throughout the months of decision in Europe, Seward exerted relentless pressure on the British and French governments. When Mercier transmitted a French offer of mediation to him in July 1862, the secretary warned that "the Emperor can commit no graver error than to mix himself in our affairs. At the rumor alone of intervention all the factions will reunite themselves against you and even in the border states you will meet resistance unanimous and desperate."[19] It was not in the French interest, he continued, to compromise the kindly feeling which the United States held for France. Mercier thereupon advised caution in Paris, adding that intervention could result in war. When he apprised Seward of Europe's reaction to McClellan's withdrawal from Richmond, the secretary stormed back: "I have noticed it but as for us it would be a great misfortune if the powers should wish to intervene in our affairs. There is no possible compromise . . . and, at any price, we will not admit the division of the Union." Seward acknowledged the kindly sentiments of Europe but replied that the best testimony of those sentiments would be Old World abstention from

---

[18]Flahault to Russell, November 5, 1862, Russell Papers, PRO 30/22/62; Malmesbury to Disraeli, November 2, 1862, Disraeli Papers, B/XX/Hs/lll; Derby to Disraeli, November 22, 1862, Disraeli Papers, B/XX/S/303; Russell to Cowley, November 12, 1862, Russell Papers, PRO 30/22/105.
[19]Seward quoted in Owsley, *King Cotton Diplomacy*, p. 333.

American affairs. When Mercier suggested that restoration of the Union was impossible, Seward told him: "Do not believe for a moment that either the Federal Congress, myself or any person connected with this government will in any case entertain any proposition or suggestion of arrangement or accommodation or adjustment from within or without upon a basis of a surrender of the Federal Union."[50]

Above all Seward sought to disabuse European leaders of their conviction that a Northern victory was impossible. Nothing had occurred, he once wrote to Dayton in Paris, to shake the confidence of the federal government in the ultimate success of its purpose. To those Europeans who insisted that the United States was too large for one nation, Seward retorted that it was too small for two. When Europe gave evidence of interventionist tendencies in August 1862, he wrote to Charles Francis Adams in London that "the nation has a right and it is its duty to live. Those who favor and give aid to the insurrection, upon whatever pretext, assail the nation in an hour of danger, and therefore they cannot be held or regarded as its friends. In taking this ground, the United States claim only what they concede to all other nations. No state can be really independent in any other position."[51]

In denying Europe the right to intervene, Seward insisted that he was defending the principle of civil government, for at stake was nothing less than the existence of the United States. "Any other principle than this," he wrote, "would be to resolve government everywhere into a thing of accident and caprice, and ultimately all human society into a state of perpetual war." American policy was dictated by the law of self-preservation, and no country, "animated by loyal sentiments and inspired by a generous ambition can ever suffer itself to debate with parties within or without a policy of self-preservation." It was not strange, therefore, that Seward instructed Adams not to debate, hear, or receive any communication from the British government which sought to advise the United States in its relations with the Confederacy. The American Republic was fighting for empire, he admitted in October 1862, but it was an empire lawfully acquired and lawfully held. "Studying to confine this unhappy struggle within our own borders," he wrote to Dayton, "we have not only invoked no foreign aid or sympathy, but we have warned foreign nations frankly and have besought them not

---

[50]Seward often expressed the view that the North would never surrender the Union. As he wrote to Adams on August 18, 1862, "The principal masses of the population are content with the present system, and cannot be brought to oppose or to surrender it." Baker, *Works of William H. Seward*, 5:350. After reviewing the events of August and September 1862, Seward wondered why the European capitals would continue to behave as if the Union would fail. See Seward to Dayton, October 20, 1862, ibid., p. 360.

[51]Seward to Adams, August 18, 1862, ibid., p. 350.

to interfere. We have practised justice towards them in every way, and conciliation to an unusual degree. But we are none the less determined for all that to be sovereign and to be free."[52]

Seward's reaction to the British cabinet debate of November 1862 revealed both confidence and dismay. It was not pleasant for a loyal American, he admitted to Adams, to observe an English cabinet discuss the future of the American Republic. But the United States enjoyed the right and possessed the power to determine its own destiny; never before was it better prepared to meet danger from abroad. The wheel of political fortune continued to turn. England and France once had desired American friendship; they would do so again. "Neither politicians nor statesmen control events," the secretary concluded. "They can moderate them and accommodate their ambitions to them, but they can do no more."[53]

Clearly the Southern struggle for independence touched tangible British and French interests; to that extent neither nation could ignore events across the Atlantic. Until the South could demonstrate its capacity to overcome the power and purpose of the North, European recognition, as an involvement in the internal affairs of another country, would have defied one of the most significant and thoroughly established traditions of modern diplomacy. Except for one fleeting period in 1862, neither Britain nor France revealed any intention of breaking from its own past and assuming commitments that would endanger its territorial and commercial interests in the New World. Had Europe supported the South before it had guaranteed its own independence, it merely would have magnified the horror and confusion of civil war. Of this Seward left no doubt, warning Europe in May 1862:

> If Europe will still sympathize with the revolution, it must now look forward to the end; an end in which the war ceases with anarchy substituted for the social system that existed when the war began. What will then have become of the interests which carried Europe to the side which was at once the wrong side and the losing one? Only a perfect withdrawal of all favor from the insurrection can now save those interests in any degree. The insurrectionary states, left hopeless of foreign intervention, will be content to stop in their career of self-destruction, and to avail themselves of the moderating power of the Federal government. If the nations of Europe shall refuse to see this, and the war must therefore go on to the conclusion I have indicated, the responsibility for that conclusion will not rest with the government of the United States.[51]

[52]Seward to Dayton, October 20, 1862, ibid., p. 364.
[53]Seward to Adams, November 4, 1862, ibid., p. 366.
[51]Seward to Sanford, ambassador to Belgium, May 23, 1862, ibid., pp. 319–20.

After November 1862 all wartime diplomacy receded into comparative insignificance. In large measure the November elections terminated the simmering diplomatic crisis that had begun six months earlier. In their triumph the Democrats made clear that the Northern population was not impatient, would no more than Seward admit separation, and possessed the confidence and determination to reforge the Union. Even the Peace Democrats, the returned Lord Lyons reported, feared that a European offer of mediation would arouse so thoroughly Northern defiance that it would compel both Peace Democrats and Republican moderates to support a more vigorous prosecution of the war. Lincoln's Emancipation Proclamation, announced in September and declared effective on January 1, 1863, had little effect on European sentiment and none on European action. Much of the British press noted accurately that as a freedom document the proclamation was an empty gesture; it freed no slaves. The *New York Times* passed final judgment on the diplomatic significance of emancipation as early as July 1862: "Those who rely on Emancipation to effect a change in our favor in foreign sentiment, lean on a broken reed. There is just one thing and only one which will work that change—and that is *success*. If we beat [the South's] armies, . . . foreign sentiment will be on our side. And nothing else will bring it there."[55] The devastating battles from Richmond to Antietam had demonstrated the South's inability to force a separation settlement on the North.

Confederate disasters at Gettysburg and Vicksburg in July 1863 shattered whatever Southern hopes of European intervention still remained. In September, Mason informed Russell by note that his mission had been terminated, to which the British secretary replied coldly: "I have on other occasions explained to you the reasons which have inclined her Majesty's Government to decline the overtures you allude to. . . . These reasons are still in force, and it is not necessary to repeat them."[56] Europe's final refusal to involve itself in the American struggle was nothing less than a total vindication of Seward's diplomacy. Whatever the North's diplomatic advantages, he had understood them and exploited them with astonishing effectiveness. He made it clear that any European nation, which committed itself to the destruction of the American Union, would pay dearly if it sought to fulfill that commitment.

[55]*New York Times*, July 17, 1862. A minority of British liberals, abolitionists, and workingmen—generally pro-Union anyway—lauded the proclamation. For the realism of the majority see Wallace and Gillespie, *Journal of Benjamin Moran*, 2:1106–07, 1110, 1116; Henry Adams to Charles Francis Adams, Jr., January 23, 27, 30, and February 13, 1863, in Ford, *Cycle of Adams Letters*, 1:243–45, 251, 252; Sumner to Bright, March 30, 1863, in Pierce, *Memoir and Letters of Charles Sumner*, 4:130.

[56]Russell is quoted in Adams, *Great Britain and the American Civil War*, 2:181.

In large measure there was nothing unique in the diplomatic issues raised by the American Civil War. Many nations had undergone internal revolution in which elements seeking power had sought either to overthrow the existing government or to establish the independence of some portion of its territory. Uprisings had succeeded and failed, but when major power was involved they had demonstrated invariably that other nations, whatever their moral and material interests, really could not intervene diplomatically without running the risk of military involvement. In reminding London and Paris of this well-established tradition, Seward touched the central issue of Europe's relationship to the conflict in America. It was within the power of the Old World to bring injury to the North; it was beyond its power to bring salvation to the South. There were no inexpensive means available to Europe to achieve the liberation of the South against the North's determination to hold it. Those Europeans who sought to cast from the South the yoke of alien rule might have been moved by the moral sentiment of Gladstone, but they had no influence on Palmerston. Since the realities of power are the determining factors in international affairs, a Gladstone in office, whatever his sentimentalism and faith in moral pressure, could have influenced the internal affairs of the United States, wrapped in civil war, with no more success than the masters of realpolitik who rejected such purpose as a matter of principle.

CHAPTER TWELVE

Bismarck's Europe:
An American View*

EMERGING FROM THEIR Civil War in 1865, the American people could view the Atlantic world with deep satisfaction. Europe's equilibrium had persisted through so many decades that it gave contemporaries the illusion of permanence. Following the Napoleonic Wars the five major European powers—Britain, France, Prussia, Austria, and Russia—had given the Continent a half century of relative peace by agreeing, effectively if not explicitly, that any change in Europe's treaty structure would require the consent of all. So devoted was the Austrian emperor to existing treaties that he allegedly threatened to declare war on any country that urged him to take one village that lay outside Austria's official boundaries.[1] Repeatedly after 1815 the great powers resolved questions that in previous centuries would have led to war. All five powers had cooperated in saving the Ottoman Empire from disintegration; all had refrained from seizing any of its territory. Memories of the Napoleonic Wars encouraged Europe's conservative mood; the Concert of Europe institutionalized it. The rules and procedures embodied in the Concert enabled the great powers to settle European questions by secretly arranging compromises behind a facade of international harmony.

At the heart of Europe's stability was the old alliance among Prussia, Austria, and Russia. The restraining influence which these three powers exercised on one another in central and eastern Europe,

*This essay was presented at the annual dinner of the Society for Historians of American Foreign Relations, American University, Washington, DC, August 5, 1981.
[1]Cited in Paul Schroeder, "The 'Balance of Power' System in Europe, 1815–1871," *Naval War College Review* 27 (March–April 1975): 22.

the Continent's most explosive region, was the key to Europe's equilibrium. As long as they preserved the stability of east-central Europe, conflicts elsewhere could not damage the European peace system. However, the Crimean War of 1854, in which Britain deserted Concert diplomacy to destroy Russia's influence in the eastern Mediterranean for a generation, went far to weaken the established order. Austria's involvement and support of Western objectives in that war effectively ended the eastern alliance. For Americans, as for Europeans, the full significance of these events was not yet apparent.[2]

Europe's general stability, added to Britain's naval supremacy, enabled the United States to maintain its interests in the Atlantic world without the necessity of military preparation or an active balance-of-power diplomacy. Despite the lingering antipathy toward Britain, shared especially by Democratic leaders, writers admitted freely that the Atlantic barrier, rendered effective by both British sea power and European diplomacy, gave the American nation its unique freedom to look inward and devote its considerable energies to the development of a rich continent. If a positive foreign policy toward Europe required alliances, military commitments, and clearly enunciated preferences for some specific order of power, as well as public disapprobation and tension, U.S. relations with Europe between 1815 and 1865 had been isolationist indeed. By such standards the powers of Europe also had pursued isolationist policies, for in that stable international environment the major European nations were equally unconcerned with military alliances and preparations for war.

Traditionally France, as the Continent's leading financial and military power, had shared with Britain major responsibility for adjusting Continental politics to changing conditions. Napoleon III, upon becoming emperor in 1852, had turned to reform, and under his guidance Paris quickly emerged as one of the world's most beautiful cities. France then joined Britain and Austria in the Crimean War to protect Turkish hegemony in the straits of the Bosporus and Dardanelles. France's victories in that war, as well as in the Austro-Sardinian War of 1859, brought Napoleon to the height of his prestige. However ambitious his foreign policies, they merely had reinforced France's dominant position in Europe's general equilibrium.[3] During the 1860s that country entered upon troubled times. Napoleon's Mexican venture with

---

[2]Ibid., pp. 25–28. Schroeder stresses the role of the old Holy Alliance in maintaining the stability of eastern-central Europe as the key to Europe's nineteenth-century stability.

[3]See J. M. Thompson, *Louis Napoleon and the Second Empire* (New York, 1955), pp. 137–95. On the brilliance of French civilization in the Second Empire see Roger L. Williams, *The World of Napoleon III* (New York, 1962), passim.

Maximilian depleted his treasury and antagonized Austria, the United States, Britain, and even French liberals. His court remained brilliant and gay, but his propensity for speculation in politics and foreign affairs no longer served him well. Suddenly, when it was too late, he discovered that he had ignored the ultimate challenge to France's primacy: the rise of Prussia to a commanding position on the European continent.

Prussia's successful assault on the traditional order of power was the triumph of one man, Otto von Bismarck, the preeminent master of realpolitik in modern times. As early as 1851 this Prussian *Junker* had seen that German greatness lay less in liberalism than in national union under the Prussian king, to be imposed by force if necessary. By 1862 Bismarck, a man of immense talent and will, had established himself as minister-president of Prussia. Firmly in command of Prussia's bid for Continental leadership, he no longer faced the old restraints on national behavior. Fully supported by King William, Bismarck defied the Prussian liberals to build a magnificent army, commanded by the military genius, General Helmuth von Moltke. By 1864 he was prepared to assert Prussian predominance in Germanic affairs. When Danish nationalists threatened to absorb the neighboring duchies of Schleswig and Holstein, Bismarck ignored the British bluff that, "if Denmark had to fight, she would not fight alone" and quickly resolved the Schleswig-Holstein issue by force.

Despite Prussia's military preponderance, Bismarck had drawn Austria into an alliance against Denmark and then permitted Austria to retain Holstein. This maneuver entangled Vienna in a German question over which Bismarck might quarrel later. By astute diplomacy he isolated Austria from its potential allies, and in 1866, using Holstein's final disposition as a casus belli, overwhelmed Austria in war.[1] Moltke's brilliant campaign, which culminated in the Prussian victory at Sadowa, rendered Prussia the unchallengeable leader of German unification and brought Bismarck to the forefront of European diplomacy. "He represents," wrote American Minister John Lothrop Motley from Vienna, "what is the real tendency and instinct of the whole Prussian people, from King William to the most pacific Spiessburger at Potsdam. They all want a great Prussia."[5] Prussia now annexed all territories that had

[1]Theodore Ayrault Dodge, "Bismarck: The Strongest Personality Since Napoleon," *Forum* 19 (May 1895): 263–64. In March 1866, Minister John Lothrop Motley reported from Vienna that Austria and Prussia were preparing for war and predicted that the old Hapsburg monarchy would be no match for the Prussian. Motley to Secretary William H. Seward, despatch no. 156, March 26, 1866, Diplomatic Despatches, Austria, General Records of the Department of State, Record Group 59, National Archives (hereafter cited as RG59).
[5]George William Curtis, ed., *The Correspondence of John Lothrop Motley* (New York, 1900), 3:107.

separated Prussia itself from its territories along the Rhine; it organized
the remaining German states north of the Main River into the North
German Confederation.

Following Sadowa the American press recognized Prussia's
supremacy and lauded the North German Confederation as a legitimate
expression of German nationalism.[6] So completely did Prussia's crushing defeat of Austria threaten Europe's equilibrium, however, that
Charles Francis Adams in London wondered whether Prussia's rapid
ascent would not require "the interposition of other great powers . . .
to save Austria from sinking too low for the general safety." In Vienna,
Motley also recognized the shift in Europe's political order. "That in
Germany a great power of the first class has suddenly risen to over-
shadowing greatness," he wrote in August 1866, "is already a historical
fact."[7] Bismarck's success in upsetting the balance of power in central
Europe challenged France's traditional interests so clearly that Motley
predicted a French effort to check Prussian military power before it
exceeded that of France itself.

II

American diplomats throughout Europe anticipated the Paris government's coming decision for war. Napoleon, they noted, was determined
to keep the leading south German states out of Prussian hands and
thereby prevent the full unification of Germany. To Americans it was
equally clear that Bismarck would never accept a French veto of German unity; only the elimination of France from Germanic affairs would
enable him to bring the remaining German states into the Prussian
fold. After 1867 both countries prepared for the inevitable showdown.
Napoleon's tottering dynasty required some stirring triumph to shore
it up. Finally, in July 1870, the French emperor employed the issue of
a possible Hohenzollern succession to the Spanish throne to provoke
a crisis. When Bismarck refused to give guarantees for the future, the
Paris government declared war.[8] Motley, now in London, predicted
France's isolation, since Austria had no interest in another war against

---

[6]For the American reaction to the German success see J. G. Gazley, *American
Opinion of German Unification, 1848–1871* (New York, 1926), pp. 230–31.

[7]Adams to Seward, July 5, 1866, in U.S., Department of State, *Papers Relating to
Foreign Affairs . . . 1861*, pt. 1 (Washington, 1867), p. 146; Motley to Seward, July 11,
and August 15, 1866, ibid., pp. 675–76, 682.

[8]Dodge, "Bismarck: The Strongest Personality Since Napoleon," pp. 265–66. To
shouts of traitor, Adolphe Thiers warned the French Assembly against approving the
war; he was overwhelmed by a voice vote. Many in the minority, including Thiers, later
became prominent in French politics. See Wickham Hoffman, *Camp, Court, and Siege: A
Narrative of Personal Adventure and Observation During Two Wars: 1861–1865, 1870–1871* (New
York, 1877), p. 136.

Prussia. "What to the eyes of the French government seems the disturbance of the equilibrium of Central Europe," he wrote, "seems to other powers only the termination of French preponderance." Some Americans urged Washington to offer diplomatic, if not military, aid to France. Instead, President Ulysses S. Grant issued a Proclamation of Neutrality toward the Franco-Prussian War with the hope that it would limit Europe's involvement as well. During August the German avalanche swept over France. In September Secretary of State Hamilton Fish offered the good offices of the United States in negotiating a peace, but Bismarck rejected the offer, reminding U.S. Minister George Bancroft in Berlin that arbitration would merely encourage French resistance.[9] Bancroft advised Washington to refrain from further efforts at intervention.

During the early weeks of the war, editorial opinion in the United States overwhelmingly favored the German cause. Even before the Civil War Napoleon had lost favor with many Americans; his pro-Southern sympathies and Mexican venture merely aggravated that mistrust. Andrew D. White recalled in his *Autobiography*: "There was not at that time any human being whom I so hated and abhorred as Napoleon III. . . . As I looked up and distinctly saw him so near to me, there flashed through my mind an understanding of some of the great crimes of political history."[10] After the outbreak of the Franco-Prussian War, *Harper's Weekly* could detect only one party in the United States: "It is a war in which Louis Napoleon is on one side and the rest of the world upon the other." Later John Sherman reminded the Senate that "certainly at the beginning of this war the universal sympathy throughout the country was with the German people." Most Americans remembered the inestimable aid that Germans, in both the United States and Europe, had rendered the Union cause. What additionally motivated this pro-German sentiment was the conviction that Germany was the victim of French aggression; who ruled Spain, declared Senator Charles Sumner, was none of Napoleon's business. That the 2 million German-Americans scattered from New York to Wisconsin were potential Republicans encouraged Republican politicians and editors especially to take up the German cause.[11]

---

[9] John Jay to Fish, despatch no. 36, September 17, 1869, Diplomatic Despatches, Austria; Motley to Fish, despatch no. 404, July 28, 1870, Diplomatic Despatches, Great Britain; Bancroft to Fish, despatch no. 160, September 11, 1870, Diplomatic Despatches, Germany, RG59. Many French leaders complained bitterly that the United States refused to aid France. See Henry Blumenthal, *A Reappraisal of Franco-American Relations, 1830–1871* (Chapel Hill, NC, 1959), pp. 194–206.

[10] Andrew Dickson White, *Autobiography* (London, 1905), 1:96.

[11] For a detailed description of American reaction to the Franco-Prussian War during its first weeks see Gazley, *American Opinion of German Unification*, pp. 322–40.

On September 1, 1870, scarcely six weeks after the war began, Moltke's Prussian forces demolished the French army at Sedan. In Paris a provisional government quickly deposed Napoleon and proclaimed the Third French Republic. War critic Adolphe Thiers emerged as its first president. "Louis Napoleon," rejoiced Walt Whitman, "fully deserves his fate—I consider him by far the meanest scoundrel . . . that ever sat on a throne." Paris held out against a German siege. During the brief conflict, the south German states voluntarily entered the German Confederation, thus enabling German leaders to proclaim the new German Empire in the Hall of Mirrors at Versailles on January 18, 1871, ten days before the city of Paris finally capitulated.[12]

For reasons of sentiment and interest, Prussia's display of military might at Sedan sent waves of anti-German emotion across the United States. Much of this reversal of opinion reflected the country's historic sympathy for France, resurrected by the realization that Prussia had badly injured French prestige and pride. German power had become too efficient, and Bismarck's military triumphs, some feared, had elevated the scale of war to the disadvantage of civilization. "The next power or combination of powers that goes to war with Germany," predicted one American analyst, "will have to begin with a million men in hand."[13] Suddenly the new Germany seemed to represent the triumph, not of nationalism but of militarism and despotism, both centering in the Prussian monarchy and the Prussian *Junker* aristocracy. Contrasted to the new French Republic, the German Empire appeared dangerously centralized. Whitman reflected the shift of opinion when he said that "as things have gone on . . . I find myself now far more for the French than I ever was for the Prussians."[14]

For Motley the French disaster at Sedan had no precedent in modern history. Minister Bancroft in Berlin predicted that France would never forgive Germany for the humiliation it had suffered. "Even though the Germans were to demand no cession of territory, no indemnity, no advantage, except the glory of their arms," he wrote in September, "there would remain the wounded self-love of the French people."[15] Thus it was not strange that American observers found Bismarck's peace terms alarming. They regarded the large indemnity imposed on

---

[12]Richard Maurice Bucke, ed., *Calamus: A Series of Letters Written During the Years 1868–1880, by Walt Whitman to a Young Friend* (Boston, 1897), p. 73; Bancroft to Fish, despatch no. 181, January 18, 1871, Diplomatic Despatches, Germany, RG59.

[13]Quoted in Gazley, *American Opinion of German Unification*, p. 418.

[14]Bucke, *Calamus*, p. 75.

[15]Jay to Fish, despatch no. 153, September 13, 1870, Diplomatic Despatches, Austria; Motley to Fish, despatch no. 472, September 29, 1870, Diplomatic Despatches, Great Britain, RG59; Bancroft to Fish, September 21, 1870, in U.S., Department of State, *Papers Relating to Foreign Affairs . . . 1870* (Washingto, 1870), p. 207.

France, as well as the German absorption of Alsace and Lorraine, unjust to France and dangerous to the peace of Europe. Journals such as *Harper's Weekly* assumed that the populations of the annexed provinces were essentially French and preferred to remain so. That France would seek revenge seemed obvious enough. William James, the noted philosopher, predicted in late December 1870 that, "if Alsace and Lorraine be taken, there *must* be another war, for them and for honor." American Minister Elihu B. Washburne reported from Paris in February 1871: "It is safe to say that today there exists all over France such feeling of hatred toward the Prussians as is almost without a parallel in the history of nations."[16]

France's decline had an immediate impact on Russo-Turkish relations in the eastern Mediterranean. Shortly after Sedan, American Minister Edward Joy Morris reported from Constantinople:

> The impaired military power and prestige of France is a source of serious apprehension to the Porte. Upon that power it has always relied when the integrity of the Empire was assailed. . . . Outside of France, England is the only other power which may be regarded as a permanent ally of Turkey. Austria aims at her spoliation on the Adriatic and Danube. . . . If Prussia shall succeed in yet further enfeebling France, the position of the Porte will become very critical, and the more so as Russia has preserved her military resources intact.

He further predicted that Russia would soon claim its reward for supporting Prussia in 1870,[17] since St. Petersburg officials resented the clauses in the Treaty of Paris (1856) which neutralized the Black Sea and closed the Bosporus and Dardanelles to Russian war vessels. On October 31, 1870, the Russian government unilaterally renounced the Black Sea clauses of the treaty. France could not respond; Britain compensated by threatening war. Bismarck refused to desert Russia and suggested an international gathering to settle the Black Sea question.

At the London Conference of January 1871, Russia agreed that no country had the right to abrogate a treaty unilaterally. In the new arrangement it gained some modification of the Black Sea clauses, but some American diplomats in Europe wondered how long Turkey, a

---

[16]William James to Henry P. Bowditch, December 29, 1870, in Henry James, ed., *The Letters of William James* (Boston, 1920), 1:159; Washburne to Fish, February 28, 1871, in U.S., Department of State, *Papers Relating to the Foreign Relations of the United States, 1871* (Washington, 1871), p. 301 (hereafter cited as *FRUS*). For a full account of Washburne's career in Paris see Dale Clifford, "Elihu Benjamin Washburne: An American Diplomat in Paris, 1870–1871," *Prologue* 3 (Winter 1970): 161–74.

[17]Morris to Fish, September 2, 1870, *Foreign Affairs, 1870*, pp. 237–38.

failing power kept alive by British and French protection, would continue to deny Russia free access to the Mediterranean and render its extensive Black Sea coast comparatively worthless. For Secretary Fish in Washington such an unnatural condition, resting solely on the power and will of two Western countries, would remain a permanent provocation to Russia. What rendered the stability of the eastern Mediterranean even more precarious was the probability that London never would again fight for Turkish interests as it did in the Crimean War. Instead, Britain would attempt to defend its interests through direct negotiations with Russia.[18]

Fish exploited the Anglo-Russian crisis by demanding a settlement of the *Alabama* claims. Britain's failure to prevent the construction of Confederate cruisers in Liverpool during the Civil War still angered much of the North. Many Americans believed, moreover, that British support of the South had unnecessarily prolonged the war; Britain, they insisted, was responsible for much of the country's indebtedness and destruction. Sumner, still chairman of the Senate Foreign Relations Committee, insisted that Britain pay not only $125,000,000 for direct Union losses at sea but also an additional $2 billion to cover the costs that resulted from Britain's contribution to Southern resistance. Sumner raised the issue of indirect claims, not because he expected payment for them but to remind the British government of its monumental folly. Such British spokesmen as Lord Granville acknowledged Britain's responsibility. "Never since the world began," he wrote in October 1870, "has there been conduct more irritating than ours to the U.S. during the civil war. Our delight at the prospect of their break-up, our insulting language when the Northerners were in distress, our scant praise when they succeeded, . . . our bungling about the Alabama which resulted in the destruction of their whole mercantile marine. They would have been angels instead of being exaggerated Britishers if they had not felt sore."[19] Despite such admission of liability, London officials insisted that Britain's behavior during the Civil War was justified by law.

Unlike Sumner and other senators the administration desired a quick settlement. By late 1870 Fish had managed to create a corresponding mood of urgency in London. During the war scare of early

[18]For the view that Russia would not long tolerate Turkish control of the Straits see Wickham Hoffman to Fish, despatch no. 37, August 12, 1869, Diplomatic Despatches, France, RG59; Fish to Wayne MacVeagh, Constantinople, May 5, 1871, in *FRUS, 1871*, p. 903. On Britain's reluctance to fight for Turkey see Jay to Fish, despatch no. 177, November 12, 1870, Diplomatic Despatches, Austria, RG59.

[19]Quoted in Charles S. Campbell, *From Revolution to Rapprochement: The United States and Great Britain, 1783–1900* (New York, 1974), pp. 111–12.

1871 the Russians scattered rumors of possible U.S.-Russian cooperation. Convinced that such rumors troubled the British, Fish advised London that the United States would not necessarily remain neutral in the event of war. Indeed, he warned the British minister in Washington, Sir Edward Thornton, that in the event of an Anglo-Russian conflict the United States would be powerless to prevent the construction of commerce raiders. In November Thornton informed Fish that Britain was prepared to settle the *Alabama* claims promptly. Still refusing to accept responsibility for war losses and to pay damages accordingly, London insisted on arbitration. To this Fish eventually agreed, and a Joint High Commission met in Washington on February 27, 1871 to conduct the final negotiations. It deliberated for two months, but finally on May 8 the two countries signed the Treaty of Washington; the Senate approved it against little opposition. Unfortunately, the agreement provided only for arbitration of the claims. In the preliminary American case, Fish again presented the indirect claims; the British insisted that he withdraw them. When the tribunal convened at Geneva in June 1872, the two sides still failed to agree on this central issue. Only when the American members withdrew the indirect claims did the British submit their arguments and enable the tribunal to hear testimony. That body, in August, found the British guilty of negligence and awarded the United States $15,500,000.[20]

III

In Berlin, Bancroft believed firmly that the German Empire created a new promising equilibrium. He defended German policy in the Franco-Prussian War and lauded the creation of a unified Germany as the necessary source of stability in central Europe. Not even Bismarck's resolve to establish universal military service for all ablebodied men troubled Bancroft. The new German army, he assured Washington, merely reinforced Europe's stability. Surrounded by potential enemies, that country had no choice but to rely on its own strength and resources.[21] No less than Bancroft, writers and officials in the United States viewed

---

[20]Ibid., pp. 117–35. For Fish's warning to the British see Fish to Jay, instruction no. 89, December 8, 1870, Diplomatic Instructions, Austria, RG59; Joseph V. Fuller, "Hamilton Fish," in Samuel Flagg Bemis, ed., *The American Secretaries of State and Their Diplomacy* (New York, 1928), 7:156. On the Washington negotiations see James P. Baxter, III, "The British High Commissioners at Washington in 1871," *Proceedings of the Massachusetts Historical Society* 65 (1934): 334–57; and Goldwin Smith, *The Treaty of Washington, 1871: A Study of Imperial History* (Ithaca, NY, 1941). For a full study of the entire postwar *Alabama* controversy see Adrian Cook, *The Alabama Claims: American Politics and Anglo-American Relations, 1865–1872* (Ithaca, NY, 1975).

[21]Bancroft to Fish, September 21, 1870, *Foreign Affairs, 1870*, p. 207.

the federal structure of the new Germany with special satisfaction. The *New York Tribune* noted that the German government resembled that of the United States more than that of any other major power.[22] In a special message to Congress in February 1871, President Grant requested a minister for Berlin of rank and salary equal to those assigned to London and Paris. In his appeal for the appropriation the president declared:

> The Union of the States of Germany into a form of government similar in many respects to that of the American Union is an event that can not fail to touch deeply the sympathies of the people of the United States. . . . In it the American people see an attempt to reproduce in Europe some of the best features of our own Constitution. . . . Germany now contains a population . . . united, like our own, under one Government for its relations with other powers, but retaining in its several members the right and power of control of their local interests, habits, and institutions. . . . The adoption in Europe of the American system of union under the control and direction of a free people, educated to self-restraint, can not fail to extend popular institutions and to enlarge the peaceful influence of American ideas.[23]

Bismarck's final triumph in establishing the German Empire merely confirmed Bancroft's earlier optimism. "The young commonwealth," he wrote in January 1871, "comes into being with every wish to maintain the most friendly relations with the United States of America." The achievement of national unity rendered Germany, in Bancroft's estimation, Europe's leading proponent of the status quo. As he explained,

> Present appearances indicate that, after the close of this war, Germany will devote itself exclusively to the employments of peace. Compared with the great objects of this war, which involved the question of national existence, all conceivable causes for future war will appear trivial and indifferent. This war has carried sorrow into almost every family. . . . For the future no motive to war that is likely to occur can seem worthy of a repetition of equal sacrifices. Indeed, people of every degree long for peace, and for its continuance. I am, therefore, of the opinion that Germany in the coming years will devote its immense energies to the improvement of its

[22]*New York Tribune*, December 23, 1870, cited in Gazley, *American Opinion of German Unification*, p. 423.

[23]Message to Congress, February 7, 1871, in James D. Richardson, ed., *A Compilation of the Messages and Papers of the Presidents* (New York, 1917), 9:4074.

laws, the establishment of its liberties, and the development of its great resources.[21]

Later that year Bancroft reported a dinner at the American Legation, attended by many German officials: "We were all delighted at the calm and sincere manner in which Prince Hohenlohe declared that it was our success in our great struggle for union which made the union of Germany possible." That aura of good feeling continued.

However reassuring Bismarck's future policies, Germany's new preponderance in central Europe would compel adjustments in the agenda of every Continental power. To John Jay, the new American minister in Vienna, it was obvious at the outset that Bismarck's triumphs ultimately would drive Europe into a system of permanent alliances; they simply had eliminated too many elements from Europe's traditional peace structure. For generations Austria had served Russia's primary purpose of preventing Prussia's domination of central Europe. Bismarck not only expelled Austria from Germanic affairs and terminated that country's role as a central European power but also in the process pushed Austria toward the Balkans and into a direct rivalry with Russia. In that potential confrontation Austria had only a limited future without German support. It was not strange that Bismarck moved quickly in 1871 to excise the memories of 1866 and cement Germany's relations with Austria. Jay observed in April that Bismarck's entente cordiale with Austria was a "fixed part of no slight importance in my study of the future of Europe." Germany's concern for Eastern stability required an effective Austria in the European equilibrium as well as Austro-Russian cooperation in the Balkans.

Unfortunately, Bismarck's intentions for Austria directly challenged Russia's ambitions. Its sympathy for the Slavs in both the Austro-Hungarian and Turkish empires, Jay predicted, would one day threaten Austrian interests and force Vienna to call for the protection of Germany. In supporting Austria, Germany would become the ultimate barrier to Russian expansion. For that reason, Jay noted in September 1871, Russian leaders admitted freely that they had blundered when they permitted Prussia to crush France, whatever their immediate success in modifying the terms of 1856. Long-term Russian interests required the resurrection of French power and prestige. To Jay it appeared equally certain that France eventually would desire an alliance with Russia, compelling Germany at last to pay a heavy price for its military and diplomatic victories of 1870 and 1871. Jay explained his reasoning in a note to Secretary Fish in March 1872:

[21]Bancroft to Fish, January 7, February 1, and March 22, 1871, *FRUS, 1871*, pp. 355–56, 374, 379–80.

France, broken and dismembered, still counts as a factor in the
European problem; and the opinion gains ground that Prussia
blundered. When preferring tribute and territory to a policy of
magnanimity and friendship, she implanted in the French people
a sense of wrong, and gave to France perhaps for generations a
policy of revenge. . . . The general impression is, that apart from
the personal affection of Czar Alexander for his uncle Kaiser William, the power of united Germany has awakened in Russia dislike,
jealousy and fear; and that this spirit . . . must sooner or later
reach to a struggle, which will probably include France, and possibly the whole of Europe.[25]

Bismarck met the immediate necessity of isolating France and
stifling Russia's Pan-Slavic ambitions by negotiating the Three
Emperors' League. During September 1872 he arranged a meeting of
Kaiser William, Czar Alexander, and Emperor Francis Joseph in Berlin. In 1873 he announced the new informal entente which would restore
German influence in St. Petersburg as well as Vienna. American diplomats followed Bismarck's diplomatic maneuvering with unguarded
approval. Central Europe, with Russia in the background, stood arrayed
against France and on the side of peace. France responded to Bismarck's additional successes by paying its indemnity and stabilizing
its government. By 1875 France, having reorganized its army, was
prosperous and strong. That year J. C. Bancroft Davis, the new American minister in Berlin, reported that France's effective forces now
exceeded those of Germany.[26] Such military preparations, added to its
scarcely concealed animosity toward Germany, unleashed a war scare
across Europe. When German newspapers predicted a French invasion,
some diplomats suspected that Bismarck would exploit the threat by
ordering an attack on France. Immediately Russia, Britain, and Austria
warned Berlin that they would not tolerate another German invasion
of France. Actually Bismarck had ruled out a preventive war. "I would,"
he addressed the kaiser, "never advise your Majesty to declare war
forthwith, simply because it appeared that our opponent would begin
hostilities in the near future. One can never anticipate the ways of

---

[25]Jay to Fish, despatch no. 122, June 7, 1870, Diplomatic Despatches, Austria;
Jay to Fish, despatch no. 275, April 15, 1871, Diplomatic Despatches, Austria; Jay to
Fish, despatch no. 346, September 6, 1871, Diplomatic Despatches, Austria; Jay to Fish,
despatch no. 426, March 29, 1872, Diplomatic Despatches, Austria, RG59. For a superb
discussion of Germany's new burden in maintaining peace between Austria and Russia
see Schroeder, "The 'Balance of Power' System in Europe," pp. 29–31.
[26]J. G. Bancroft Davis to Fish, despatch no. 164, August 23, 1875, Diplomatic
Despatches, Germany, RG59.

divine providence securely enough for that."[27] American observers discounted the rumors; neither France nor Germany, they noted, desired war. "On my own judgment," wrote Davis in April 1875, "peace will be preserved so long as there continues to be a good understanding between Russia, Austria, and Germany."[28]

IV

Even as Europe's war scare abated, Turkey's impending retreat from the Balkans again endangered the peace. Several communities in Bosnia and Herzegovina, two provinces south of Austria, revolted against the Turks. In 1876 Bulgaria entered the rebellion. When the Turks crushed the Bulgarian uprising with immense cruelty, Serbia and Montenegro, in June, declared war on Turkey. Historically, the Turkish Empire in Europe had served Austrian no less than British interests in the Balkans. "If it were not for Turkey," admitted the noted Austrian Foreign Minister Count Andrássy in January 1875, "all these nationalist aspirations would fall down on our heads. . . . If Bosnia-Herzegovina should go to Serbia or Montenegro, or if a new state should be formed there which we cannot prevent, then we should be ruined and should ourselves assume the role of the 'Sick Man.' "[29] What troubled American observers in the new Balkan crisis was its threat to the survival of the Three Emperors' League. Russia could not rescue the revolting Slavs without confronting Austria, and Bismarck refused to make a choice. Turkey responded to the Balkan challenge by annihilating the Serbs, massacring the Bulgarians, and imposing terms that even London thought outrageous. Whereas the British, French, and Austrians sympathized with the Slavs, all three peoples had a primary interest in perpetuating Turkish rule in Europe. As one American journalist explained in August 1876,

> England has always been jealous of Russia, and has always thwarted her measures regarding Turkey, because Russia, enthroned at Constantinople, would seriously affect the balance of power, and would greatly reduce the influence of England in the Mediterranean. France has in general sympathized with England, and taken the same course for substantially the same reasons. Austria, the

[27]Bismarck quoted in Bernard Brodie, *Strategy in the Missile Age* (Princeton, NJ, 1959), p. 234.

[28]Davis to Fish, despatch no. 98, April 13, 1875, Diplomatic Despatches, Germany, RG59.

[29]Andrássy quoted in George H. Rupp, *A Wavering Friendship: Russia and Austria, 1876–1878* (Cambridge, MA, 1941), p. 39.

only other power seriously interested, has been opposed to Russia not so much because she favored the policy of France and England as because the dismemberment of Turkey might prove detrimental to the integrity of her own dominions. These are the reasons— these the motives which brought about the Crimean war. These are reasons—these the motives which at this time have made active interference in the affairs of Turkey by the Great Powers impossible, and which have induced them all to stand aloof and allow the Sultan and his subjects to settle their own difficulties.[30]

London invited the powers to Constantinople in December 1876 to discuss Turkey's peace terms. There it became clear that Turkey, supported by Britain, would reject any compromise with its defeated subjects. German leaders questioned Europe's perennial defense of Turkey, convinced that Britain had vastly overestimated Turkey's importance to its position in the eastern Mediterranean. Russia was now determined to rescue the Slavs; therefore, to encourage Austrian neutrality in a possible Russo-Turkish conflict, it promised Vienna control of Bosnia and Herzegovina. Then, in April 1877, Russia invaded Turkey. Britain and France refused to shoulder Turkey's resistance, as neither power had any interest in fighting another Crimean War. Late in the year Russian forces smashed the Turkish army and sent it into wild retreat toward Constantinople, while Bulgarian forces avenged the horrors of the previous year. Despite Turkey's military collapse, British officials in Constantinople encouraged the Turkish government to avoid direct negotiations with Russia. At the end London advised the Porte to obtain the best terms possible, although it reserved the right to protest later.[31] During February 1878 both London and Vienna urged Bismarck to call a conference as the last remaining chance to preserve Europe's peace. The Treaty of San Stefano, signed on March 3, recognized the independence of Romania, Serbia, and Montenegro. It created a large autonomous Bulgaria which extended from the Black Sea to the Aegean, but it did not deliver Bosnia and Herzegovina to Austria. Turkey had failed to defend British interests in the eastern Mediterranean and Austrian interests in the Balkans. From Constantinople, U.S. Minister Horace Maynard predicted yet another war.[32]

[30]Davis to Fish, despatch no. 184, October 11, 1875, Diplomatic Despatches, Germany; Edwards Pierrepont to Fish, despatch no. 58, October 25, 1876, Diplomatic Despatches, Great Britain, RG59; "The Insurrection in Turkey," *Frank Leslie's Illustrated Weekly* 42 (August 12, 1876): 370–71.
[31]Davis to Fish, despatch no. 598, February 26, 1877, Diplomatic Despatches, Germany, RG59; Freiherr von Werther to Bülow, Constantinople, January 14, 1877, in E. T. S. Dugdale, ed., *German Diplomatic Documents, 1871–1914* (London, 1928), 1:46; Prince Henry VII of Reuss to Bülow, Constantinople, January 15, 1878, ibid., pp. 59–60.
[32]Bismarck to Schweinitz, St. Petersburg, February 20, 1878, ibid., p. 65; Horace Maynard to Secretary William M. Evarts, March 6, April 3, 1878, in *FRUS, 1878* (Washington, 1878), pp. 859, 866.

To prevent Turkey's disintegration from creating another dangerous Russo-British confrontation, Bismarck called the Treaty of Paris signatories of 1856 to Berlin. Prime Minister Benjamin Disraeli, who agreed to represent Britain, declined to attend the conference until Russia agreed to place all peace conditions on the agenda. Britain opposed Bulgaria's extension to the Aegean and the Sea of Marmara, as well as Austria's claim to Bosnia and Herzegovina.[33] The spectacular Congress of Berlin, which convened in June 1878, marked the high point in the noted careers of Bismarck, Disraeli, and Andrássy. With Bismarck presiding, the British and Austrian leaders asserted their countries' interests in the Balkans. Bismarck, to protect the Three Emperors' League, hoped to defend Austrian demands without antagonizing Russia; ultimately, the Berlin settlement permitted him no easy escape. Britain and Austria managed to reduce the size of a still autonomous Bulgaria and deny it frontage on the Aegean. As a result, Austria gained administrative control of Bosnia and Herzegovina, thereby inaugurating its extension into the Balkans, and Britain acquired Cyprus and a protectorate over Asiatic Turkey. At Berlin, Britain reaffirmed its retreat from Turkey's defense, leaving Austria to pursue its interests in the Balkans with German support alone. American Minister Bayard Taylor in Berlin observed that the settlement would not guarantee the stability of the Balkans: "While the treaty of Berlin practically removes Turkey from the list of European powers, it established no permanent basis of peace."[34]

V

In the wake of the Congress of Berlin, Bismarck's efforts to isolate France and prevent conflict between Austria and Russia became more and more fragile. The court of St. Petersburg, convinced that Bismarck had been less than sympathetic, turned away from Berlin. Much of the Russian press complained that the Treaty of Berlin failed to recognize Russia's friendliness toward Prussia during the wars of 1866 and 1870. Bismarck responded to Russian coolness by going to Vienna and offering Austria a defensive treaty, signed in October 1879. Andrew D. White, now U.S. minister in Berlin, lauded the Dual Alliance as a guarantee of the status quo in eastern-central Europe; it was

---

[33]Count Munster to Bülow, London, March 9, 1878, in Dugdale, *German Diplomatic Documents*, 1:73; Count Munster to German Foreign Office, March 10, 1878, ibid., p. 76; Bülow to Count Munster, March 11, 1878, ibid., pp. 76–77; Count Munster to Bülow, May 2, 25, 1878, ibid., pp. 96–97; John A. Kasson to Evarts, March 30, 1878, in *FRUS, 1878*, pp. 34–35.

[34]Bayard Taylor to Evarts, despatch no. 32, July 15, 1878, Diplomatic Despatches, Germany, RG59.

not an anti-Russian pact. To German officials, White reported, the alliance "is strictly what it claims to be, that is, one between the two German speaking nations with reference to dangers which may beset them, and that it shall not be developed into anything more offensive to Russia than it now is. It is felt that the Emperor of Germany, in view of his close personal connection with the Russian Imperial family, has gone quite as far as he can be expected to go."[35] White noted accurately that London's distrust of Russia assured British support of the Dual Alliance. Lord Salisbury, Britain's foreign secretary, declared in October that "I believe that in the strength and independence of Austria lie the best hopes of European stability and peace. What has happened in the last few weeks justified us in hoping that Austria, if attacked, would not be alone."[36] The Paris government regarded the Dual Alliance as a further assault on French leadership and prestige. Bismarck's renewal of the Three Emperors' League in 1881 relieved the Austro-Russian rivalry in the Balkans by including a mutual agreement to defend the Bosporus and Dardanelles against any attempt of another power to force a passage through them in defiance of the Treaty of Paris.[37]

During the following year Bismarck completed his defense of Austria with the Triple Alliance of Germany, Austria, and Italy. For him the chief purpose of the new alliance was to cover Austria's Italian frontier in the event of war. What drove Italy into the Bismarckian system was its rivalry with France over the occupation of Tunis in North Africa. Bismarck, however, assured the London government that the Triple Alliance was in no way aimed at British interests in the Mediterranean.[38] With Britain again placing its concern for European stability in German hands, France's isolation seemed complete. In Berlin, U.S. Minister Aaron A. Sargent admitted that the Triple Alliance revealed the hand of a master statesman, but it seemed to obscure, rather than clarify, Europe's diplomatic future. He expressed his doubts in a letter of May 7, 1883:

> While war is not likely to result, in that the war-game is too costly to be hastily commenced, and the real interests of Europe counsel peace; and while the real motive of the recently announced Triple

[35]White to Evarts, November 18, 1879, in *FRUS, 1880* (Washington, 1880), pp. 392–93; "The German-Austrian Alliance," *Nation* 29 (October 23, 1879): 269–70.

[36]W. J. Hoppin to Evarts, despatch no. 78, October 18, 1879, Diplomatic Despatches, Great Britain, RG59.

[37]Bismarck to Prince Henry VII of Reuss, January 29, 1880, in Dugdale, *German Diplomatic Documents*, 1:107–08.

[38]Bismarck to German Foreign Office, May 22, 1882, ibid., p. 125; Count Hatzfeldt to Prince Henry VII of Reuss, Vienna, May 4, 1882, ibid., p. 122.

Alliance is to secure peace, and perhaps may tend to make a war extra hazardous to France, still the announcement of this alliance has stirred up ill-feeling in the latter country and compelled it to realize that it is isolated in Europe, and must keep quiet under the penalty of receiving the blows of all its Continental neighbors. This condition of things is galling to a high-spirited nation; and however it may have been inclined to peace, and may still, from policy, so continue, there is a necessary revival of the old antagonisms, a setting of the teeth, and the muttered remark that France can wait.[39]

For American observers in Europe the Austro-German alliance remained Europe's primary diplomatic reality; its very importance held Russia in the German orbit and directed its energies toward Asia Minor and Central Asia. During the 1880s Britain and Italy settled their differences in the Mediterranean, and only France's continuing quarrel over Tunis prevented it from forming a three-power entente. In March 1885, the *Nation* predicted the eventual formation of this new power alignment in Europe. "The frivolous encouragements of Germany, her caresses, her demonstrations on all colonial questions," ran its conclusion, "cannot blind a serious mind to the brutal fact that sooner or later there must be a new trial of strength between France and Germany. It would be therefore for the interest of France, without committing herself to any important course, to draw nearer to England and to Italy, since England and Italy are allied by necessity."[40] American diplomats, still placing their hopes for peace on Bismarck's diplomacy, approved the renewal of the Triple Alliance in 1887. Bismarck that year succeeded in negotiating the Reinsurance Treaty with Russia in which the two countries promised to remain neutral if one went to war. To him the arrangement was comforting because it eliminated, during its existence, the possibility of a Franco-Russian alliance.

Bismarck assaulted Britain's isolation from the Continent in January 1889 by offering that country a mutual defense pact against France. His reasoning was acute:

England and Germany are not threatened with an attack by any Power except France. Nothing but Austro-Russian complications could drive Germany into war with Russia, and as a war even at the best offers Germany no acceptable compensation, we must do our utmost to avoid Austria being involved in war. The only element, threatening to these two friendly powers, is seen to be France,

[39]Aaron A. Sargent to Secretary Frederick T. Frelinghuysen, despatch no. 148, May 7, 1883, Diplomatic Despatches, Germany, RG59.
[40]"England and Italy," *Nation* 40 (March 1885): 198.

the only neighbor common to both. . . . British foreign policy will enjoy freedom of movement in all directions, if only she is fully protected from the French war-danger by alliances. . . . Neither France nor Russia will break the peace, if they are told officially that, if they do so, they will at once find England against them for a certainty. They will only break it, if they are allowed to hope that it may be possible to attack the peaceable nations of Europe one after the other. Once it is clearly understood that England would be protected against a French attack by a German alliance and Germany against a French attack by an English alliance, I consider the peace of Europe assured for the duration of such a published Treaty.[11]

Lord Salisbury in London acknowledged the importance of British-German friendship to Europe's peace but had no inclination to defy Britain's established policy of "splendid isolation." He postponed his decision long enough to consign Bismarck's proposal to oblivion.[12]

Germany's Kaiser William I died in the spring of 1888, and three months later Crown Prince William succeeded him. The young man ascended to the throne deeply prejudiced against Russia; his immediate trips to Rome and Vienna demonstrated his special faith in the Triple Alliance. Despite Bismarck's entreaties, William II refused to renew the Russian treaty in 1890, as he saw no future in German-Russian relations. Having lost control of an essential element of German policy, Bismarck tendered his resignation in March 1890. In St. Petersburg, U.S. minister George W. Wurts reported Russia's reaction: "It is at last acknowledged here—as in France—that the tenure of office of the late Chancellor of the German Empire was a guarantee of peace; and in this respect the Russian press . . . has, with some few exceptions, rendered an unexpected tribute to the benefit derived from his influence."[13]

From France came a similar tribute. "Since the war," wrote one American observer, "the chief object of Bismarck has been the preservation of peace. He has always shown the greatest courtesy to all the men, whoever they are, who have been in power in France. A conviction

---

[11]Bismarck to Count Hatzfeldt, January 11, 1889, in Dugdale, *German Diplomatic Documents*, 1:370–71.

[12]Count Hatzfeldt to Bismarck, January 16, 1889, ibid., pp. 372–73.

[13]George W. Wurts to Secretary James G. Blaine, despatch no. 85, March 24, 1890, Diplomatic Despatches, Russia, RG59. Russian leaders, Wurts reported, did not anticipate any immediate change in Russo-German relations, but he noted that the impulsive nature of the young kaiser caused uneasiness in St. Petersburg. Fears were general that a termination of the Russo-German alliance would unsettle Europe. See, for example, "The European Equilibrium," *Nation* 50 (January 16, 1890): 46; Sir Charles W. Dilke, "Critics of 'Problems of Greater Britain,' " *North American Review* 151 (July 1890): 44–46; and "The Peace of Europe," *New York Times*, September 4, 1891.

has thus by degrees been formed in all French minds that the policy
of Bismarck with regard to France was defensive, not offensive; he was
even anxious to soothe the wounded feelings of France."[14] British leaders agreed; for instance, Sir Charles W. Dilke commented in the *North
American Review* that "one great influence on the side of peace, indeed,
has lately gone, for Prince Bismarck in the last fourteen years has been
a powerful factor on the side of peace preservation throughout the
continent of Europe."[15] It was left for *Puck*, on April 2, 1890, to pass
judgment on the passing of Bismarck from the European diplomatic
scene:

> Strange ending of it all! The Iron Hand
> That swept up states into an Empire, held
> The hammer of unchallenged power, to weld
> Disunion into strength, make weakness grand,
> And forge the war-sword of a Fatherland—
> This mighty hand whose lightest sign compelled
> The will of Europe; hand that smote and felled,
> Made or unmade, as the stern spirit planned—
> This hand at last is loosed, nor more shall hold
> Its guiding grasp upon a nation's arm,
> Or mark for her the path of peace again.
> Let him go—an Emperor is come too bold
> To need him, or to heed the land's alarm—
> A boy who plays at making over Men!

VI

Germany's renewal of the Triple Alliance in May 1891 inaugurated
the diplomacy that led to the Franco-Russian alliance of 1894. Still,
the Russian desertion of its former connection with Germany came
hard. Nikolai Karlovich Giers, Russia's brilliant foreign minister from
1882 to 1895, favored the Three Emperors' League to an alliance with
France; indeed, he attempted without success to renew the eastern
alliance in March 1890. Thereafter he opposed Russian membership
in any military arrangement aimed at Germany, but Czar Alexander
III, not he, controlled Russian policy. Alexander compelled Giers to
negotiate the Franco-Russian entente of August 27, 1891, which awarded
France a consultative pact against Germany, and Russian support
against Britain in the eastern Mediterranean. The Russian foreign office

[14]*Nation* 50 (April 17, 1890): 311.
[15]Dilke, "Critics of 'Problems of Greater Britain,' " pp. 44–45.

assured new American Minister White that the entente would enable Russia to restrain France and thereby contribute to Europe's stability.[16] In the Franco-Russian convention of August 1892, France acquired further guarantees against Germany, while Russia gained promises of support against Austria. Alexander, favoring still closer ties to France, permitted the Russian squadron to visit Toulon in October 1893. The French were delighted; Franco-Russian cooperation in the Mediterranean would at last enable France to challenge Anglo-Italian naval supremacy along the North African coast. Paris acquired no naval agreement but pushed for mutual guarantees against Germany, without which it could not support Russia in the east. Alexander accepted the French demands, but he reminded the French that Russia had no interest in a war of revenge against Germany. The pact freed both France and Russia to pursue their ambitions in Africa, Asia, and the Middle East, largely in competition with Britain. On January 4, 1894, the French government approved a military convention; the Franco-Russian alliance, still largely secret, was now complete.[17]

To American diplomats and writers Russia's gradual alignment with France between 1891 and 1894 did not presage immediate war; instead, it multiplied enormously the burdens of European diplomacy. At the heart of Europe's stability had been Bismarck's capacity to control the policies of Germany's allies. The Three Emperors' League had compelled Russia to recognize Austrian interests in the Balkans. The Triple Alliance limited both Franco-Italian rivalry in the Mediterranean and Austro-Italian rivalry in Europe. By isolating France on the Continent, Bismarck eliminated the danger of an open Franco-German conflict. Franco-Russian diplomacy, however, broke the restraints of the Bismarckian system. As early as October 1890, W. J. Stillman warned that two, and only two, possible aggressions endangered the peace of Europe. "The first and most menacing of these," he wrote, "is the attempt of the Russians to regain control of Bulgaria, Servia, and the South Slavic tribes generally, and the other is the determination of France to recover the lost provinces of Alsace and Lorraine. I defy the worst alarmist in France to point out any other."[18]

---

[16]George F. Kennan, *The Decline of Bismarck's European Order: Franco-Russian Relations, 1875–1890* (Princeton, NJ, 1979), pp. 407–10. Kennan lamented Giers's failure to save the Russo-German treaty: "Giers was thus left pitifully alone with his doubts and anxieties: the only one to regret the collapse of a structure of relationships on which the peace of Europe had reposed for a decade; the only one to sense in this development the preparation of the eventual German-Russian war from which no good *could* come, only the destruction of both Empires" (p. 409). For White's observation see White, *Autobiography*, 2:32.

[17]On the Franco-Russian negotiations see A. J. P. Taylor, *The Struggle for Mastery in Europe* (Oxford, 1954), pp. 325–45.

[18]W. J. Stillman, "Italy and the Triple Alliance," *Nation* 51 (October 30, 1890), p. 340.

The U.S. minister in Vienna, Bartlett Tripp, feared that the Franco-Russian alliance would unleash the ambitions of both powers. "The Alliance of France and Russia," he noted, "is . . . of possible alarm to the nations composing the *Triple Alliance*. . . . They see in the recent fetes and receptions at Toulon and Paris, a re-opening of the Eastern question as well as that of Alsace and Lorraine."[49]

At stake in the former threat was peace between Austria and Russia, even Austria's survival as a factor in the European equilibrium. Austria's primary interest in Balkan stability consigned to Russia alone the promising and glorious task of delivering the Slavs from Austrian and Turkish rule. The triumph of Slavic nationalism, whether inspired by Russia or not, would destroy Austria's polyglot empire. Beyond Austria's consequent decline as a major power loomed the ultimate confrontation between Germans and Slavs, with consequences for eastern-central Europe that few cared to predict. Some American observers questioned the shortsightedness of Austria's Slavic minorities who blindly opposed Austrian unification when that country, in alliance with Germany, comprised the only barrier to Russian expansion into central Europe and the Balkans.[50] Any disintegration of the Austro-Russian equilibrium in the Balkans would set off a war. "The Eastern question," editorialized the *Nation*, "cannot be reopened without endangering the peace of the world. The smallest spark may set fire to the combustible materials which for the last twenty years have been accumulating in Europe."[51]

Of czarist Russia the American people knew little. Throughout the nineteenth century the United States had enjoyed friendly relations with this remote empire; the two countries converged in their mutual desire to protect their interests against the ambitions of western Europe. Russia had adopted the values, style, and professionalism of the other European powers, but still that nation remained, for western Europeans and Americans alike, a strange, remote, and unknown land. Much of that immense region stayed in social and political darkness.[52] For centuries, diplomats complained, the principle of territorial expansion had

[49]Tripp to Secretary Walter Q. Gresham, despatch no. 62, January 4, 1894, Diplomatic Despatches, Austria, RG59.

[50]Stillman, "Italy and the Triple Alliance," p. 340; Edward A. Freeman, "Dangers to the Peace of Europe," *Forum* 12 (November 1891): 304–09.

[51]"The European Equilibrium," p. 47.

[52]Travelers and writers throughout the century noted the general social, economic, and political backwardness of Russia. William R. Thayer observed in November 1891 that Russian power had no relationship to Russian civilization: "What the riches of Italy were to the Germans of the fifth century, what the settlements of Germany were to the Huns in the eleventh century, what the plains of Hungary . . . were to the Turks of the seventeenth century,—such is civilized Europe to the Russians to-day." See William R. Thayer, "The Armed Truce of the Powers," *Forum* 12 (November 1891): 322.

guided Russian policy. Momentarily halted in Europe, Russia continued to exploit the weakness of Asiatic Turkey, strengthen its position
in northern Persia, and push across central Asia toward Afghanistan
and India. So enormous were Russia's territories, so great its population, so expansive its tradition, that many Westerners regarded Russia
as the ultimate danger to their security. Scarcely reassuring was its
declining intellectual, political, and commercial dependence on the
West.[53] British diplomat Cecil Spring-Rice reminded Theodore Roosevelt in September 1896:

> It looks like the gathering of great forces for a struggle, not in the
> immediate (that would be better) but in the far future. . . . Russia
> is self sufficient. She is also practically invulnerable to attack. She
> is growing and has room to grow. . . . Owing to Alsace and Lor-
> raine, Europe is hopelessly divided, and it looks as if commercial
> and colonial jealousies would divide England and Germany in a
> similar manner. Taking all these things together, it is not at all
> improbable that Europe may be in a given period at the mercy of
> a power really barbarous but with a high military organization. . . .
> No power will attack Russia—no one can afford to. Russia there-
> fore has simply to bide her time.[54]

For Roosevelt, Russia was an appalling problem. "It has always seemed
to me," he had written in August, "that the Germans showed shortsightedness in not making some alliance that would enable them to
crush Russia. Even if in the dim future Russia should take India and
become the preponderant power of Asia, England would merely be
injured in one great dependency; but when Russia grows so as to crush
Germany, the crushing will be once for all."[55]

French *revanche* menaced Europe only as it allied itself with the
other elements of European conflict: Russia's ambitions in eastern
Europe and the Balkans. "Every schoolboy in America," Stillman noted,
"must know by this time that France will declare war on the first
convenient opportunity, and attack Germany with a fury such as she
has never shown in any previous war." Other American observers

[53]On Russian expansionism see Theodore Ayrault Dodge, "A Glance at the Euro-
pean Armies," *Forum* 13 (July 1892): 563; Arminius Vambery, "Russia and England,"
North American Review 160 (May 1895): 561–66; and George Washburn, "The Coming
of the Slav," *American Monthly Review of Reviews* 17 (February 1898): 200. Washburn of
Robert College, Constantinople, regarded Russia as already the dominant power of
Europe.

[54]Spring-Rice to Roosevelt, September 14, 1896, in Stephen Gwynn, ed., *The Letters
and Friendships of Sir Cecil Spring Rice: A Record* (London, 1929), 1:210–11.

[55]Roosevelt to Spring-Rice, August 5, 1896, in Elting E. Morison, ed., *The Letters
of Theodore Roosevelt* (Cambridge, MA, 1951), 1:555.

agreed that France's ultimate objectives in Europe rendered war inevitable. "It does not follow," cautioned Edward A. Freeman in the *Forum*, "that every Frenchman is eager to go to war with Germany to-day or to-morrow; but assuredly every Frenchman longs to win back the lands which were recovered by Germany in 1871, and every Frenchman is ready to go to war with Germany for that end at any favorable moment."[56] Except for French ambition, Slavic and central Europe might face the Eastern question with comparative ease. What gave the impending crisis its special character was the fact that the Russian and French threats would break on central Europe at the same moment. Nothing would unleash Russian power across eastern Europe and the Balkans more assuredly than a massive French assault on Germany. No American saw the essentially tragic nature of the Franco-Russian alliance more clearly than did William R. Thayer, who observed in November 1891:

> Russia is . . . the center of the warlike storm-area to-day. Eliminate her from European politics, and the other powers would have no plausible excuse for keeping up their armaments, because France, in spite of her grievances and wrath, would see the hopelessness of dashing her head against Germany supported by Austria and Italy. The possibility of winning Russia as an ally to strike Germany "between the hammer and the anvil" has given French revenge a concrete practical form, and has forced Germany to stand by her guns. But the Russian monster threatens not only Germany; as Napoleon discerned eighty years ago, he endangers all western Europe.

One day, Thayer predicted, France and Germany would forget their lesser quarrels and stand together against the Cossack invader.[57] Perhaps Russian control of Slavic Europe would force a coalition of all the Western powers.

What gave American observers a special sense of foreboding in the mid-1890s was not merely the clash of national purposes but also the power that sustained it. Never before had Europe's leading nations embarked on such an insatiable quest for weapons. The Continental powers possessed 20 million men trained for war, 3 million under arms prepared to march. "Every city," wrote Thayer, "has its barracks and parade-ground; every frontier frowns with a double row of fortifications. At the end of the nineteenth century, Europe, from the Douro to the

---

[56]Stillman, "Italy and the Triple Alliance," p. 340; Freeman, "Dangers to the Peace of Europe," p. 301.
[57]Thayer, "The Armed Truce of the Powers," pp. 321, 323.

Don, is a camp whereon ten times three hundred thousand of her able-bodied men are bivouacking, ready at a sign to spring to arms and slay each other. This spectacle is without parallel in the history of the world."[58] The mobilization of such huge quantities of manpower and resources required the constant incitement of nationalistic emotions, certain to create insecurity in other states and provoke them to additional measures of defense. Armaments and preparations of such magnitude sustained a crisis mood. "Europe is one great armed camp," Tripp reported from Vienna, "and every lightning flash from diplomatic wires is like the firing of a sentry gun—a call to arms."[59]

Many Americans blamed Germany for this state of military preparedness and tension, but not all. Its new constitution of 1871 provided for the military training of all ablebodied men. Whatever Bismarck's responsibility for inaugurating the system of peace-time military conscription, it was the zeal of other powers to match or excel Germany's military program that sustained the competition. By the 1890s some observers regarded France as more responsible than Germany for Europe's military expenditures. According to Stillman, "the present policy of France is to exhaust the finances of the triple alliance by the necessity of constantly increasing its armaments to keep pace with hers; and, trusting to her greater wealth to hold out longest, she goes on increasing her army and spending for new guns."[60] Russia's army was huge, disciplined, poorly equipped, and largely illiterate. Not even Napoleon's army, wrote American military analyst Theodore Ayrault Dodge, was as sound as the French army of the 1890s, whose infantry was superb and its artillery the best in Europe. The German army was magnificent but not necessarily better than the French. Both armies possessed a remarkable esprit de corps; the choice between the two, wrote Dodge, was narrow. The Austrian and Italian armies were smaller and inferior in training and spirit. Never had Europe been so perfectly prepared for war; never was the morale of its leading armies so high. "But Europe," Dodge noted, "stands aghast at her own weapons. War is *quasi*-suicide; and Europe gazes at the blade she holds against her vitals and shrinks from the thrust. The dread is born of certainty that a war will be a general one, of the uncertainty of its issue."[61] War among powers so heavily armed would endanger territorial and political arrangements that had held for generations.

[58]Ibid., p. 312; "Italy's Burdens Under the Triple Alliance," *Nation* 50 (April 17, 1890): 312–13.
     [59]Tripp to Secretary Richard Olney, despatch no. 175, January 18, 1896, Diplomatic Despatches, Austria, RG59.
     [60]Stillman, "Italy and the Triple Alliance," p. 341.
     [61]Dodge, "A Glance at the European Armies," pp. 561–73.

Europe's division into two alliance systems, each confident of its military superiority, placed future peace on the altar of diplomatic inflexibility and the deterrent power of the alliance structure. It was not strange that Tripp predicted a troubled future for Europe, explaining in his report from Vienna of January 4, 1894 that

> I see no possibility of the great nations of Russia and Germany at present submitting to a peaceful solution of the questions of international differences now impending; political differences must therefore continue to be settled by resort to arms, and the slightest provocation on the part of some of the smaller nations, is liable at any moment to bring on a general engagement of all the armies of Europe. Nothing but wise statesmanship and the existing fear on the part of the nations of the terrible result of such a contest can avert the impending conflict which each moment becomes more imminent.[62]

VII

Peace rested on the capacity of the central alliance to neutralize the Franco-Russian danger. British membership alone, Bismarck had argued, would give it the necessary preponderance of power. "England's neutrality," observed Dodge, "would leave the scales very evenly balanced between the rival alliances; England casting her lot with the Triple Alliance would make this the stronger and tend toward peace, which England has also every motive to desire." The *Nation* agreed, believing that any attack on such a combination of powers would be hopeless.[63] So obvious appeared the British interest in the success of the Triple Alliance that the *New York Times* predicted, on August 15, 1892, that a European war would bring Britain into the Triple Alliance to preserve what remained of European stability.

Actually, Britain's policy toward the Continent remained ambivalent. The decline of eastern European stability, as dramatized by the collapse of the former Russo-German entente, disturbed British officials but not sufficiently to make policy changes. Britain limited its interests to western Europe and the Mediterranean and acknowledged no similar interest east of the Rhine. London accepted German dominance of central Europe; it recognized Austria's importance to Eastern stability

---

[62]Tripp to Gresham, despatch no. 62, January 4, 1894, Diplomatic Despatches, Austria, RG59.
[63]Dodge, "A Glance at the European Armies," p. 573; *Nation* 58 (January 25, 1894): 59; Arthur Silva White, "An Anglo-American Alliance," *North American Review* 158 (April 1894): 486–88.

and assumed that it would maintain its position in alliance with Germany. Historically, what protected eastern Europe and the Balkans against extensive aggression had been a variety of agreements, partnerships, and mutual interests—all rendered tenuous by the declining stability of the Balkans—that gave the region some cohesion at the price of progress and self-determination. Freeman observed that Europe's peace and stability could "be kept only by crushing the hopes of nations and by refusing them their lawful rights."[64] Britain had not created the eastern European peace system and perhaps only partially understood it. This system, however, enabled Britain decade after decade to experience the stability of a vital portion of Europe where it had a minimum of immediate concern and no control. Ultimately, it was the stability of eastern Europe that permitted Britain its autonomous foreign policy. British isolation would not survive the breakdown of eastern European or Balkan stability, or any war fought over the political and territorial status of eastern Europe.[65]

Britain's refusal to define its interests in Europe's changing configuration of power deeply troubled Berlin. London's elusiveness denied the German government every possibility of creating a consistent policy toward that important country. Unable to achieve an understanding with the British regarding Europe's future, German officials hoped to prevent one between Britain and France. In July 1891, Leo von Caprivi, the new German chancellor, noted the English-French rivalry in Africa. "So long as England and France still *want* something in that part of the world," he wrote, "the uncertainty will keep them in rivalry. But if they *get* it they will live at peace beside one another—a condition which we ought not to hurry on." Thereafter the German kaiser noted repeatedly his pleasure at Anglo-French misunderstandings. Following a French and Russian rejection of the British proposal regarding Egypt in 1896, William II noted that "England has made a move and is compromised. Her flirtation with Gallo-Russia is upset. That is all I wanted. I am delighted." That year the German foreign minister, Baron von Marschall, looked forward to the time when all the Continental powers "would be united in one thought, which is that England is never any help and often does harm."[66] If they could not turn Britain into a friend, German officials sought to avoid quarrels and to induce London

---

[64]Freeman, "Dangers to the Peace of Europe," p. 299.

[65]For an analysis of British policy toward eastern Europe in the nineteenth century see Paul W. Schroeder, "Munich and the British Tradition," *Historical Journal* 19 (March 1976): 234–41.

[66]Memorandum by Chancellor Caprivi for Baron von Rotenhan and Holstein, July 20, 1891, Dugdale, *German Diplomatic Documents* (London, 1929), 2:143; Baron von Marschall to Count zu Eulenburg, February 23, 1896, ibid., p. 429. Many writers of the time resented Britain's refusal to accept any responsibility toward the Continent.

with concessions to pursue policies that conformed to German interests.[67] Such diplomatic maneuvering failed to solidify the fundamental
German-British interest in European stability, or to commit Britain to
any understandable or predictable course of action toward the Continent.

Despite the size of the Atlantic, the relationship of the United
States to Europe in the late nineteenth century differed only in degree
and tradition from that of isolated Britain. However determined its
avoidance of a balance-of-power diplomacy, the United States, like
Britain, had powerful economic, political, and intellectual ties to Europe.
The country had its scholars, editors, political writers, and diplomats
who understood that the United States had been the special beneficiary
of the European equilibrium. They understood as well that America's
perennial freedom to concentrate on its domestic concerns, with little
commitment to armaments and none to the definition or defense of
interests in Europe, rested on the persistence of the Continent's fundamental stability. Americans also recognized that the disintegration
of the precise conditions within Europe which had preserved the peace
rendered the concept of isolation, as embodied in the Monroe Doctrine,
obsolete. American interests were becoming too universal, too enmeshed
in the affairs of Europe to be entrusted to the oceans alone; no longer
was the European equilibrium self-contained. In a narrowly balanced
continent unable to resolve the issues that divided it, the policies of
the uncommitted countries carried the burden of future peace and
security. For some, including Alfred Thayer Mahan, the United States
had arrived at that stage in its development where it could influence
events and policies in regions that lay well beyond its own shores. By
the nature of their reach and interests, powerful nations touch the
interests of others more decidedly than do the weak. American power
alone had created objectives and obligations that did not exist in previous decades. No less than other countries, said Mahan, the United
States must "assume an inevitable task, an appointed lot in the work
of upholding the common interests of civilization."[68]

One powerful coterie of writers, mindful of the diplomatic barriers, concluded logically that the United States and Britain, acting
together, could still protect their interests from the burgeoning dangers
posed by the predictable clash of Europe's two alliance systems. Such
writers agreed that the major concerns of the two countries lay essentially in the inviolability of the world's ocean routes. So intertwined
were those interests on the seas that any circumstances that promoted

[67]Ibid., p. xii.
[68]Alfred T. Mahan, "Possibilities of an Anglo-American Reunion," *North American Review* 159 (November 1894): 558.

or endangered the interests of one would affect similarly the interests of the other.[69] In the Atlantic especially the objectives of the two powers had been identical. The defense of established interests there seemed to demand a high level of Anglo-American cooperation. No power other than the United States, observed some writers, would enable Britain to defend its interests in south Africa, the Middle East, and south Asia. What Britain and the United States might achieve in alliance, Sidney Sherwood described in the *Forum* of March 1896:

> To attack this alliance would mean to attack at once the strongest navy in the world and the country which could furnish unlimited men of the best fighting quality and with inexhaustible economic resources behind them. It would be folly for any power short of united Europe to attack at once the whole English-speaking world— a folly which Europe would not be likely to commit. . . . The British Empire and the United States acting together would literally control the industries and commerce of the world. Add to this the probable fact that the states of Central and South America would for the most part join with us in an alliance which guaranteed the principles of the Monroe Doctrine, the combination would be absolutely irresistible.[70]

This advocacy of Anglo-American cooperation anticipated only the defense of maritime interests. Even those who proposed a league of armed neutrality between the United States and Britain argued that it would serve the interests of peace, not in Europe but throughout the oceans of the world. Almost invariably British and American writers who favored closer British-American ties, no less than the foreign offices, defended policies of abstention from Europe's alliance arrangements.[71] Defending interests on the high seas appeared far less dangerous and costly than assuming responsibility for the peace of Europe.

Unfortunately, those who advocated a larger American role in world politics, if only to strengthen the nation's historic ties to Britain in the Atlantic, did not dispel the illusions of isolation created by successive decades of actual noninvolvement in European politics. International stability, based on the European equilibrium and anchored

---

[69]Sidney Sherwood, "An Alliance with England the Basis of a Rational Foreign Policy," *Forum* 21 (March 1896): 95, 98–99.

[70]Ibid., pp. 96–97; Lord Charles Beresford, "Possibilities of an Anglo-American Reunion," *North American Review* 159 (November 1894): 572. Admiral Beresford argued that a British-American alliance "would deter other nations from attacking that which for the moment appeared inadequately defended."

[71]Sir George S. Clarke, "A Naval Union with Great Britain," *North American Review* 158 (March 1894): 363–64; White, "An Anglo-American Alliance," pp. 485–86, 490–93; Mahan, "Possibilities of an Anglo-American Reunion," pp. 552–53.

elsewhere to British power and diplomacy, was ultimately taken for granted, and its essential contribution to American security all but forgotten. By the 1890s Americans generally no longer recognized the nation's vital stake in Europe's peace. The restoration of the Continent after the Napoleonic Wars created conditions of such stability that the average citizen of the United States, enjoying perennial security at relatively little cost, began to put his faith in the reality of geographic isolation itself. That isolation, resting on the vast ocean that separated Europe from America, wrote Sherwood, "was the great fact which lay at the bottom of our traditional foreign policy of isolation."[72] This gradual identification of American security with the Atlantic, rather than with a body of precise political conditions in Europe, which after 1890 were subject to vast dislocations, created the foundations of the pervading U.S. isolationism. Whatever happened in Europe, ran the burgeoning isolationist argument, it could not challenge the historic security of the American people.

---

[72]Sherwood, "An Alliance with England," p. 92.

CHAPTER
THIRTEEN

World Power:
The McKinley Years*

AMERICA'S EXPLOSIVE RISE to industrial greatness during the closing decades of the nineteenth century produced ambivalent reactions in the minds of European statesmen. A nation's significance in world politics hinges not only upon its intrinsic power but also upon the judgment of others as to how and under what circumstances that power will be employed. That the United States possessed enormous productive energy was illustrated by its amazing internal development as well as by its burgeoning commercial activities all over the globe. The profound significance of the nation's territorial expansion, moreover, had not escaped the attention of British and French officials. Indeed, the acquisition of Texas and California rendered the United States so completely dominant in the Western Hemisphere that some European editors and diplomats had favored direct European intervention to maintain some balance of power in the New World. America's Civil War demonstrated the country's unique capacity to sustain a determined and large-scale military action and to emerge from that war as potentially the most powerful nation in the world. Few wars of modern times had involved more men or created more death and destruction. The American economy had revealed the capacity to supply large armies with food and clothing as well as the best in military equipment without demanding drastic sacrifices from the civilian population. The Civil War also had increased the power of business and government

*This essay is an expanded version of "The Reluctant World Power," in *Ideas and Diplomacy: Readings in the Intellectual Tradition of American Foreign Policy* (New York: Oxford University Press, 1964). Reprinted by permission.

313

to harness the country's vast wealth and energy and direct them toward the achievement of national purposes. After the war its unprecedented internal expansion would enable the United States to project immense power abroad; it had become by the 1890s a nation of consequence in world affairs.

Even then the United States, as a nation among nations, was an unknown quantity. Despite its energy and latent power, it had engaged in no actions abroad that proved its willingness to recognize and defend economic, political, or moral commitments distant from its own shores. Protected by two oceans, both secured by the British navy, post-Civil War Americans had long deserted the Founding Fathers' intellectual concern for the European balance of power. American involvement in the politics of Europe and Asia had become a matter of choice, one which the government of the United States, in the absence of any direct threats to U.S. economic or security interests, generally had refused to exercise. Avoiding an active diplomacy in the affairs of the world, Americans too readily viewed the competitive, often cynical, mode of European politics as something to be shunned, even condemned. For them isolationism had come to reflect not a favorable geographic position and a satisfactory international equilibrium but a superior morality. Lord Bryce, the brilliant English critic of American life, attributed America's strange aversion to power politics to special geographic and political conditions that would one day disappear:

> America lives in a world of her own. . . . Safe from attack, safe even from menace, she hears from afar the warring cries of European races and faiths, as the gods of Epicurus listened to the murmurs of the unhappy earth spread out beneath their golden dwellings. . . . Had Canada or Mexico grown to be a great power, had France not sold Louisiana, or had England, rooted on the American continent, become a military despotism, the United States could not indulge the easy optimism which makes them tolerate the faults of their government. . . . Since the War of Secession ended, no serious danger has arisen either from within or from without to alarm transatlantic statesmen. Social convulsions from within, warlike assaults from without, seem now as unlikely to try the fabric of the American Constitution, as an earthquake to rend the walls of the Capitol.[1]

Thus for Europe's foreign offices the United States remained a remote and comparatively unimportant country whose foreign policies mattered little. As late as 1895 the contrast between the United States as

---

[1] James Bryce [Lord Bryce], *The American Commonwealth* (London, 1888), 1:412–13.

a potentially first-class military power and the United States as an active and predictable component in a worldwide balance of power presented a profound dichotomy.

Still, events in the Pacific and the Caribbean slowly, almost imperceptibly, were pushing the United States onto the world stage. American commercial expansionists of the 1840s had predicted accurately the impact which the acquisition of San Francisco Bay and Juan de Fuca Strait would have on U.S. relations with the Pacific. By mid-century trading vessels, emerging from these harbors, sailed the entire region. The French consul at San Francisco predicted in 1852 that "all the archipelagoes of the Pacific Ocean, the entire American continent from Sitka to the Strait of Magellan, China, Japan, are destined to submit to the influence of this state [and] to be attracted into the sphere of its commercial activity."[2] Also by mid-century Boston traders, and their missionary allies, had transformed the Hawaiian Islands, with their port of Honolulu, into an important Pacific depot. The American Hawaiians were not annexationists, but the strategic significance of the islands to the future importance of the United States in the Pacific Ocean was obvious. Eugène Duflot de Mofras, French explorer of the early 1840s, regarded Hawaii as an appendage of California and predicted that the nation which controlled one would also control the other. Sir George Simpson, in his *Narrative of a Journey Round the World* (1847), described the island group as "a stepping-stone from the whole of the American coast to the Celestial Empire."

What attracted Americans to the immense world of the Pacific were not only the possibilities of trade and investment but also the exotic qualities of Polynesian and Asian life. The region comprised ancient societies incapable of resisting the superior power, technology, and organization of the Western World. Scattered throughout the Pacific and around its periphery were villages and cities of cultural excitement, economic challenge, and easy access where Western merchants, missionaries, travelers, and officials could acquire exquisite goods and personal services at little cost. It was not strange that the American invasion of the Pacific from west coast bases revealed an absence of the restraints which guided the United States in its relations with Europe. The application of American will in the Orient appeared so effortless that it led to expanded objectives and assumptions of omnipotence that ultimately demanded a price far in excess of the nation's needs or benefits.

---

[2]French consul, quoted in Norman A. Graebner, *Empire on the Pacific: A Study in American Continental Expansion* (New York, 1955), p. 226.

From the beginning America's invasion of China demonstrated a propensity for defying the rules of diplomatic practice. After 1860 China hung low on the American horizon, largely because of its domestic infirmities. The Taiping Rebellion, which had ravished that country in the 1850s, totally undermined its power and prestige, although British and French victories against the rebels had saved the ruling Manchu dynasty. The Treaties of Tientsin, imposed on China in 1858 by the two powers, opened additional treaty ports, established the right of diplomatic representation in Peking, and recognized the right of missionaries to proselytize freely.[3] Western powers secured control of border areas of historic concern to China, while Russia gained a large region south of the Amur and east of the Ussuri rivers in 1860. Between 1862 and 1867 France annexed Indochina; Britain occupied Burma, attached it to India, and imposed on China a new Indo-Chinese boundary favorable to India. Despite this powerful presence on Chinese soil, the Peking government responded slowly to Western infringements on its sovereignty. Gradually the British and French imposed on China the system of unequal treaties, managed largely from London, which granted foreigners a vast array of specific privileges for trade and residence. The Chinese experienced the foreign impact in all the treaty ports, but especially in Shanghai. In time these foreign impositions reduced China almost to the state of a protectorate.[4]

Anson Burlingame, the first U.S. minister to China (1861), embraced the growing American concern for China's independence from foreign domination. Under him the United States assumed the role of special protector of the Chinese nation. Burlingame devoted himself to securing pledges from the great powers to preserve what remained of China's political integrity, and in 1867 he entered the service of the Peking government to head its special mission to the West. In July 1868 he negotiated a special treaty in Washington, whereby the United States agreed formally to respect China's territorial and administrative integrity.[5] In Europe, however, he met failure. After

[3]For the Taiping Rebellion see Philip A. Kuhn, "The Taiping Rebellion," in John K. Fairbank, ed., *The Cambridge History of China* (Cambridge, England, 1978), 10:264–317.

[4]Fairbank traces the evolution of the treaty system and describes its operation in "The Creation of the Treaty System," ibid., pp. 213–63.

[5]On Burlingame see David L. Anderson, "Anson Burlingame: American Architect of the Cooperative Policy in China, 1861–1871," *Diplomatic History* 1 (Summer 1977): 239–55; Anderson, "Anson Burlingame: Reformer and Diplomat," *Civil War History* 25 (December 1979): 293–308. For Burlingame's decision to enter the Chinese service see Burlingame to William H. Seward, December 14, 1867, in U.S., Department of State, *Papers Relating to Foreign Affairs, 1868*, pt. 1 (Washington, 1869), p. 494; and S. Wells Williams to Seward, December 23, 1867, ibid., pp. 495–97. For Burlingame's treaty with the United States see Frederick Wells Williams, *Anson Burlingame and the First Chinese Mission to Foreign Powers* (New York, 1912), pp. 127–52.

the 1860s the United States at times followed the British-French lead in exerting pressure on a resistant China to maintain Western interests and at other times moved unilaterally to protect it against the combined demands of the European powers. In practice, though, the United States, while proclaiming its innocence and its humanitarian concern for China's welfare, shared all the advantages offered by the treaty system, the international settlement at Shanghai, the British-controlled Chinese Imperial Maritime Customs Service, and the presence of the British navy in Chinese waters. American interests dictated the persistent search for a strong position in China, in part because the China market seemed to offer untold, if reluctant, possibilities for American business, and in part because U.S. missionary activity there created in the American mind a pervasive attitude of paternalism toward that amorphic empire. Protecting China's integrity against external pressures became the keystone of America's policy in the Far East.

Meanwhile, the invasion of the north Pacific by New England whalers, the increased traffic between California and China, the projected San Francisco-Shanghai steamship line, plus Commodore Matthew C. Perry's own penchant for expansion, led by 1854 to the breakdown of Japanese isolation. Perry's treaty with Japan in that year was devoid of the conventional unequal clauses that the Western powers had imposed on China; it anticipated a U.S.-Japanese relationship based on the concept of two equal and independent nations. Four years later the Townsend Harris treaty reverted in phraseology to the older pattern of extraterritoriality and treaty ports.[6] These impositions drove Japan toward the modernization of its legal, administrative, economic, and military systems in its determination to achieve equality with the West. This intense effort at modernization culminated during the 1890s in the emergence of Japan as the first Asian nation to achieve the status of a world power. Its railway system now reached every important point in the country, expanding industries produced goods of all descriptions, and steamship lines under Japan's control connected its ports with all the principal coastal cities of East Asia. One Japanese writer boasted in 1895 that "the whole Empire, in every department of labor and enterprise, has partaken of the forward movement which began with Japan's emergence from the sleep of centuries, and . . . the

---

[6] Perry's treaty with Japan is in Payson J. Treat, *Diplomatic Relations Between the United States and Japan, 1853-1895*, 2 vols. (Stanford, CA, 1932), 1:15-17. For the Convention of Shimoda and the Harris treaty of 1858 see ibid., pp. 48-60; and Carl Crow, *Harris of Japan* (London, 1939), pp. 196-97, 260-94. The Convention of Shimoda of June 1857 opened the port of Nagasaki, permitted residencies at Shimoda and Hakodate, and established the principle of extraterritoriality in Japan. In the treaty of 1858, Harris gained every important concession he wanted. When he was criticized for demanding the extraterritoriality clauses in both of his agreements, he pointed out that the principle had entered the Japanese treaties with Holland and Russia.

general advance has been so marked and so successful as to afford the amplest promise of future prosperity and continued progress."[7] Such achievements won the overwhelming approval of the American people.

By the 1880s expanding U.S. interests in the Pacific had involved the United States in a scramble with other powers for position in a variety of strategic areas. As early as 1867 an American naval officer had claimed the Midway Islands to the north of Hawaii, about half the distance between San Francisco and Yokohama, for the United States. Hawaii itself could not escape the consequences of U.S. expansion into the Pacific. In 1867 the Senate had rejected a commercial treaty with Hawaii which would have opened the American market to its sugar. In 1875 the United States finally accepted such a treaty, extracting from Hawaii the pledge to maintain its integrity and independence. In the 1884 renewal of that treaty the United States secured the exclusive right to a naval base at Pearl Harbor. Korea, like Japan a hermit nation, also attracted Americans in search of trade and ports of call. Unable to communicate with Korean authorities, the United States left to Japan the task of breaking down Korean seclusion. The Korean government in 1875 had received a Japanese minister and shortly thereafter had opened three ports, thus granting the Japanese extraterritorial rights. In return, Japan recognized Korea as an independent state. Finally, in May 1882, an American naval officer negotiated a similar treaty in Seoul, again recognizing that country's independence. Still, American concerns in Korea were so negligible, compared to those of Japan and Russia, that the United States made no effort to counter the pressures that those two countries were willing to exert on Seoul in order to have their way.[8]

America's interest in Samoa was not new; for over half a century its navigators had called at these important islands in the South Pacific in search of items for the China trade. The Samoan Islands possessed a special attractiveness because they commanded several important sea-lanes between San Francisco and Australia. In Pago Pago, on the island of Tutuila, the Samoans had one of the world's most beautiful and capacious harbors—and the possible site of a great naval base.[9]

[7]S. Kurino, "The Future of Japan," *North American Review* 160 (May 1895): 630. Kurino was the Japanese minister in Washington.

[8]For the Hawaiian treaties of 1867, 1875, and 1884 see Merze Tate, *Hawaii: Reciprocity or Annexation* (East Lansing, MI, 1968), pp. 52–77, 108–17, 160–91. The Japanese treaty with Korea seemed to break Korea's isolation, permitting the United States and other countries—Britain, Germany, France, and Russia—to move in. See Han Wookuen, *The History of Korea*, ed. Grafton K. Mintz (Honolulu, 1970), pp. 371–87.

[9]For a contemporary view of Samoa see Hervey W. Whitaker, "Samoa: The Isles of the Navigators," *Century Magazine*, New Series 16 (May–October 1889): 12–25. The standard account of American policy toward Samoa is George H. Ryden, *The Foreign Policy of the United States in Relation to Samoa* (New Haven, 1933).

Finally in 1878 Secretary of State William M. Evarts negotiated with a representative of the Samoan chiefs a treaty that granted the United States a coaling and naval station at Pago Pago in return for an American promise to protect the islands from the encroachments of other foreign countries. But American rights in the Samoan Islands were not exclusive. Germany gained special privileges at Saluafata near Apia, while the British acquired the right to a naval base anywhere except at Saluafata and the American site at Pago Pago. Thus Samoa became the center of a three-nation rivalry. The American diplomat, John A. Kasson, observed that the United States would not be in competition for such valuable islands had it ventured earlier into the Pacific with a large navy and converted that ocean into an American lake. "Instead of this," he complained, "we have now everywhere the flag of the three embattled nations of Europe still grasping for the insular fragments left unappropriated, and exposing every American interest of the present and future on the Pacific, to embroilment in their wars."[10]

Germany's consul created a minor crisis in 1884 when he raised the nation's flag over Apia and proclaimed a German protectorate over the islands. For George H. Bates, who went to Samoa as American commissioner in 1886, the islands were too strategically important to give up. "The construction of the Isthmian canal," he wrote, "is now a mere matter of time, and when the world's commerce floats through such a channel it needs no prophet to assure us that Hawaii will resign to Samoa the key to maritime dominance of the Pacific."[11] To guarantee American claims to Samoa with a three-power agreement, Secretary of State Thomas F. Bayard invited British and German representatives to confer in Washington, but the conference, convening in 1887, settled nothing. The Germans continued to demand a mandate over the islands; the British, in exchange for German cooperation elsewhere, supported the German cause. By 1888 Germany's repeated efforts to control Samoan politics aroused both Congress and the American press. The *New York Evening Post* reminded its readers that the United States not only had valuable interests in the islands but also had practically guaranteed their independence. "It can afford a step toward war in defending one and redeeming the other," ran its conclusion.[12] Congress appropriated special funds to strengthen the American defenses at Pago Pago. "When the foreign governments see that the United States has

---

[10]Kasson is quoted in Edward Younger, *John A. Kasson: Politics and Diplomacy from Lincoln to McKinley* (Iowa City, 1955), p. 340.

[11]George H. Bates, "Some Aspects of the Samoan Question," *Century Magazine*, New Series 15 (November 1888–April 1889): 947. Bates suggested that the United States extend the Monroe Doctrine to include all of Polynesia. See Bates to Bayard, December 10, 1886, in U.S., Department of State, *Papers Relating to the Foreign Relations of the United States, 1889* (Washington, 1890), pp. 276–77 (hereafter cited as *FRUS*).

[12]*New York Evening Post*, reprinted in *New York Herald*, January 9, 1889.

appropriated money," predicted a leading member of Congress, "they will understand that we mean business."[13] The president ordered three naval vessels to Apia. There the Americans faced three German and one British warship with decks cleared for action. Meanwhile, some Americans wondered why the United States would sacrifice its good relations with Bismarck's Germany over the Samoan Islands. The crisis suddenly ended when a fierce Samoan hurricane, on March 16, 1889, wrecked all the German and American ships; the British vessel alone managed to ride out the storm. At the Berlin Conference of April–June 1889, the three powers agreed to respect the independence of the islands, but the treaty did not terminate the American-German rivalry over Samoa.[14]

II

Behind America's accelerating involvement in the Pacific were intellectual, social, and economic developments of the first magnitude. Throughout the Western World expansion had become the order of the day. By the 1880s Britain, France, Belgium, Holland, and even Germany had inaugurated policies of partitioning Africa and converting the islands of the Pacific into colonies. Much of this new imperialistic spirit and the rivalries it generated resulted from the Darwinian notion of a competitive order in which only the fittest—whether individuals or nations—could survive. Such American writers as Josiah Strong and John Fiske urged the U.S. government to enter the race for empire, for no other nation's power, energy, productivity, and institutions, they said, appeared to be so completely the products of natural selection. No country seemed more fit to bring the backward and disorganized regions of the world under the protection or control of Western civilization. For Strong, spiritual Christianity and civil liberty, as the keys to Western civilization, had contributed most to the elevation of the human race. "It follows, then," he wrote in 1885, "that the Anglo-Saxon, as the great representative of these two ideas . . . , is divinely commissioned to be, in a peculiar sense, his brother's keeper. Add to this the fact of his rapidly increasing strength in modern times, and we have well nigh a demonstration of his destiny."[15] Fiske boasted

[13]Quoted in *New York World*, February 13, 1889.
[14]For a detailed study of American opinion and the Samoan crisis see Clara Eve Schieber, *The Transformation of Sentiment Toward Germany, 1870–1914* (Boston, 1923), pp. 39–88. Some newspapers, Schieber noted, registered strong protests against any American move to acquire the Samoan Islands. The *Boston Daily Globe*, for example, insisted that the United States had "no rights and business there." Ibid., p. 68.
[15]Josiah Strong, *Our Country* (New York, 1885), p. 161.

that year that the "work which the English race began when it colonized America is destined to go on until every land on the earth's surface that is not already the seat of an old civilization shall become English in its language, its religion, in its political habits and traditions, and to a predominant extent in the blood of its people."[16] Religious groups entered this civilizing mission with enthusiasm, demanding the participation of government to carry Christianity to the "barbarian" peoples of Asia, Africa, and the South seas.

Perhaps a more tangible incentive to American activity in the Pacific lay in the sometimes depressed state of its economy. After 1865 American business had pushed the nation's industrial capacity beyond domestic demand. So speculative was most of the railroad and industrial construction that it repeatedly toppled the national economy into periodic depressions, the worst of them blanketing the years 1873 to 1878 and 1893 to 1897. Each depression stimulated business consolidation and strengthened the hand of the strongest enterprises, but it also seemed to demonstrate the need for foreign markets if the economy were ever again to perform at full capacity. To meet the challenge the country had no apparent choice but to reconstruct its economy or compete for foreign markets and points of strategic significance, especially in the Pacific. Accepting in principle their obligation to secure the needs of American business abroad, the nation's leaders were careful to limit official policy to the quest for markets, not acquisitions. James G. Blaine emphasized this distinction in August 1890 when he said that "under the beneficent policy of protection we have developed a volume of manufactures which, in many departments, overruns the demands of the home market. . . . Our great demand is expansion. I mean expansion of trade with countries where we can find profitable exchanges. We are not seeking annexation of territory." Blaine himself had conformed to this principle during the previous year when, as secretary of state, he called the Pan-American Conference in Washington to acquaint the Latin American representatives with the variety and quality of U.S. productions.[17]

Alfred Thayer Mahan, in his book *The Influence of Sea Power Upon History* (1890), expanded the requirements of national greatness to include not only production and shipping to ensure the exchange of products but also colonies "which facilitate and enlarge the operations of shipping and tend to protect it by multiplying points of safety." He

[16]John Fiske, "Manifest Destiny," *Harper's New Monthly Magazine* 70 (March 1885): 578–90.
[17]On the quest for markets as an important factor in American foreign policy see Walter LaFeber, *The New Empire: An Interpretation of American Expansion, 1860–1898* (Ithaca, NY, 1963), passim.

advocated, as a logical corollary, the creation of a navy adequate to protect the nation's commerce and to intercept the shipping of the enemy, thus giving it command of the sea. For Mahan it was essential that the United States control an important maritime route of its own, extending from the cities of the Atlantic coast, through an isthmian canal, into the Pacific.[18] The United States, bordered by two oceans, enjoyed an advantageous position, but one that could prove vulnerable in time of war. Mahan foresaw future conflict in the Pacific between the Occident and the Orient. In preparation for this eventuality the United States, in his view, required a large navy and a canal as well as island outposts in the mid-Pacific.

Clearly the United States was replete with proponents of the new manifest destiny. Still, as a group they did not present a vision of empire. Such leading social Darwinists as Strong and Fiske, or even Herbert Spencer, were not expansionists at all, for nowhere did they advocate territorial acquisitions through the use of force. For them expansion was a cultural process; they assumed the expansion of Anglo-Saxon civilization, not because of its superior power but because of its superior humanity. Nor did missionary societies assume that their endeavors could succeed only under the aegis of the American flag. Even Mahan, as a realist, was concerned that the United States not acquire territories that it could not adequately defend. For him coaling stations would contribute to the development of national power without committing the nation to extensive and costly defenses. With this judgment the commercial expansionists agreed.[19]

In large measure Mahan reflected, rather than guided, the expansionist outlook of the Harrison administration which took office in March 1889. Benjamin Harrison's secretary of the navy, Benjamin F. Tracy, soon recommended the construction of two large battle fleets with twenty battleships, one for the Atlantic-Caribbean area, one for the Pacific. The Naval Policy Board went far beyond Tracy in advocating thirty-five battleships. Actually, he inaugurated the construction of three new steel battleships—the *Maine*, *Oregon*, and *Olympia*—but only the *Oregon* patrolled the Pacific.[20] Meanwhile, the Harrison administration found the concept of "strategic bases" appealing. The president admitted to Secretary of State Blaine in October 1891 that "as to

---

[18]Alfred Thayer Mahan, "The United States Looking Outward," *Atlantic Monthly* 66 (December 1890): 816–24.

[19]Paul S. Holbo had developed the theme that the expansionism of the 1880s, and even the 1890s, has been greatly exaggerated. If the sentiments were often expansive, they did not recommend the annexation of any specific territories. See Holbo, "Economics, Emotion, and Expansion: An Emerging Foreign Policy," in H. Wayne Morgan, ed., *The Gilded Age* (Syracuse, NY, 1970), pp. 213–21.

[20]William Reynolds Braisted, *The United States Navy in the Pacific, 1897–1909* (Austin, TX, 1958), pp. 6–7.

naval stations and points of influence, we must look forward to a departure from the too conservative opinions which have been held heretofore." In the late spring of 1889 the administration had concluded the arrangements on Samoa; thereafter, it looked to other possible bases in the Caribbean and the Pacific. In August 1891, Blaine suggested to Harrison that "there are only three places that are of value enough to be taken, that are not continental. One is Hawaii and the others are Cuba and Porto Rico. Cuba and Porto Rico are not now imminent and will not be for a generation. Hawaii may come up for decision at any unexpected hour and I hope we shall be prepared to decide it in the affirmative."[21]

America's expanding interest in Hawaii approached its consummation in the Hawaiian revolution of 1893. Through three generations of missionary and commercial encroachment, a small group of American investors had gained a dominant position in the island's sugar industry as well as its foreign trade. The McKinley tariff of 1890, in terminating reciprocal tariff arrangements with Hawaii, apparently had doomed that island to lower property values and depression. Still, many planters feared annexation to the United States because of the possible effect of American labor and immigration laws on the importation of cheap contract labor from China and Japan.[22] As late as January 1893 the large planters opposed annexation when Hawaii's Queen Liliuokalani announced a new constitution designed to return the islands to native rule. The foreign planter-merchant community retaliated by establishing a provisional government and turning to John L. Stevens, the American minister, for protection. Stevens promptly landed marines from the warship *Boston*, recognized the provisional government as the de facto government of Hawaii, and proclaimed Hawaii a protectorate of the United States. Now the leading planters, in the interest of stable government, agreed to take their chances on the labor question rather than on the continued independence of the islands. On February 14, Secretary of State John W. Foster signed an annexation treaty with Hawaiian commissioners. President Harrison then forwarded it to the Senate where it faced strong Democratic opposition. The session ended with the Hawaiian treaty still awaiting approval.[23]

[21]Harrison to Blaine, October 1, 1891, in Albert T. Volwiler, "Harrison, Blaine, and American Foreign Policy, 1889–1893," *Proceedings of the American Philosophical Society* 79 (1938): 638–39; Blaine to Harrison, August 10, 1891, in Volwiler, *Correspondence Between Benjamin Harrison and James G. Blaine, 1882–1893* (Philadelphia, 1940), p. 174.

[22]See Richard D. Weigle, "Sugar and the Hawaiian Revolution," *Pacific Historical Review* 16 (February 1947): 41–58.

[23]For detailed studies of the Hawaiian revolution and the treaty of 1893 see Merze Tate, *The United States and the Hawaiian Kingdom* (New Haven, CT, 1965), pp. 155–218; and Ralph S. Kuykendall, *The Hawaiian Kingdom* (Honolulu, 1967), 3:582–620.

For Grover Cleveland, the new president, these events in Hawaii were a serious reflection on American justice, and he immediately dispatched James H. Blount, a former congressman from Georgia, to Honolulu to conduct an investigation. Blount hauled down the American flag and ordered the marines back to their ship. In his report of July 1893, he accused Stevens of supporting the revolution to overthrow the queen. The Cleveland administration favored the queen, but it possessed no means to restore her to power. The president and his secretary of state, Walter Q. Gresham, were equally critical of the previous administration's involvement in Samoa, and Gresham expressed his displeasure:

> It is in our relations to Samoa that we have made the first departure from our traditional and well-established policy of avoiding entangling alliances with foreign powers in relation to objects remote from this hemisphere. . . . If the departure was justified, there must be some evidence of detriment suffered before its adoption, or of advantage since gained, to demonstrate the fact. . . . Every nation, and especially every strong nation, must sometimes be conscious of an impulse to rush into difficulties that do not concern it, except in a highly imaginary way. To restrain the indulgence of such a propensity is not only the part of wisdom, but a duty we owe to the world as an example of the strength, the moderation, and the beneficence of popular government.[21]

Cleveland refused to defend American interests in Samoa and withdrew U.S. warships from Pago Pago. Republican spokesman Henry Cabot Lodge accused Gresham of attempting to nullify the Berlin treaty by refusing to send Congress an estimate for the appropriation necessary to carry out the treaty provisions. Only the perversity of the German kaiser and American public opinion, charged Lodge, prevented the administration from altogether surrendering U.S. interests in Samoa.[25]

Other Americans joined members of the Cleveland administration in denouncing the expansionist tendencies of the Harrison years as an unwarranted departure from the nation's established policies. In March 1893, *Harper's Weekly* accused the previous administration of needlessly multiplying the country's entanglements abroad. "Are we ready," asked the writer, "to alter the whole character of the Government, with its beneficial traditional policies, to impose upon the people

---

[21]Cleveland's conservative policies are discussed in Tate, *The United States and the Hawaiian Kingdom*, pp. 228–57; and Kuykendall, *The Hawaiian Kingdom*, pp. 620–31. An analysis of Gresham's conservatism is in Matilda Gresham, *Life of Walter Q. Gresham* (Chicago, 1919), 2:740–68.

[25]For a contemporary critique of Cleveland's policies toward Hawaii and Samoa see Henry Cabot Lodge, "Our Blundering Foreign Policy," *Forum* 19 (March 1895): 10.

the burdens entailed by the building up and maintaining of immense armaments, and to expose this republic to all the political and economic consequences which such a policy would bring in its train?" Similarly, Carl Schurz, the noted Republican, warned the American people in *Harper's New Monthly Magazine* in October 1893 that the United States, should it annex Hawaii, would give up the advantages of geographic insulation which gave it a security possessed by no other nation on the globe. "Hawaii," he wrote, "would be our Achilles' heel. Other nations would observe it, and regard us no longer as invulnerable. If we acquire Hawaii, we acquire not an addition to our strength, but a dangerous element of weakness."[26] William Graham Sumner, the conservative Yale sociologist, extended Schurz's argument against territorial expansion: "The sum of the matter is that colonization and territorial extension are burdens, not gains." Of all imperial states, he added, only Great Britain had the power to derive some compensation from its imperial burdens. Lord Bryce noted that America's strength, like that of Russia, lay in the absence of insular territories to defend. Neither had possessions that could be cut off by a naval enemy, nor could any country think of invading either of them successfully.[27]

During the depressed 1890s spokesmen of the conservative Cleveland administration perpetuated the distinction between the country's need for enlarged markets and the dangers involved in the acquisition of insular possessions. Gresham readily acknowledged in 1894 the need for new commercial opportunities. Opposed to the annexation of islands in the Pacific, he suggested that the United States negotiate for coaling stations that would serve its commerce without creating military and political responsibilities. Schurz accepted this formula, writing that "there is little doubt that we can secure by amicable negotiation sites for coaling stations which will serve us as well as if we possessed the countries in which they are situated. In the same manner we can obtain . . . all sorts of commercial advantages . . . without assuming any responsibilities."[28] Richard Olney, who succeeded Gresham as secretary of state in 1895, shared his predecessor's preference for trade expansion through limited commercial arrangements. The widespread desire for markets suggested no precise actions of government which might acquire them. That the spokesmen for the nation's business and

[26]*Harper's Weekly*, March 18, 1893, quoted in Volwiler, "Harrison, Blaine, and American Foreign Policy," p. 637; Carl Schurz, "Manifest Destiny," *Harper's New Monthly Magazine* 87 (October 1893): 743–44.

[27]William Graham Sumner, "The Fallacy of Territorial Extension," *Forum* 21 (June 1896): 419; James Bryce [Lord Bryce], "The Policy of Annexation for America," ibid. 24 (December 1897): 385–95.

[28]Schurz, "Manifest Destiny," p. 746.

agriculture wanted enlarged foreign markets was beyond question. Still, it seems clear that trade expansion received little encouragement from the actual policies the government pursued, and that the pressure for markets had at best a generalized, not a specific, influence on American territorial expansion.

American conservatism continued to stall the annexation of Hawaii. On July 4, 1894, the leaders of Hawaii established a republic, prepared either to maintain their independence or to accept annexation. Events played into the hands of the annexationists. To secure additional cheap labor the sugar planters gained a treaty with Japan in 1896 to ensure the flow of Japanese laborers, but so huge was the Japanese invasion that the Hawaiian government halted the movement in defiance of the treaty. Tokyo protested and dispatched a warship to Honolulu, thereby pressuring the Hawaiians to relent.[29] With William McKinley's inauguration in March 1897, the Washington mood again became expansionist. Secretary of State John Sherman in June negotiated a treaty with Hawaiian commissioners similar to that of February 1893, but without provisions for compensation to the former queen and the heir presumptive. The new treaty released a burst of expansionism. One Pacific coast newspaper proclaimed: "We are exclusively a land power no longer. We are a sea power as well. . . . It is especially necessary that we make ourselves strong in the Pacific, and the Hawaiian Islands are the key to the Pacific." McKinley sent the treaty to the Senate for approval; Queen Liliuokalani, then in Washington, pleaded with the State Department to withdraw it. What she could not prevent the Senate did by overwhelmingly rejecting the treaty. Once more the anti-imperialists had demonstrated their power.[30]

III

Of more immediate consequence for American expansion into the Pacific was the Cuban revolt which broke out in February 1895. Without delay the junta, with headquarters in New York, supported by the Cuban League, its American counterpart with branches in all the large cities, launched a campaign to involve the United States in this renewal of the Cuban struggle for independence. Cuban revolutionaries understood the peculiar appeal of humanitarian causes to nineteenth-century Americans; the Spanish government, by employing measures of extreme

[29]For the crisis in Hawaii see Tate, *The United States and the Hawaiian Kingdom*, pp. 258–68.

[30]The negotiation and rejection of the Hawaiian treaty of 1897 receive a detailed analysis in ibid., pp. 269–84.

repression, played into their hands. Indeed, the Madrid government damaged its image almost beyond recall when in 1896 it dispatched General Valeriano Weyler to Cuba where he proceeded to herd civilians suspected of rebel leanings into concentration camps.[31] The junta promoted mass meetings to belabor Spanish policy in Cuba, thus creating a powerful anti-Spanish sentiment in the United States. Unable to mount a successful revolution, Cuban leaders knew from the beginning that their success hinged on American support. To aggravate Spanish hostility toward the United States, the junta organized filibustering expeditions which failed to influence events in Cuba but brought the anticipated Spanish complaints that the United States, in permitting such expeditions to outfit on American soil, served the cause of the revolution. The newspaper press, led by Joseph Pulitzer's *New York World* and William Randolph Hearst's *New York Journal*, supported the Cuban cause, stressing not only Spanish atrocities, actual and fabricated, but also Spain's threat to American commercial, financial, and property interests in the Caribbean.[32] By mid-summer 1896 the junta's demand for action had won the support of Republican editors who discerned the political implications of the nation's latest humanitarian crusade.

Cleveland, resentful of the junta's filibustering activities and embarrassed by the legitimacy of the Spanish complaints, announced a policy of strict neutrality in June 1895 and again in June 1896. In his annual message of December 1895, the president had explained to the nation why he refused to be guided by liberal sentiment. It was the duty of government, he said, "to observe in good faith the recognized obligations of international friendship." He admonished the American people to uphold the neutrality which they were obligated to observe toward a friendly sovereign state.[33] In February 1896 the Senate passed a resolution recognizing Cuban belligerence; in April the House concurred. Cleveland ignored the resolution, while Democratic editors accused Republicans of introducing the issue of belligerency merely to embarrass the president. With McKinley's election in November, such

[31] See Sherman to Stewart L. Woodford, July 16, 1897, in *FRUS, 1898* (Washington, 1901), pp. 558–59; and David F. Trask, *The War with Spain in 1898* (New York, 1981), pp. 1–10.

[32] For the role of the newspapers in the Cuban crisis see George W. Auxier, "Middle Western Newspapers and the Spanish-American War, 1895–1898," *Mississippi Valley Historical Review* 26 (March 1940): 523–34; Joseph E. Wisan, *The Cuban Crisis as Reflected in the New York Press* (New York, 1934); Marcus M. Wilkerson, *Public Opinion and the Spanish-American War: A Study in War Propaganda* (Baton Rouge, LA, 1932).

[33] Cleveland's message to Congress, December 2, 1895, in James D. Richardson, ed., *A Compilation of the Messages and Papers of the Presidents*, 10 vols. (Washington, 1896–1899), 9:636.

Republican newspapers as the *Chicago Tribune* boasted that the next administration would adopt a more humane, civilized, and patriotic policy. Cleveland responded to the pressure. The utter ruin of an adjoining territory, he acknowledged in his December 1896 message to Congress, was not only a question of philanthropic concern but also one of primary interest. Both issues had led to vehement demands that the strife in Cuba "be terminated by our intervention, even at the cost of war between the United States and Spain." Should the insurrection degenerate into a hopeless struggle, presaging nothing but endless destruction, the president concluded, American obligations to Spanish sovereignty would be superseded by higher obligations "which we can hardly hesitate to recognize and discharge."[34]

McKinley entered the White House determined to avoid a war for Cuban rights. With much of the press clamoring for intervention, the new president assured the nation that he would seek only what was due it.[35] He would pursue the country's minimum objectives in Cuba and without armed intervention, if possible. Like Cleveland, McKinley reserved the ultimate right of the United States to stop the bloodshed in Cuba if Spain could not do so in a reasonable length of time; unlike Cleveland, he insisted that Spain conduct its campaign in Cuba in accordance with "the military codes of civilization." In his attack on Weyler and his policies, McKinley recognized no merit at all in Spanish behavior. Whereas the previous administration would accept an agreement with Spain without reference to Cuban demands, McKinley opposed any arrangement for Cuba unacceptable to its revolutionaries who had long made independence their minimum objective.[36] Whatever the president's preference for peace, he offered Spain no choice except capitulation to Cuba's requests or war with the United States.

McKinley launched his diplomatic offensive in July 1897. His new minister to Spain, Stewart L. Woodford, left Washington that summer armed with instructions that condemned Spanish methods of warfare and demanded that Spain, in the interests of humanity, "put a stop to this destructive war and make proposals of settlement honorable to herself and just to her Cuban colony and to mankind."[37] The United States, added the president, would offer its good offices to help Spain bring the war to an end. McKinley, for good reasons, did not suggest how the United States would exercise its good offices, since

[34]Cleveland's message to Congress, December 7, 1896, ibid., pp. 719, 722.
[35]McKinley's inaugural, March 4, 1897, ibid., 8:6241.
[36]John A. S. Grenville and George Berkeley Young make these distinctions between the McKinley and Cleveland policies, in *Politics, Strategy, and American Diplomacy: Studies in Foreign Policy, 1873–1917* (New Haven, CT, 1966), pp. 248–49.
[37]Sherman to Woodford, July 16, 1897, in *FRUS, 1898,* pp. 559–60.

Spanish officials in Madrid understood the limited choices before them. The new Liberal ministry, which gained power in October 1897, was determined to avoid a war which it could not win. It recalled Weyler and instructed his successor to revoke the concentration policy. Then in November the new regime, in its search for peace, offered autonomy to the Cubans. Neither the Liberal leaders nor the Spanish queen, Woodford informed McKinley, could do more without wounding the country's pride and violating its tradition.[38] Spain's only hope for a peaceful solution lay in the willingness of Cubans to settle for autonomy rather than full independence.

For McKinley the prospects seemed propitious. In his December message to Congress, he asserted that Spain deserved every reasonable chance to prove the efficacy of its policies, but he warned that if its policy failed—and it had no chance of success—the United States, in response to the demands of humanity, might be duty bound to intervene with force.[39] McKinley had not departed from his initial position. Woodford, like the president, questioned the sincerity of the Spanish proposals; even if they were genuine, he feared, the Cuban rebels would not accept them. Indeed, in January 1898 revolts broke out in Havana in defiance of Spain's offer of autonomy. McKinley dispatched the USS *Maine* to lend material support to the American consul general in his effort to protect U.S. citizens and property in Havana.

Spanish officials acknowledged readily enough that the Havana riots demonstrated at last the failure of their policy. They also knew that American encouragement of the Cuban insurgents had eliminated any possibility of compromise. On January 17 the queen informed Woodford that Cleveland had promised to sever all official U.S. support for the rebels if Spain would grant autonomy.[40] McKinley's refusal to desert the rebels, a decision reinforced by reports of continued repression in Cuba, rendered the Spanish position hopeless. On February 1 the Madrid government gave vent to its frustration by condemning the United States for harboring revolutionary organizations which labored freely for the separation of Cuba from Spain; it denied the United States the right to interfere in Cuban affairs: "The Spanish government does not admit the right of neighboring country to limit duration of

[38]For a statement of Spain's new policy see Pio Gullon, the new Spanish foreign minister, to Woodford, October 23, 1897, ibid., pp. 582–89. The offer of autonomy is in Woodford to Sherman, November 13, 1897, ibid., pp. 600–01.
[39]McKinley's message to Congress, December 6, 1897, in *FRUS, 1897* (Washington, 1898), p. xxi.
[40]Spanish leaders recognized their problem; they had done everything they believed they could do, including the offer of autonomy. What rendered their position untenable, they told Woodford, was McKinley's refusal to accept autonomy as the basis of a settlement. See Woodford to McKinley, March 9, 1898, in *FRUS, 1898*, pp. 682–83.

struggle. . . . Foreign intrusion and interferences are never and in no way justified. These might lead to the intervention which every country that respects itself must repel with force. Peace . . . can be found only in the formula of colonial self-government and Spanish sovereignty."[41] Cuba was a Spanish, not an American, concern, but U.S. policy had become the determinant of Cuba's future. Spain had no choice but to grant Cuban independence, turn to Europe for moral and military support, or prepare for war. The Liberal ministry, playing for time, attempted to rally popular sentiment behind its determination to defend what remained of Spanish policy.

During February and March 1898 a series of events ended the drift, beginning when a private letter written by Enrique Dupuy de Lôme, the Spanish minister in Washington, fell into the hands of the press. Published on February 9 in the *New York Journal*, it condemned the president for weakness in seeking public approval and ridiculed much of the recent U.S.-Spanish diplomacy. The publication aggravated the country's anti-Spanish sentiment and forced the minister's recall.[42] Far more dangerous to U.S.-Spanish relations was the destruction of the battleship *Maine* in Havana harbor on February 15, with heavy loss of life. Spanish behavior following the incident was impeccable, and officials in Washington, including the president, accepted the news with remarkable restraint. However, widespread public opinion, anchored to the cry "Remember the *Maine*" and whipped up by the press, demanded war; thereafter, the events that brought conflict closer came in rapid succession. Congress, early in March, voted $50 million to assist the administration in strengthening the nation's defenses. On March 17, Senator Redfield Proctor of Vermont reported to Congress what he had seen on a recent tour to Cuba, describing in detail the appalling conditions he had witnessed among the hundreds of thousands of starving and emaciated Cubans confined to concentration camps. The new Spanish minister warned Madrid accurately that Proctor's speech, because of the senator's known temperance on the Cuban question, would have a profound effect on American opinion. Then on March 28 the Naval Board of Inquiry, appointed by McKinley to investigate the *Maine* tragedy, issued its report. Without attributing responsibility, the board concluded nevertheless that the battleship had been destroyed by a mine. Congressional and public opinion now reached

---

[41]Gullon to Woodford, February 1, 1898, ibid., pp. 663–64; Woodford to Sherman, February 8, 9, 1898, ibid., pp. 657–58; Woodford to McKinley, February 26, 1898, ibid., p. 665. Quotation is on p. 657.

[42]For the de Lôme affair see H. Wayne Morgan, *America's Road to Empire: The War with Spain and Overseas Expansion* (New York, 1965), pp. 40–44.

a new level of intensity. Meanwhile, the secretary of state again urged Spain to revoke the *reconcentrado* order and to make peace with Cuba even at the price of independence.[43]

As the crisis mounted in April, Republican congressmen and editors warned the president that, if he did not lead the country into a popular war, others would. One cabinet member criticized the president's hesitancy: "He is making a great mistake. He is in danger of ruining himself and the Republican Party by standing in the way of the people's wishes. Congress will declare war in spite of him. He'll get run over and his party with him." The *Chicago Tribune* also warned McKinley against further procrastination: "The people want no disgraceful negotiations with Spain. Should the President plunge his administration into that morass, he and his administration would be swept out of power in 1900 by a fine outburst of popular indignation. An administration which strains the national honor never will be forgiven."[44] Now McKinley, in the interest of both party unity and executive control of foreign policy, assumed responsibility for leading the nation to war. Woodford reported on April 5 that the queen had agreed to a six-months' unconditional suspension of hostilities in Cuba, providing time for the establishment of permanent peace. Finally, on April 10, Woodford assured the president that by August 1 he could obtain peace by negotiation on the basis of either autonomy or independence. "I hope," he added, "that nothing will now be done to humiliate Spain, as I am satisfied that the present Government is going . . . as fast and far as it can. With your power of action sufficiently free you will win the fight on your own lines."[45] One day later McKinley sent his war message to Congress, which debated it for one week before adopting four resolutions that recognized Cuban independence, demanded a Spanish withdrawal, and authorized the president to employ the nation's military forces to achieve American purpose. Last, in the famed Teller Resolution, Congress asserted its determination to leave the Cuban people in possession of their own government. By April 21

[43]Day to Woodford, March 20, 26, 27, 1898, in *FRUS, 1898*, pp. 692–93, 704, 711–12. In these letters William R. Day, the new secretary of state, warned the Spanish government that, if it did not quickly settle the Cuban revolution, the United States would intervene. Woodford reported that Spain would do "all that highest honor and justice require in the matter of the *Maine*"; clearly, it wanted to avoid war. Throughout the crisis the Madrid government insisted that the majority of Cubans favored autonomy and peace, but that the insurgents, backed by the United States, made such a settlement impossible. See Woodford to McKinley, March 25, 1898, ibid., 703–04; Polo de Bernabé to Sherman, April 1, 1898, ibid., pp. 728–29.

[44]*Chicago Tribune*, February 27, 1898. For another version of the White House scene see Morgan, *America's Road to Empire*, p. 55.

[45]Woodford to McKinley, April 5, 10, 1898, in *FRUS, 1898*, pp. 734–35, 747.

the United States had broken diplomatic relations with Spain and entered its war for Cuban independence.[46]

Few Americans attempted to justify the war against Spain except in terms of humanitarianism. Such motives were not strange to American liberal thought, but before 1898 they had never governed action. With the Spanish-American War, moral abstraction as a mass phenomenon was substituted for the political realism that had circumscribed previous American diplomacy. Whether it was a people's war, forced on a reluctant administration, or one reflecting a slow, steady evolution of presidential policy, it did not result from any deliberate weighing of interests and responsibilities. The president asked for the declaration of war in the name of humanity and civilization as well as endangered American interests. "Our own direct interests [in Cuba] were great," observed Theodore Roosevelt in his *Autobiography*, "but even greater were our interests from the standpoint of humanity. Cuba was at our very doors. It was a dreadful thing for us to sit supinely and watch her death agony."[47] Similarly, Senator George F. Hoar acknowledged on April 12 that the American people could not "look idly on while hundreds of thousands of innocent human beings, women and children and old men, die of hunger close to our doors. If there is ever to be war it should be to prevent such things as that."[48] Such dictates of humanity impelled the United States to ignore Spain's contention that the established rules of international conduct gave it the right to manage Cuban affairs in accordance with its own interests and purposes. But had Cuba lain off the coast of Asia Minor there would

[46]The Teller Amendment declared that the United States would recognize the independence of Cuba after it had been freed of Spanish control. The defeated Turpie-Foraker Amendment would have recognized Cuban independence as a means of removing Spain without war. Had Congress adopted that course, the *New York Herald* observed, it would have assumed that the United States could have what it wanted in world affairs simply by recognizing and supporting revolutionaries that favored its views. For an excellent analysis of the Turpie-Foraker Amendment see Paul S. Holbo, "Presidential Leadership in Foreign Affairs: William McKinley and the Turpie-Foraker Amendment," *American Historical Review* 72 (July 1967): 1321–35.

[47]Theodore Roosevelt, *An Autobiography* (New York, 1913), p. 228; Hoar is quoted in Morgan, *America's Road to Empire*, p. 63.

[48]To measure the extent to which the United States, in its Cuban involvement, departed from the country's own traditions, one need only to recall the arguments of Seward employed to forestall European intervention in the American Civil War and the similar arguments which Secretary of State Hamilton Fish used to explain why the United States would not interfere in the Cuban revolt of the 1870s. The specific emotional, geographic, and power factors of 1898 rendered the departure from the past so easy that most Americans were hardly conscious of the fact that they were breaking with tradition. Some Europeans noted that the United States defied not only its own past but international law as well. See, for example, *Saturday Review* (London) 86 (December 3, 1898); 725.

have been no war of liberation in 1898. Previous generations of Americans had sought new deals for Greeks and Hungarians in vain. In 1898 such sentiment mattered because it was directed at oppression by a weak power in an adjacent region where the United States held the clear strategic advantage.

IV

On May 1, 1898, Commodore George Dewey's U.S. squadron sailed into Manila Bay and destroyed Spain's Pacific fleet at anchor. This victory did not presage an annexationist movement; it was logical that the United States should strike Spanish naval power wherever it existed and thereby protect American commerce. Dewey's orders to attack Manila originated in the Navy Department and received the president's approval on April 24. The orders anticipated the momentary retention of Manila and other Philippine ports "as an inducement to Spain to make peace after the liberation of Cuba." They did not contemplate any territorial acquisitions in the western Pacific.[49] Still, this sudden display of U.S. naval power and the possibilities it opened for American empire building were not lost on a small but well-placed and influential body of expansionists in Washington. Even before the news of Dewey's victory reached the capital, such men as Senator Albert J. Beveridge of Indiana and Senator Lodge of Massachusetts had expansion in mind. On April 27, four days before Dewey's victory, Beveridge had declared before a Boston audience that "in the Pacific is the true field of our earliest operations. There Spain has an island empire, the Philippine Archipelago. It is poorly defended. . . . In the Pacific the United States has a powerful squadron. The Philippines are logically our first target." Lodge wrote several days later: "If, as now seems certain, we have captured Manila, we ought I think, to hold that great strategic point in the East, which would enable us to get our share of the Pacific trade."[50] There is no evidence that the president shared such ambitions.

During the weeks following Dewey's victory, events moved with a logic of their own. Washington acted quickly to establish American control of the Philippines. Dewey himself maintained a blockade of Manila Bay and kept a close surveillance of the German squadron under Admiral Otto von Diedrichs. A Spanish army held Manila, but a successful Filipino insurgency had freed the islands of Spanish control

[49]See Grenville and Young, *Politics, Strategy, and American Diplomacy*, pp. 269–72.
[50]Beveridge is quoted in Claude J. Bowers, *Beveridge and the Progressive Era* (Boston, 1932), pp. 69–70; Lodge to L. S. Amonson, May 3, 1898, in Grenville and Young, *Politics, Strategy, and American Diplomacy*, p. 268.

and was already closing in on the capital. Ignoring the clouded political status of the islands, McKinley on May 4 ordered General Wesley Merritt to Manila to complete the reduction of Spanish power and to secure the islands while they remained in the possession of the United States.[51] During June and July a contingent of more than ten thousand American soldiers reached Manila. These forces, supported by Emilio Aguinaldo's insurgents, assaulted the city, but the Spaniards by prear-rangement surrendered it on August 13 only to the American forces. Thereafter, the Filipinos viewed the United States as the enemy and prepared to fight for their independence.

This display of American power in the Pacific sealed the fate of Hawaii. Those who had vainly pushed Hawaiian annexation during 1897 had not allowed the issue to die. In January 1898, Roosevelt declared in *Gunton's Magazine*: "We must take Hawaii. . . . If we do not take Hawaii ourselves we will have lost the right to dictate what shall be her fate. . . . Hawaii cannot permanently stand alone, and we have no right to expect other powers to be blind to their own interests because we are blind to ours. If Hawaii does not become American then we may as well make up our own minds to see it become European or Asiatic." On May 4, three days after the battle of Manila Bay, the annexationists brought before Congress a joint resolution for Hawaii's annexation. Two months later the measure had gone through com-mittees onto the floor of both houses. Requiring no more than a bare majority, the measure passed the House on June 15 by a vote of 209 to 91, with 49 abstentions. The Senate concurred, after a determined debate staged by the Democratic minority, by 42 to 21. The nation's overwhelming expansionist sentiment, as reflected in Congress, cen-tered in the Republican leadership of the Northeast and the Upper Middle West. "We need Hawaii," McKinley wrote, "as much and a good deal more than we did California. . . . It is manifest destiny."[52]

Unlike Samoa and Hawaii (two independent island groups), the Philippines, as Spanish territory, had been of necessity off limits to prewar American imperialist ambitions. Prior to Dewey's victory there could have been absolutely no sentiment for Philippine annexation. Finley Peter Dunne's "Mr. Dooley" remarked that the American people "did not know whether the Philippines were islands or canned goods." President McKinley himself had to resort to a globe to discover their

[51] Richard E. Welch, Jr., *Response to Imperialism: The United States and the Philippine-American War, 1899–1902* (Chapel Hill, NC, 1979), pp. 4–6.
[52] McKinley is quoted in Charles S. Olcott, *The Life of William McKinley*, 2 vols. (Boston, 1916), 1:379.

location; he could not, he admitted, have described it within two thousand miles. Against the immediate background of the country's burgeoning interests in the Pacific, however, the reduction of Spanish power in the Philippines confronted the United States with the unanticipated dilemma of what was to be the disposition of the islands, now no longer under Spanish control. At the outset the United States had four clear choices: it could return the islands to Spain, or it could grant them independence, as it had promised Cuba; it could transfer the islands to another power, or it could retain them as possessions of the United States. That the United States reluctantly acquired the Philippines did not mean that it had no freedom of choice, but the decision to destroy Spanish power in Manila had been crucial because it closed all easy avenues of retreat from a self-imposed dilemma. Once the islands had been liberated, they had either to be restored to Spain or brought under the control of the United States.

Among American editors, politicians, intellectuals, and businessmen, Dewey's victory at Manila had unleashed an expansionist drive toward the Philippines. Both northern commercial groups and Protestant missionary societies had concluded as early as May 1898 that the acquisition of these islands would serve the nation's interests by enlarging the American naval, mercantile, and cultural role in the western Pacific. "We think the retrocession of the islands," declared the *New York Times* on May 24, "would bring severe censure upon us. It would be a scandal to return the people of the Philippines to oppression and barbarism at the end of the war which began in the name of humanity." Lyman Abbott, New England's noted clergyman, agreed: "We did not mean to free the Philippine Islands, but we have done it, and the responsibility of the Philippine Islands is upon us, whether we like it or not."[53] The *New York Herald* averred that the return of the Philippines to Spain would be as "reckless and inexcusable as giving up the Louisiana Purchase." National expansion, concluded the *New York Sun*, "is the American idea of 1898."[54] By August such expansionist sentiment dominated the press; still, official U.S. policy toward the Philippines evolved slowly. Throughout May and June 1898 expansionists in Congress and the administration had argued with McKinley on the necessity of acquiring the Philippines. Lodge reported to Roosevelt in late May that the president seemed to be grasping the essentials of a Philippine policy. In June, Secretary of State William R. Day

[53]*New York Times*, May 24, 1898; Lyman Abbott, "The Duty and Destiny of America," *Plymouth Morning Pulpit*, June 15, 1898, pp. 14–20.
[54]*New York Herald*, August 13, 1898; *New York Sun*, August 14, 1898.

informed Lodge that perhaps the nation could not escape its destiny
in the Philippines.[55]

Gradually a national policy emerged. At the end of July the
president announced that any truce with Spain must include the stipulation that the United States continue to occupy Manila until the
conclusion of a treaty. Finally, on September 16, the administration
clarified its intentions in the instructions to its peace commissioners:

> Without any original thought of complete or even partial acqui-
> sition, the presence and success of our arms at Manila imposes
> upon us obligations which we cannot disregard. The march of
> events rules and over-rules human action. . . . We cannot be
> unmindful that without any desire or design on our part the war
> has brought us new duties and responsibilities which we must
> meet and discharge as becomes a great nation on whose growth
> and career from the beginning the Ruler of Nations has plainly
> written the high command and pledge of civilization.[56]

Thereafter, the president faced the task of defining his precise objectives
in the Philippines, a task that he entrusted to his peace commission.
Like the Spanish-American War itself, McKinley rationalized his ultimate decision to annex the Philippines in terms of humanitarianism.
There was no alternative, the president explained to a group of visiting
clergymen, "but to take them all, and to educate the Filipinos, and
uplift and Christianize them, and by God's grace do the very best we
could by them, as our fellowmen, for whom Christ also died."[57]

McKinley, with the support of Congress, had destroyed American
continental isolation by the annexation of Hawaii. The acquisition of
the Philippines, however, threatened to extend U.S. political and military commitments across the Pacific, where other nations possessed
greater naval power than did the United States. Despite the magnitude
of this distant commitment, the president continued to rationalize his
decision to annex the Philippines by citing the nation's obligation to

[55]Lodge to Roosevelt, May 24, 1898, in Henry Cabot Lodge, ed., *Selections from the Correspondence of Theodore Roosevelt and Henry Cabot Lodge, 1884–1918*, 2 vols. (New York, 1925), 1:299; Lodge to Roosevelt, June 24, 1898, ibid., p. 313. Roosevelt wrote to Lodge: "You must get Manila and Hawaii; you must prevent any talk of peace until we get Porto Rico and the Philippines." See Roosevelt to Lodge, June 12, 1898, ibid., p. 309. For a study of these expansionists see Julius W. Pratt, "The 'Large Policy' of 1898," *Mississippi Valley Historical Review* 19 (September 1932): 219–42.

[56]McKinley to peace commissioners, September 16, 1898, in *FRUS, 1898*, pp. 906–08.

[57]McKinley's interview with the Methodist clergymen took place on November 21, 1899. In explaining the Philippine decision, the president insisted that he did not want to take the islands but had no choice. For the interview see Olcott, *Life of William McKinley*, 2:109–11.

humanity. This theme dominated his speeches during his tour of the Midwest in October 1898. Always he dwelt on the accidental nature of the country's de facto possession of the Philippines and its special responsibility to the Filipinos which, he insisted, flowed from that possession. For example, he declared at Cedar Rapids, Iowa, that "we accepted war for humanity. We can accept no terms of peace which shall not be in the interests of humanity." He repeated his appeal at Omaha: "The war was no more invited by us than were the questions which are laid at our door by its results. Now as then we will do our duty . . . , seeking only the highest good of the nation, and recognizing no other obligation, pursuing no other path, but that of duty." Still later in Boston he declared that "our concern was not for territory or trade or empire, but for the people whose interests and destiny, without our willing, had been put into our hands."[58] The president simply refused to dwell on the burdens of empire at all. It was not strange that the American people, given the simple choice between humanity and inhumanity, assured him of their overwhelming support.

From late October until December 1898, McKinley faced a divided peace commission, then deliberating in Paris. On October 25 he requested the opinions of the commissioners on the issue of annexation. "There is a very general feeling," he wrote, "that the United States, whatever it might prefer as to the Philippines, is in a situation where it cannot let go, . . . and it is my judgment that the well-considered opinion of the majority would be that duty requires we should take the archipelago."[59] Four members of the commission—Whitelaw Reid, editor of the *New York Tribune*, Senators Cushman K. Davis of Minnesota and William P. Frye of Maine, and former Secretary of State Day, chairman of the commission—favored the annexation of all or part of the Philippines; however, Senator George Gray of Delaware, the only Democrat on the commission, was absolutely opposed. He warned McKinley that annexation would "make necessary a navy equal to the largest of powers, a greatly increased military establishment, immense sums for fortifications and harbors, multiple occasions for dangerous complications with foreign nations, and increased burdens of taxation. . . . On the whole, instead of indemnity—injury."[60] Despite such advice, McKinley instructed the commission to claim all the Philippine Islands. To leave any of the islands in Spanish hands, he advised, would create later problems and oppose the interests of humanity. Unable to establish the right of conquest, the commissioners overcame

[58]*New York Times*, October 12, 13, 1898, ibid.
[59]McKinley to Day, October 25, 1898, ibid., pp. 107–08.
[60]George Gray to Hay, October 28, 1898, in *FRUS, 1898*, p. 934.

their dilemma by offering an indemnity. Late in November they framed the final demands on the Spanish government: the cession of Puerto Rico, Guam, and the entire Philippine archipelago to the United States in exchange for $20 million. Spain reluctantly accepted these terms and signed the Treaty of Paris on December 10, 1898.

Opponents of expansion—and they were legion—placed powerful intellectual obstacles in the path of the annexationists. In November a group of distinguished citizens, including former President Cleveland and industrialist Andrew Carnegie, formed the Anti-Imperialist League. Members of the league detected in the acquisition of the Philippines a serious violation of the nation's democratic principles. David Starr Jordan, the noted American educator, told a San Francisco audience that there was great danger that in their easy victory the American people "might lose sight of the basal principles of the Republic, a co-operative association in which 'all just government is derived from the consent of the governed.'" Former President Cleveland professed amazement at the extent to which the nation tolerated "the fatal un-American idea of imperialism and expansion. . . . The extent of this," he added, "presents to me a new startling phase in our national character, and a craze which, like a fever, must have its course." Senator Hoar anchored his speech of January 9, 1899 against annexation to this sentiment: "You cannot subjugate [the Filipinos] . . . because you think it is for their own good. . . . You have no right at the cannon's mouth to impose on an unwilling people your Declaration of Independence . . . your notions of freedom [and] . . . of what is good."[61]

More serious was the charge that the acquisition of the Philippines was a departure from America's traditional conservatism in foreign policy. The assertion that the United States was overextending itself in the Pacific raised issues from which there was no escape. The acquisition of distant territories would entail financial and military burdens with few rewards. The United States, wrote Carnegie, lacked not only the naval power to protect the Philippines but also the will to create it.[62] Some antiexpansionists conceded the need for a coaling station in the Philippines; they denied that the United States needed more. "Must Great Britain own the whole of Spain," demanded Schurz, "in order

[61]For a general discussion of the anti-imperialist movement see Fred Harvey Harrington, "The Anti-Imperialist Movement in the United States, 1898–1900," *Mississippi Valley Historical Review* 22 (September 1935): 211–30. Hoar's speech is in *Congressional Record*, 55th Cong., 3d sess., pt. 1, pp. 494–503; the quotation is on p. 503. Hoar insisted that he stood for the principles of Alexander Hamilton, George Washington, John Adams, John Quincy Adams, and Daniel Webster in denying that the United States had any obligation to distant peoples.

[62]Andrew Carnegie, "Distant Possessions—The Parting of the Ways," *North American Review* 167 (August 1898): 239–48.

to hold Gibraltar?" Schurz feared that Philippine annexation so completely overcommitted the nation that it would reduce the United States
to utter reliance on the British fleet. Such indebtedness would demand
a price of its own. "If we do take the Philippines," he concluded, "and
thus entangle ourselves in the rivalries of Asiatic affairs, the future will
be . . . one of wars and rumors of wars, and the time will be forever
past when we could look down with condescending pity on the nations
of the old world groaning under militarism and its burdens."[63] Senator
Augustus O. Bacon of Georgia foresaw "peace at evening, perhaps,
with no certainty but that the morrow will find us participants in a
world's war." Against such arguments Senate approval came hard, but
it came. The final vote was 57 to 27, one more than necessary to gain
the required two thirds. On February 9, 1899, Lodge reported the
victory to Roosevelt: "It was the closest, hardest fight I have ever
known, and probably we shall never see another in our time when there
was so much at stake."[64]

Almost forgotten in the euphoria was the mounting political crisis
in the Philippines which erupted into war before the end of February.
To repress the Filipino insurrection the United States required three
years of fighting, much of it a bitter, costly, and divisive guerrilla war
that employed almost eight times the military forces needed to defeat
the Spaniards in Cuba. Ultimately, the drastic antiguerrilla tactics, the
atrocities, the destruction of villages, and the concentration camps to
control the population captured the world's press, tarnished the nation's
reputation, and produced its share of scandals.[65] But the more fundamental costs of the Philippine annexation lay elsewhere. That decision destroyed the nation's basic isolation from the Eastern Hemisphere
by extending the Monroe Doctrine to the western Pacific. Only the
splendid victory over the Spanish squadron at Manila Bay obscured
the magnitude of the nation's new obligations. So remote were the
burdens of empire that many Americans assumed that the acquisition
of the Philippines strengthened the nation. Unfortunately, this would
have been true only if the cost of maintaining an adequate defense of
the islands were offset by sources of power in the new territories which

[63]Carl Schurz, "American Imperialism," a convocation address at the University
of Chicago, January 4, 1899, pp. 20–21. See also Schurz, "American Imperialism," in
W. J. Bryan, ed., *Republic or Empire? The Philippine Question* (Chicago, 1899), pp. 332–36.
Perhaps most telling was William Graham Sumner's conservative attack on Philippine
annexation, in "The Conquest of the United States by Spain," *Yale Law Journal* 8 (January
1899): 168–93.

[64]Lodge to Roosevelt, February 9, 1899, in Lodge, *Correspondence of Roosevelt and
Lodge*, 1:391.

[65]For details of the war see Welch, *The United States and the Philippine-American War*,
passim.

equaled or exceeded the power required for their defense. Actually the Philippines were so distant and defenseless that only a massive American defense effort could render them secure. As Thucydides, the Greek historian, wrote many centuries ago, "You cannot decline the burdens of empire and still expect to share its honours."[66] For this challenge of empire there was no precedent in the American experience. The occasional warnings that the United States possessed no naval forces adequate for the defense of its far-flung commitments passed almost unnoticed. The suddenness and completeness of the changes wrought by expansion measured the extent to which illusions emanating from the habit of easy success had supplanted analysis in the conduct of the nation's foreign relations.

V

Soon events in China drew the United States even deeper into the politics of the western Pacific. American commercial and missionary activity in China had long sustained an interest in Washington and elsewhere in that country's internal peace and stability. Japan's successful assault on China in 1894, following a long confrontation over Korea, demonstrated that China could not protect its political and territorial integrity against external pressure. In the subsequent peace treaty, Japan dispossessed China of Formosa, the Pescadores, and the strategic Liaotung Peninsula. Moreover, Japan forced China to recognize the independence of Korea and to grant Japanese citizens the same trading privileges in China enjoyed by citizens of the Western powers. Neither the United States nor Great Britain chose to interfere, but Russia, Germany, and France, at China's request, demanded that Japan, in the interest of peace, return the Liaotung Peninsula to China. The U.S. minister to China, Charles Denby, warned Peking that European intervention was "more likely to produce dismemberment [of China] than any action that may be taken by Japan." He added his conviction that "unless Russia and England and France are more disinterested than history shows them to be they will each demand heavy

---

[66]In similar fashion the *Saturday Review* (London) noted that the United States had entered the war and acquired the Philippines light-heartedly and without mental or physical preparation. It had warned in December 1898 that "to the United States it is the beginning of a new era in which her moral as well as her material power will be sharply tested." *Saturday Review* 86 (December 17, 1898): 802. Two weeks later it observed: "It is not inconceivable that, when they realise what a colonial empire means, the Americans may sell their new acquisitions." Ibid. (December 31, 1898): 869. The United States had achieved much in 1898, the publication agreed, but declared that the real costs still lay in the future. What the country needed, therefore, was more humility. Ibid. (December 10, 1898): 774.

compensation for any services rendered to China." Denby advised the Chinese to follow their true policy and seek "a sincere, friendly rapprochement with Japan,"[67] but they ignored his advice. Japan, unable to resist the combined powers of Europe, complied with their demand.

As Denby predicted, China's troubles had only begun. Russia's ambitions toward China were at least the equal of Japan's. Having gained possession of Vladivostok and undertaken the construction of the Trans-Siberian Railway to strengthen its presence in East Asia, Russia now joined Germany and France in dividing China "like a melon" into spheres of influence. During March 1897, France gained control of the island of Hainan. In November German troops, employing the murder of two German Catholic priests as a pretext, seized Kiaochow, a port on the Shantung Peninsula, a seizure legalized in March 1898 as a leasehold. Not to be outdone, Russia that month forced from the Chinese government a twenty-five-year lease to the fine harbor at Port Arthur. China seemed in danger of disappearing piecemeal.[68]

American business groups operating in China, especially exporters of cotton goods and the American-China Development Company, viewed these developments with grave concern. Left unopposed the European powers eventually would wipe out the equal trading and investment privileges which Americans enjoyed in China. In January 1898, Denby reminded the McKinley administration that present trends toward exclusive economic spheres would tend to destroy American markets in China: "We should urge on China the reform of all evils in her government which touch American interests, and the adoption of vigorous measures in the line of material progress." He believed it essential that the U.S. government officially denounce the actions in China of Germany, Russia, and France. The United States, having only commercial, financial, and missionary interests in China, could best protect those interests through a Chinese government strong and efficient enough to defend the principle of equal opportunity among

[67]For the Sino-Japanese War and peace treaty see Hilary Conroy, *The Japanese Seizure of Korea, 1868–1910: A Study of Realism and Idealism in International Relations* (Philadelphia, 1960), passim; William L. Langer, *The Diplomacy of Imperialism* (New York, 1951), pp. 170–72; and Treat, *Diplomatic Relations Between the United States and Japan*, 2:443–544. For Denby's advice to China see Denby to Gresham, February 26, 1895, Diplomatic Despatches, China, 97, No. 2148, National Archives. For this communication I am indebted to James A. Busselle.

[68]"European Aggressions in China," *Nation* 71 (July 26, 1900): 65–66. French agreement with China on Hainan, March 15, 1897, German lease of Kiaochow, March 6, 1898, Russian lease of the Liaotung Peninsula, with the port of Port Arthur, March 27, 1898, in John V. A. MacMurray, ed., *Treaties and Agreements with and Concerning China, 1894–1919*, 2 vols. (New York, 1921), pp. 98, 112, 119–21.

foreign groups operating there.[69] Speaking for American business interests in China, the New York Chamber of Commerce memorialized the federal government in February 1898:

> That there are important changes now going on in the relations of European powers to the Empire of China . . . affecting the privileges enjoyed under existing treaty rights by American citizens trading in and with China. That the trade of the United States to China is now rapidly increasing, and is destined, with the further opening of that country, to assume large proportions unless arbitrarily debarred by the action of foreign governments. . . . That, in view of the changes threatening to future trade development of the United States in China, the Chamber of Commerce . . . respectfully and earnestly urge that such proper steps be taken as will commend themselves to your wisdom for the prompt and energetic defence of the existing treaty rights of our citizens in China, and for the preservation and protection of their important commercial interests in that Empire.

Whatever the concern of U.S. business groups in China's future, they offered no specific prescriptions for a new American China policy.[70]

Britain's interests in China were far more extensive than those of the United States. Britain had long dominated the foreign commerce of China through the British-operated Chinese Imperial Maritime Customs Service. Unwilling to use force to maintain its free access to all Chinese ports, London sought to interest the United States in a joint defense of the Open Door in China. In March 1898 the British government, through its minister in Washington, approached the McKinley administration for a cooperative policy "in opposing any action of foreign powers which would tend to restrain the opening of China to the commerce of all nations."[71] The president expressed sympathy with British purpose, but, having been assured by Germany and Russia that they had no intention of defying the principle of open trade in China,

[69]On Denby's efforts to defend American commercial interests in China see Charles S. Campbell, *Special Business Interests and the Open Door Policy* (New Haven, CT, 1951), pp. 25–29, 33–34.

[70]Marilyn Blatt Young has developed this theme in "American Expansion, 1870–1900: The Far East," in Barton J. Bernstein, ed., *Towards a New Past: Dissenting Essays in American History* (New York, 1968), pp. 189–90. Charles Beresford, Britain's noted advocate of the Open Door, wrote that, while the Japanese desired to act in some practical manner, he "could discover no desire on the part of the commercial communities in the United States to engage in any practical effort for preserving what to them might become in the future a trade, the extent of which no mortal can conjecture." Ibid., p. 190.

[71]Quoted in R. G. Neale, "Anglo-American Relations During the Spanish-American War" (M.A. thesis, University of Melbourne, 1955), pp. 108–09. Lord Bryce urged British-American cooperation in China, in "Some Thoughts on the Policy of the United States," *Harper's New Monthly Magazine* 97 (September 1898): 609–18.

he informed the British that he saw no reason to depart from America's traditional policy of noninvolvement. That spring, moreover, the United States faced the immediate problem of Cuba. During 1898 the British government encouraged the United States to acquire the Philippines, but it reversed its policies in China. Convinced that the Peking government was too weak to protect British interests in China, London officials acquired a lease of Weihaiwei, a port on the Shantung Peninsula opposite Port Arthur. Next, they acquired special concessions in the Yangtze River Valley and at Kowloon, opposite Hong Kong. Britain thus retreated in self-defense to the policy of leaseholds which initially it had condemned.[72]

When Secretary of State John Hay in September 1899 finally issued the famous Open Door Notes, his action was largely unilateral. The occasion for the actual formulation of the notes was the visit of Alfred E. Hippisley to Washington. Hippisley, a private British citizen employed by the Chinese Maritime Customs Service, was completely devoted to Chinese interests. He saw that European and British policy in China was reducing the customs receipts of Peking and, with that loss, any hope of building an effective Chinese administration. Members of the McKinley administration fully shared his bitter opposition to the trends within China. Thus when Hippisley, during a visit to his wife's relatives in Baltimore, renewed his acquaintance with William W. Rockhill, Hay's adviser on Far Eastern matters, he found a receptive audience. Hippisley doubted that Washington could terminate the spheres of influence in China; he hoped merely that the United States, by restating its treaty rights in China, might encourage the other powers to maintain the principle of commercial equality in the ports which they controlled. Rockhill forwarded the gist of Hippisley's memorandum to Hay, whereupon the secretary instructed Rockhill to prepare notes to be sent to the European powers.[73]

Hay's Open Door Notes, sent originally to Russia, Great Britain, and Germany (later to Italy, France, and Japan), requested assurances from each nation that it would not interfere with the treaty rights or special interests of other countries within its spheres of influence in

---

[72]For the British agreements with China on the Yangtze Valley, the new territories beyond Kowloon, and the port of Weihaiwei see MacMurray, *Treaties and Agreements with and Concerning China*, pp. 104, 130, 152. The lease to Weihaiwei was to extend as long as the Russians held Port Arthur. Even some American journals agreed that since China was falling apart the British were wise to take a piece rather than fight other powers on the question of leaseholds. See *Nation* 66 (April 14, 1898): 277.

[73]On the role of Hippisley and others in the formulation of the Open Door Notes see Paul A. Varg, *Open Door Diplomat: The Life of W. W. Rockhill* (Urbana, IL, 1952), pp. 26–32; A. Whitney Griswold, *The Far Eastern Policy of the United States* (New York, 1938), pp. 36–76.

China. Hay asked, moreover, that each country involved in China in no way interfere with any treaty port or vested interest; that it allow the collection of existing Chinese tariffs, irrespective of spheres of influence; and that it treat its own citizens and other nationals alike in making such assessments as harbor dues.[74] He made no effort to terminate the established spheres of influence, although he made clear in his note to Britain that he opposed them. The replies, especially from Britain and Russia, approved the Open Door for China in principle; otherwise, they were evasive.[75] Still, the secretary chose to announce to the world in March 1900 that his notes had brought favorable responses from all six countries. The acceptance of his proposals, Hay declared, was "final and definite." Some three months later, when China's Boxer Rebellion compelled the powers to dispatch troops to rescue their nationals from the besieged legations at Peking, the secretary reiterated, in a new round of notes, that the American purpose in China included preserving Chinese territorial and administrative integrity, as well as the safeguarding for all nations "the principle of equal and impartial trade with all parts of the Chinese Empire."[76] Hay's second Open Door Notes were unilateral declarations; they did not ask the powers for their agreement.

Much of the American and European press took Hay's diplomatic exchanges at face value. Never before, it seemed, had the United States gained such unlimited commercial and humanitarian objectives at such negligible cost. For some Americans Hay's contribution to the Open Door ranked him with the greatest of nineteenth-century American diplomats. Senator Shelby M. Cullom of Illinois offered a characteristic eulogy: "The magnitude of the man [Hay] will only appear in the magnitude of his work when it reaches its colossal proportions in the proper perspective of the past. . . . It is claiming nothing not fully accorded to him to say that at home he has long held a position beside John Quincy Adams, Daniel Webster and Seward, the greatest of our Secretaries of State. . . . It is suggestively true that his genius for statecraft has gained fuller recognition in the Old World than among his

---

[74]Open Door Notes: Hay to White (Germany), September 6, 1899, in *FRUS, 1899* (Washington, 1901), pp. 129–30; Hay to Choate (England), September 6, 1899, ibid., pp. 131–33; Hay to Tower (Russia), September 6, 1899, ibid., pp. 140–41.

[75]The British and Russian replies made no concessions on leaseholds but agreed to the Open Door principle within their spheres of influence. See Salisbury to Choate, November 30, 1899, ibid., p. 136; and Count Mouravieff to Tower, December 18–30, 1899, ibid., pp. 141–42. Russia's reply was more evasive than Britain's. Hay wrote in April 1900 that Russia was "opposed to the whole business from the beginning; and did what she could to block our game." See Allan Nevins, *Henry White* (New York, 1930), p. 168.

[76]Hay's note to the powers of March 20, 1900, ibid., p. 142. For the second Open Door Note of July 3, 1900 see *FRUS, 1901*, Appendix 1, p. 18.

own countrymen." Much of the press lauded the secretary for his momentous success. The *New York Journal of Commerce* called the Open Door episode "one of the most important diplomatic negotiations of our time." The *London Daily Chronicle* viewed the Open Door Notes as "to some extent a guarantee against the dismemberment of China." The *Nation* joined other journals in praising the Open Door policy as a great national triumph. "Our intervention in China," ran its conclusion, "has given the world a transcendent exhibition of American leadership in the world of ideas and the world of action. We have proved that we are guided by a diplomacy unsurpassed in its grasp of the situation, in its clear and consistent policy, in its patient moderation, its firmness, its moral impulse."[77]

Actually, as others noted, Hay's apparent achievements on behalf of China carried the seeds of disaster. They, like the acquisition of the Philippines, confirmed the illusion that the United States could have its way in the Orient at little or no cost to itself. More realistic observers saw that Hay's diplomacy either had committed the United States to the use of force in a disorganized region of the Far East, or it had achieved nothing; no nation would have compromised its essential interests in China merely at his request. "Diplomacy has done nothing to change the situation," warned the *Springfield Republican*, "while the Government has gone far toward placing itself in a position where, to be consistent, it must guarantee by military force the territorial integrity of China, or share in a possible partition."[78] Similarly, Alfred Thayer Mahan observed in November 1900 that the United States could not "count upon respect for the territory of China unless we are ready to throw not only our moral influence but, if necessity arise, our physical weight into the conflict, to resist an expropriation, the result of which might be to exclude our commerce and neutralize our influence." Mahan noted that both Russia and Japan, the two dominant powers in the Far East, had far greater interests in China than did the United States.[79] But the Open Door policy, by establishing a powerful and exaggerated American concern for the commercial and territorial integrity of China, rendered any country that might challenge Chinese will the potential enemy of the United States.

[77]*Public Opinion* 28 (April 5, 1900): 419–21; *Literary Digest* 20 (January 13, 1900): 35; *Times* (London), January 15, 1900; *London Daily Chronicle*, quoted in *New York Times*, January 3, 1900; *Nation* 70 (April 5, 1900): 254; ibid. 71 (July 19, 1900): 41; John Barrett, "America's Duty in China," *North American Review* 171 (August 1900): 154.

[78]*Springfield Republican* (Massachusetts), quoted in *Public Opinion* 28 (April 5, 1900): 420.

[79]Alfred Thayer Mahan, "Effects of Asiatic Conditions Upon International Policies," *North American Review* 171 (November 1900): 618; Mahan, *The Problem of Asia* (Boston, 1900), p. 179.

Editors, politicians, and businessmen looked confidently to the Far East as the new stage for American activity; they revealed no hesitancy in assigning to Washington the major responsibility for the management of that region's future evolution. In January 1900, Senator Beveridge dramatically acknowledged the new U.S. interest in the Pacific:

> The Philippines are ours forever.... And just beyond the Philippines are China's illimitable markets. We will not retreat from either.... We will not renounce our part in the mission of our race, trustee, under God, of the civilization of the world.... The Pacific is our ocean.... The power that rules the Pacific ... is the power that rules the world. And, with the Philippines, that power is and will forever be the American Republic.[80]

The possible, even probable, consequences of such optimism for American foreign relations were clear only to a minority of intellectuals who warned that no American interests in the Pacific merited carte blanche commitments. Indeed, U.S. expansion in that area triumphed with such negligible national effort that it failed completely to challenge the American people's isolationist habits of mind. It never occurred to most citizens, or even to their leaders, that these new obligations in the Pacific one day might make exorbitant demands on the Republic. Americans understood only that they were on the road to world prominence and could not turn back. The war with Spain and subsequent expansion had struck a responsive chord, feeding national and racial pride, promising lucrative trade, and redeeming the traditional belief in the nation's mission to humanity.

VI

Developments in both Europe and East Asia at the turn of the century uncovered a full spectrum of Anglo-American interests which previous decades of experience had denied. Britain's relationship to the European continent was not reassuring. For fifty years that country had pursued a policy of strict isolation, but in 1898 the older assumptions of a stable and balanced Europe were no longer valid. Britain confronted a continent heavily armed and divided by the Triple Alliance of Germany, Austria, and Italy, and the Franco-Russian alliance of recent vintage. All Continental countries were in varying degrees jealous

---

[80]Beveridge's speech in the Senate, January 9, 1900, *Congressional Record*, 56th Cong., 1st sess., p. 704.

of Britain's power and wealth, colonial possessions, and remarkable progress. London officials could not predict how Europe's great powers— France, Germany, and Russia—would fit into future British policies. For Joseph Chamberlain, Britain's noted colonial secretary, the answer to Europe's puzzle lay in drawing all parts of the empire into closer unity and in maintaining "the bonds of permanent unity with our kinsmen across the Atlantic."[81] During the spring of 1898 many in Britain speculated openly on the possible alliance between Great Britain and the United States. Lord Charles Beresford, a member of Parliament, declared that "an Anglo-American alliance would be the most powerful factor in the world for peace and the development of commerce." The most dramatic appeal for an alliance came from Chamberlain himself. "There is a powerful and generous nation speaking our language, bred of our race, and having interests identical with ours," he reminded a Birmingham audience on May 13. "I would go so far as to say that, terrible as war may be, even a war itself would be cheaply purchased if, in a great and noble cause, the Stars and Stripes and the Union Jack should wave together over an Anglo-Saxon alliance."[82]

American leaders no more than the country generally were prepared in 1898 to link the fate of the United States directly and permanently to that of Britain, yet some understood that the United States, no more than Britain, could act any longer on the world stage in total disregard of the European powers. Roosevelt responded to the demands of the changing international environment by asserting that the English-speaking people "are now closer together than for a century and a quarter, and that every effort should be made to keep them close together; for their interests are really fundamentally the same, and they are most closely akin . . . in feeling and principle, than either is akin to any other people in the world."[83] Ambassador Hay had declared publicly in London on April 20 that "we are bound by ties we did not forge and that we can not break. We are joint ministers in the same sacred mission of freedom and progress, charged with duties we can not evade." The Lansing Journal, in response to Chamberlain's Birmingham speech, admonished Washington that "the statesmen of the United States would be matchless ingrates if they did not reciprocate Mr. Chamberlain's sentiments and consider his proposals in the same

---

[81]Chamberlain is quoted in Literary Digest 16 (May 28, 1898): 634.

[82]Beresford is quoted in ibid. (April 30, 1898): 511; Chamberlain in ibid. (May 28, 1898): 634.

[83]Roosevelt to Arthur Hamilton Lee, November 25, 1898, in Elting E. Morison, ed., The Letters of Theodore Roosevelt, 8 vols. (Cambridge, MA., 1951–1954), 2:890.

frank and lofty spirit in which they are so obviously proffered."[84] For some American observers this apparent Anglo-American rapprochement guaranteed both the security of the two nations and the peace of the world. *Munsey's Magazine* observed in July 1898 that "a mutual understanding between Britain and America would be more likely to assure the world's tranquility than to break it; but whether the future is one of war or of peace, the influence of such a rapprochement would be tremendous. . . . With all the English speaking races standing together, there would not be much doubt as to the hegemony of the world." For Samuel E. Moffett, writing in *Forum*, a reunion of the English-speaking peoples would reduce international relations to their ultimate stability.[85]

What fueled Anglo-American apprehension was Germany's naval expansion. In January 1897, Admiral Alfred von Tirpitz became head of naval planning in Germany and quickly committed the Reichstag to an impressive building program. The Naval Act of 1898 provided for nineteen battleships and more than forty large and small cruisers. Then in 1900 the Reichstag allowed for a much larger navy with four squadrons of eight battleships each in addition to numerous lighter craft. Unfortunately, Germany hardly could become a great power in the Atlantic without acquiring naval stations in the Caribbean in direct defiance of the Monroe Doctrine. For that reason it required no more than Tirpitz's appointment to inaugurate a broad anti-German reaction in the United States. As early as January 1897, Poulteny Bigelow warned his readers in the *North American Review* that "Germany can do nothing outside of her borders without ships-of-war, and that she is building up her navy can only mean that she intends to participate actively in events beyond the seas." He added that "it should not surprise us if we read some morning that the German flag had been hoisted on St. Thomas or Curacao as a practical protest to our pretensions."[86] The *Review of Reviews* observed in May 1897 that German leaders had their eyes on South America and were increasing their navy for the purpose of seizing territory in the Western Hemisphere.[87] By contrast Anglo-American relations in Latin America had improved steadily in the late 1890s. Britain wanted only the protection of its

[84]Hay is quoted in *Literary Digest* 16 (April 30, 1898): 512; *Lansing Journal* (Michigan), quoted in ibid. (May 28, 1898): 637.

[85]"Britain and America," *Munsey's Magazine* 19 (July 1898): 603; Samuel E. Moffett, "Ultimate World Politics," *Forum* 27 (August 1899): 667–68.

[86]For German naval policy see Gerard Fiennes, *Sea Power and Freedom: A Historical Study* (New York, 1918), pp. 260ff. See Poulteny Bigelow's warning, in Bigelow, "The German Press and the United States," *North American Review* 164 (January 1897): 20–21.

[87]"The German Menace," *Review of Reviews* 15 (May 1897): 585.

possessions and its commercial access to the region. Having no territorial ambitions in Latin America, the British welcomed the Monroe
Doctrine as a status quo policy that served British as well as American
interests. Roosevelt detected this mutuality of concern when he wrote
in February 1898: "I feel most we should . . . beware of letting a foolish
hatred of England blind us to our own honor and interests. . . . Germany, and not England, is the power with whom we are most apt to
have trouble over the Monroe Doctrine."[88]

At issue in Germany's alleged threat to the Monroe Doctrine was
the continued dominance of the British navy in the Atlantic. Until
Germany could strike down British naval supremacy, observed the
Review of Reviews in July 1897, it would be "cabined, cribbed, and conned
between the fortress-guarded frontiers of the German Empire in Europe."
The *Contemporary Review* warned that Germany could achieve its goal
of becoming the leading commercial and colonial power in the world
only by securing the downfall of Britain.[89] In acknowledging Germany's
challenge to England's naval position, Roosevelt warned Sir Cecil Spring-
Rice in August 1897 that Great Britain must eventually "crush the
German Navy and the German commercial marine out of existence."
For Roosevelt, Britain, with its naval power, remained an essential
defender of the Monroe Doctrine. As he wrote to Elihu Root in January
1900, "If the disaster to the British Empire . . . should come about, it
may very well be that in but a few years we shall be face to face with
the question of either abandoning the Monroe Doctrine and submitting
to acquisition of American territory by some great military power or
going to war."[90] For countless observers the burgeoning anti-Germanism
of the late 1890s submerged the fears of previous years that Russia,
not Germany, was the ultimate danger to Europe's equilibrium and
thus to Anglo-American security.

German naval and territorial ambitions apparently created a body
of mutual Anglo-American interests in the Far East as well. When
London in 1898 encouraged the United States to acquire the Philippines, the *Boston Herald* saw British policy for what it was: an effort to
make Anglo-American friendship a predominant factor in the western
Pacific. "[Britain] is seeking our favour now," the *Herald* explained,
"because she is out of favour with her sister powers in Europe and

[88]Roosevelt to Charles Arthur Moore, February 14, 1898, in Morison, *Letters of Roosevelt*, 1:772.

[89]*Review of Reviews* 16 (July 1897): 81; *Contemporary Review*, quoted in "The Kaiser's Designs on England," ibid. 19 (January 1899): 86.

[90]Roosevelt to Cecil Spring-Rice, August 13, 1897, in Morison, *Letters of Roosevelt*, 1:645; Roosevelt to Elihu Root, January 29, 1900, ibid., 2:1151. Roosevelt wondered why Germany would threaten the interests of Britain and the United States in the Atlantic when its real danger lay in Russia. Ibid., 1:645.

would like us for an ally in her conflict with them. As the field of such conflict is likely to be the East, she would like us to go there and hence her reason for advising us to take the Philippines."[91] At the same time, the English *Saturday Review*, in December 1898, observed that the American peace negotiators involved in acquiring the Philippines were "making their bargain . . . under the protecting naval strength of England. And we shall expect, to be quite frank, a material *quid pro quo* for this assistance. We shall expect to be remembered when [the United States] comes into her kingdom in the Philippines. . . . For the young imperialist has entered upon a path where she will require a stout friend."[92]

Commodore Dewey and Admiral von Diedrichs avoided a confrontation at Manila in 1898, but the presence of the German squadron suggested that Germany was determined to establish a strong presence in the western Pacific. Indeed, Hay reported from London on August 2, after conversing with the German ambassador, that Spain had ambitions in the Philippines. Such suppositions reinforced Washington's determination to hold the Philippines and London's to support that decision. In 1899 Germany gained several significant bases in the north Pacific when it purchased the Carolines and Ladrones from Spain; its known ambitions in China recommended closer Anglo-American cooperation in that region as well. Mahan argued that need in the *North American Review*: "Of all the nations we shall meet in the East, Great Britain is the one with which we have by far the most in common." Roosevelt acknowledged his agreement in a letter to Mahan in which he asserted that the United States and Britain should work together in China, using their combined naval power to ensure especially the proper development of the Yangtze Valley as essential for China's growth.[93] Thus Britain's undiminished role as a world power, supported by Anglo-American cooperation, seemed to ensure the maintenance of three fundamental American purposes: the balance of power in Europe, the Monroe Doctrine for the Western Hemisphere, and the Open Door for China. A rapprochement between Great Britain and the United States had become, for much of the old established American foreign policy elite, the essential foundation for a secure and peaceful future. Together the two English-speaking countries would ensure the advance of their civilization, for themselves and for the rest of the world.

[91] *Boston Herald*, quoted in Neale, "Anglo-American Relations During the Spanish-American War," p. 105.

[92] "The New-Comer in High Politics," *Saturday Review* 86 (December 3, 1898): 725.

[93] Mahan, "Effects of Asiatic Conditions Upon International Policies," p. 620; Roosevelt to Mahan, March 18, 1901, in Morison, *Letters of Roosevelt*, 3:23.

VII

In 1900 the American people could look back on a century of diplomatic success unparalleled in history. What appeared to serve its interests abroad the nation had achieved both quickly and cheaply. The Republic had freed the Mississippi Valley of British and Spanish intrigue, and the Mediterranean of piratical attacks on American seamen; it had relieved the French of Louisiana, the Spaniards of Florida, the British of Oregon, and the Russians of Alaska; it had driven the Mexicans out of Texas, New Mexico, and California; and more recently, it had deprived Spain of Cuba, Puerto Rico, and the Philippines. When on occasion the nation had gone to war, its measurable gains always seemed to exceed the price of victory. Never was this more true than for the Civil War itself. Despite that struggle's physical cost to North and South alike, few Americans in 1900 would have regarded the price of reforging the Union excessive. Thus no nation of modern times had achieved its purposes more consistently, completely, and at less cost to its people.

These triumphs in diplomacy and war were not accidental. What mattered was the continuing relationship of ends to means. The quality of American power and energy, when contrasted to the actual goals which the nation pursued, always placed the United States in the commanding position, both diplomatically and militarily. American successes had not been extracted from a perennial struggle against powerful neighbors that might have prevented those successes entirely or have forced the country to pay an exorbitant price for them. Instead, the country's advance to greatness had comprised, in large measure, the clearing of forests, the tilling of soil, the occupying of a vast, rich continental domain. In this experience the American people had faced no opposing forces more demanding than the scattered Indian tribes, which on occasion fought to protect their tribal hunting grounds. When the nation moved beyond its private preserve to achieve its ends through diplomacy or war, it faced, after 1815, enemies no more powerful than Mexico and Spain. By limiting its objectives to the North American continent, where it possessed a total strategic advantage, the United States, in its conflicts with such dominant nations as England and France, always had benefited from the weakening effect of distance.

The country's almost unprecedented security, maintained at such little expense, resulted essentially from factors that lay outside the Western Hemisphere. Never in history had a nation been so completely the beneficiary of all fundamental trends in world politics as was the United States in the nineteenth century. The nation's strength—relative to Europe's great powers the greatest that it ever wielded—took its precise character, first of all, from the sheer size of the oceans. The Atlantic alone would have demanded an excess of power and productivity to establish a European presence in the Western Hemisphere commensurate with that of the United States. However, what made the Atlantic an even greater barrier to European encroachment was the British navy, as much a defender of U.S. interests in the Atlantic as if the American people had paid for every ship. Behind the British navy lay the European balance of power. Indeed, any successful venture by a Continental power into the Western Hemisphere would have comprised such a massive threat to the European balance that the foreign powers themselves would have resorted to war to terminate such a venture.[94] So completely did American purpose in maintaining the political independence of the Latin American states conform to the realities of power in the Atlantic world that the United States required neither war nor the threat of one to protect its basic hemispheric interests. The countries of Asia were too remote and backward to challenge any established American interests either in the Western Hemisphere or in the Pacific. These elements in world politics, all of which served the security interests of the United States, did not determine the quality of the country's behavior, but they ensured the success of policies that were otherwise politically and conceptually sound.

American success flowed from the character of the nation's goals as much as from the varied sources of its power. All of the essential objectives of U.S. policy in the nineteenth century, especially those which measured the country's genuine external achievements, were always limited and precise. All were tangible, comprising territorial adjustment, monetary compensation, or defensive and commercial arrangements. Officials responsible for American policy before 1898, without exception, refrained from committing the United States to the pursuit of abstractions such as liberty, democracy, or justice. Those in power who insisted that the country carried a special burden for humanity thought less of involvement in revolutions abroad than in the creation of a society at home that might be worthy of emulation. For Thomas Jefferson, James Madison, John Quincy Adams, and Abraham Lincoln the United States was never more than an example setter for the world.

Tragically, in the critical years at the turn of the century, U.S. leadership managed to uproot a thoroughly established diplomatic tradition without conveying to that generation of Americans the realization that anything significant had occurred at all. But some

---

[94]For American consciousness of the role of the European balance of power in underwriting the security of the United States see "The United States as a Great Power," *Harper's Weekly* 39 (April 27, 1895): 386.

contemporaries sensed that the decisions of the McKinley years were a turning point in the history of the Republic. What mattered for them was not that the United States had become a world power but that it had deserted, in the process of acquiring the Philippines and committing itself to the territorial and administrative integrity of China, those principles of statecraft which had guided it through its first century of independence. The defiance of American diplomatic experience lay not in the mere absence of a precedent for expansion into the western Pacific. It lay, instead, in the decision to anchor such unprecedented national behavior to abstract moral principles rather than to the political wisdom and common sense of the past. The newly acquired sense of moral obligation which propelled the nation on its new course in world affairs was totally incompatible with the assumptions and methods that had permitted earlier generations of Americans to defend the perennial interests of the United States with style and distinction. After the events of 1899 the nation no longer possessed an unblurred diplomatic tradition that reached deeply into its own history, or which alone could enlighten the thought and decisions of the future.

Not only had the United States assumed vast new commitments without regard to the means required to protect them, but also it faced a world in which all the old sources of national security were rapidly receding from the scene. The country's major antagonists after 1900 were not to be characterized by Mexico and Spain. Two first-class powers, Germany and Japan, had mounted the world stage with the United States. Already Washington's declared preferences in both Europe and the Far East had marked the two countries as potential enemies. Roosevelt expressed the sentiments of many Americans when he addressed his friend, George Von Lengerke Meyer, in 1901: "It seems to me that Germany's attitude toward us makes her the only power with which there is any reasonable likelihood or possibility of our clashing within the future."[95] Soon American interests in Manchuria, added to the country's purposes toward China (as embodied in the principle of the Open Door), would transform Japan into the special antagonist of the United States in the Far East. Not only did the country enter the new century at odds with two of the strongest nations in the world, but also it had chosen to contest their purposes in the Eastern Hemisphere where its interests were seldom clear and where others could more easily bring their power to bear. No longer did the British navy and the traditional European equilibrium guarantee the United States its former protection in the Atlantic world.

---

[95]Roosevelt to George Von Lengerke Meyer, April 12, 1901, in Morison, *Letters of Roosevelt*, 3:52.

These nineteenth-century elements of power had been assumed for so long that the American people were no longer conscious of their contribution to the country's security. Soon the United States would carry the full burden of its policies, whether the policies squared with the nation's historic interests or not.

Finally, the United States entered the new century as a territorially satiated power, satisfied with its possessions and its status among the nations of the world. Enjoying a favored position at little cost to itself (and seemingly unmindful of its potentially costly commitments abroad), the nation began to discard its precise and limited approaches of the nineteenth century, conducted through diplomacy and power. It sought rather those global conditions that would serve its peculiar interests in trade, investment, and peace. This gradual dedication to the status quo completed the silent revolution that the years of expanding interests had wrought in the country's external relations. To preserve its international position without expensive or dangerous foreign policies, the United States required a new world order that would limit further change to peaceful processes, preferably through a system of contractual arrangements among nations. It was logical, therefore, that the United States, as the world's major satisfied nation, would assume the lead in the advocacy of nonpower devices, such as arbitration and conciliation, or even a world court, as the only legitimate means for settling international disputes. Such devices, if universally accepted, would guarantee the country its international advantages without the necessity of war or extensive military preparations.

Such dedication to peaceful procedures universalized the nation's external objectives. Until the Spanish-American War the foreign policies of the United States were rendered solvent by ample power to cover limited, largely hemispheric, goals. The reliance on physical power, always a limited entity, had confined, rather than expanded, American ambition. National interests, equally limited, were no less restrictive. By contrast, moral purposes embodied in the quest for universal peace, democracy, and justice, operating in a supposedly rational world, created endless expectations among those who claimed the selfless obligation to serve mankind. After 1900 the country's official phraseology gradually embraced global abstract objectives which no traditional power could achieve. At the same time, much of the nation's emerging foreign policy elite denied the necessity, even the legitimacy, of force in international affairs. The notion that the United States could achieve a world order based on an effective system of international law made a powerful impact on the country's outlook. It created that strange dichotomy between the advance of the United States to industrial greatness, between its determination to extend its pervasive economic influence into much of the external world, and the price which the country was prepared to pay to sustain even those specific international relationships that had once assured its favored position in world politics. Confronted after the turn of the century, both in Europe and in Asia, by powers that identified their interests with change and accepted the legitimacy of force to achieve it, American leadership could escape its dilemma only by hasty improvisation which often succeeded in protecting the nation's interests but seldom in establishing its precepts.

Articles and Essays by Norman A. Graebner

"Thomas Corwin and the Election of 1848: A Study in Conservative Politics," *Journal of Southern History* 17 (May 1951): 162–79.

"United States Gulf Commerce with Mexico 1822–1848," *Inter-American Economic Affairs* 5 (Summer 1951): 36–51.

"Maritime Factors in the Oregon Compromise," *Pacific Historical Review* 20 (November 1951): 331–45.

"James K. Polk's Wartime Expansionist Policy," East Tennessee Historical Society's *Publications* 23 (1951): 1–14.

"James K. Polk: A Study in Federal Patronage," *Mississippi Valley Historical Review* 38 (March 1952): 613–32.

"Depression and Urban Votes," *Current History* 23 (October 1952): 234–38.

"Polk, Politics, and Oregon," East Tennessee Historical Society's *Publications* 24 (1952): 11–25.

"American Interest in California, 1845," *Pacific Historical Review* 22 (February 1953): 13–27.

"Party Politics and the Trist Mission," *Journal of Southern History* 19 (May 1953): 137–56.

"A Bipartisan Foreign Policy," *Current History* 24 (June 1953): 327–32.

"Political Parties and the Presidency," *Current History* 25 (September 1953): 138–43.

"The American Presidential Tradition," in *Selecting the President: The Twenty-Seventh Discussion and Debate Manual* (1953). Prepared by the National University Extension Association.

"Farm Welfare, 1954," *Current History* 26 (January 1954): 111–16.

"The Farm Issue," *Current History* 27 (October 1954): 249–55.

"Politics in Foreign Policy," *Current History* 28 (January 1955): 7–14.

"Consequences of the China Debate," *World Affairs Quarterly* 26 (October 1955): 255–74.

"The Roots of Our Immigration Policies," *Current History* 29 (November 1955): 285–92.

"New Books on American Foreign Policy," *Current History* 30 (March 1956): 172–75.

"Foreign Policy in '52," *World Affairs Quarterly* 27 (April 1956): 3–26.

"The Changing Nature of the Democratic Party," *Current History* 31 (August 1956): 70–76.

"Foreign Aid and American Policy," *Current History* 31 (October 1956): 212–17.

"The Truman Administration and the Cold War," *Current History* 35 (October 1958): 223–28.

"The West and the Soviet Satellites," *Current History* 36 (April 1959): 193–99.

"The China Illusion," *Current History* 37 (October 1959): 222–27.

"United States: Foreign Relations," *Collier's Year Book, 1960*, for the year 1959. These surveys continued each year until 1975.

"The Cold War: An American View," *International Journal* 15 (Spring 1960): 95–112.

"Alliances and Free World Security," *Current History* 38 (April 1960): 214–19.

"Eisenhower's Popular Leadership," *Current History* 39 (October 1960): 230–36.

"Lincoln and the National Interest," in O. Fritiof Ander, ed., *Lincoln Images: Augustana College Centennial Essays*. Rock Island, IL: Augustana College Library, 1960.

"Northern Diplomacy and European Neutrality," in David Donald, eds., *Why the North Won the Civil War*. Baton Rouge: Louisiana State University Press, 1960.

"Lincoln's Humility," in Ralph G. Newman, ed., *Lincoln for the Ages*. Garden City, NJ: Doubleday and Company, 1960.

"Politics and the Oregon Compromise," *Pacific Northwest Quarterly* 52 (January 1961): 7–14.

"China and Asian Security: An American Dilemma," *International Journal* 16 (Summer 1961): 213–30.

"Nebraska's Missouri River Frontier, 1854–1860," *Nebraska History* 42 (December 1961): 213–35.

"World Report," in *Contemporary Civilization 2*. Chicago: Scott, Foresman and Company, 1961.

"James K. Polk," in Morton Borden, ed., *America's Ten Greatest Presidents.* Chicago: Rand McNally and Company, 1961.

"China: Unanswered Challenge," *Current History* 42 (January 1962): 36–42.

"1848: Southern Politics at the Crossroads," *The Historian* 25 (November 1962): 14–35.

"The United States and the Indochina Crisis: 1954," *World Review* 2 (July 1963): 12–22.

"Can a Nuclear World War Be Avoided?" *The Annals of the American Academy of Political and Social Science* 351 (January 1964): 132–39.

"The United States and European Unity," in Jack D. Dowell, ed., *The Unity of Western Europe.* Pullman: Washington State University Press, 1964.

"U.S. Foreign Policy and Presidential Politics: 1964," *World Review* 4 (March 1965): 14–29.

"Obligation v. Interest in American Foreign Policy," *Australian Journal of Politics and History* 11 (August 1965): 137–49.

"The Limits of Military Aid," *Current History* 50 (June 1966): 353–57.

"United States: Civil War and Reconstruction," in *Encyclopaedia Britannica* (1967).

"American Nominating Politics and the Failure of Consensus: 1968," *Australian Journal of Politics and History* 14 (December 1968): 393–408.

"The University Student and Political Action," *Proceedings of the Fourth Annual Faculty Assembly.* Faculty Senate, State University of New York, 1968, pp. 89–111.

"History and Politics," in Malcolm B. Parsons, ed., *Perspectives in the Study of Politics.* Chicago: Rand McNally and Company, 1968.

"The Uses of Diplomatic History," in Mary B. Humphreys, ed., *Approaches to the Study of International and Intercultural Relations.* Chicago: North Central Association of Colleges and Secondary Schools, 1968.

"Cold War Origins and the Continuing Debate: A Review of Recent Literature," *Journal of Conflict Resolution* 13 (March 1969): 123–32.

"Whither Containment?" *International Journal* 24 (Spring 1969): 246–63.

"Global Containment: The Truman Years," *Current History* 57 (August 1969): 77–83.

"NATO: An Uneasy Alliance," *Current History* 58 (May 1970): 298–303.

"The United States and the Evolution of NATO, 1949–1951," *Teaching History* 4 (May 1970): 15–28.

"The United States and the Soviet Union: The Elusive Peace," *Current History* 59 (October 1970): 193–98.

"The Vitality of Libraries," *Illinois Libraries* 52 (November 1970): 885–90.

"Vietnam and the Intellectual Crisis," *Virginia Journal of International Law* 11 (March 1971): 281–89.

"Germany Between East and West," *Current History* 62 (May 1972): 225–28.

"Diplomacy from the Outside: American Intervention in Vietnam," in Robin Higham, ed., *Civil Wars in the Twentieth Century*. Lexington: University of Kentucky Press, 1972.

"Presidential Politics in a Divided America: 1972," *Australian Journal of Politics and History* 19 (April 1973): 28–47.

"Europe and the Superpowers," *Current History* 64 (April 1973): 145–49.

"World Politics in the New Age," *World Review* 12 (July 1973): 8–21.

"Hoover, Roosevelt, and the Japanese," in Dorothy Borg and Shumpei Okamoto, eds., *Pearl Harbor as History: Japanese-American Relations 1931–1941*. New York: Columbia University Press, 1973.

"How Isolationist Was Nineteenth-Century American Foreign Policy?" in Milton O. Gustafson, ed., *The National Archives and Foreign Relations Research*. Athens: Ohio University Press, 1974.

"Introduction," in Richard Dean Burns and Edward M. Bennett, eds., *Diplomats in Crisis: United States-Chinese-Japanese Relations, 1919–1941*. Santa Barbara: CA: ABC-Clio Press, 1974.

"Japan: Unanswered Challenge, 1931–1941," in Margaret F. Morris and Sandra L. Myres, eds., *Essays on American Foreign Policy*. Austin: University of Texas Press, 1974.

"United States Policy and NATO's Southern Flank," *The Globe* 13 (August 1975): 1–4.

"History, Society, and the Right to Privacy," *Proceedings of the First Rockefeller Archive Center Conference*, 1975, pp. 20–24.

"The Manchurian Crisis, 1931–1932," in Robin Higham, ed., *Intervention or Abstention: The Dilemma of American Foreign Policy*. Lexington: University of Kentucky Press, 1975.

"Presidential Power and Foreign Affairs," in Charles W. Dunn, ed., *The Future of the American Presidency*. Morristown, NJ: General Learning Press, 1975.

An Essay on Freedom. University Park: Pennsylvania State University, 1975.

The Records of Public Officials. New York: American Assembly, 1975.

"European Interventionism and the Crisis of 1862," *Journal of the Illinois State Historical Society* 69 (February 1976): 35–45.

"Henry Kissinger and American Foreign Policy: A Contemporary Appraisal," *Australian Journal of Politics and History* 22 (April 1976): 7–22.

"America's Search for World Order," *Virginia Quarterly Review* 52 (Spring 1976): 161–82.

"Christianity and Democracy: Tocqueville's Views of Religion in America," *Journal of Religion* 56 (July 1976): 263–73.

"America in the World," in William T. Alderson, ed., *American Issues: Understanding Who We Are*. Nashville: American Association for State and Local History, 1976.

"The Spirit of Expansion: 'Fifty-four Forty or Fight,' " in Henry Steele Commager, ed., *The American Destiny: An Illustrated Bicentennial History of the United States*. London: Danbury Press, 1976.

"Thomas Corwin and the Sectional Crisis," *Ohio History 86* (Autumn 1977): 229–47.

"The Limits of Victory," *Studies in Modern European History and Culture* 3 (1977): 75–93.

"Morgenthau as Historian," in Kenneth Thompson and Robert J. Myers, eds., *Truth and Tragedy: A Tribute to Hans Morgenthau*. Washington, DC: New Republic Book Company, 1977.

"Changing Perceptions of China Since Midcentury," in John Chay, ed., *The Problems and Prospects of American-East Asian Relations*. Boulder, CO: Westview Press, 1977.

"Lessons of the Mexican War," *Pacific Historical Review* 47 (August 1978): 325–42.

"Government Without Consensus," *Virginia Quarterly Review* 54 (Autumn 1978): 648–64.

"The Apostle of Progress," in Cullom Davis, Charles B. Strozier, and Rebecca Monroe Veach, eds., *The Public and the Private Lincoln*. Carbondale: Southern Illinois University Press, 1979.

"Lutherans and Politics," in John E. Groh and Robert H. Smith, eds., *The Lutheran Church in North American Life*. St. Louis: Clayton Publishing House, 1979.

"Teaching and Learning at Oxford," *British Association of American Studies Newsletter*, no. 41 (January 1980): 2–3.

"The Mexican War: A Study in Causation," *Pacific Historical Review* 49 (August 1980): 405–26.

"Moralism and American Foreign Relations," in Kenneth W. Thompson, ed., *Herbert Butterfield: The Ethics of History and Politics*. Washington, DC: University Press of America, 1980.

"Human Rights and Foreign Policy: The Historic Connection," in Kenneth W. Thompson, ed., *The Moral Imperatives of Human Rights:*

A World Survey. Washington, DC: University Press of America, 1980.

Roosevelt and the Search for a European Policy 1937–1939. Oxford: Clarendon Press, 1980. (Harmsworth Lecture)

"From Carter to Reagan: An Uneasy Transition," *Australian Journal of Politics and History* 27, no. 3 (1981): 304–29.

"The United States and NATO, 1953–69," in Lawrence S. Kaplan and Robert W. Clawson, eds., *NATO After Thirty Years*. Wilmington, DE: Scholarly Resources, 1981.

"Between the Wars: The Intellectual Climate of American Foreign Relations," in John N. Schacht, ed., *Three Faces of Midwestern Isolationism*. Iowa City: Center for the Study of the Recent History of the United States, 1981.

"America's Limited Power in the Contemporary World," Phi Beta Kappa, *Key Reporter* 47 (Spring 1982): 2–5.

"The Decline of America: A Countering Appraisal," *Virginia Quarterly Review* 58 (Summer 1982): 369–91.

"Coming to Terms with Reality," *Naval War College Review* 36 (September–October 1983): 91–113.

"Public Opinion and Foreign Policy: A Pragmatic View," in Don C. Piper and Ronald J. Terchek, eds., *Interactions: Foreign Policy and Public Policy*. Washington, DC: American Enterprise Institute for Public Policy Research, 1983.

"Divided America in Search of Security." Reynolds Lecture delivered at Davidson College, October 18, 1982. Published by Davidson College, 1983.

"Western Disunity: Its Challenge to America." Reynolds Lecture delivered at Davidson College, October 19, 1982. Published by Davidson College, 1983.

"The Soviet-American Conflict: A Strange Phenomenon," *Virginia Quarterly Review* 60 (Autumn 1984): 565–86.

Adams and Jefferson in Europe, 1783–1789. Three essays. The 1982 Carroll Lectures, Mary Baldwin College. Published by Mary Baldwin College, 1984.

"Zachary Taylor and Millard Fillmore," in Henry F. Graff, ed., *The Presidents: A Reference History*. New York: Charles Scribner's Sons, 1984.

"The Illinois Country and the Treaty of Paris of 1783," *Illinois Historical Journal* 78 (Spring 1985): 2–16.

"American Foreign Policy After Vietnam," *Parameters* 15 (Autumn 1985).

"The United States, Russia, and the International Order," in Ulrich Goebel and Irmgard Elsner Hunt, eds., *War and Peace: Perspectives in the Nuclear Age*. Lubbock: Texas Tech Press, 1985.

"Eisenhower, Congress, and the Cold War Consensus," in Richard A. Melanson, ed., *The Domestic Consensus and American Foreign Policy.* Lanham, MD: University Press of America, 1985.

"Eisenhower and China: A Public View," in Richard A. Melanson and David A. Mayers, eds., *Reevaluating Eisenhower: American Foreign Policy in the 1950s.* Champaign: University of Illinois Press, 1986.

Index

Fitzsimmons, Thomas, 102
Fletcher, Charles, 215
Florida: as issue in American Revolution, xxx, xxxii; weakness of under Spanish rule, 158–59; negotiations over, 159–61; acquired by United States, 161
Floridablanca, Count of, xxx, 79
Fort Donelson, 271
Fort Duquesne, xix
Fort Henry, 271
Fort Jesup, 227
Fort Niagara, xix, 12, 13
Fort Oswego, xix, 12
Fort Sumter, 259, 263
Fort Warren, 267, 268
Foster, Augustus J., 133–36
Foster, John W., 323
France: rivalry with Hapsburgs, xvii–xviii; rivalry with Britain, xvii–xx; opposed by British Americans, xviii–xx; committed to American independence, xxvi, xxix; allied with Spain, xxix–xxx; allied with America, xxiv–xxix, 78, 100, 103; and problem of trade, 2, 48–51; and Farmers–General, 50–51; and Directory, 99–100, 109; undeclared war with America, 101–02; interest in Louisiana, 109; commercial policy of, 116–20; responds to nonimportation (1809), 128–29; misleading policies of, 131–36, 140; and balance of power in 1815, 151–52; enters Quadruple Alliance, 152; no threat to America, 153; grants new commercial arrangements, 156–57; policy toward Latin America, 166–68; and American Civil War, 261–62; recognizes Southern belligerency, 264; warned by Seward, 265–67, 278–80; refuses to support South, 273–74, 277–78; in Concert of Europe, 284; under Napoleon III, 284; ventures into Mexico, 284–85; faces rising power of Prussia, 285–86; in Franco-Prussian War, 286–88; Republic proclaimed, 288; animosity toward Germany, 288–89, 293–94; American opinion toward, 287–89; isolated by the Dual Alliance, 297–99; enters alliance with

Russia, 301–02; endangers European balance by supporting Russia, 304–05; military preparations of, 306; rivals Britain in Africa, 308; gains Indochina, 316; expands into Africa, 320; supports China, 340; gains control of Hainan, 341. *See also* French and Indian War; French Revolution
Francis Joseph, emperor of Austria, 294
Franklin, Benjamin: begins peace negotiations (1782), xiii; opposes France in America, xix–xx; and French alliance, xxvi–xxvii; summons Jay to Paris, xxxi; favors France over Britain and neutrality, xxxiv–xxxv; on future of American commerce, 2–3; views Barbary pirates, 6; and Treaty of Paris, 7, 16; appointed to joint commission, 17; complains of British policy, 20–21; returns to America, 22–23; favors Constitutional Convention, 63; and American mission, 67
Frederick the Great, king of Prussia, xx
Freeman, Edward A., 305, 308
Frémont, John C., 204, 231
French and Indian War, xix–xx
French Revolution, American reaction to, 83–90
Friedland, battle of, 119
Frye, William P., 337

Gadsden, James, 188
Gallatin, Albert, 123–25, 155, 157, 174, 246, 256
Geismar, Baron, 53–54
Genêt, Edmond Charles, 87–88, 91
Gentry, Meredith P., 215
Gentz, Friedrich von, xiv
George III, king of England, xxiii–xxiv, xxx, 28–29, 31, 45, 55
Gérard de Rayneval, Joseph Mathias, xxxi
German, Obadiah, 142
German Empire: proclaimed, 288; faces French animosity, 288–89; lauded by Bancroft, 291–93; and European stability, 292–94
Germany: in Dual Alliance, 297–98; and Triple Alliance, 298–99; ends alliance with Russia, 300; military preparedness of, 306; troubled by

NORMAN A. GRAEBNER is recognized as one of the leading historians of American diplomacy. A former president of the Society of Historians of American Foreign Relations and author of eight books, including **EMPIRE ON THE PACIFIC** and **THE AGE OF GLOBAL POWER**, and over one hundred articles, Professor Graebner is Randolph P. Compton Professor of History and Public Affairs at the University of Virginia.